WEIRDOS FROM ANOTHER PLANET

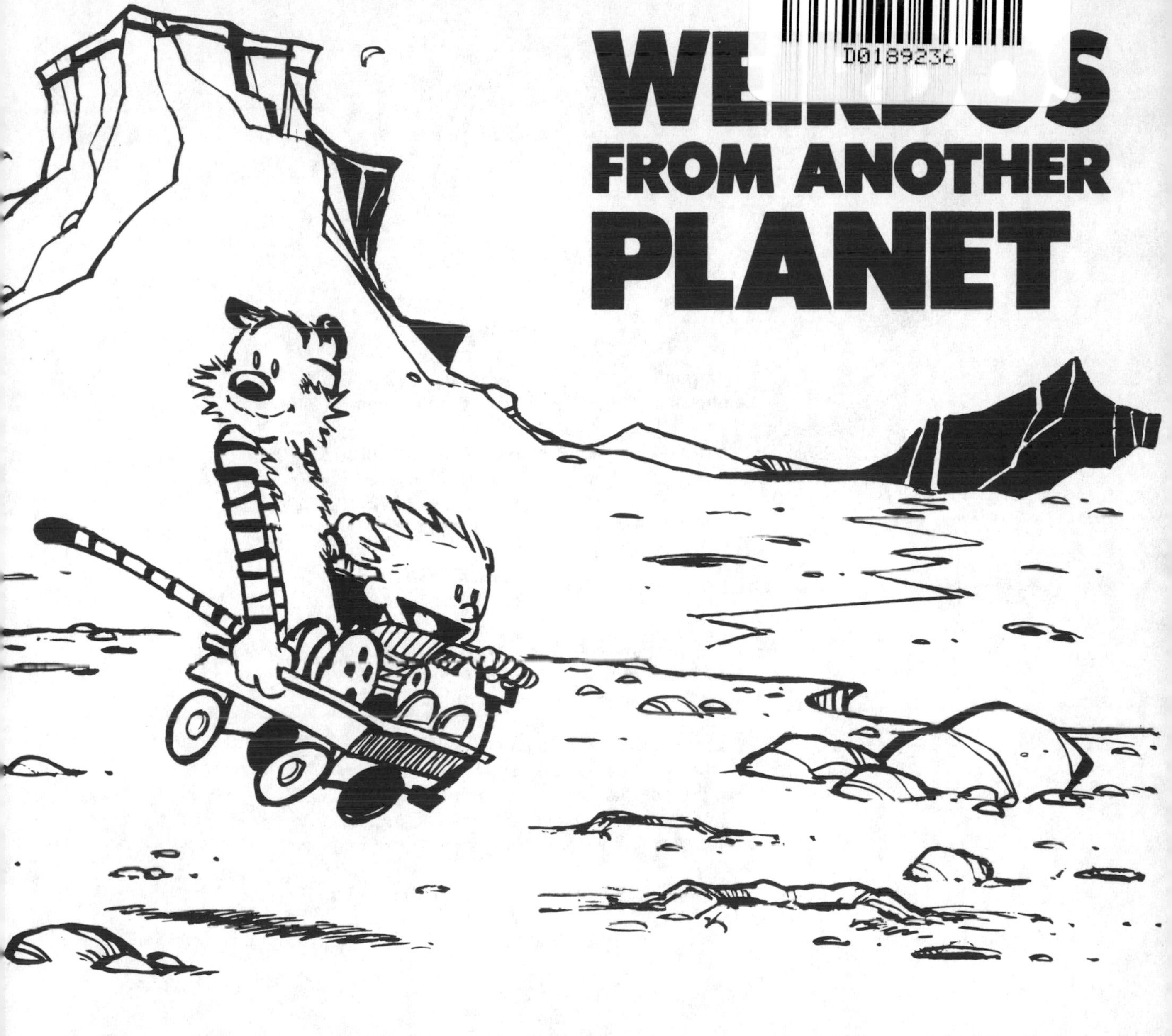

A Calvin and Hobbes Collection by Bill Watterson

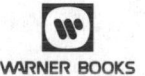

WARNER BOOKS

A *Warner* Book

First published in the United States of America by
Andrews and McMeel, Kansas City, Missouri, 1990

First published in Great Britain by Sphere Books Ltd, 1990
Reprinted 1990, 1991
Reprinted by Warner Books 1992
Reprinted 1993, 1994, 1995

Copyright © 1990 by Bill Watterson
distributed by Universal Press Syndicate

Printed in England by Clays Ltd, St Ives plc

ISBN 0 7515 0424 6

Warner
A Division of
Little, Brown and Company (UK)
Brettenham House
Lancaster Place
London WC2E 7EN

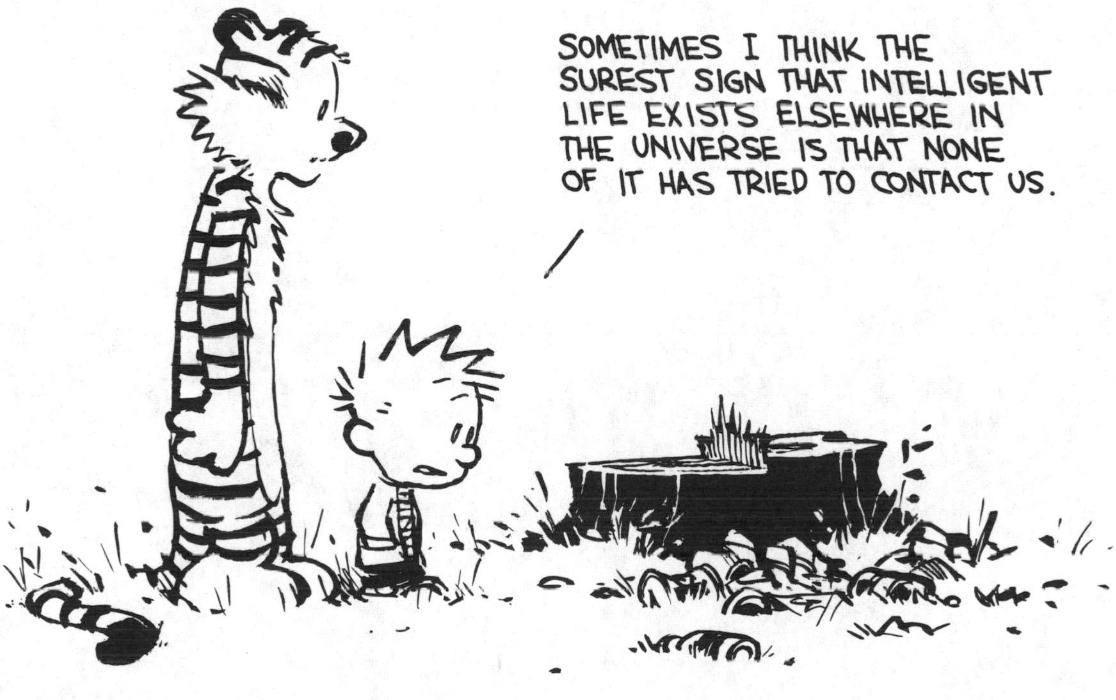
SOMETIMES I THINK THE SUREST SIGN THAT INTELLIGENT LIFE EXISTS ELSEWHERE IN THE UNIVERSE IS THAT NONE OF IT HAS TRIED TO CONTACT US.

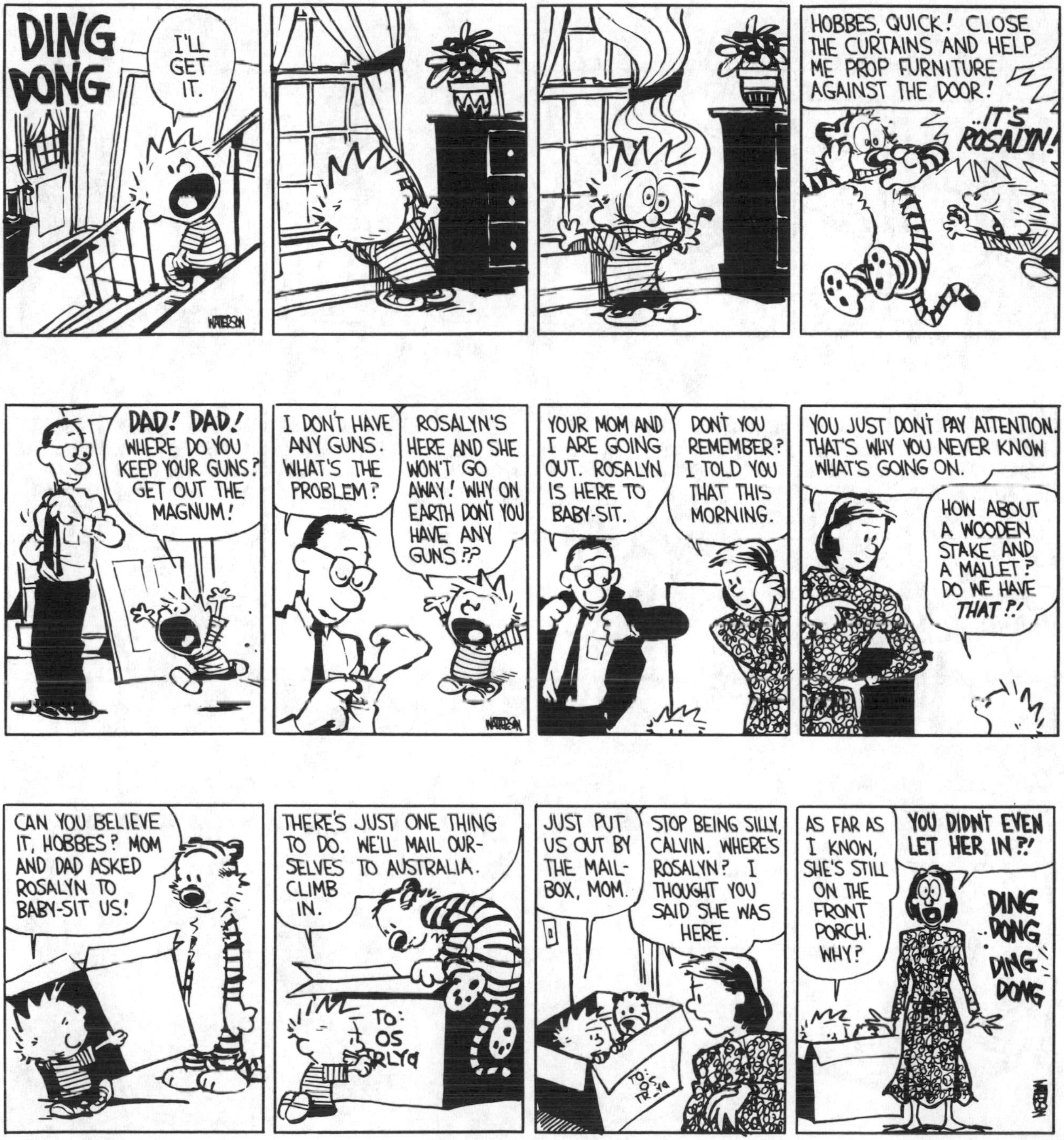
DING DONG
I'LL GET IT.
HOBBES, QUICK! CLOSE THE CURTAINS AND HELP ME PROP FURNITURE AGAINST THE DOOR!
..IT'S ROSALYN!
DAD! DAD! WHERE DO YOU KEEP YOUR GUNS? GET OUT THE MAGNUM!
I DON'T HAVE ANY GUNS. WHAT'S THE PROBLEM?
ROSALYN'S HERE AND SHE WON'T GO AWAY! WHY ON EARTH DON'T YOU HAVE ANY GUNS ??
YOUR MOM AND I ARE GOING OUT. ROSALYN IS HERE TO BABY-SIT.
DON'T YOU REMEMBER? I TOLD YOU THAT THIS MORNING.
YOU JUST DON'T PAY ATTENTION. THAT'S WHY YOU NEVER KNOW WHAT'S GOING ON.
HOW ABOUT A WOODEN STAKE AND A MALLET? DO WE HAVE THAT?!
CAN YOU BELIEVE IT, HOBBES? MOM AND DAD ASKED ROSALYN TO BABY-SIT US!
THERE'S JUST ONE THING TO DO. WE'LL MAIL OURSELVES TO AUSTRALIA. CLIMB IN.
TO: OS
JUST PUT US OUT BY THE MAILBOX, MOM.
STOP BEING SILLY, CALVIN. WHERE'S ROSALYN? I THOUGHT YOU SAID SHE WAS HERE.
AS FAR AS I KNOW, SHE'S STILL ON THE FRONT PORCH. WHY?
YOU DIDN'T EVEN LET HER IN?!
DING DONG
DING DONG

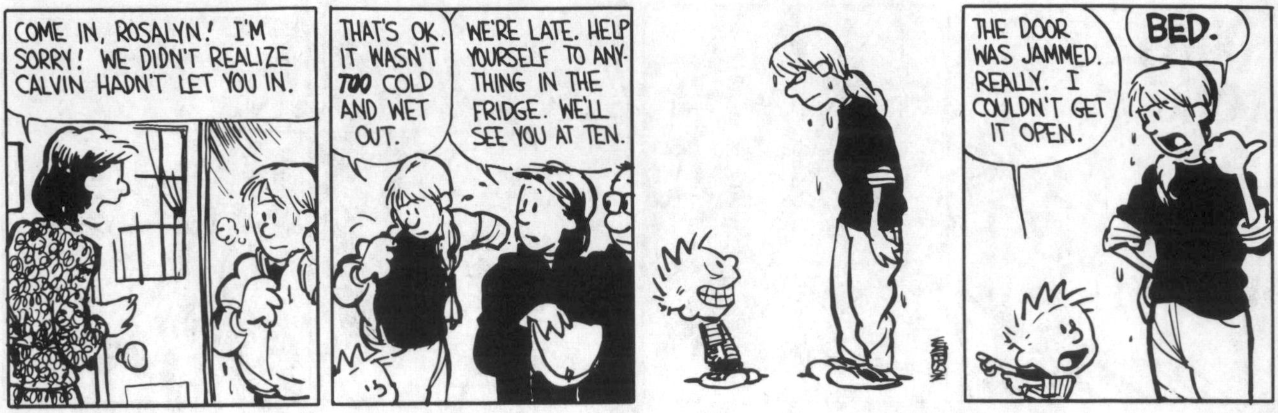
COME IN, ROSALYN! I'M SORRY! WE DIDN'T REALIZE CALVIN HADN'T LET YOU IN.
THAT'S OK. IT WASN'T TOO COLD AND WET OUT.
WE'RE LATE. HELP YOURSELF TO ANYTHING IN THE FRIDGE. WE'LL SEE YOU AT TEN.
THE DOOR WAS JAMMED. REALLY. I COULDN'T GET IT OPEN.
BED.

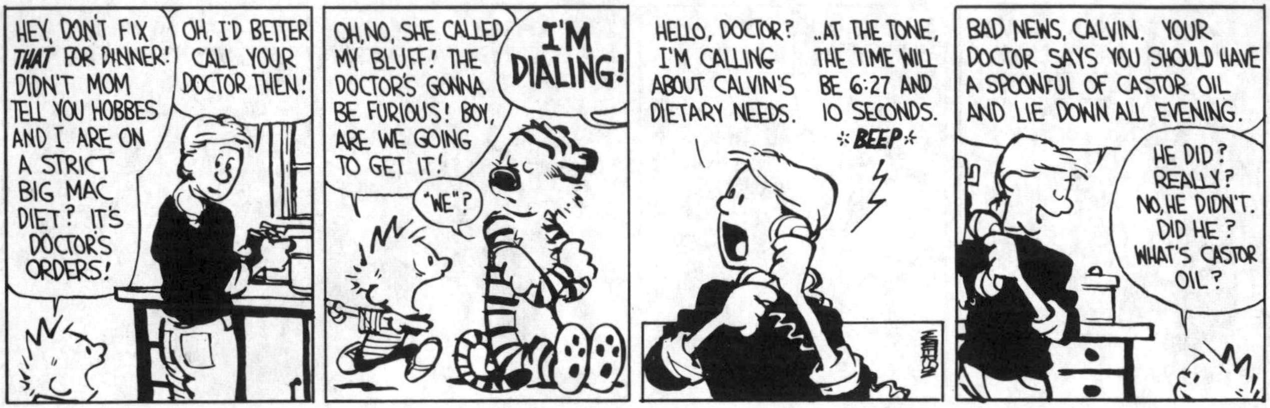
HEY, DON'T FIX THAT FOR DINNER! DIDN'T MOM TELL YOU HOBBES AND I ARE ON A STRICT BIG MAC DIET? IT'S DOCTOR'S ORDERS!
OH, I'D BETTER CALL YOUR DOCTOR THEN!
OH, NO, SHE CALLED MY BLUFF! THE DOCTOR'S GONNA BE FURIOUS! BOY, ARE WE GOING TO GET IT!
I'M DIALING!
"WE"?
HELLO, DOCTOR? I'M CALLING ABOUT CALVIN'S DIETARY NEEDS.
..AT THE TONE, THE TIME WILL BE 6:27 AND 10 SECONDS.
BEEP
BAD NEWS, CALVIN. YOUR DOCTOR SAYS YOU SHOULD HAVE A SPOONFUL OF CASTOR OIL AND LIE DOWN ALL EVENING.
HE DID? REALLY? NO, HE DIDN'T. DID HE? WHAT'S CASTOR OIL?

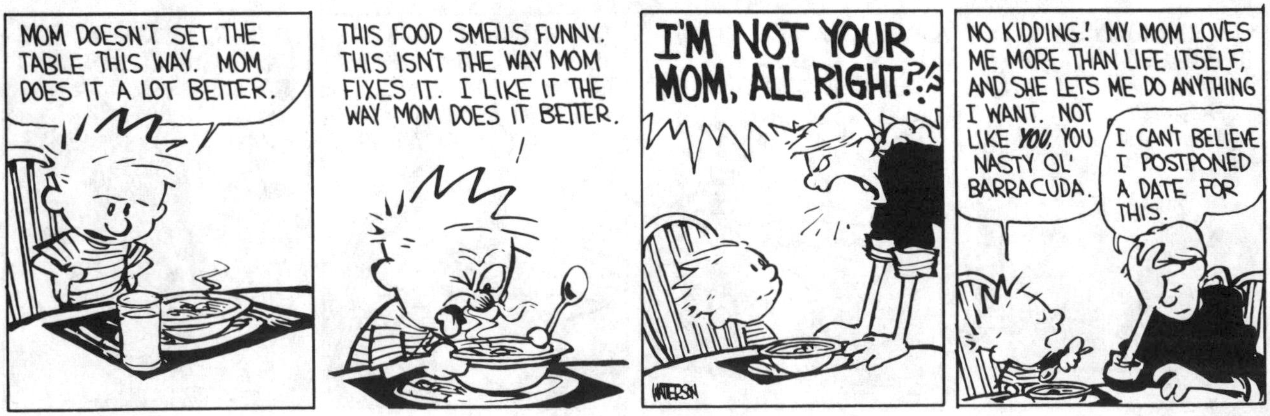
MOM DOESN'T SET THE TABLE THIS WAY. MOM DOES IT A LOT BETTER.
THIS FOOD SMELLS FUNNY. THIS ISN'T THE WAY MOM FIXES IT. I LIKE IT THE WAY MOM DOES IT BETTER.
I'M NOT YOUR MOM, ALL RIGHT?!
NO KIDDING! MY MOM LOVES ME MORE THAN LIFE ITSELF, AND SHE LETS ME DO ANYTHING I WANT. NOT LIKE YOU, YOU NASTY OL' BARRACUDA.
I CAN'T BELIEVE I POSTPONED A DATE FOR THIS.

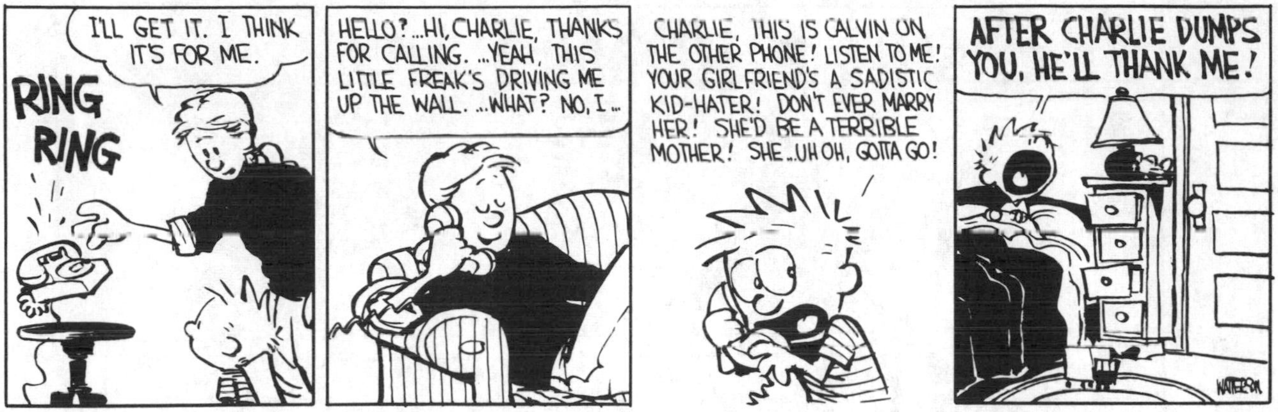
I'LL GET IT. I THINK IT'S FOR ME.
RING RING
HELLO? ...HI, CHARLIE, THANKS FOR CALLING. ...YEAH, THIS LITTLE FREAK'S DRIVING ME UP THE WALL. ...WHAT? NO, I...
CHARLIE, THIS IS CALVIN ON THE OTHER PHONE! LISTEN TO ME! YOUR GIRLFRIEND'S A SADISTIC KID-HATER! DON'T EVER MARRY HER! SHE'D BE A TERRIBLE MOTHER! SHE...UH OH, GOTTA GO!
AFTER CHARLIE DUMPS YOU, HE'LL THANK ME!
WATTERSON

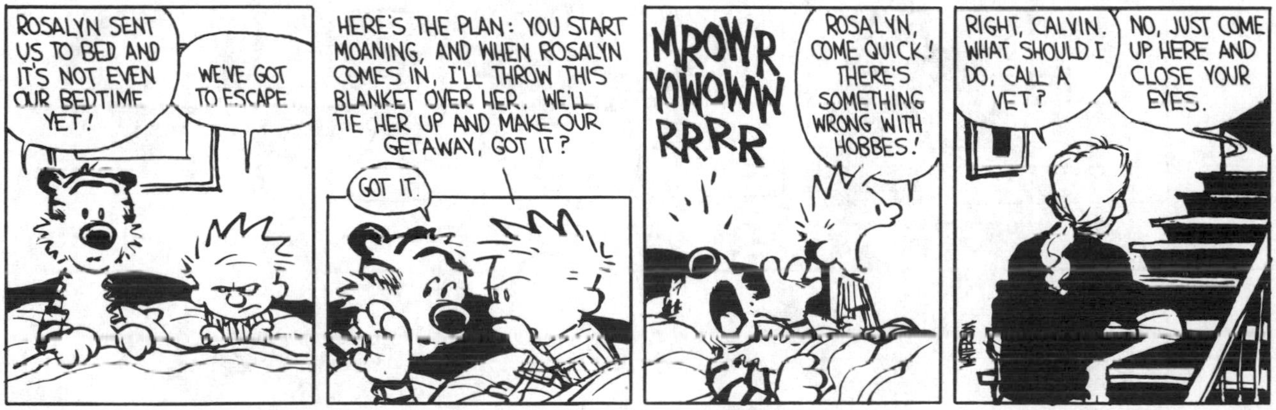
ROSALYN SENT US TO BED AND IT'S NOT EVEN OUR BEDTIME YET!
WE'VE GOT TO ESCAPE.
HERE'S THE PLAN: YOU START MOANING, AND WHEN ROSALYN COMES IN, I'LL THROW THIS BLANKET OVER HER. WE'LL TIE HER UP AND MAKE OUR GETAWAY, GOT IT?
GOT IT.
MROWR YOWOWW RRRR
ROSALYN, COME QUICK! THERE'S SOMETHING WRONG WITH HOBBES!
RIGHT, CALVIN. WHAT SHOULD I DO, CALL A VET?
NO, JUST COME UP HERE AND CLOSE YOUR EYES.
WATTERSON

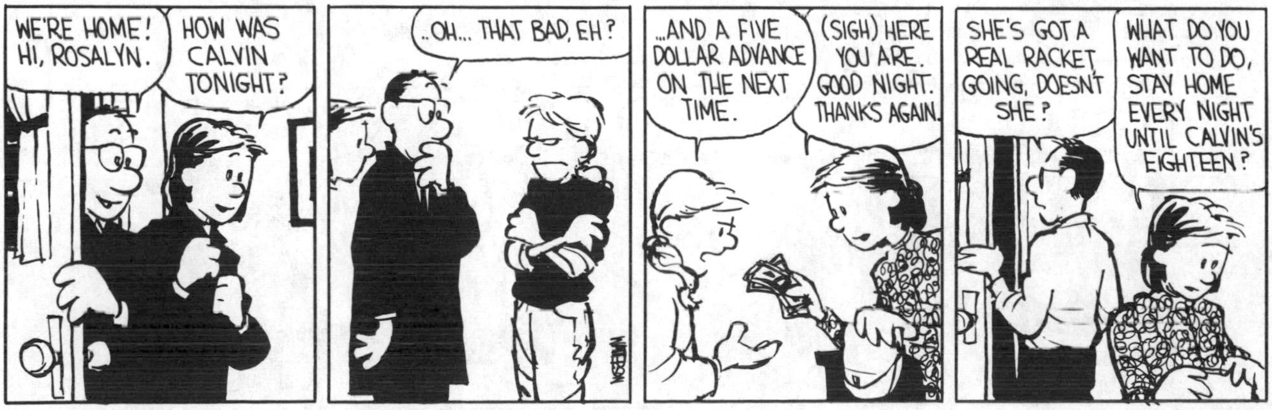
WE'RE HOME! HI, ROSALYN.
HOW WAS CALVIN TONIGHT?
..OH... THAT BAD, EH?
WATTERSON
...AND A FIVE DOLLAR ADVANCE ON THE NEXT TIME.
(SIGH) HERE YOU ARE. GOOD NIGHT. THANKS AGAIN.
SHE'S GOT A REAL RACKET GOING, DOESN'T SHE?
WHAT DO YOU WANT TO DO, STAY HOME EVERY NIGHT UNTIL CALVIN'S EIGHTEEN?

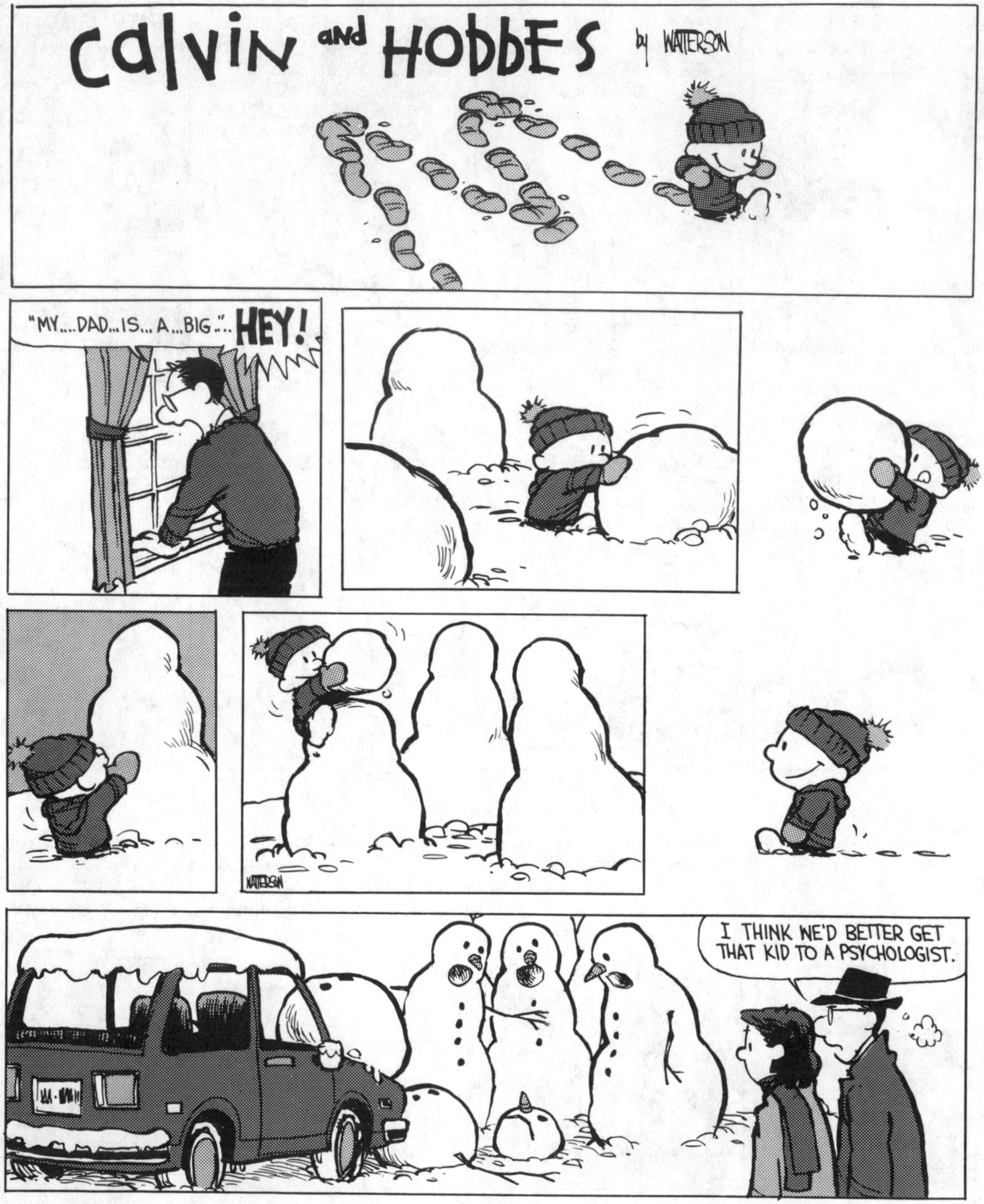
Calvin and HOBBES
by WATTERSON
"MY....DAD...IS...A...BIG...". HEY!
WATTERSON
I THINK WE'D BETTER GET THAT KID TO A PSYCHOLOGIST.

Hey, Calvin, guess what we're doing in gym today. We're wrestling!
Next period you'll be so covered with mat burns you'll need skin grafts! Ha ha ha! See ya then, twinky.
SIGHHHHH...
PHYSICAL EDUCATION IS WHAT YOU LEARN FROM HAVING YOUR FACE IN SOMEONE'S ARMPIT RIGHT BEFORE LUNCH.

KAPWIINGGG! IT'S CALVIN, THE HUMAN LIGHT PARTICLE!
IN THE BLINK OF AN EYE, HE'S 165,000 MILES AWAY!
NOTHING IN THE UNIVERSE IS FASTER THAN CALVIN!
...I HOPE!

MUCH AS I LOVE MY "CHOCOLATE FROSTED CRUNCHY SUGAR BOMBS," THE BEST PART IS AFTER THE CEREAL IS GONE.
THAT'S WHEN YOU EAT THE LEFTOVER MILK THAT'S ALL SLUDGY FROM THE EXTRA SUGAR YOU ADDED.
SOMETIMES I EAT TWO OR THREE BOWLS OF THIS.
I CAN HEAR YOUR HEART RACING FROM HERE.
THEY MAKE THIS CEREAL WITH MARSHMALLOW BITS, TOO, BUT MOM WON'T BUY IT FOR ME.

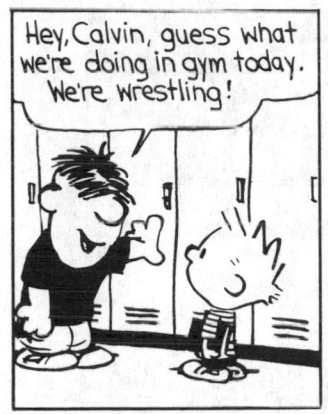

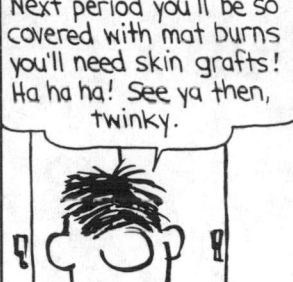

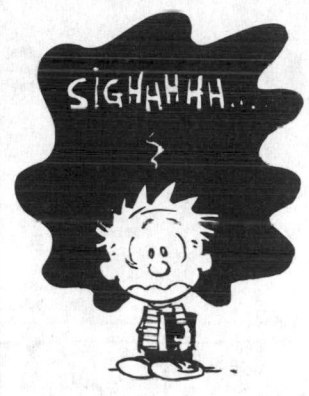

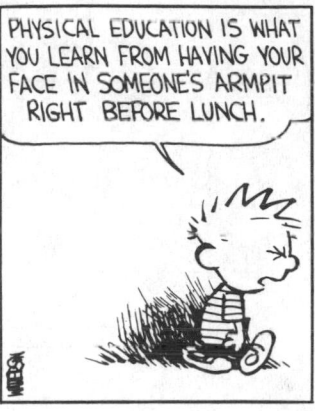

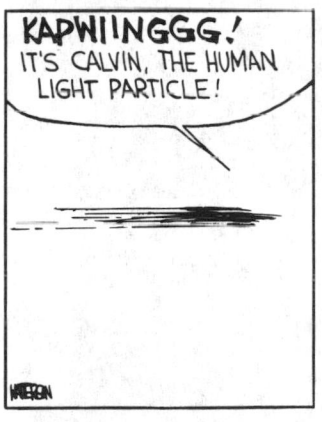

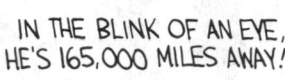

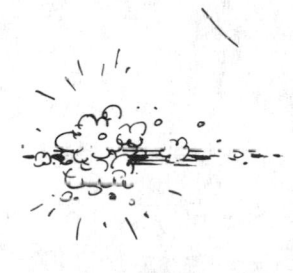

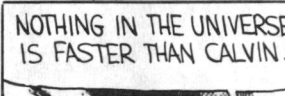

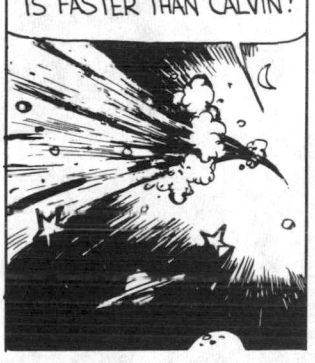

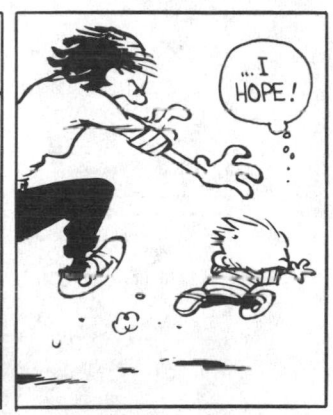

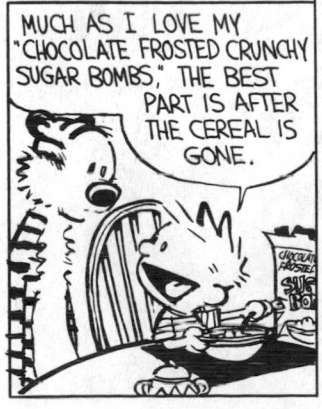

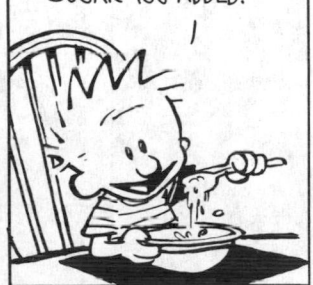

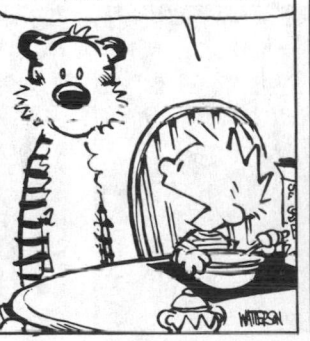

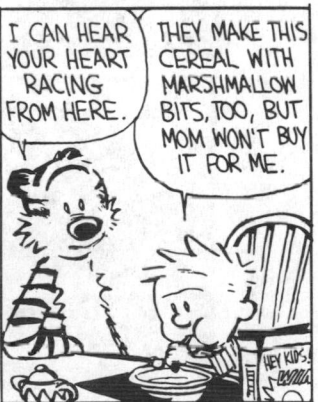

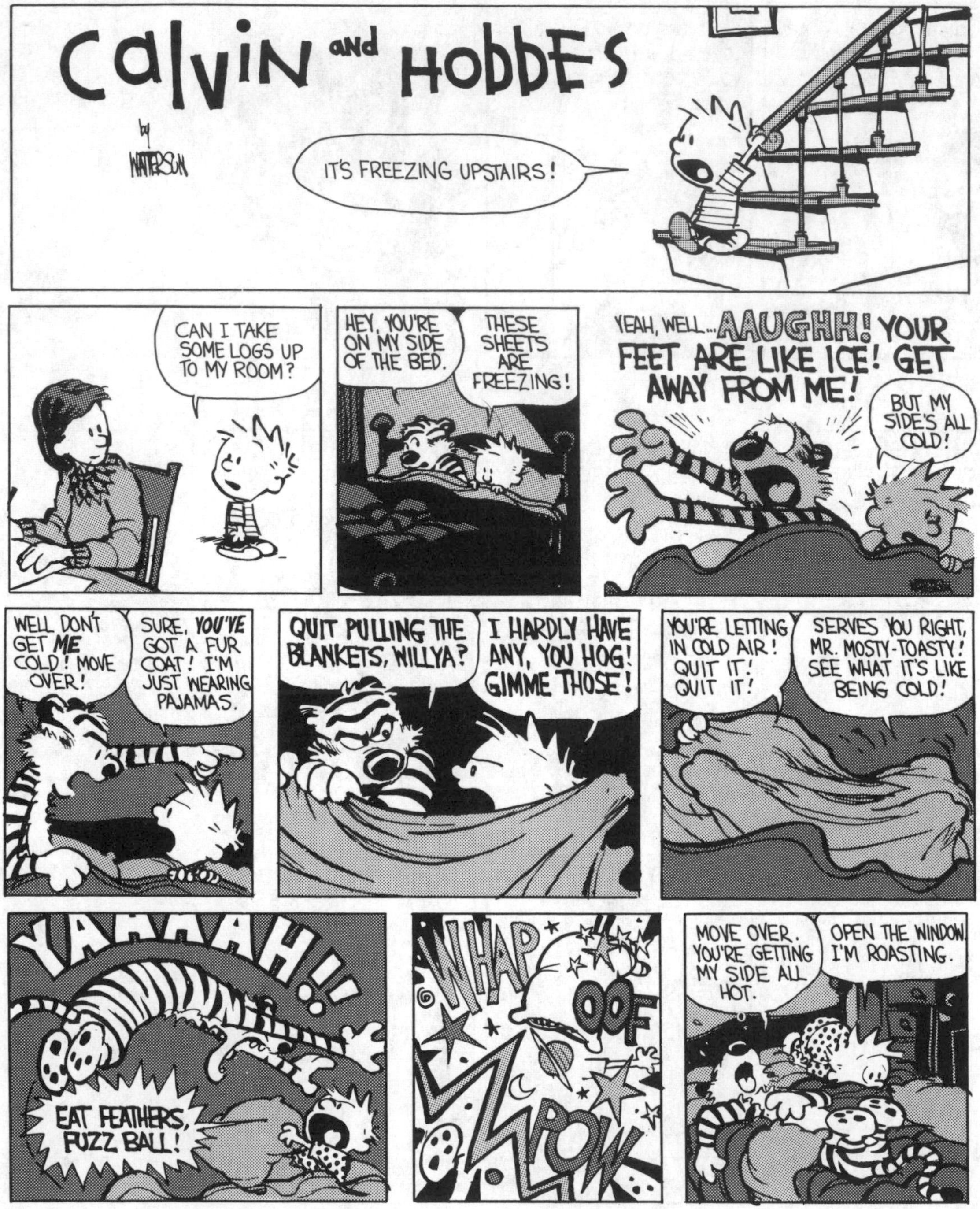
Calvin and HOBBES
by WATTERSON
IT'S FREEZING UPSTAIRS!
CAN I TAKE SOME LOGS UP TO MY ROOM?
HEY, YOU'RE ON MY SIDE OF THE BED.
THESE SHEETS ARE FREEZING!
YEAH, WELL... AAUGHH! YOUR FEET ARE LIKE ICE! GET AWAY FROM ME!
BUT MY SIDE'S ALL COLD!
WELL DON'T GET ME COLD! MOVE OVER!
SURE, YOU'VE GOT A FUR COAT! I'M JUST WEARING PAJAMAS.
QUIT PULLING THE BLANKETS, WILLYA?
I HARDLY HAVE ANY, YOU HOG! GIMME THOSE!
YOU'RE LETTING IN COLD AIR! QUIT IT! QUIT IT!
SERVES YOU RIGHT, MR. MOSTY-TOASTY! SEE WHAT IT'S LIKE BEING COLD!
YAAAAH!!!
EAT FEATHERS, FUZZ BALL!
WHAP
OOF
POW
MOVE OVER. YOU'RE GETTING MY SIDE ALL HOT.
OPEN THE WINDOW. I'M ROASTING.

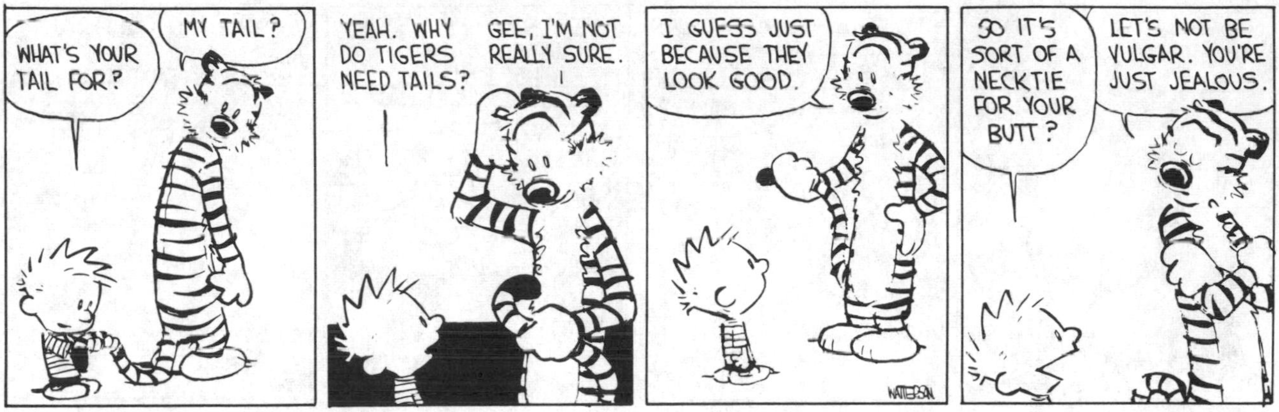
WHAT'S YOUR TAIL FOR?
MY TAIL?
YEAH. WHY DO TIGERS NEED TAILS?
GEE, I'M NOT REALLY SURE.
I GUESS JUST BECAUSE THEY LOOK GOOD.
SO IT'S SORT OF A NECKTIE FOR YOUR BUTT?
LET'S NOT BE VULGAR. YOU'RE JUST JEALOUS.
WATTERSON

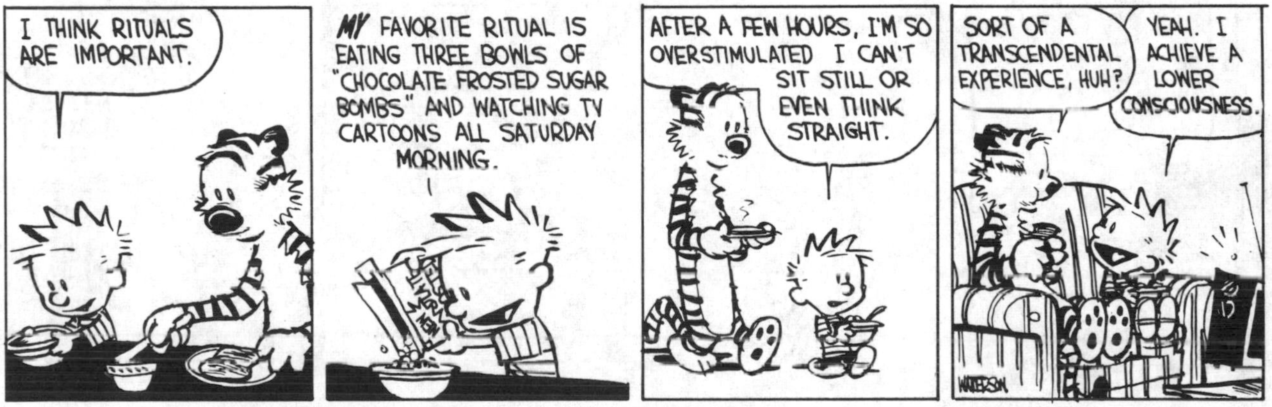
I THINK RITUALS ARE IMPORTANT.
MY FAVORITE RITUAL IS EATING THREE BOWLS OF "CHOCOLATE FROSTED SUGAR BOMBS" AND WATCHING TV CARTOONS ALL SATURDAY MORNING.
AFTER A FEW HOURS, I'M SO OVERSTIMULATED I CAN'T SIT STILL OR EVEN THINK STRAIGHT.
SORT OF A TRANSCENDENTAL EXPERIENCE, HUH?
YEAH. I ACHIEVE A LOWER CONSCIOUSNESS.
WATTERSON

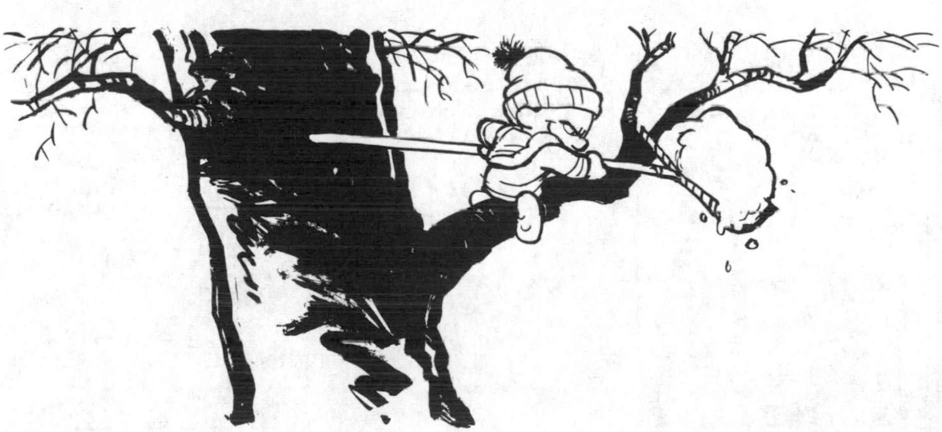

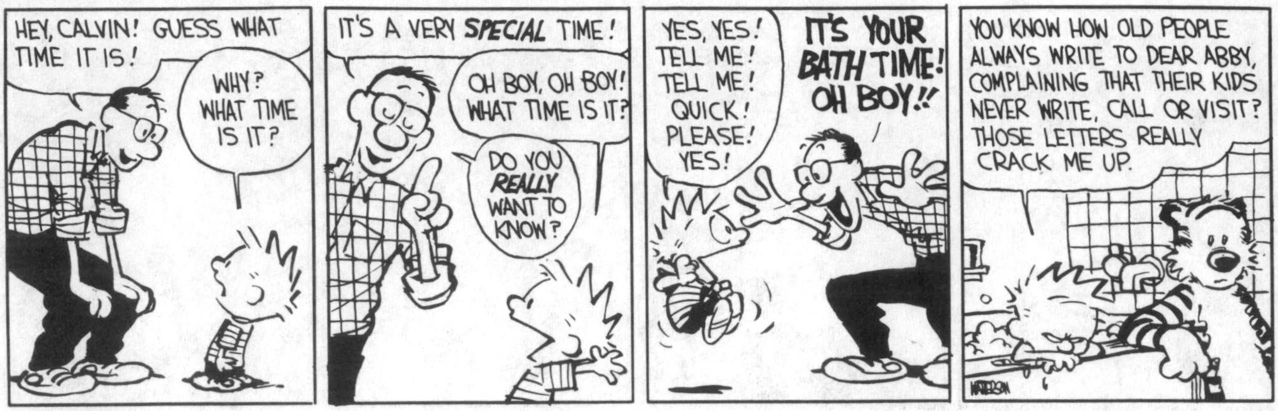
HEY, CALVIN! GUESS WHAT TIME IT IS!
WHY? WHAT TIME IS IT?
IT'S A VERY SPECIAL TIME!
OH BOY, OH BOY! WHAT TIME IS IT?
DO YOU REALLY WANT TO KNOW?
YES, YES! TELL ME! TELL ME! QUICK! PLEASE! YES!
IT'S YOUR BATH TIME! OH BOY!!
YOU KNOW HOW OLD PEOPLE ALWAYS WRITE TO DEAR ABBY, COMPLAINING THAT THEIR KIDS NEVER WRITE, CALL OR VISIT? THOSE LETTERS REALLY CRACK ME UP.
WATTERSON

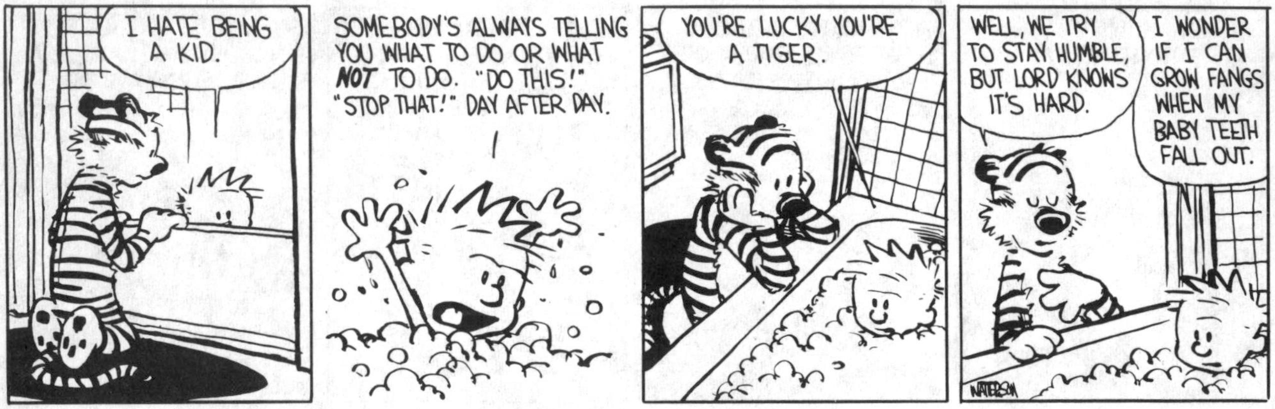
I HATE BEING A KID.
SOMEBODY'S ALWAYS TELLING YOU WHAT TO DO OR WHAT NOT TO DO. "DO THIS!" "STOP THAT!" DAY AFTER DAY.
YOU'RE LUCKY YOU'RE A TIGER.
WELL, WE TRY TO STAY HUMBLE, BUT LORD KNOWS IT'S HARD.
I WONDER IF I CAN GROW FANGS WHEN MY BABY TEETH FALL OUT.
WATTERSON

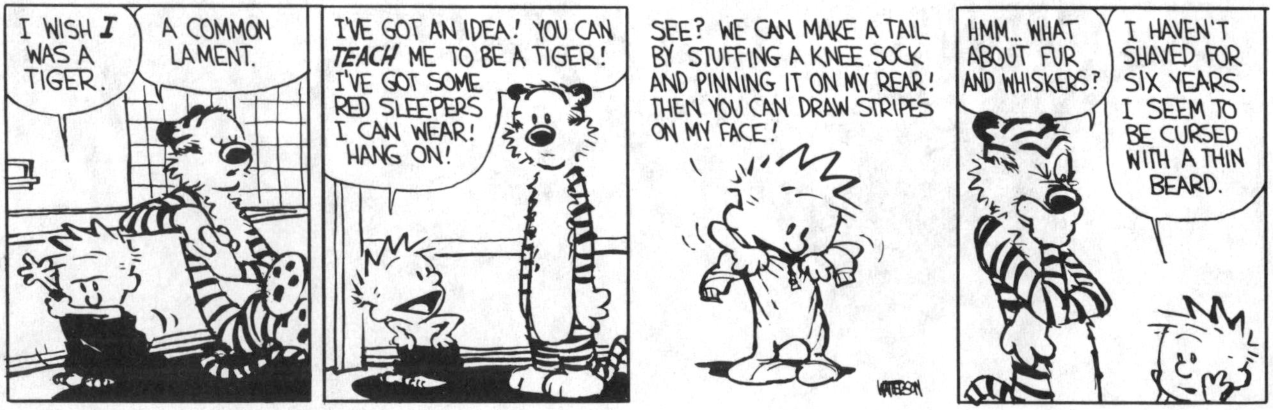
I WISH I WAS A TIGER.
A COMMON LAMENT.
I'VE GOT AN IDEA! YOU CAN TEACH ME TO BE A TIGER! I'VE GOT SOME RED SLEEPERS I CAN WEAR! HANG ON!
SEE? WE CAN MAKE A TAIL BY STUFFING A KNEE SOCK AND PINNING IT ON MY REAR! THEN YOU CAN DRAW STRIPES ON MY FACE!
WATTERSON
HMM... WHAT ABOUT FUR AND WHISKERS?
I HAVEN'T SHAVED FOR SIX YEARS. I SEEM TO BE CURSED WITH A THIN BEARD.

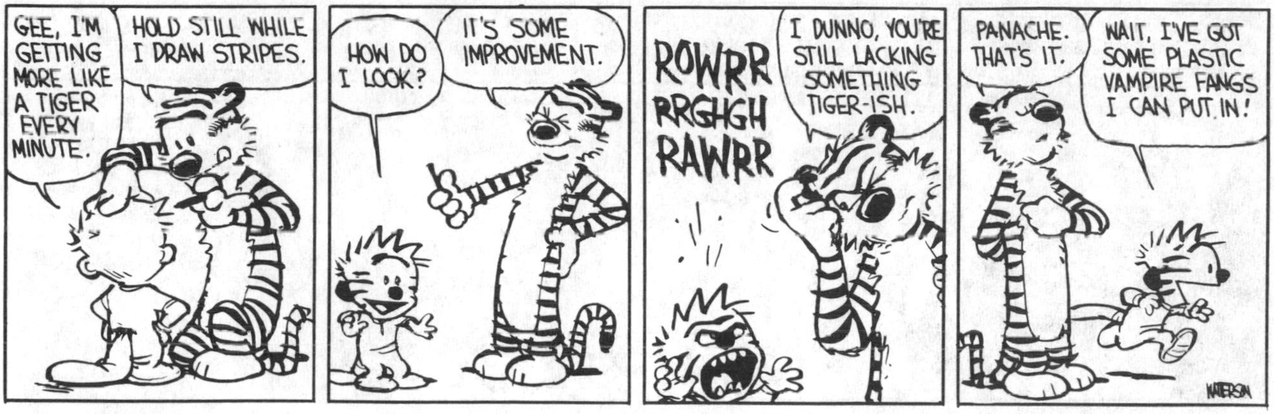
GEE, I'M GETTING MORE LIKE A TIGER EVERY MINUTE.
HOLD STILL WHILE I DRAW STRIPES.
HOW DO I LOOK?
IT'S SOME IMPROVEMENT.
ROWRR RRGHGH RAWRR
I DUNNO, YOU'RE STILL LACKING SOMETHING TIGER-ISH.
PANACHE. THAT'S IT.
WAIT, I'VE GOT SOME PLASTIC VAMPIRE FANGS I CAN PUT IN!

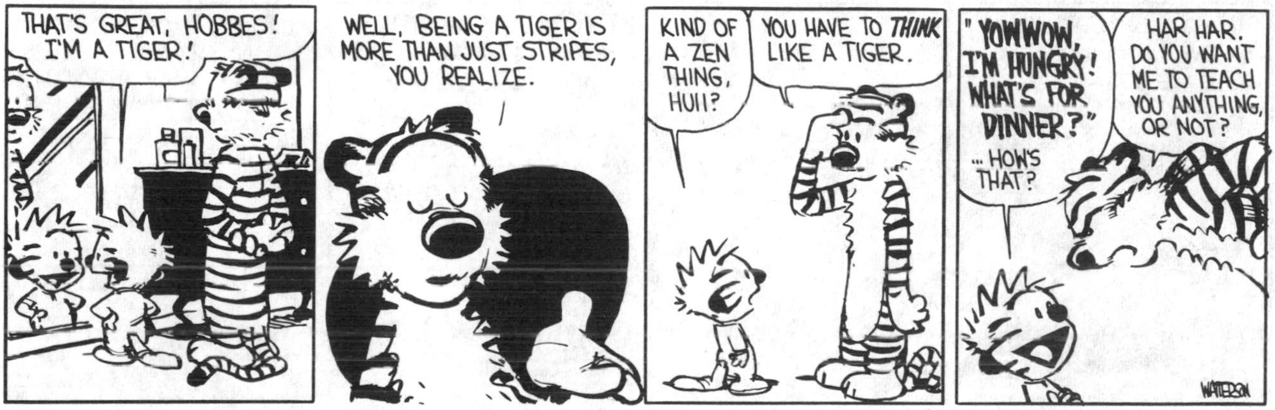
THAT'S GREAT, HOBBES! I'M A TIGER!
WELL, BEING A TIGER IS MORE THAN JUST STRIPES, YOU REALIZE.
KIND OF A ZEN THING, HUH?
YOU HAVE TO THINK LIKE A TIGER.
"YOWWOW, I'M HUNGRY! WHAT'S FOR DINNER?" ... HOW'S THAT?
HAR HAR. DO YOU WANT ME TO TEACH YOU ANYTHING, OR NOT?

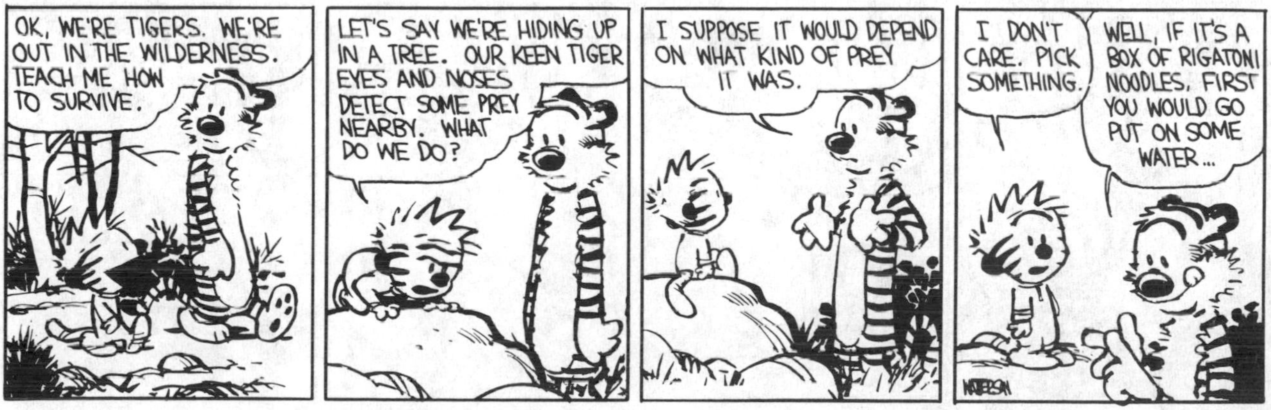
OK, WE'RE TIGERS. WE'RE OUT IN THE WILDERNESS. TEACH ME HOW TO SURVIVE.
LET'S SAY WE'RE HIDING UP IN A TREE. OUR KEEN TIGER EYES AND NOSES DETECT SOME PREY NEARBY. WHAT DO WE DO?
I SUPPOSE IT WOULD DEPEND ON WHAT KIND OF PREY IT WAS.
I DON'T CARE. PICK SOMETHING.
WELL, IF IT'S A BOX OF RIGATONI NOODLES, FIRST YOU WOULD GO PUT ON SOME WATER...

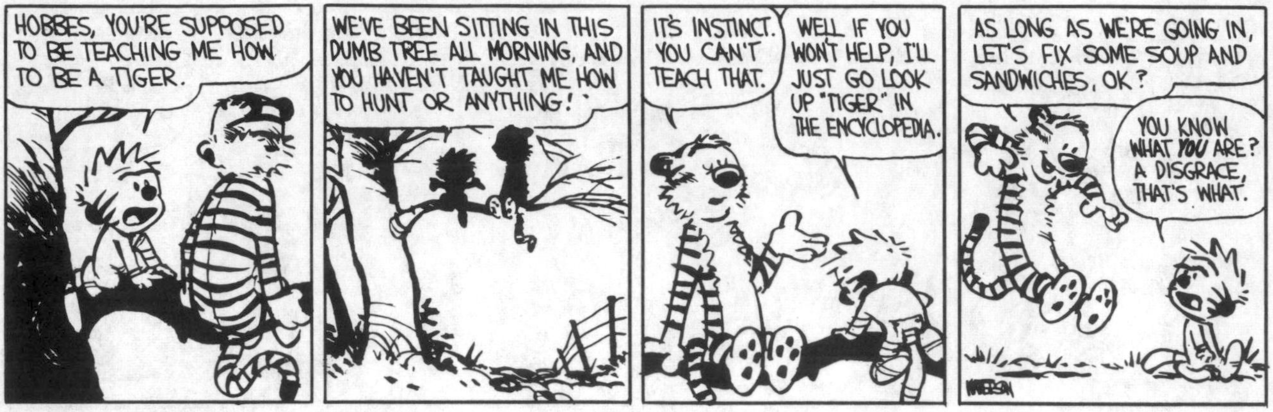
HOBBES, YOU'RE SUPPOSED TO BE TEACHING ME HOW TO BE A TIGER.
WE'VE BEEN SITTING IN THIS DUMB TREE ALL MORNING, AND YOU HAVEN'T TAUGHT ME HOW TO HUNT OR ANYTHING!
IT'S INSTINCT. YOU CAN'T TEACH THAT.
WELL IF YOU WON'T HELP, I'LL JUST GO LOOK UP "TIGER" IN THE ENCYCLOPEDIA.
AS LONG AS WE'RE GOING IN, LET'S FIX SOME SOUP AND SANDWICHES, OK?
YOU KNOW WHAT **YOU** ARE? A DISGRACE, THAT'S WHAT.

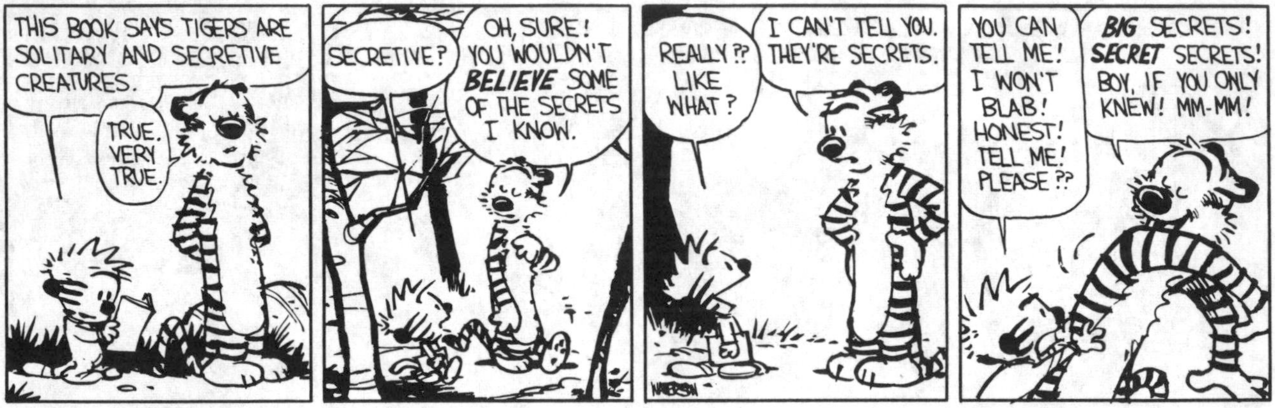
THIS BOOK SAYS TIGERS ARE SOLITARY AND SECRETIVE CREATURES.
TRUE. VERY TRUE.
SECRETIVE?
OH, SURE! YOU WOULDN'T **BELIEVE** SOME OF THE SECRETS I KNOW.
REALLY?? LIKE WHAT?
I CAN'T TELL YOU. THEY'RE SECRETS.
YOU CAN TELL ME! I WON'T BLAB! HONEST! TELL ME! PLEASE??
BIG SECRETS! **SECRET** SECRETS! BOY, IF YOU ONLY KNEW! MM-MM!

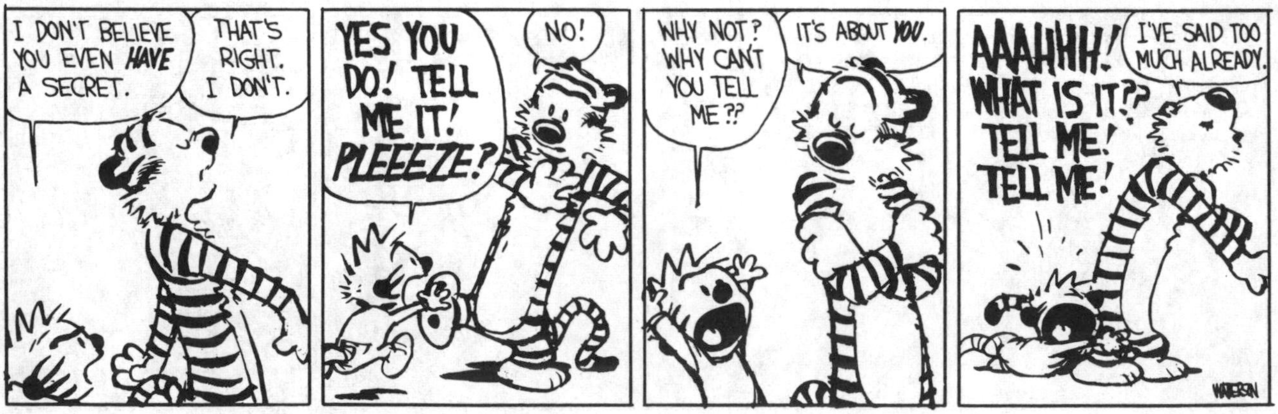
I DON'T BELIEVE YOU EVEN **HAVE** A SECRET.
THAT'S RIGHT. I DON'T.
YES YOU DO! TELL ME IT! PLEEEEZE?
NO!
WHY NOT? WHY CAN'T YOU TELL ME??
IT'S ABOUT **YOU**.
AAAHHH! WHAT IS IT?? TELL ME! TELL ME!
I'VE SAID TOO MUCH ALREADY.

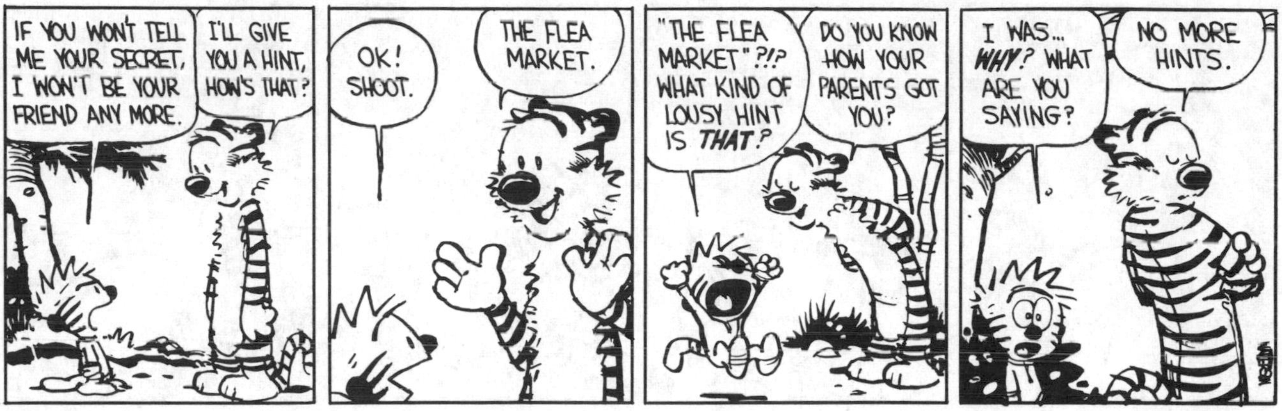
IF YOU WON'T TELL ME YOUR SECRET, I WON'T BE YOUR FRIEND ANY MORE.
I'LL GIVE YOU A HINT, HOW'S THAT?
OK! SHOOT.
THE FLEA MARKET.
"THE FLEA MARKET"?!? WHAT KIND OF LOUSY HINT IS *THAT*?
DO YOU KNOW HOW YOUR PARENTS GOT YOU?
I WAS... *WHY?* WHAT ARE YOU SAYING?
NO MORE HINTS.

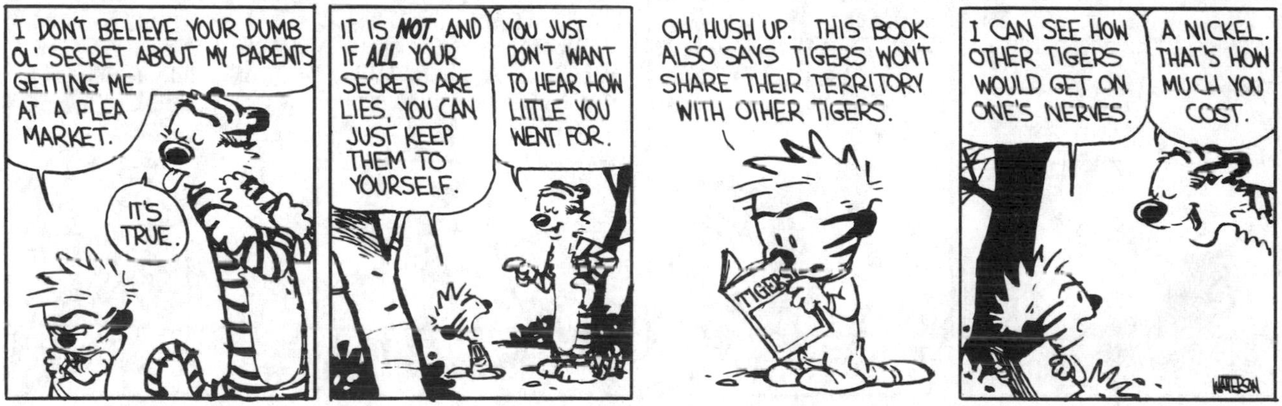
I DON'T BELIEVE YOUR DUMB OL' SECRET ABOUT MY PARENTS GETTING ME AT A FLEA MARKET.
IT'S TRUE.
IT IS ***NOT***, AND IF ***ALL*** YOUR SECRETS ARE LIES, YOU CAN JUST KEEP THEM TO YOURSELF.
YOU JUST DON'T WANT TO HEAR HOW LITTLE YOU WENT FOR.
OH, HUSH UP. THIS BOOK ALSO SAYS TIGERS WON'T SHARE THEIR TERRITORY WITH OTHER TIGERS.
TIGERS
I CAN SEE HOW OTHER TIGERS WOULD GET ON ONE'S NERVES.
A NICKEL. THAT'S HOW MUCH YOU COST.

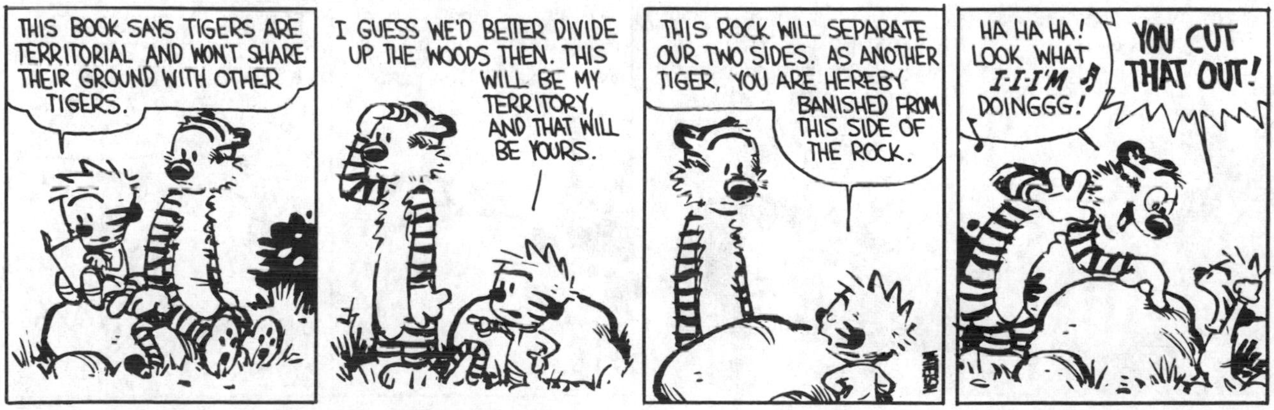
THIS BOOK SAYS TIGERS ARE TERRITORIAL AND WON'T SHARE THEIR GROUND WITH OTHER TIGERS.
I GUESS WE'D BETTER DIVIDE UP THE WOODS THEN. THIS WILL BE MY TERRITORY, AND THAT WILL BE YOURS.
THIS ROCK WILL SEPARATE OUR TWO SIDES. AS ANOTHER TIGER, YOU ARE HEREBY BANISHED FROM THIS SIDE OF THE ROCK.
HA HA HA! LOOK WHAT *I-I-I'M* DOINGGG!
YOU CUT THAT OUT!

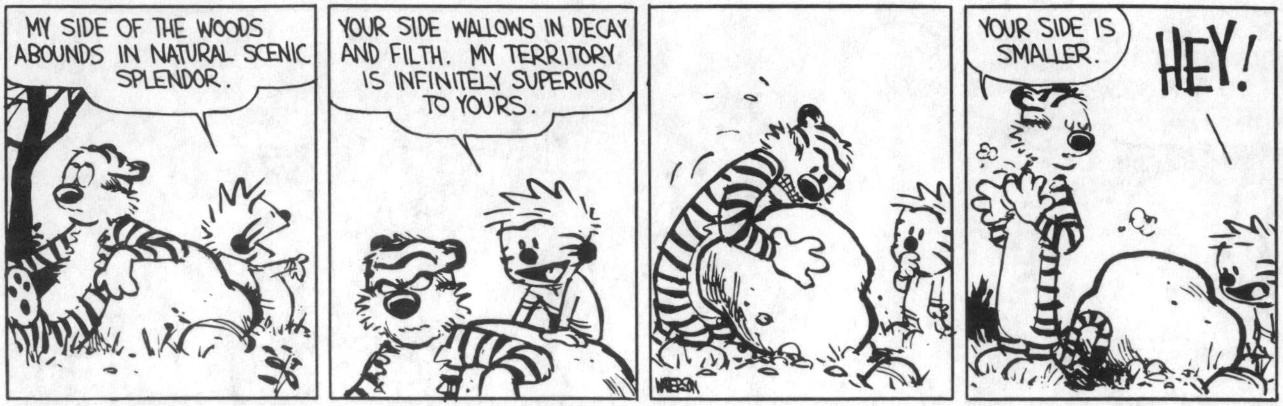
MY SIDE OF THE WOODS ABOUNDS IN NATURAL SCENIC SPLENDOR.
YOUR SIDE WALLOWS IN DECAY AND FILTH. MY TERRITORY IS INFINITELY SUPERIOR TO YOURS.
YOUR SIDE IS SMALLER.
HEY!

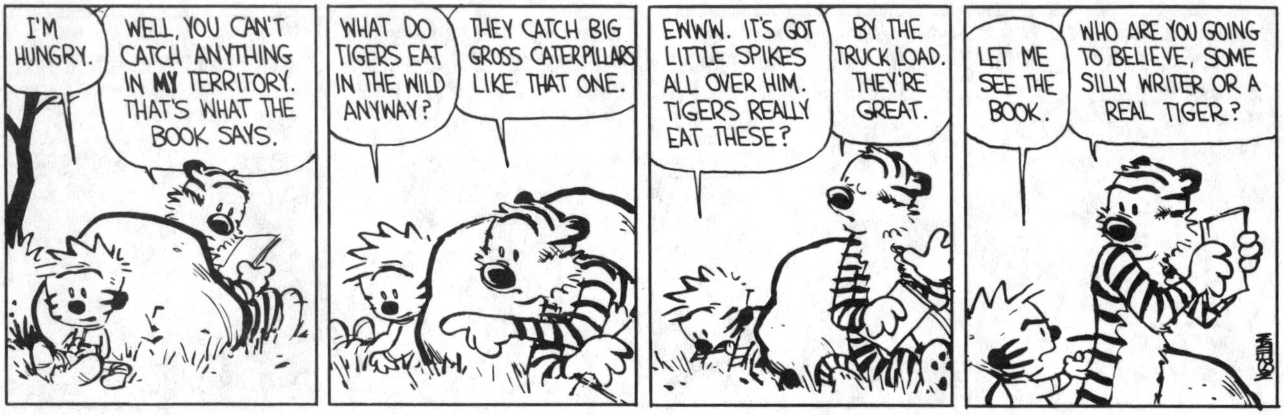
I'M HUNGRY.
WELL, YOU CAN'T CATCH ANYTHING IN MY TERRITORY. THAT'S WHAT THE BOOK SAYS.
WHAT DO TIGERS EAT IN THE WILD ANYWAY?
THEY CATCH BIG GROSS CATERPILLARS LIKE THAT ONE.
EWWW. IT'S GOT LITTLE SPIKES ALL OVER HIM. TIGERS REALLY EAT THESE?
BY THE TRUCK LOAD. THEY'RE GREAT.
LET ME SEE THE BOOK.
WHO ARE YOU GOING TO BELIEVE, SOME SILLY WRITER OR A REAL TIGER?

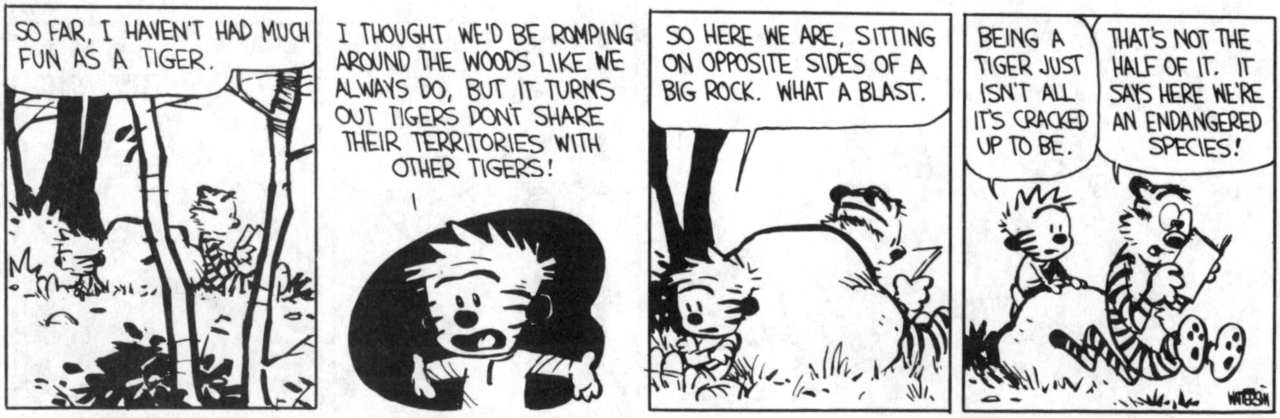
SO FAR, I HAVEN'T HAD MUCH FUN AS A TIGER.
I THOUGHT WE'D BE ROMPING AROUND THE WOODS LIKE WE ALWAYS DO, BUT IT TURNS OUT TIGERS DON'T SHARE THEIR TERRITORIES WITH OTHER TIGERS!
SO HERE WE ARE, SITTING ON OPPOSITE SIDES OF A BIG ROCK. WHAT A BLAST.
BEING A TIGER JUST ISN'T ALL IT'S CRACKED UP TO BE.
THAT'S NOT THE HALF OF IT. IT SAYS HERE WE'RE AN ENDANGERED SPECIES!

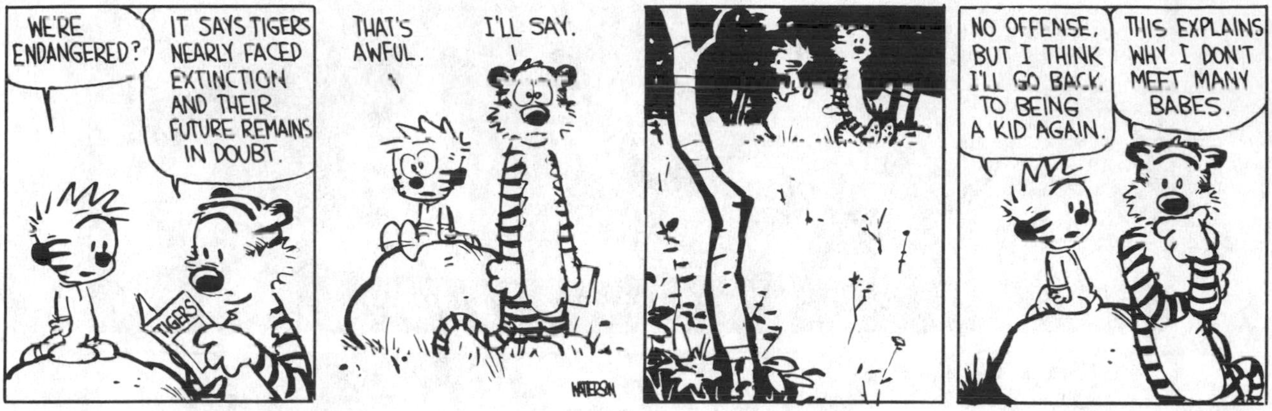
WE'RE ENDANGERED?
IT SAYS TIGERS NEARLY FACED EXTINCTION AND THEIR FUTURE REMAINS IN DOUBT.
TIGERS
THAT'S AWFUL.
I'LL SAY.
NO OFFENSE, BUT I THINK I'LL GO BACK TO BEING A KID AGAIN.
THIS EXPLAINS WHY I DON'T MEET MANY BABES.

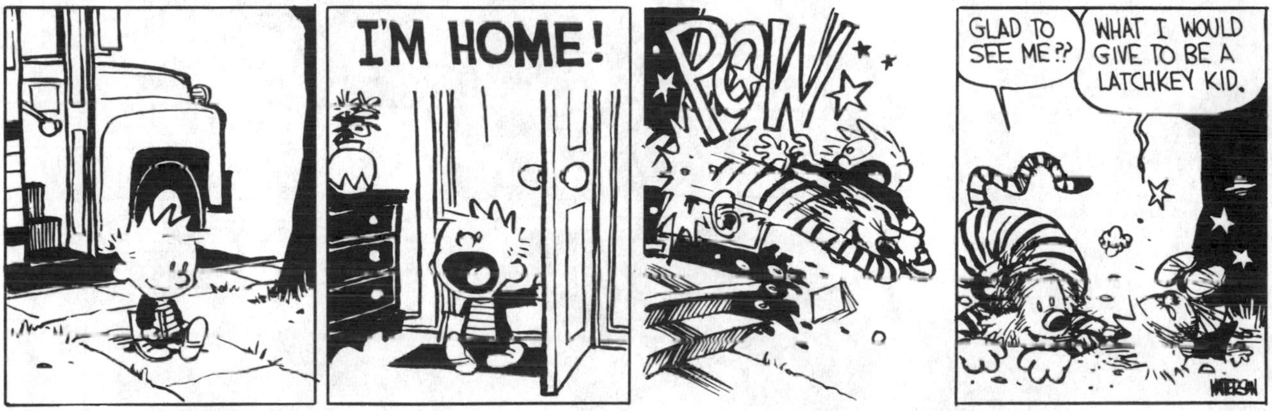
I'M HOME!
POW
GLAD TO SEE ME??
WHAT I WOULD GIVE TO BE A LATCHKEY KID.

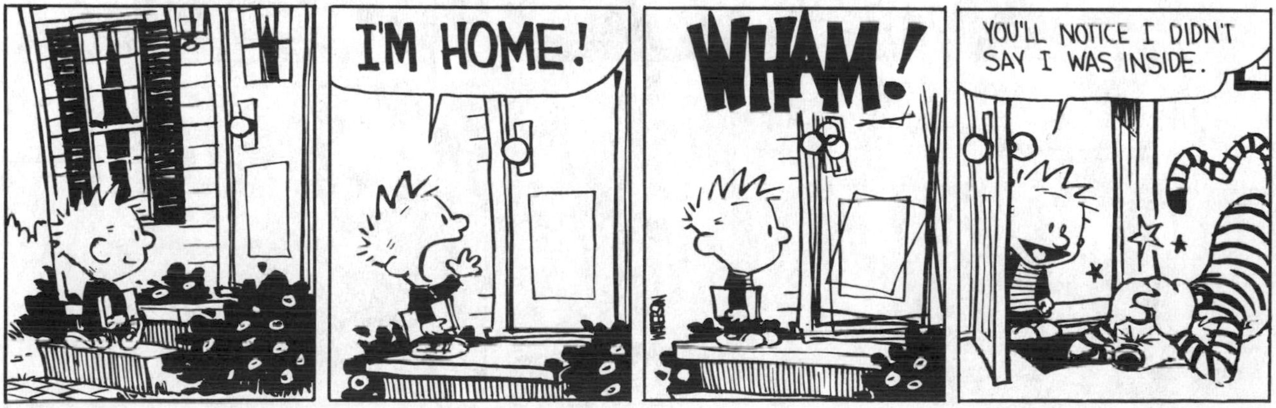
I'M HOME!
WHAM!
YOU'LL NOTICE I DIDN'T SAY I WAS INSIDE.

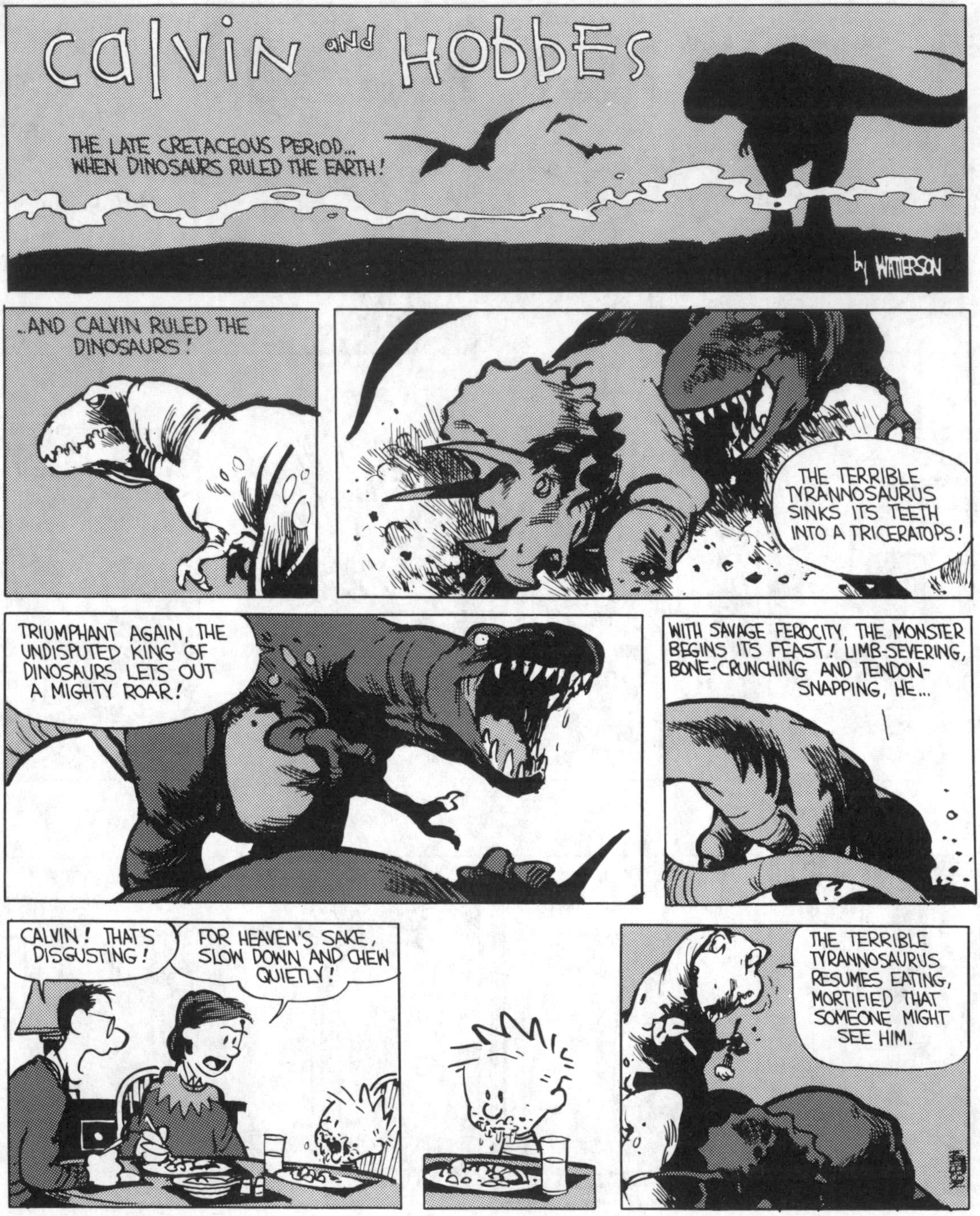
Calvin and Hobbes
THE LATE CRETACEOUS PERIOD... WHEN DINOSAURS RULED THE EARTH!
by WATTERSON
..AND CALVIN RULED THE DINOSAURS!
THE TERRIBLE TYRANNOSAURUS SINKS ITS TEETH INTO A TRICERATOPS!
TRIUMPHANT AGAIN, THE UNDISPUTED KING OF DINOSAURS LETS OUT A MIGHTY ROAR!
WITH SAVAGE FEROCITY, THE MONSTER BEGINS ITS FEAST! LIMB-SEVERING, BONE-CRUNCHING AND TENDON-SNAPPING, HE...
CALVIN! THAT'S DISGUSTING!
FOR HEAVEN'S SAKE, SLOW DOWN AND CHEW QUIETLY!
THE TERRIBLE TYRANNOSAURUS RESUMES EATING, MORTIFIED THAT SOMEONE MIGHT SEE HIM.

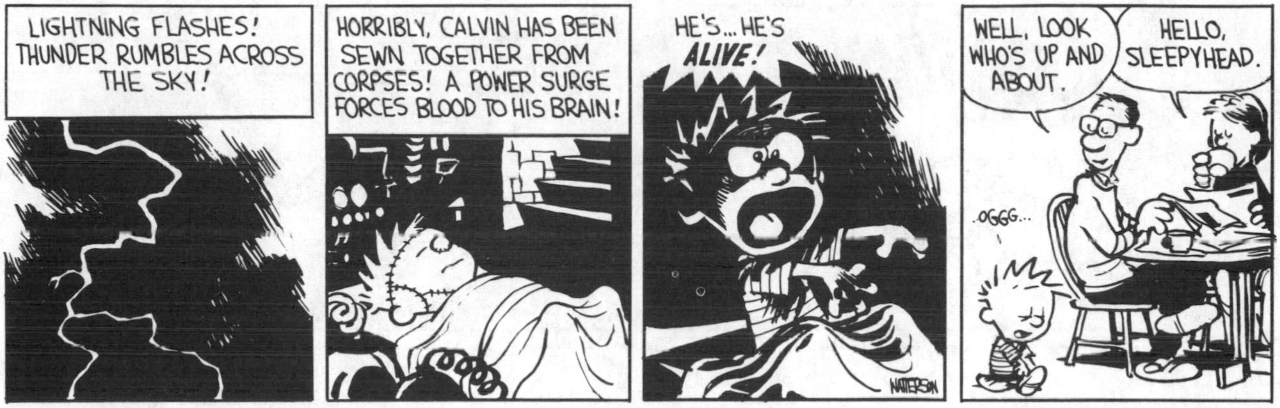
LIGHTNING FLASHES! THUNDER RUMBLES ACROSS THE SKY!
HORRIBLY, CALVIN HAS BEEN SEWN TOGETHER FROM CORPSES! A POWER SURGE FORCES BLOOD TO HIS BRAIN!
HE'S... HE'S ALIVE!
WELL, LOOK WHO'S UP AND ABOUT.
HELLO, SLEEPYHEAD.
..OGGG...

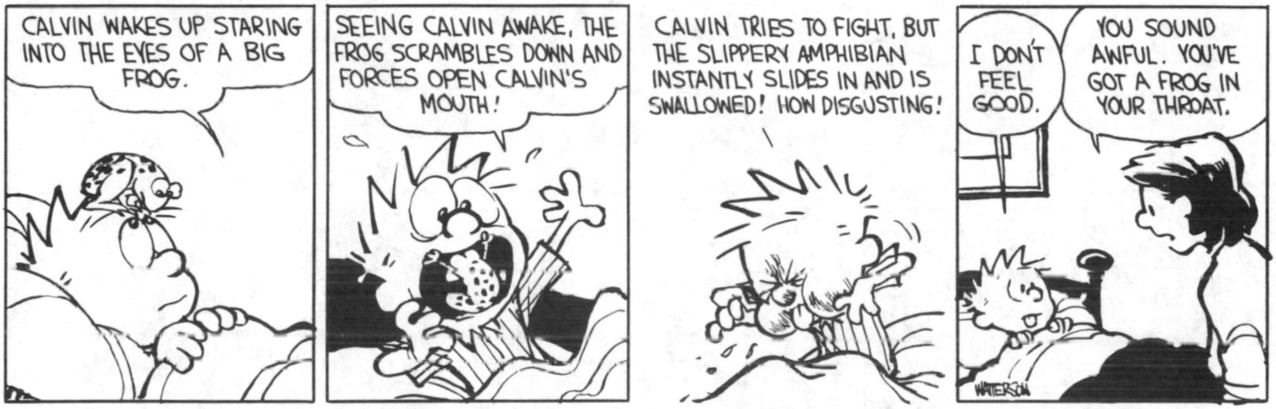
CALVIN WAKES UP STARING INTO THE EYES OF A BIG FROG.
SEEING CALVIN AWAKE, THE FROG SCRAMBLES DOWN AND FORCES OPEN CALVIN'S MOUTH!
CALVIN TRIES TO FIGHT, BUT THE SLIPPERY AMPHIBIAN INSTANTLY SLIDES IN AND IS SWALLOWED! HOW DISGUSTING!
I DON'T FEEL GOOD.
YOU SOUND AWFUL. YOU'VE GOT A FROG IN YOUR THROAT.

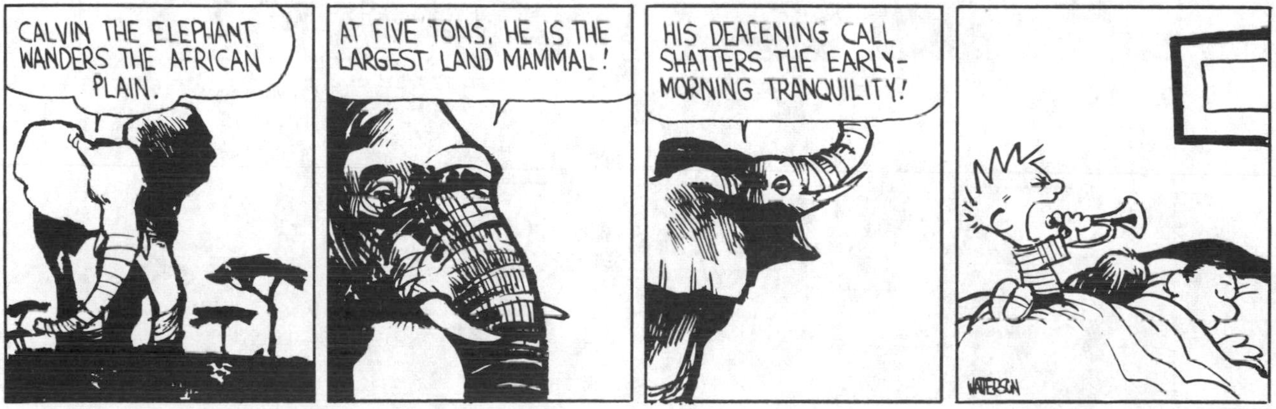
CALVIN THE ELEPHANT WANDERS THE AFRICAN PLAIN.
AT FIVE TONS, HE IS THE LARGEST LAND MAMMAL!
HIS DEAFENING CALL SHATTERS THE EARLY-MORNING TRANQUILITY!

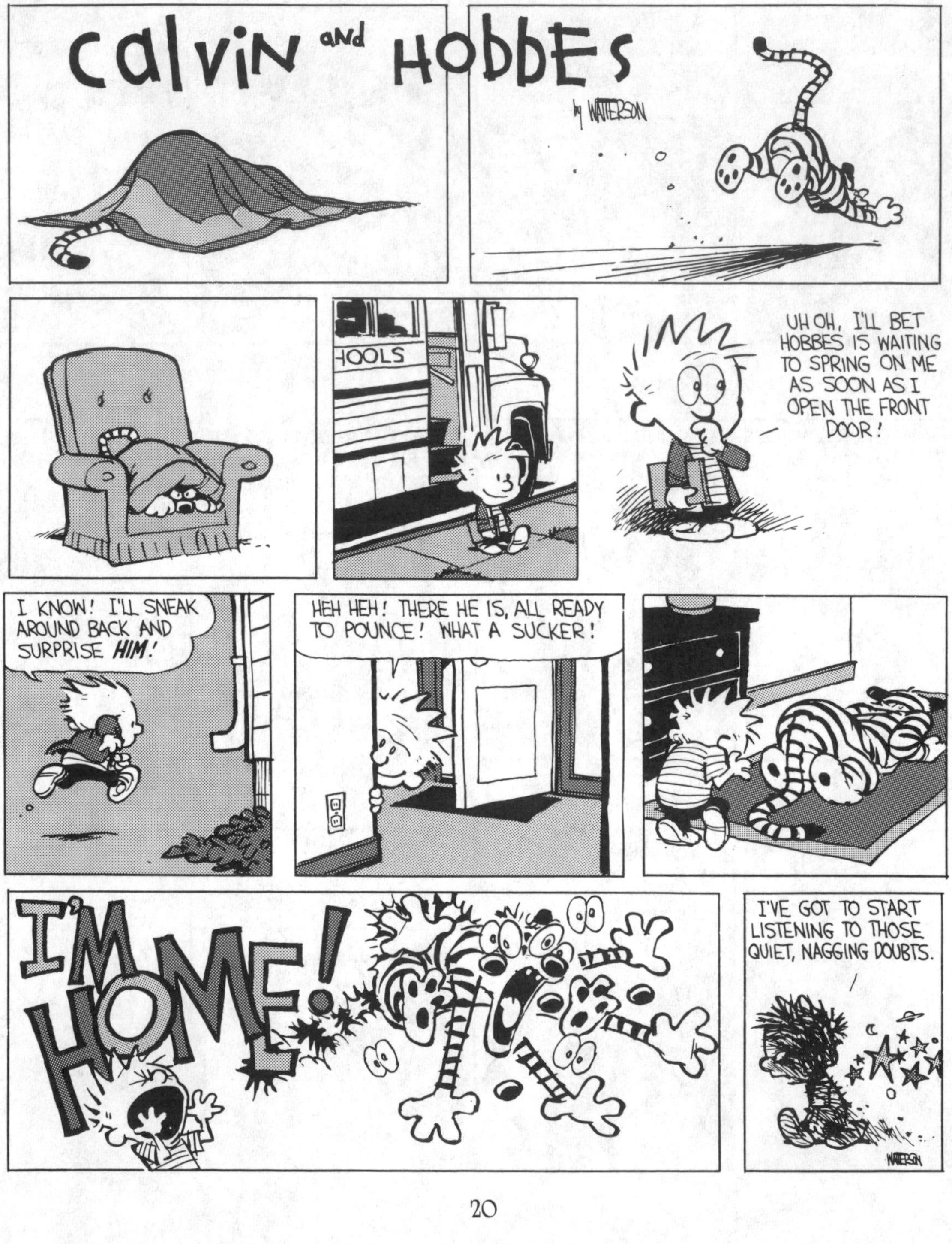
Calvin and HOBBES
by WATTERSON
HOOLS
UH OH, I'LL BET HOBBES IS WAITING TO SPRING ON ME AS SOON AS I OPEN THE FRONT DOOR!
I KNOW! I'LL SNEAK AROUND BACK AND SURPRISE HIM!
HEH HEH! THERE HE IS, ALL READY TO POUNCE! WHAT A SUCKER!
I'M HOME!
I'VE GOT TO START LISTENING TO THOSE QUIET, NAGGING DOUBTS.
WATTERSON

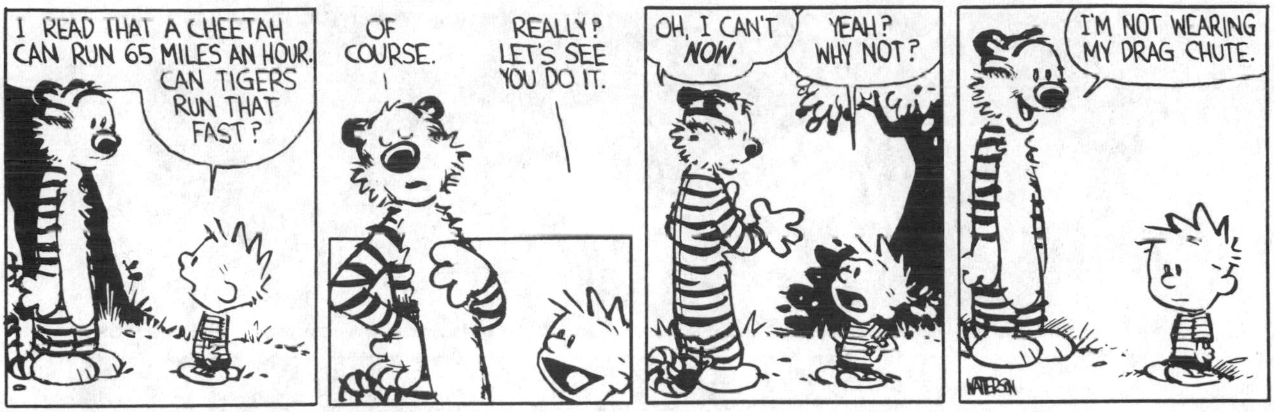
I READ THAT A CHEETAH CAN RUN 65 MILES AN HOUR. CAN TIGERS RUN THAT FAST?
OF COURSE.
REALLY? LET'S SEE YOU DO IT.
OH, I CAN'T NOW.
YEAH? WHY NOT?
I'M NOT WEARING MY DRAG CHUTE.

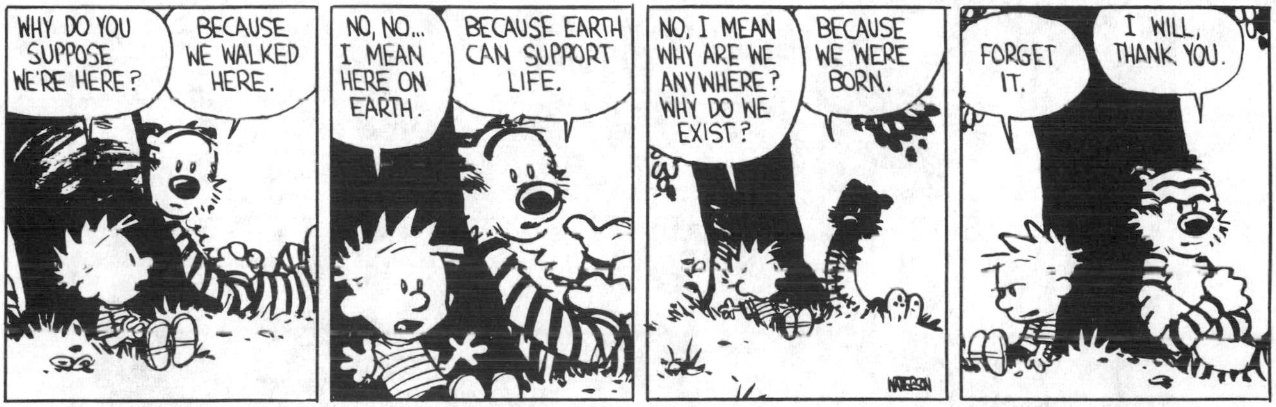
WHY DO YOU SUPPOSE WE'RE HERE?
BECAUSE WE WALKED HERE.
NO, NO... I MEAN HERE ON EARTH.
BECAUSE EARTH CAN SUPPORT LIFE.
NO, I MEAN WHY ARE WE ANYWHERE? WHY DO WE EXIST?
BECAUSE WE WERE BORN.
FORGET IT.
I WILL, THANK YOU.

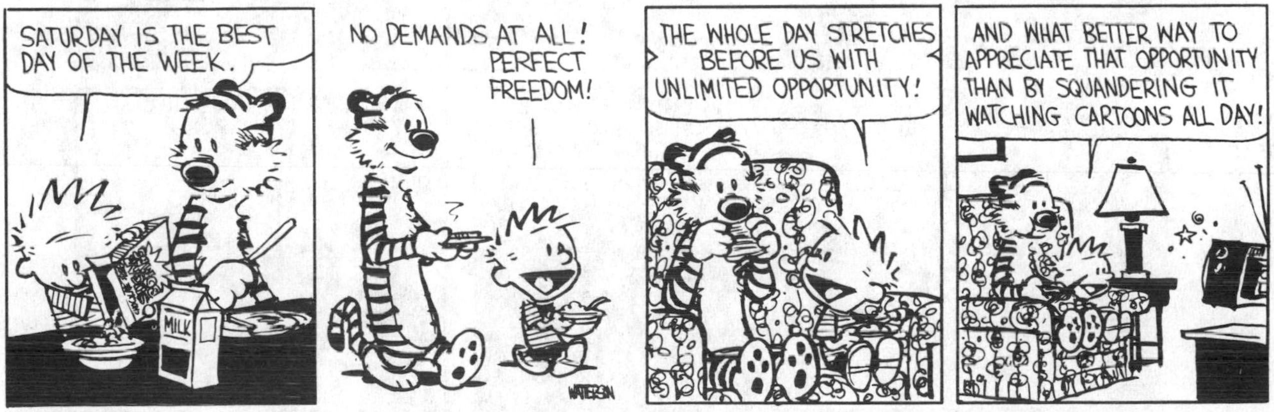
SATURDAY IS THE BEST DAY OF THE WEEK.
MILK
NO DEMANDS AT ALL! PERFECT FREEDOM!
THE WHOLE DAY STRETCHES BEFORE US WITH UNLIMITED OPPORTUNITY!
AND WHAT BETTER WAY TO APPRECIATE THAT OPPORTUNITY THAN BY SQUANDERING IT WATCHING CARTOONS ALL DAY!

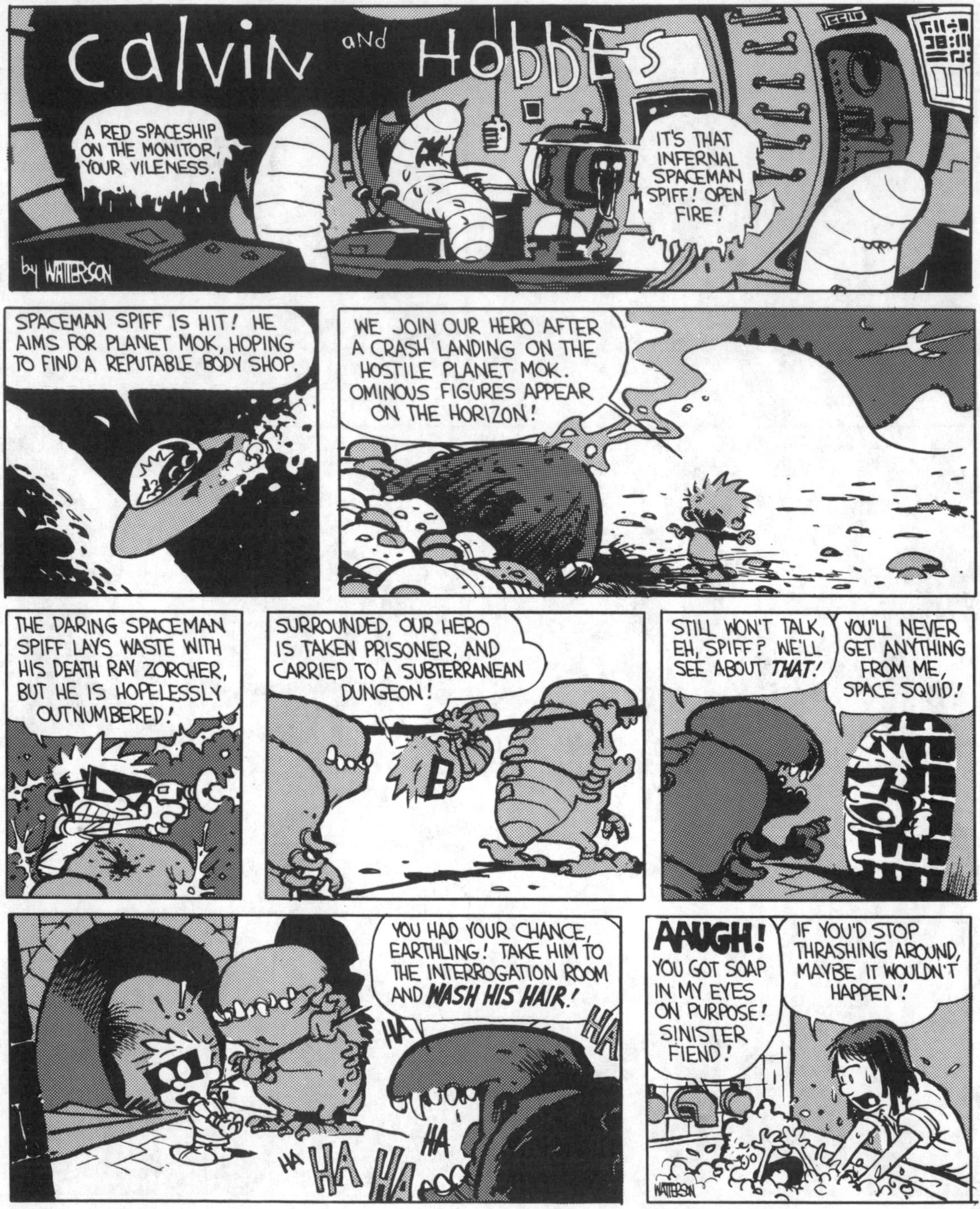
Calvin and Hobbes
by WATTERSON
A RED SPACESHIP ON THE MONITOR, YOUR VILENESS.
IT'S THAT INFERNAL SPACEMAN SPIFF! OPEN FIRE!
SPACEMAN SPIFF IS HIT! HE AIMS FOR PLANET MOK, HOPING TO FIND A REPUTABLE BODY SHOP.
WE JOIN OUR HERO AFTER A CRASH LANDING ON THE HOSTILE PLANET MOK. OMINOUS FIGURES APPEAR ON THE HORIZON!
THE DARING SPACEMAN SPIFF LAYS WASTE WITH HIS DEATH RAY ZORCHER, BUT HE IS HOPELESSLY OUTNUMBERED!
SURROUNDED, OUR HERO IS TAKEN PRISONER, AND CARRIED TO A SUBTERRANEAN DUNGEON!
STILL WON'T TALK, EH, SPIFF? WE'LL SEE ABOUT THAT!
YOU'LL NEVER GET ANYTHING FROM ME, SPACE SQUID!
YOU HAD YOUR CHANCE, EARTHLING! TAKE HIM TO THE INTERROGATION ROOM AND WASH HIS HAIR!
HA HA HA HA HA HA HA
AAUGH! YOU GOT SOAP IN MY EYES ON PURPOSE! SINISTER FIEND!
IF YOU'D STOP THRASHING AROUND, MAYBE IT WOULDN'T HAPPEN!
WATTERSON

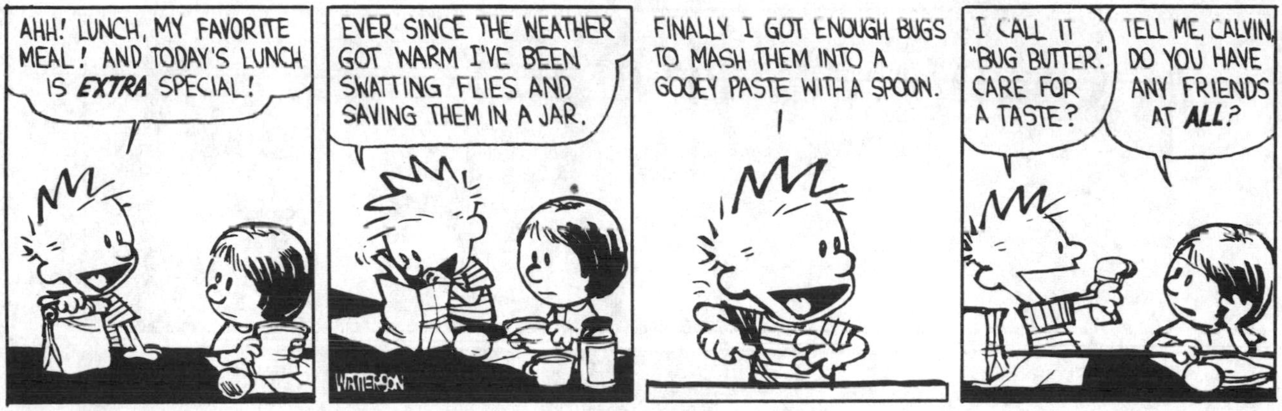
AHH! LUNCH, MY FAVORITE MEAL! AND TODAY'S LUNCH IS *EXTRA* SPECIAL!
EVER SINCE THE WEATHER GOT WARM I'VE BEEN SWATTING FLIES AND SAVING THEM IN A JAR.
FINALLY I GOT ENOUGH BUGS TO MASH THEM INTO A GOOEY PASTE WITH A SPOON.
I CALL IT "BUG BUTTER." CARE FOR A TASTE?
TELL ME, CALVIN, DO YOU HAVE ANY FRIENDS AT *ALL*?

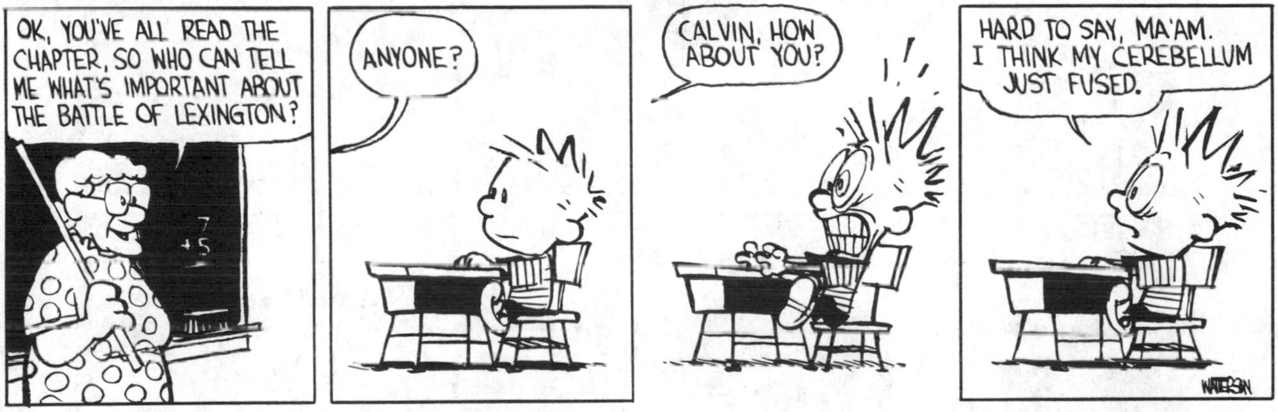
OK, YOU'VE ALL READ THE CHAPTER, SO WHO CAN TELL ME WHAT'S IMPORTANT ABOUT THE BATTLE OF LEXINGTON?
ANYONE?
CALVIN, HOW ABOUT YOU?
HARD TO SAY, MA'AM. I THINK MY CEREBELLUM JUST FUSED.

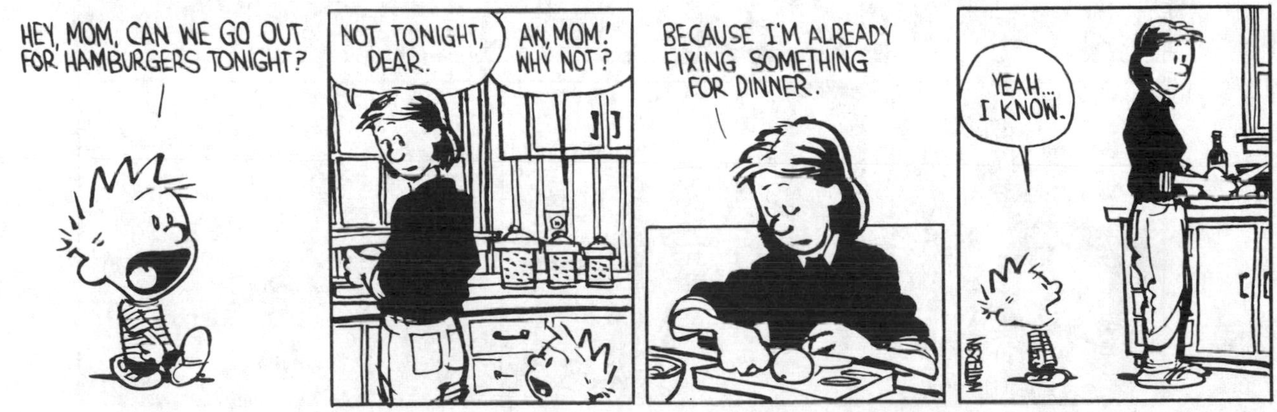
HEY, MOM, CAN WE GO OUT FOR HAMBURGERS TONIGHT?
NOT TONIGHT, DEAR.
AW, MOM! WHY NOT?
BECAUSE I'M ALREADY FIXING SOMETHING FOR DINNER.
YEAH... I KNOW.

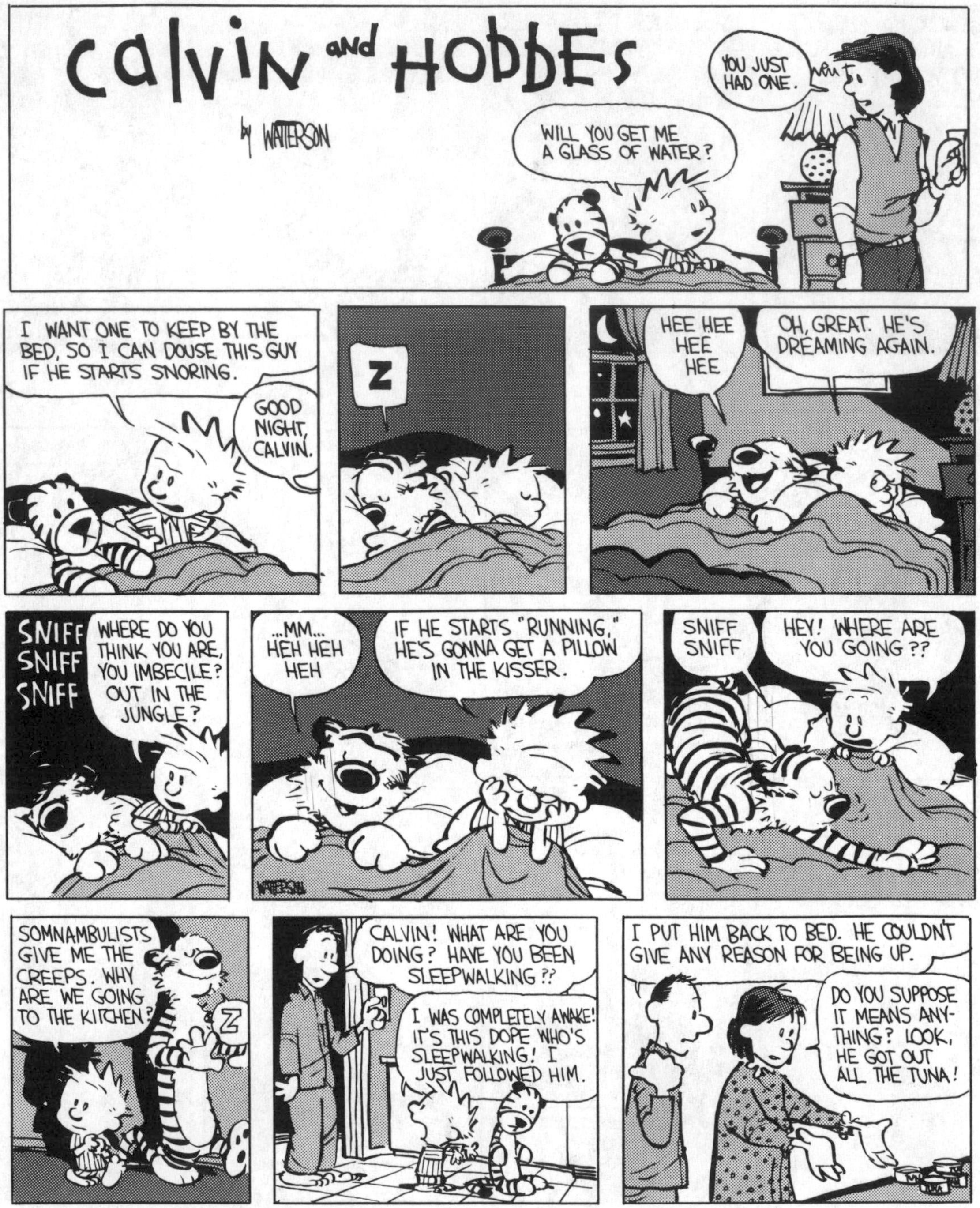
Calvin and HOBBES
by WATTERSON
WILL YOU GET ME A GLASS OF WATER?
YOU JUST HAD ONE.
I WANT ONE TO KEEP BY THE BED, SO I CAN DOUSE THIS GUY IF HE STARTS SNORING.
GOOD NIGHT, CALVIN.
Z
HEE HEE HEE HEE
OH, GREAT. HE'S DREAMING AGAIN.
SNIFF SNIFF SNIFF
WHERE DO YOU THINK YOU ARE, YOU IMBECILE? OUT IN THE JUNGLE?
...MM... HEH HEH HEH
IF HE STARTS "RUNNING," HE'S GONNA GET A PILLOW IN THE KISSER.
SNIFF SNIFF
HEY! WHERE ARE YOU GOING??
SOMNAMBULISTS GIVE ME THE CREEPS. WHY ARE WE GOING TO THE KITCHEN?
Z
CALVIN! WHAT ARE YOU DOING? HAVE YOU BEEN SLEEPWALKING??
I WAS COMPLETELY AWAKE! IT'S THIS DOPE WHO'S SLEEPWALKING! I JUST FOLLOWED HIM.
I PUT HIM BACK TO BED. HE COULDN'T GIVE ANY REASON FOR BEING UP.
DO YOU SUPPOSE IT MEANS ANYTHING? LOOK, HE GOT OUT ALL THE TUNA!

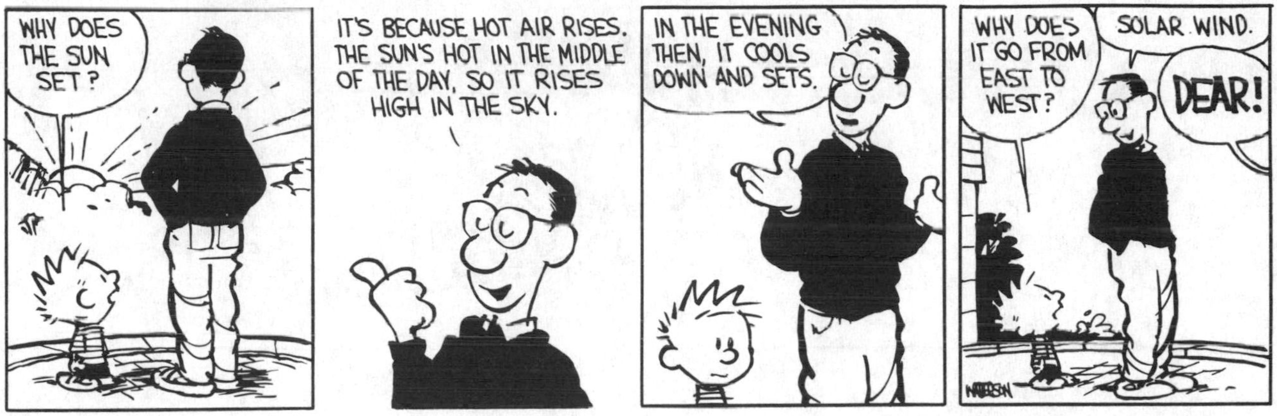
WHY DOES THE SUN SET?
IT'S BECAUSE HOT AIR RISES. THE SUN'S HOT IN THE MIDDLE OF THE DAY, SO IT RISES HIGH IN THE SKY.
IN THE EVENING THEN, IT COOLS DOWN AND SETS.
WHY DOES IT GO FROM EAST TO WEST?
SOLAR WIND.
DEAR!

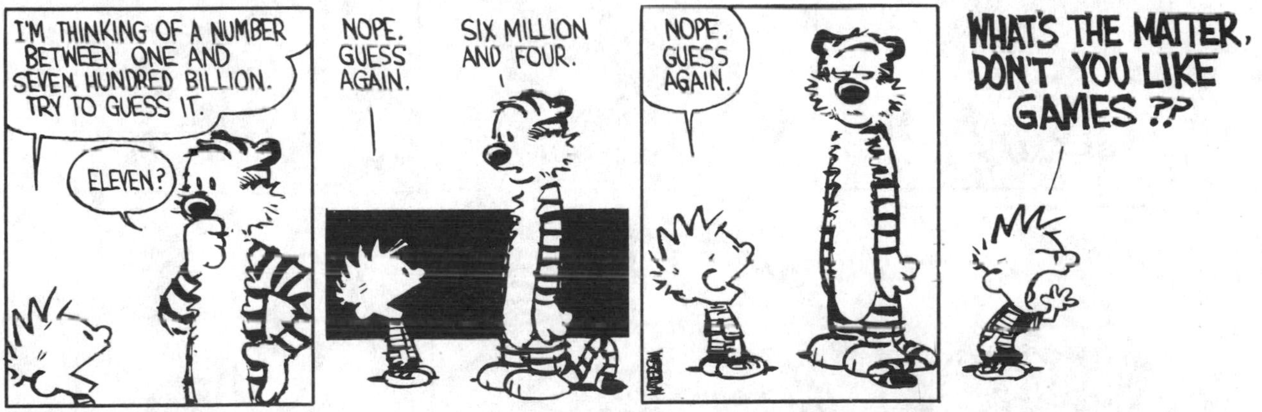
I'M THINKING OF A NUMBER BETWEEN ONE AND SEVEN HUNDRED BILLION. TRY TO GUESS IT.
ELEVEN?
NOPE. GUESS AGAIN.
SIX MILLION AND FOUR.
NOPE. GUESS AGAIN.
WHAT'S THE MATTER, DON'T YOU LIKE GAMES ??

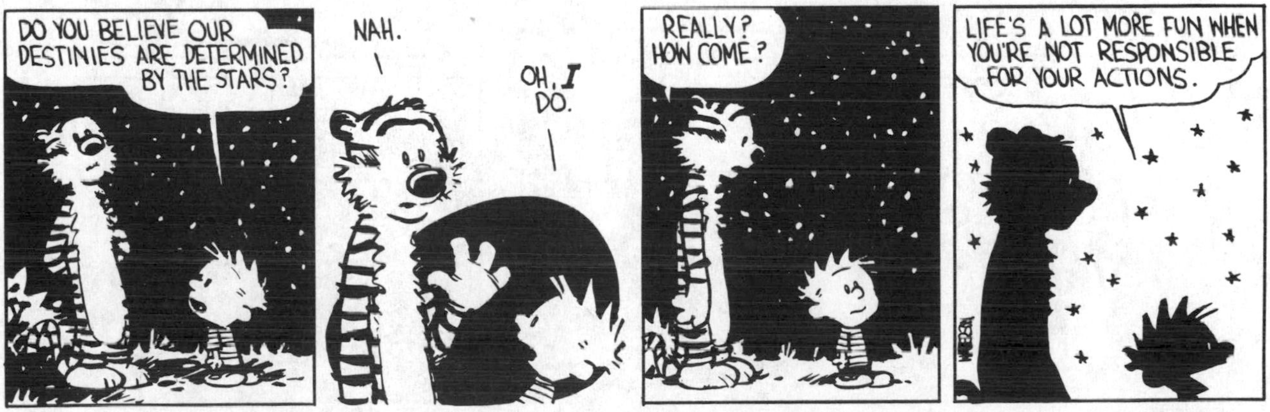
DO YOU BELIEVE OUR DESTINIES ARE DETERMINED BY THE STARS?
NAH.
OH, I DO.
REALLY? HOW COME?
LIFE'S A LOT MORE FUN WHEN YOU'RE NOT RESPONSIBLE FOR YOUR ACTIONS.

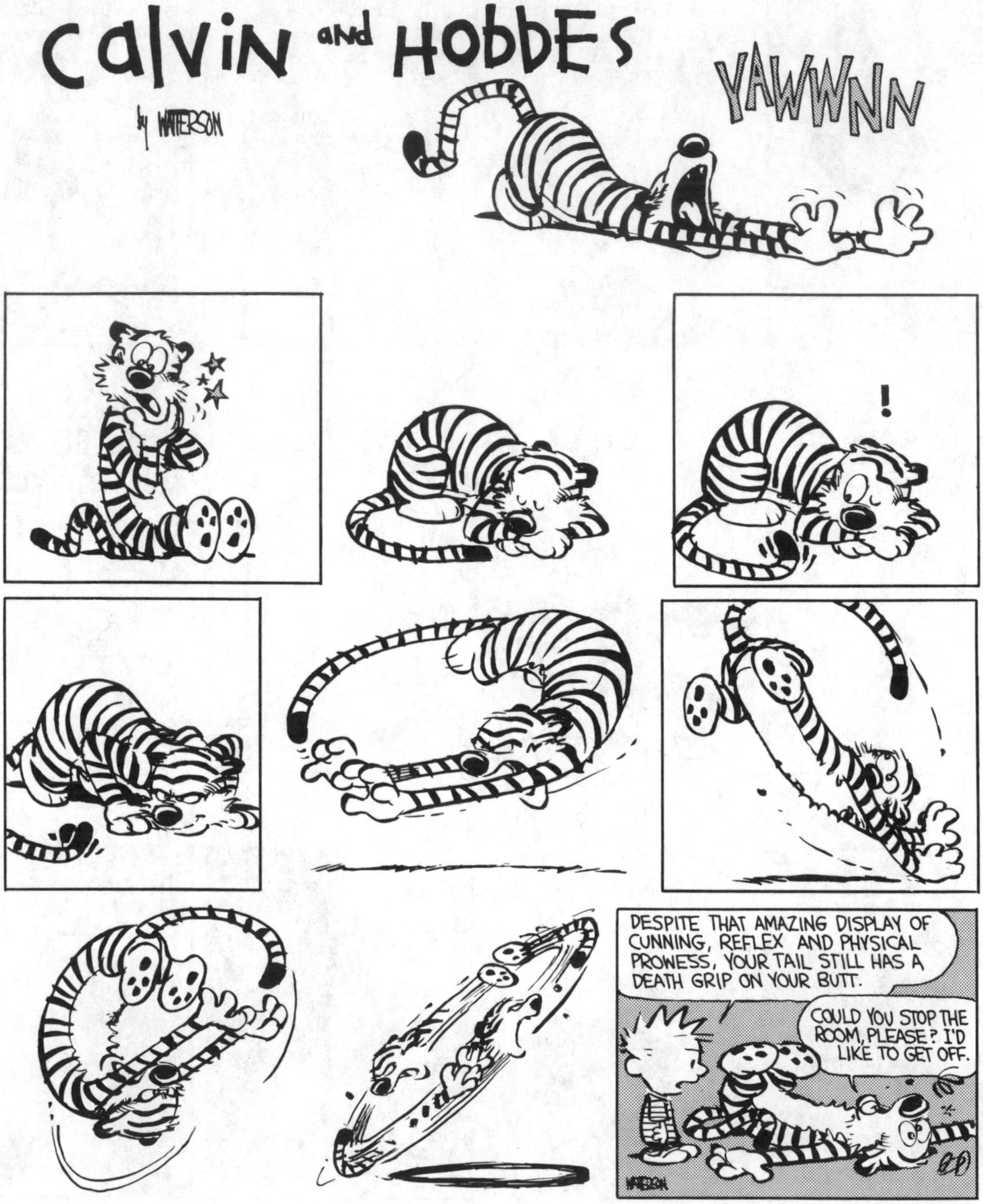
Calvin and HOBBES
by WATTERSON
YAWWNN
!
DESPITE THAT AMAZING DISPLAY OF CUNNING, REFLEX AND PHYSICAL PROWESS, YOUR TAIL STILL HAS A DEATH GRIP ON YOUR BUTT.
COULD YOU STOP THE ROOM, PLEASE? I'D LIKE TO GET OFF.
WATERSON

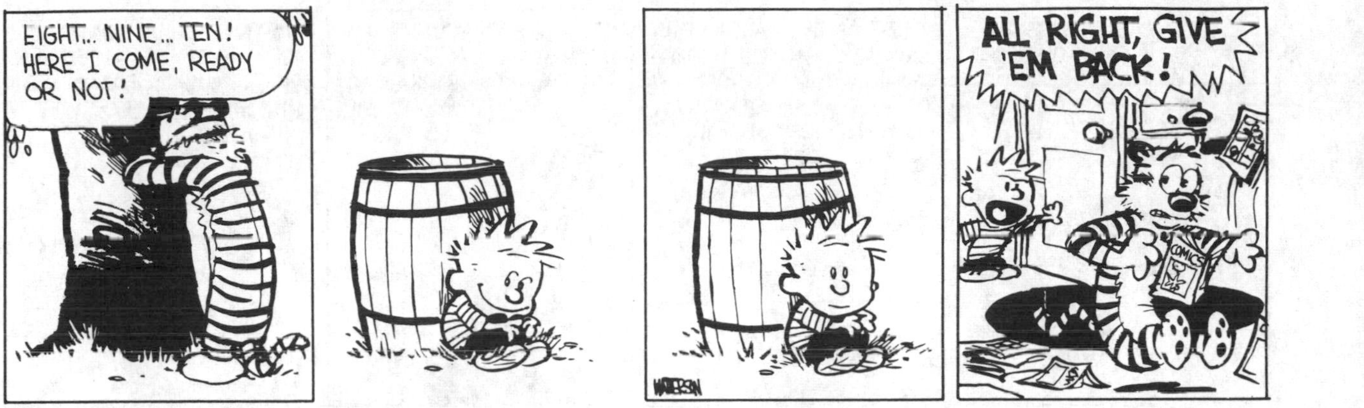
EIGHT... NINE... TEN! HERE I COME, READY OR NOT!
ALL RIGHT, GIVE 'EM BACK!
COMICS

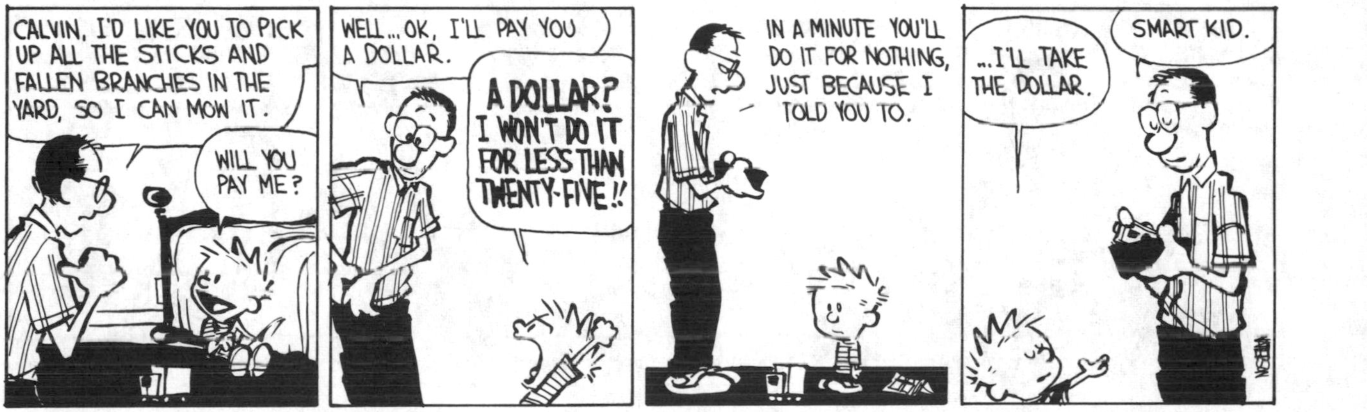
CALVIN, I'D LIKE YOU TO PICK UP ALL THE STICKS AND FALLEN BRANCHES IN THE YARD, SO I CAN MOW IT.
WILL YOU PAY ME?
WELL... OK, I'LL PAY YOU A DOLLAR.
A DOLLAR? I WON'T DO IT FOR LESS THAN TWENTY-FIVE!!
IN A MINUTE YOU'LL DO IT FOR NOTHING, JUST BECAUSE I TOLD YOU TO.
...I'LL TAKE THE DOLLAR.
SMART KID.

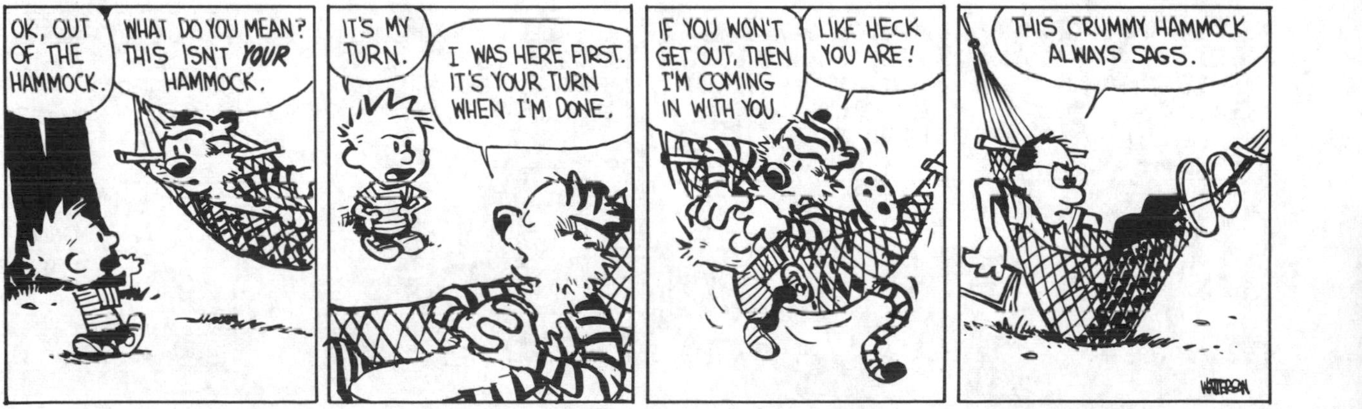
OK, OUT OF THE HAMMOCK.
WHAT DO YOU MEAN? THIS ISN'T YOUR HAMMOCK.
IT'S MY TURN.
I WAS HERE FIRST. IT'S YOUR TURN WHEN I'M DONE.
IF YOU WON'T GET OUT, THEN I'M COMING IN WITH YOU.
LIKE HECK YOU ARE!
THIS CRUMMY HAMMOCK ALWAYS SAGS.

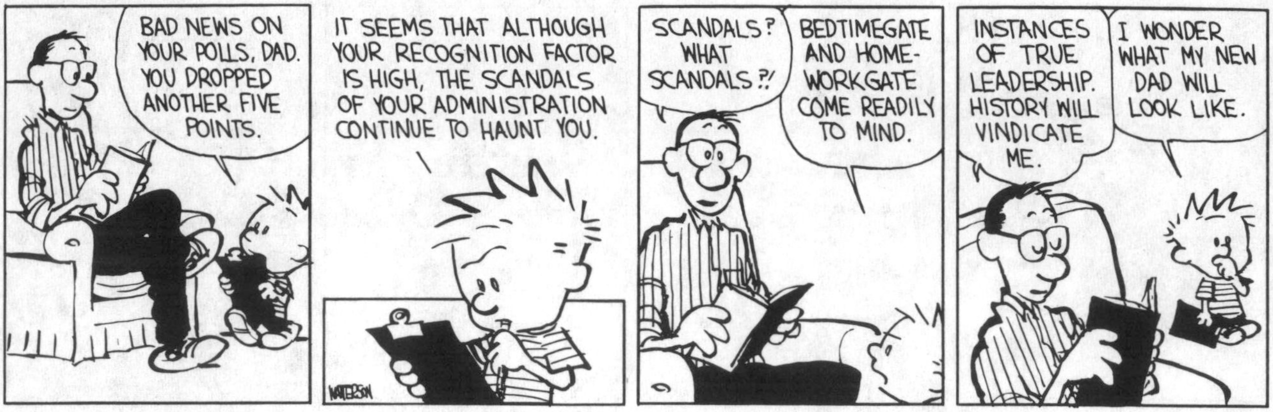
BAD NEWS ON YOUR POLLS, DAD. YOU DROPPED ANOTHER FIVE POINTS.
IT SEEMS THAT ALTHOUGH YOUR RECOGNITION FACTOR IS HIGH, THE SCANDALS OF YOUR ADMINISTRATION CONTINUE TO HAUNT YOU.
SCANDALS? WHAT SCANDALS?!
BEDTIMEGATE AND HOME-WORKGATE COME READILY TO MIND.
INSTANCES OF TRUE LEADERSHIP. HISTORY WILL VINDICATE ME.
I WONDER WHAT MY NEW DAD WILL LOOK LIKE.

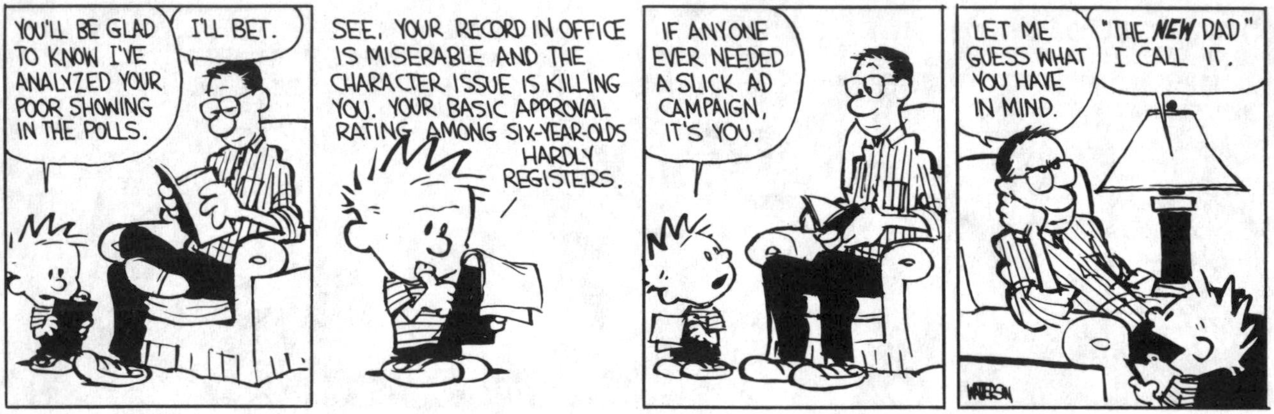
YOU'LL BE GLAD TO KNOW I'VE ANALYZED YOUR POOR SHOWING IN THE POLLS.
I'LL BET.
SEE, YOUR RECORD IN OFFICE IS MISERABLE AND THE CHARACTER ISSUE IS KILLING YOU. YOUR BASIC APPROVAL RATING AMONG SIX-YEAR-OLDS HARDLY REGISTERS.
IF ANYONE EVER NEEDED A SLICK AD CAMPAIGN, IT'S YOU.
LET ME GUESS WHAT YOU HAVE IN MIND.
"THE NEW DAD" I CALL IT.

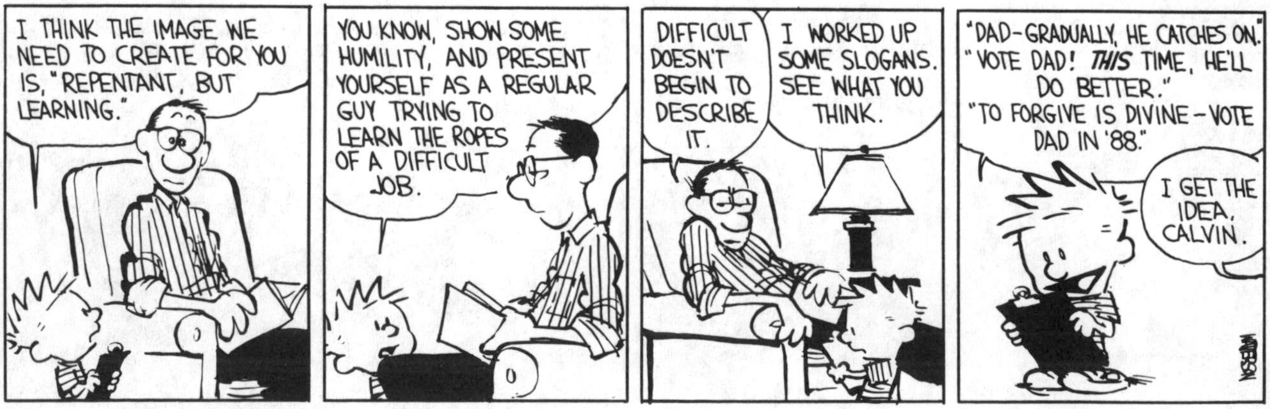
I THINK THE IMAGE WE NEED TO CREATE FOR YOU IS, "REPENTANT, BUT LEARNING."
YOU KNOW, SHOW SOME HUMILITY, AND PRESENT YOURSELF AS A REGULAR GUY TRYING TO LEARN THE ROPES OF A DIFFICULT JOB.
DIFFICULT DOESN'T BEGIN TO DESCRIBE IT.
I WORKED UP SOME SLOGANS. SEE WHAT YOU THINK.
"DAD-GRADUALLY, HE CATCHES ON." "VOTE DAD! THIS TIME, HE'LL DO BETTER." "TO FORGIVE IS DIVINE-VOTE DAD IN '88."
I GET THE IDEA, CALVIN.

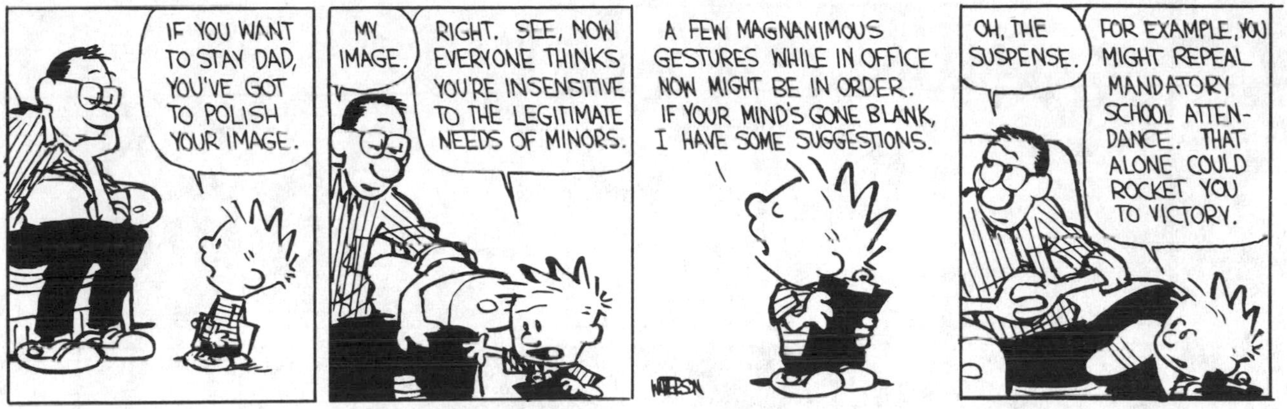
IF YOU WANT TO STAY DAD, YOU'VE GOT TO POLISH YOUR IMAGE.
MY IMAGE.
RIGHT. SEE, NOW EVERYONE THINKS YOU'RE INSENSITIVE TO THE LEGITIMATE NEEDS OF MINORS.
A FEW MAGNANIMOUS GESTURES WHILE IN OFFICE NOW MIGHT BE IN ORDER. IF YOUR MIND'S GONE BLANK, I HAVE SOME SUGGESTIONS.
OH, THE SUSPENSE.
FOR EXAMPLE, YOU MIGHT REPEAL MANDATORY SCHOOL ATTENDANCE. THAT ALONE COULD ROCKET YOU TO VICTORY.

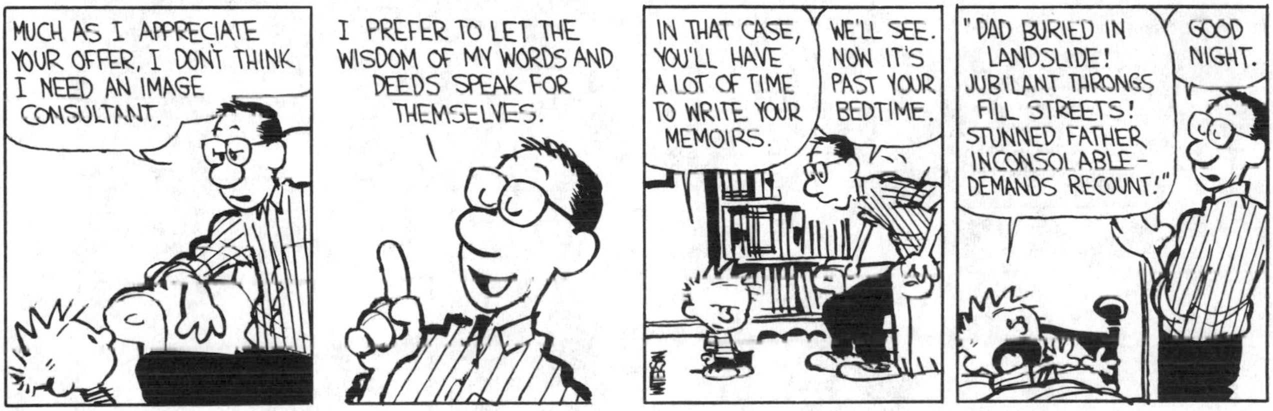
MUCH AS I APPRECIATE YOUR OFFER, I DON'T THINK I NEED AN IMAGE CONSULTANT.
I PREFER TO LET THE WISDOM OF MY WORDS AND DEEDS SPEAK FOR THEMSELVES.
IN THAT CASE, YOU'LL HAVE A LOT OF TIME TO WRITE YOUR MEMOIRS.
WE'LL SEE. NOW IT'S PAST YOUR BEDTIME.
"DAD BURIED IN LANDSLIDE! JUBILANT THRONGS FILL STREETS! STUNNED FATHER INCONSOLABLE - DEMANDS RECOUNT!"
GOOD NIGHT.

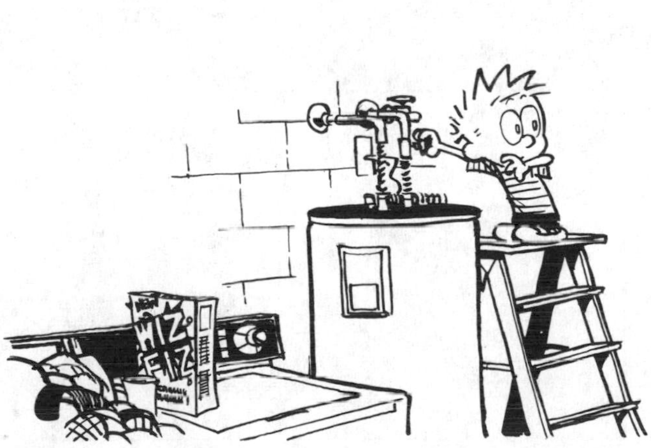

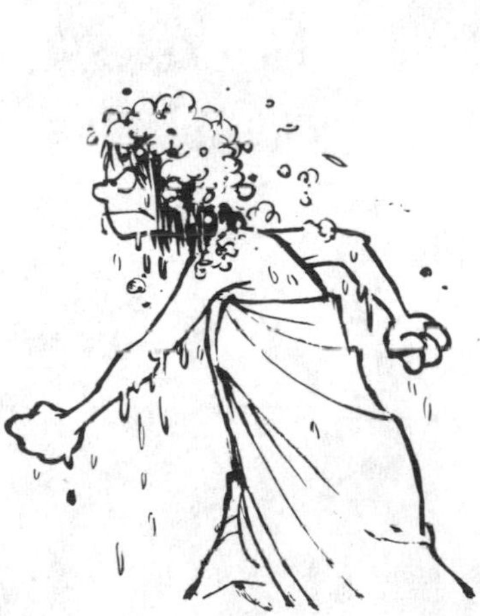

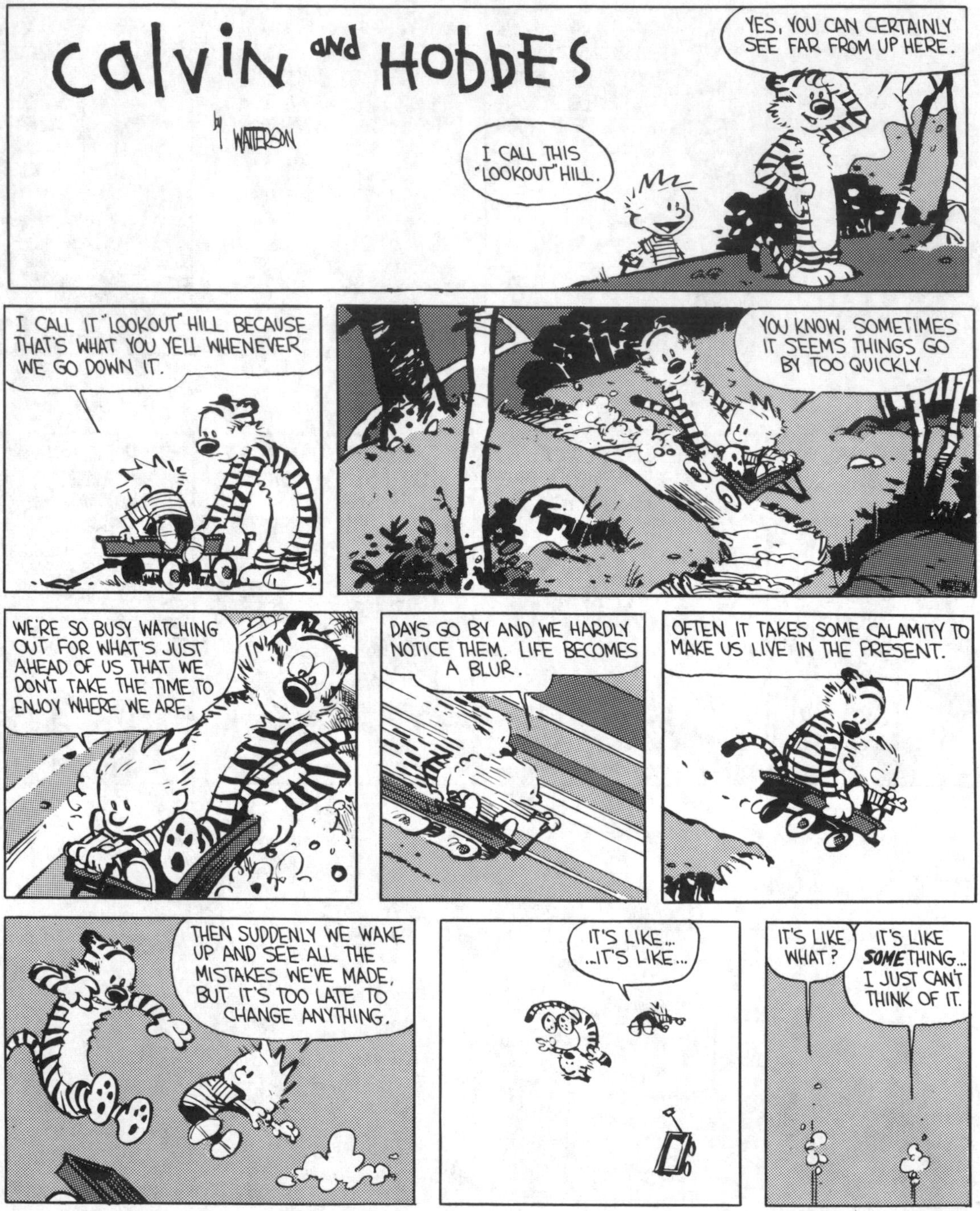
Calvin and HOBBES
by WATTERSON
I CALL THIS "LOOKOUT" HILL.
YES, YOU CAN CERTAINLY SEE FAR FROM UP HERE.
I CALL IT "LOOKOUT" HILL BECAUSE THAT'S WHAT YOU YELL WHENEVER WE GO DOWN IT.
YOU KNOW, SOMETIMES IT SEEMS THINGS GO BY TOO QUICKLY.
WE'RE SO BUSY WATCHING OUT FOR WHAT'S JUST AHEAD OF US THAT WE DON'T TAKE THE TIME TO ENJOY WHERE WE ARE.
DAYS GO BY AND WE HARDLY NOTICE THEM. LIFE BECOMES A BLUR.
OFTEN IT TAKES SOME CALAMITY TO MAKE US LIVE IN THE PRESENT.
THEN SUDDENLY WE WAKE UP AND SEE ALL THE MISTAKES WE'VE MADE, BUT IT'S TOO LATE TO CHANGE ANYTHING.
IT'S LIKE... ...IT'S LIKE...
IT'S LIKE WHAT?
IT'S LIKE SOMETHING... I JUST CAN'T THINK OF IT.

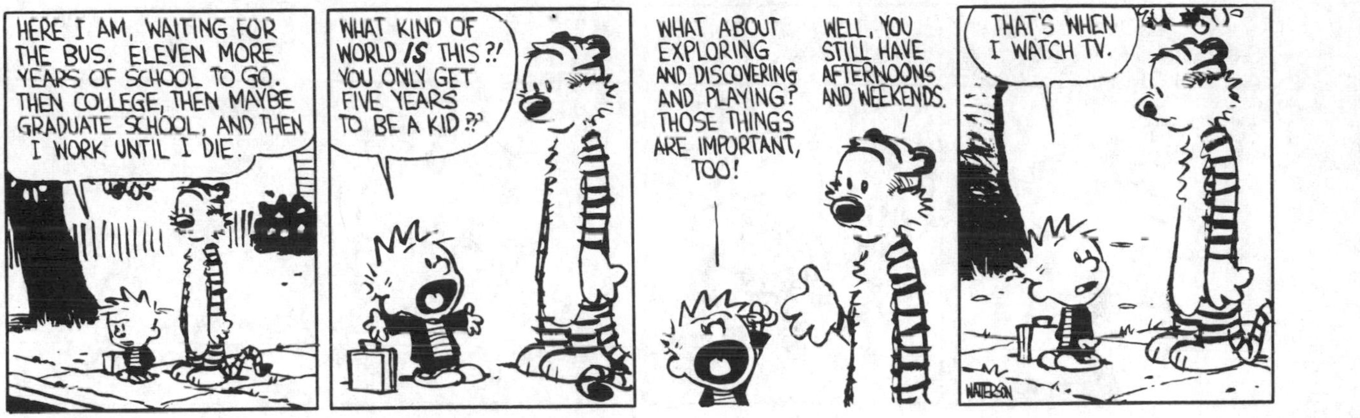
HERE I AM, WAITING FOR THE BUS. ELEVEN MORE YEARS OF SCHOOL TO GO. THEN COLLEGE, THEN MAYBE GRADUATE SCHOOL, AND THEN I WORK UNTIL I DIE.
WHAT KIND OF WORLD *IS* THIS?! YOU ONLY GET FIVE YEARS TO BE A KID?!
WHAT ABOUT EXPLORING AND DISCOVERING AND PLAYING? THOSE THINGS ARE IMPORTANT, TOO!
WELL, YOU STILL HAVE AFTERNOONS AND WEEKENDS.
THAT'S WHEN I WATCH TV.

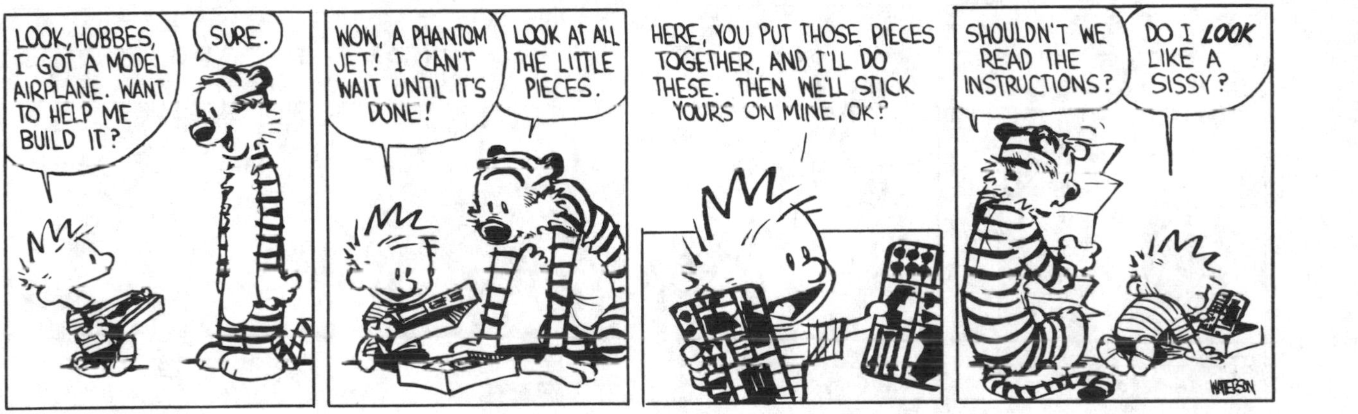
LOOK, HOBBES, I GOT A MODEL AIRPLANE. WANT TO HELP ME BUILD IT?
SURE.
WOW, A PHANTOM JET! I CAN'T WAIT UNTIL IT'S DONE!
LOOK AT ALL THE LITTLE PIECES.
HERE, YOU PUT THOSE PIECES TOGETHER, AND I'LL DO THESE. THEN WE'LL STICK YOURS ON MINE, OK?
SHOULDN'T WE READ THE INSTRUCTIONS?
DO I *LOOK* LIKE A SISSY?

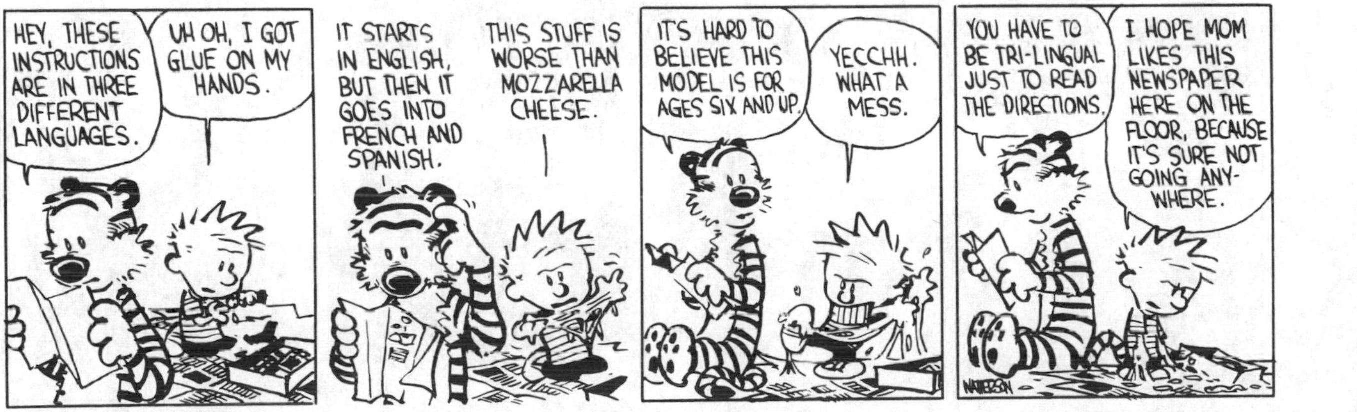
HEY, THESE INSTRUCTIONS ARE IN THREE DIFFERENT LANGUAGES.
UH OH, I GOT GLUE ON MY HANDS.
IT STARTS IN ENGLISH, BUT THEN IT GOES INTO FRENCH AND SPANISH.
THIS STUFF IS WORSE THAN MOZZARELLA CHEESE.
IT'S HARD TO BELIEVE THIS MODEL IS FOR AGES SIX AND UP.
YECCHH. WHAT A MESS.
YOU HAVE TO BE TRI-LINGUAL JUST TO READ THE DIRECTIONS.
I HOPE MOM LIKES THIS NEWSPAPER HERE ON THE FLOOR, BECAUSE IT'S SURE NOT GOING ANY-WHERE.

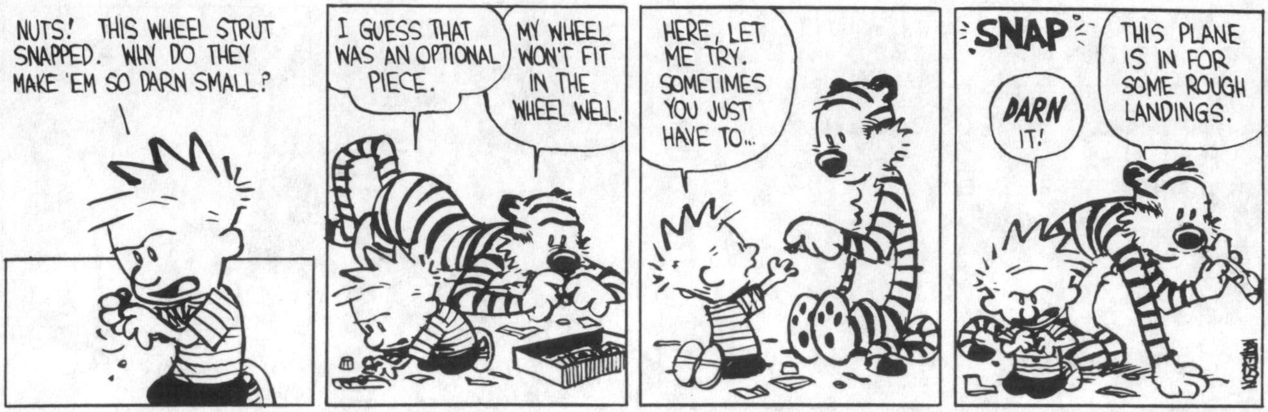
NUTS! THIS WHEEL STRUT SNAPPED. WHY DO THEY MAKE 'EM SO DARN SMALL?
I GUESS THAT WAS AN OPTIONAL PIECE.
MY WHEEL WON'T FIT IN THE WHEEL WELL.
HERE, LET ME TRY. SOMETIMES YOU JUST HAVE TO...
SNAP
DARN IT!
THIS PLANE IS IN FOR SOME ROUGH LANDINGS.

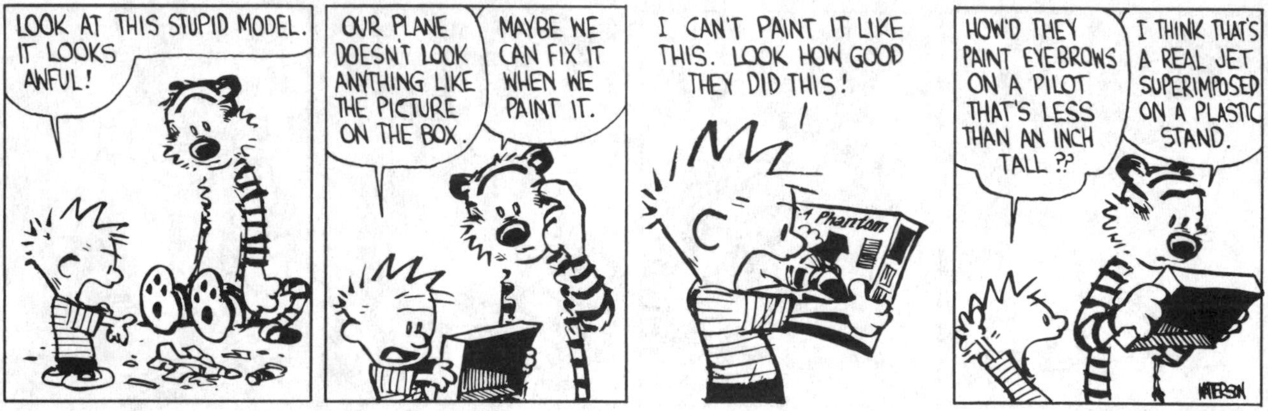
LOOK AT THIS STUPID MODEL. IT LOOKS AWFUL!
OUR PLANE DOESN'T LOOK ANYTHING LIKE THE PICTURE ON THE BOX.
MAYBE WE CAN FIX IT WHEN WE PAINT IT.
I CAN'T PAINT IT LIKE THIS. LOOK HOW GOOD THEY DID THIS!
Phantom
HOW'D THEY PAINT EYEBROWS ON A PILOT THAT'S LESS THAN AN INCH TALL ??
I THINK THAT'S A REAL JET SUPERIMPOSED ON A PLASTIC STAND.

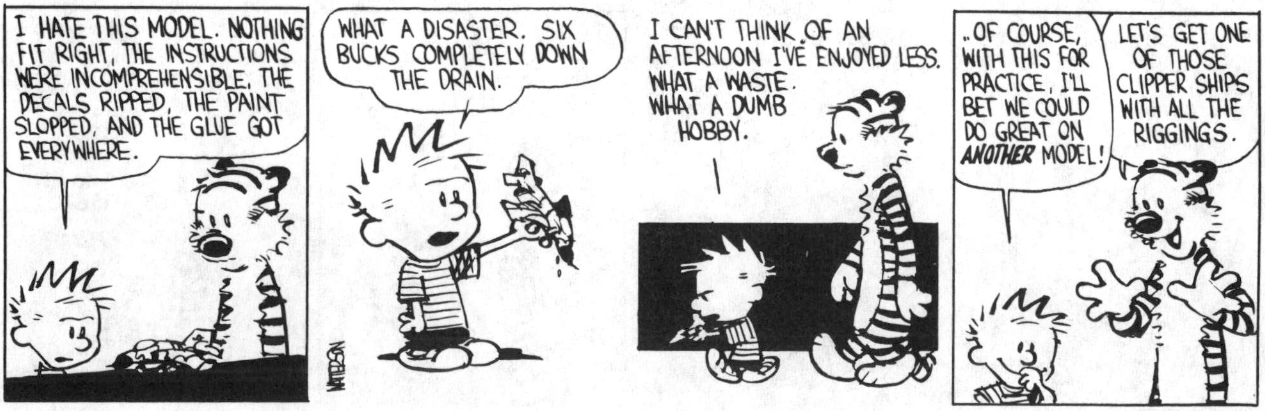
I HATE THIS MODEL. NOTHING FIT RIGHT, THE INSTRUCTIONS WERE INCOMPREHENSIBLE, THE DECALS RIPPED, THE PAINT SLOPPED, AND THE GLUE GOT EVERYWHERE.
WHAT A DISASTER. SIX BUCKS COMPLETELY DOWN THE DRAIN.
I CAN'T THINK OF AN AFTERNOON I'VE ENJOYED LESS. WHAT A WASTE. WHAT A DUMB HOBBY.
..OF COURSE, WITH THIS FOR PRACTICE, I'LL BET WE COULD DO GREAT ON ANOTHER MODEL!
LET'S GET ONE OF THOSE CLIPPER SHIPS WITH ALL THE RIGGINGS.

Calvin and HOBBES
by WATTERSON
A VOICE CACKLES IN CALVIN'S RADIO. "ENEMY FIGHTERS AT TWO O'CLOCK!"
ROGER. WHAT SHOULD I DO UNTIL THEN?
CALVIN'S F-4 PHANTOM SCREAMS ACROSS THE SKY!
BUT WHAT'S THIS? THE CANOPY GLASS IS ALL SMEARED! HE CAN HARDLY SEE THROUGH IT!
OH, NO! THE THROTTLE SNAPS OFF IN HIS HAND!
CALVIN'S ONLY HOPE IS TO LAND, BUT THE WHEELS REFUSE TO OPEN! THEY'RE STUCK!
FRANTICALLY CALVIN TRIES TO EJECT, BUT THE COCKPIT IS FUSED TOGETHER! HIS JET IS A HOPELESS MESS! EVERYTHING IS GOING WRONG!
WATTERSON
STUPID MODEL.

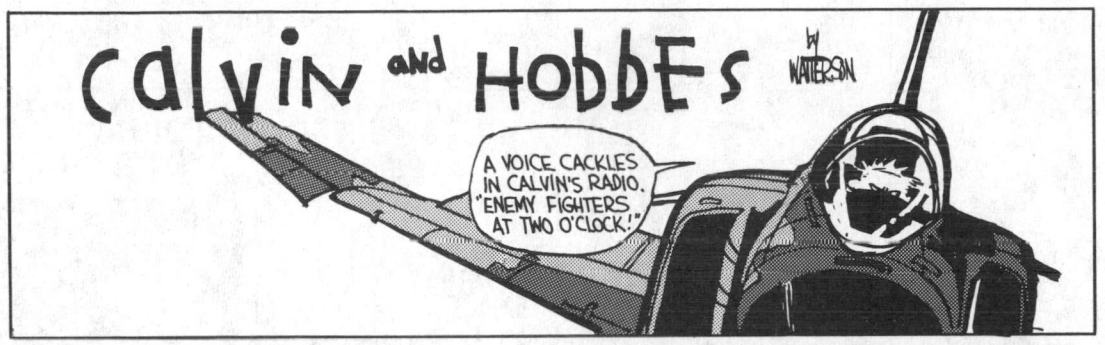

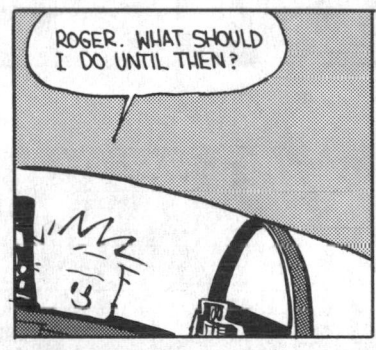

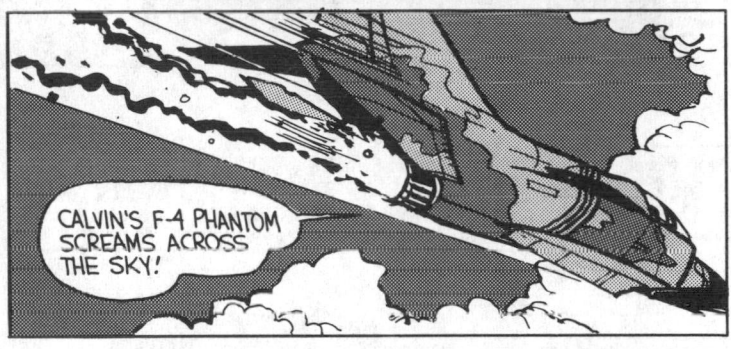

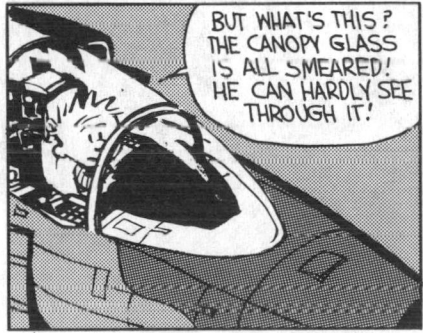

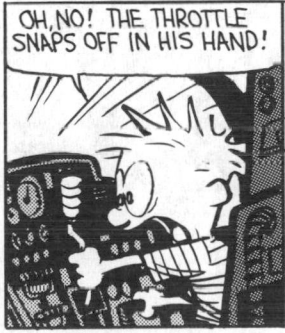

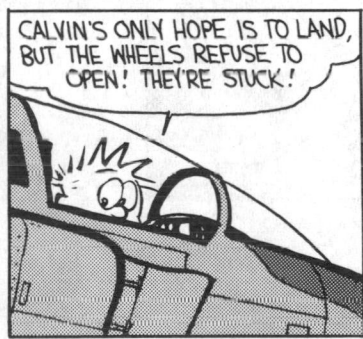

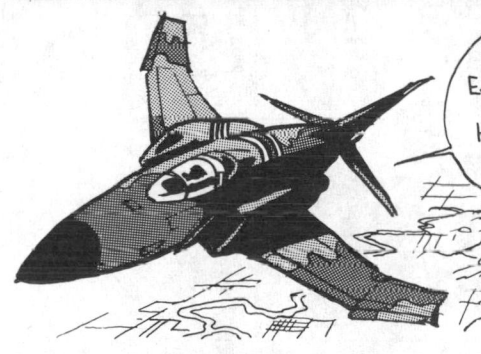

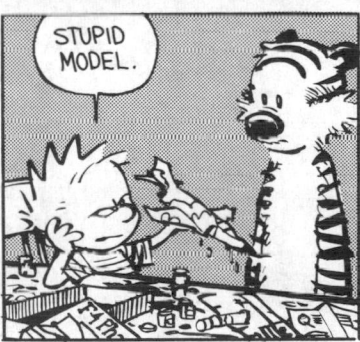

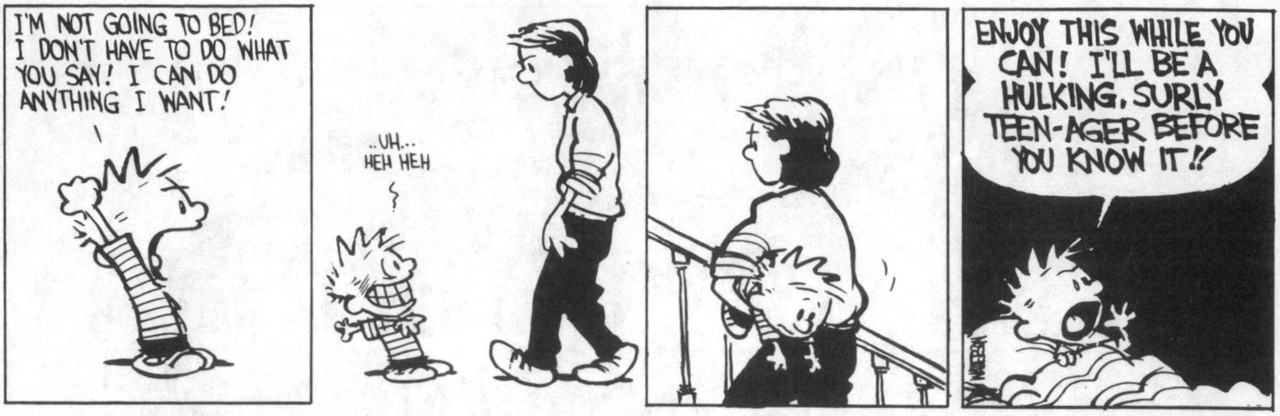
I'M NOT GOING TO BED! I DON'T HAVE TO DO WHAT YOU SAY! I CAN DO ANYTHING I WANT!
..UH.. HEH HEH
ENJOY THIS WHILE YOU CAN! I'LL BE A HULKING, SURLY TEEN-AGER BEFORE YOU KNOW IT!!

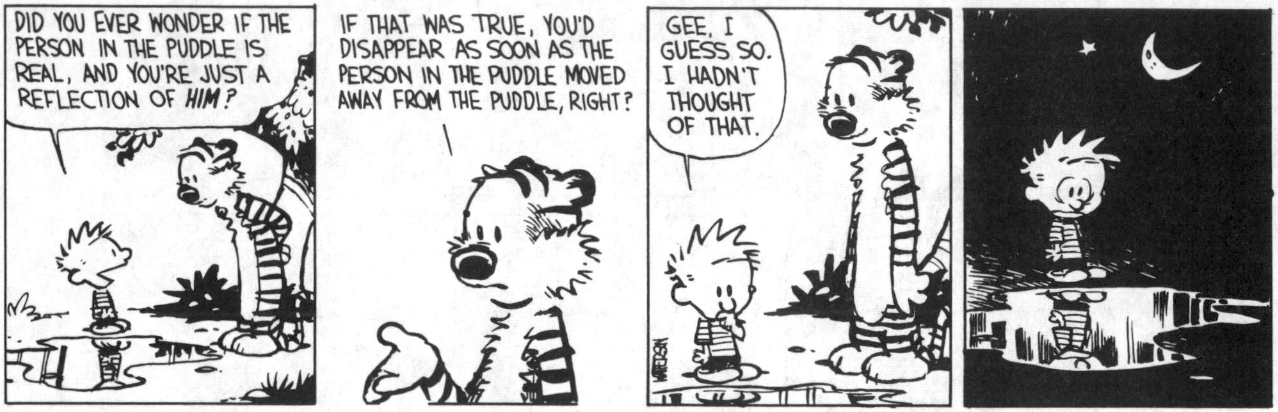
DID YOU EVER WONDER IF THE PERSON IN THE PUDDLE IS REAL, AND YOU'RE JUST A REFLECTION OF HIM?
IF THAT WAS TRUE, YOU'D DISAPPEAR AS SOON AS THE PERSON IN THE PUDDLE MOVED AWAY FROM THE PUDDLE, RIGHT?
GEE, I GUESS SO. I HADN'T THOUGHT OF THAT.

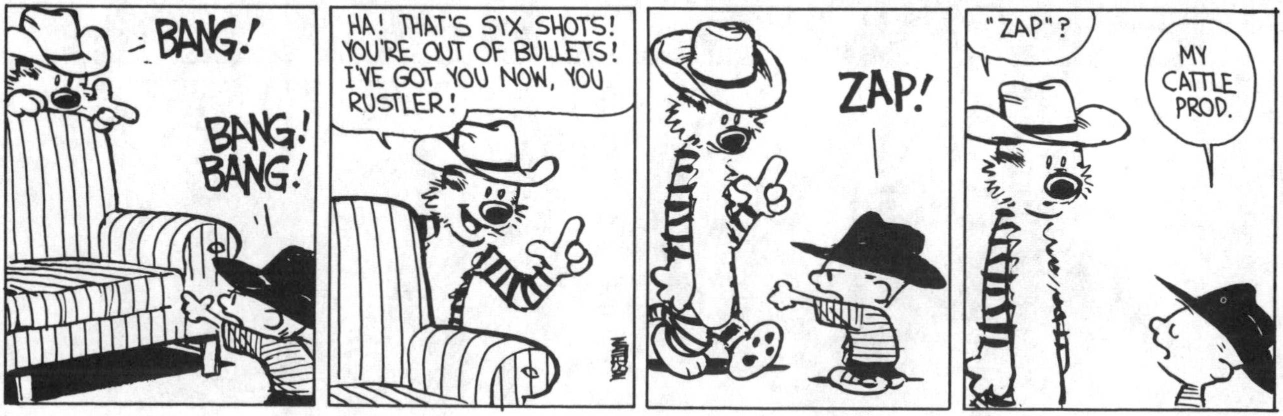
BANG!
BANG! BANG!
HA! THAT'S SIX SHOTS! YOU'RE OUT OF BULLETS! I'VE GOT YOU NOW, YOU RUSTLER!
ZAP!
"ZAP"?
MY CATTLE PROD.

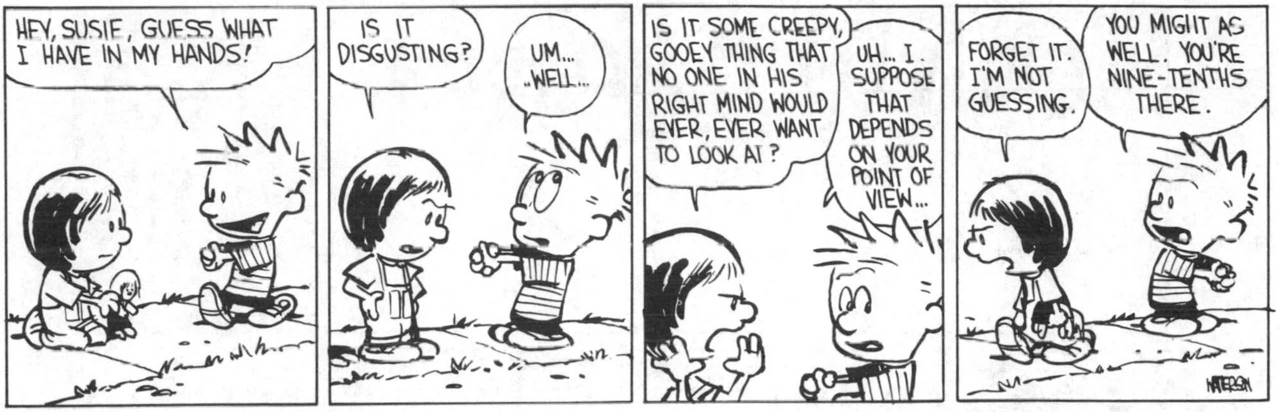
HEY, SUSIE, GUESS WHAT I HAVE IN MY HANDS!
IS IT DISGUSTING?
UM... ..WELL...
IS IT SOME CREEPY, GOOEY THING THAT NO ONE IN HIS RIGHT MIND WOULD EVER, EVER WANT TO LOOK AT?
UH... I SUPPOSE THAT DEPENDS ON YOUR POINT OF VIEW...
FORGET IT. I'M NOT GUESSING.
YOU MIGHT AS WELL. YOU'RE NINE-TENTHS THERE.

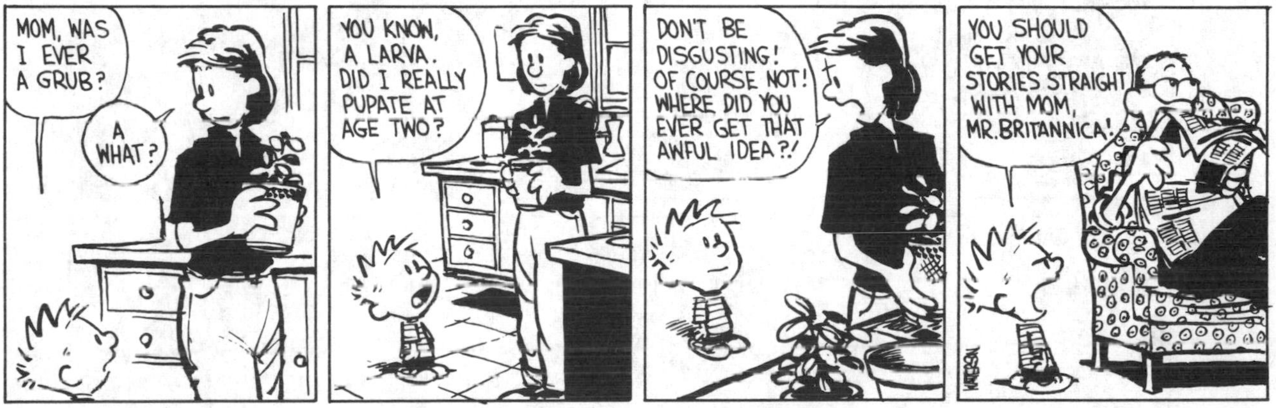
MOM, WAS I EVER A GRUB?
A WHAT?
YOU KNOW, A LARVA. DID I REALLY PUPATE AT AGE TWO?
DON'T BE DISGUSTING! OF COURSE NOT! WHERE DID YOU EVER GET THAT AWFUL IDEA?!
YOU SHOULD GET YOUR STORIES STRAIGHT WITH MOM, MR. BRITANNICA!

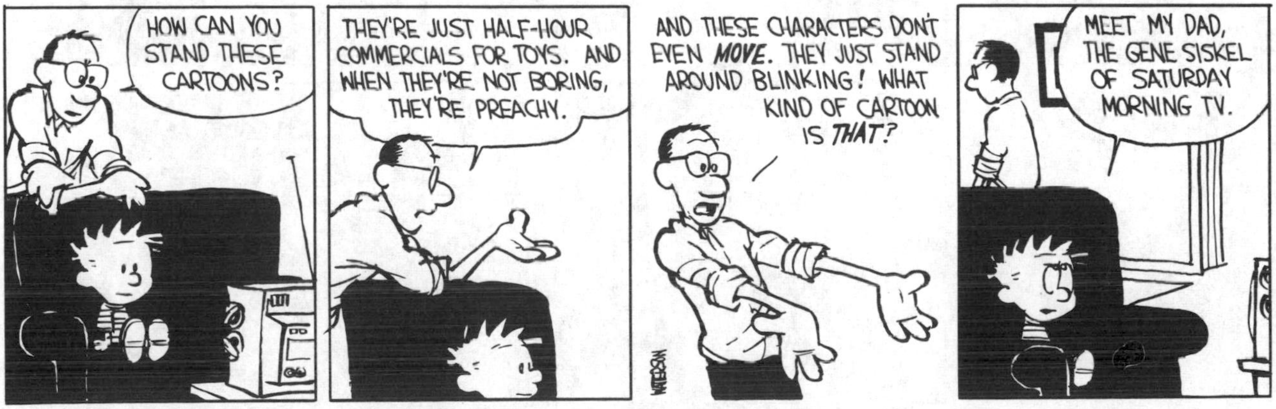
HOW CAN YOU STAND THESE CARTOONS?
THEY'RE JUST HALF-HOUR COMMERCIALS FOR TOYS. AND WHEN THEY'RE NOT BORING, THEY'RE PREACHY.
AND THESE CHARACTERS DON'T EVEN *MOVE*. THEY JUST STAND AROUND BLINKING! WHAT KIND OF CARTOON IS *THAT*?
MEET MY DAD, THE GENE SISKEL OF SATURDAY MORNING TV.

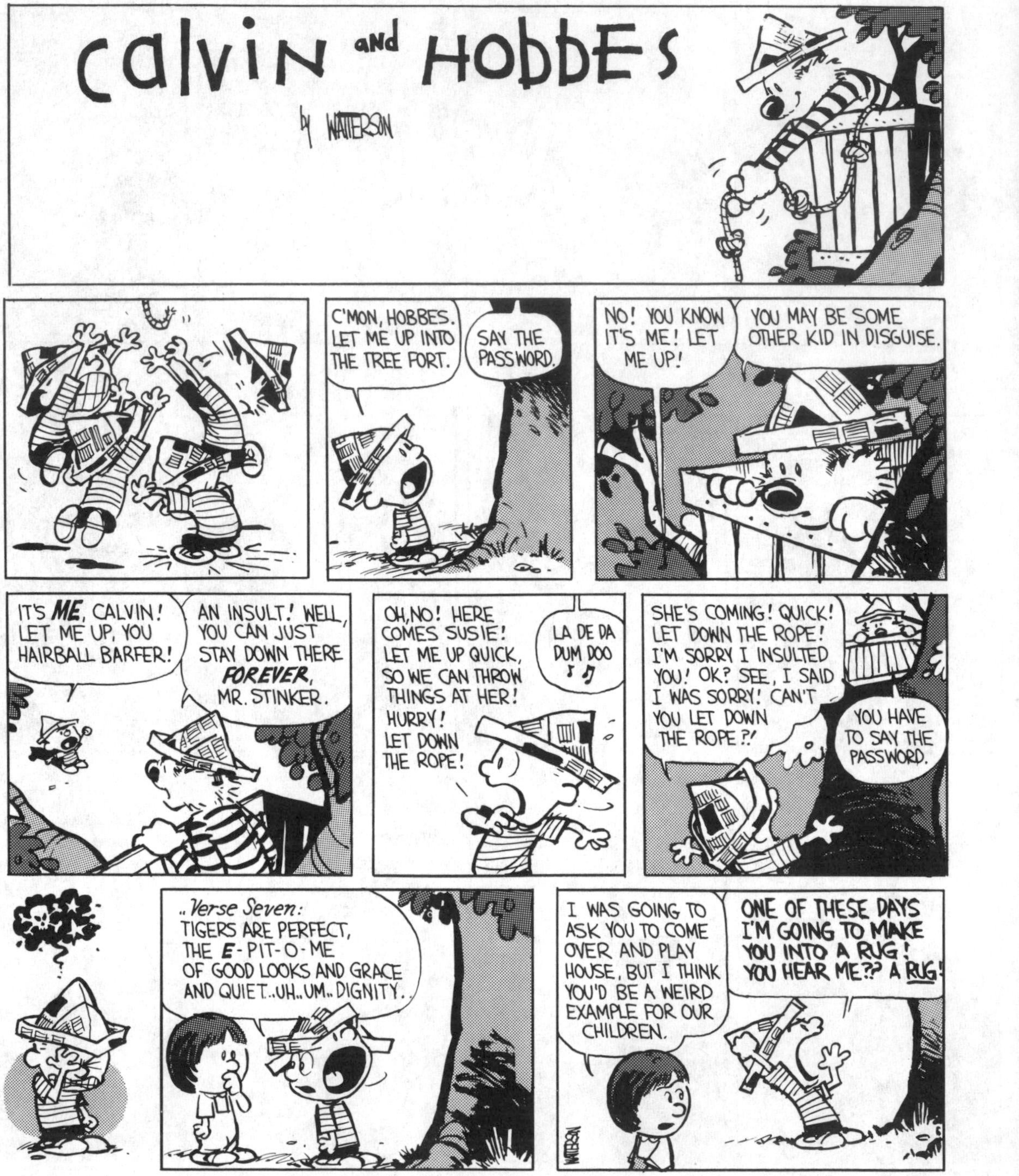

Calvin and HOBBES
by WATTERSON
C'MON, HOBBES. LET ME UP INTO THE TREE FORT.
SAY THE PASSWORD.
NO! YOU KNOW IT'S ME! LET ME UP!
YOU MAY BE SOME OTHER KID IN DISGUISE.
IT'S **ME**, CALVIN! LET ME UP, YOU HAIRBALL BARFER!
AN INSULT! WELL, YOU CAN JUST STAY DOWN THERE ***FOREVER***, MR. STINKER.
OH, NO! HERE COMES SUSIE! LET ME UP QUICK, SO WE CAN THROW THINGS AT HER! HURRY! LET DOWN THE ROPE!
LA DE DA DUM DOO
SHE'S COMING! QUICK! LET DOWN THE ROPE! I'M SORRY I INSULTED YOU! OK? SEE, I SAID I WAS SORRY! CAN'T YOU LET DOWN THE ROPE?!
YOU HAVE TO SAY THE PASSWORD.
..*Verse Seven:* TIGERS ARE PERFECT, THE **E**-PIT-O-ME OF GOOD LOOKS AND GRACE AND QUIET..UH..UM..DIGNITY..
I WAS GOING TO ASK YOU TO COME OVER AND PLAY HOUSE, BUT I THINK YOU'D BE A WEIRD EXAMPLE FOR OUR CHILDREN.
ONE OF THESE DAYS I'M GOING TO MAKE YOU INTO A RUG! YOU HEAR ME?? A RUG!
WATTERSON

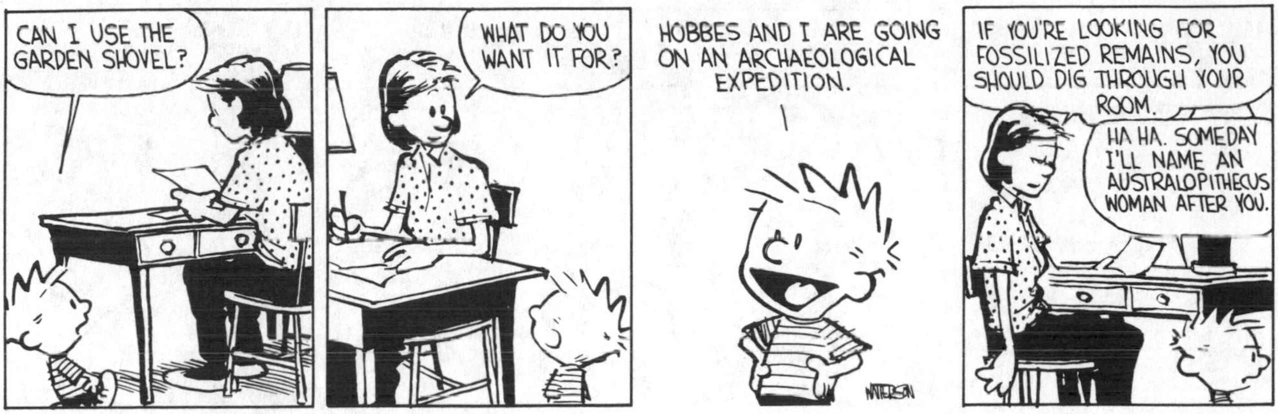
CAN I USE THE GARDEN SHOVEL?
WHAT DO YOU WANT IT FOR?
HOBBES AND I ARE GOING ON AN ARCHAEOLOGICAL EXPEDITION.
IF YOU'RE LOOKING FOR FOSSILIZED REMAINS, YOU SHOULD DIG THROUGH YOUR ROOM.
HA HA. SOMEDAY I'LL NAME AN AUSTRALOPITHECUS WOMAN AFTER YOU.

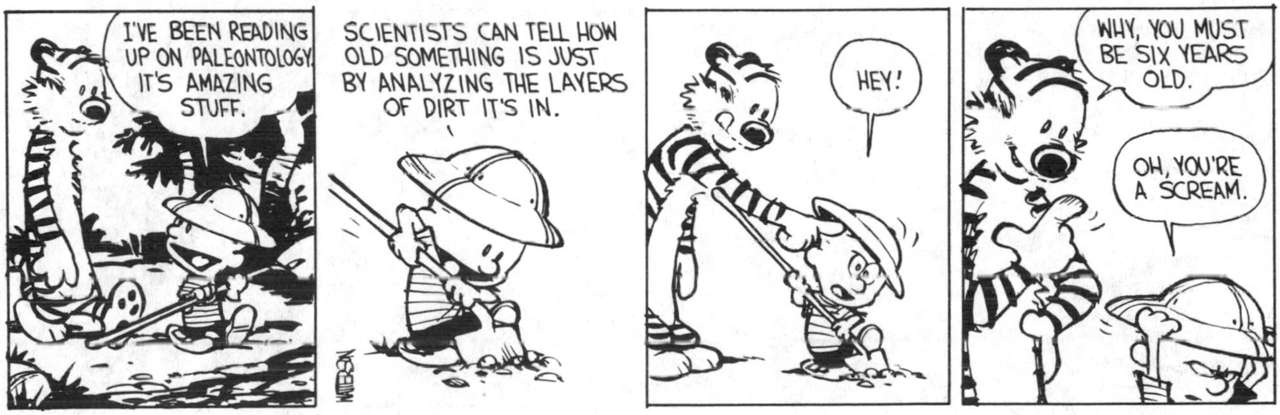
I'VE BEEN READING UP ON PALEONTOLOGY. IT'S AMAZING STUFF.
SCIENTISTS CAN TELL HOW OLD SOMETHING IS JUST BY ANALYZING THE LAYERS OF DIRT IT'S IN.
HEY!
WHY, YOU MUST BE SIX YEARS OLD.
OH, YOU'RE A SCREAM.

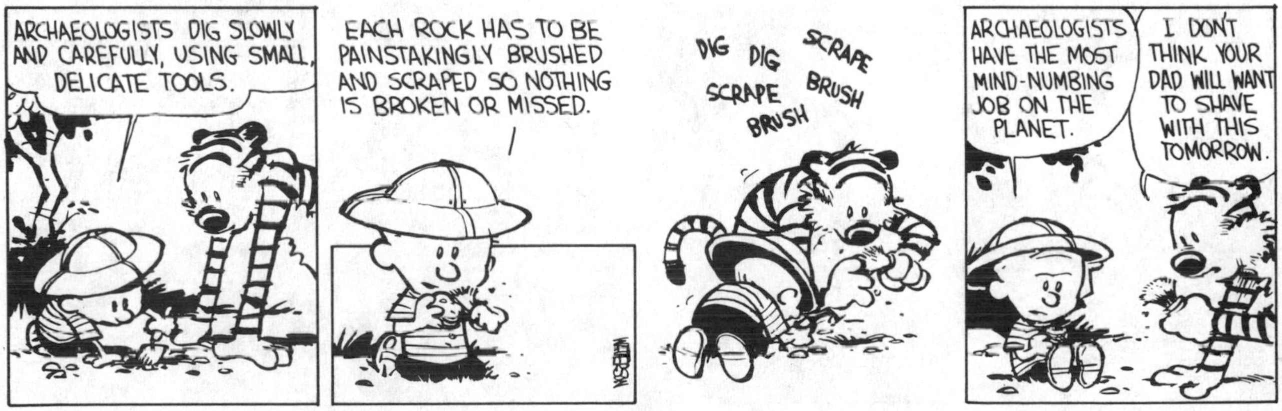
ARCHAEOLOGISTS DIG SLOWLY AND CAREFULLY, USING SMALL, DELICATE TOOLS.
EACH ROCK HAS TO BE PAINSTAKINGLY BRUSHED AND SCRAPED SO NOTHING IS BROKEN OR MISSED.
DIG DIG SCRAPE SCRAPE BRUSH BRUSH
ARCHAEOLOGISTS HAVE THE MOST MIND-NUMBING JOB ON THE PLANET.
I DON'T THINK YOUR DAD WILL WANT TO SHAVE WITH THIS TOMORROW.

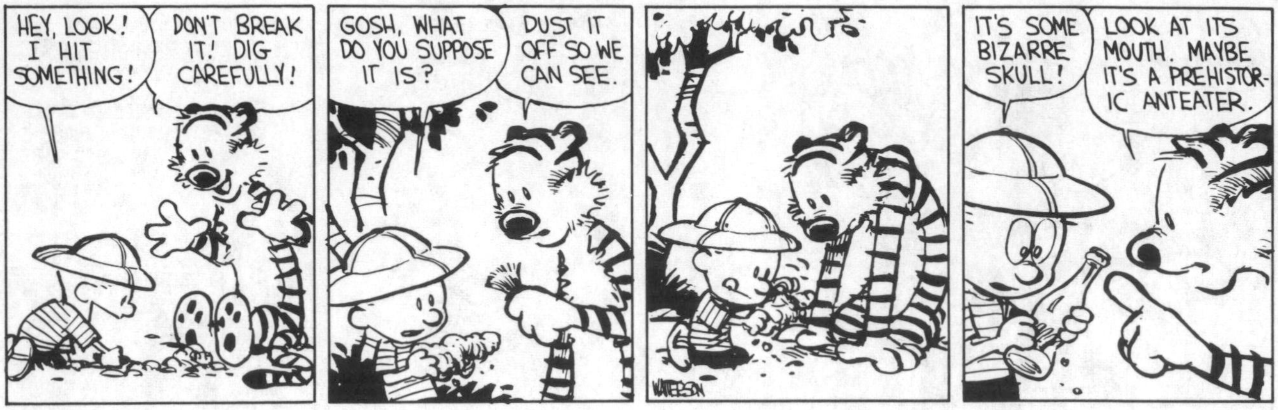
HEY, LOOK! I HIT SOMETHING!
DON'T BREAK IT! DIG CAREFULLY!
GOSH, WHAT DO YOU SUPPOSE IT IS?
DUST IT OFF SO WE CAN SEE.
IT'S SOME BIZARRE SKULL!
LOOK AT ITS MOUTH. MAYBE IT'S A PREHISTORIC ANTEATER.

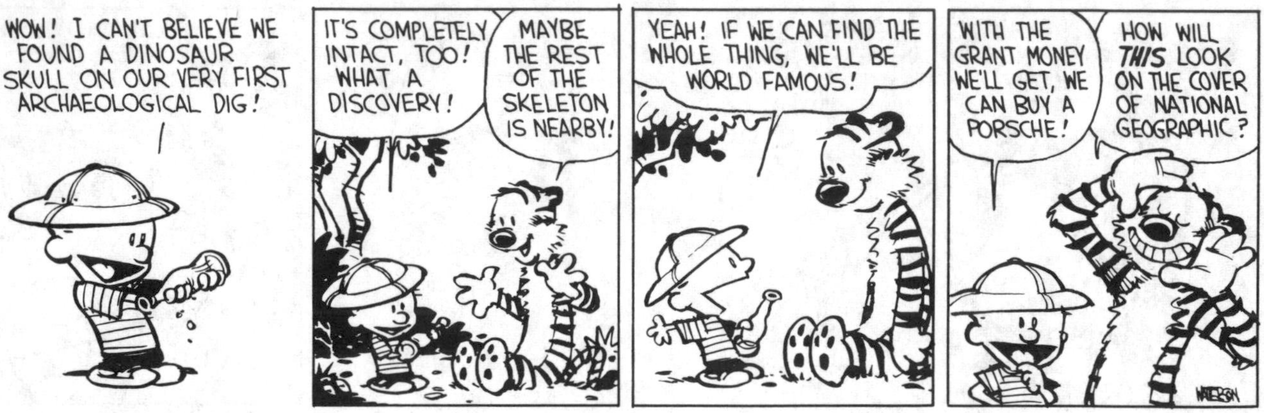
WOW! I CAN'T BELIEVE WE FOUND A DINOSAUR SKULL ON OUR VERY FIRST ARCHAEOLOGICAL DIG!
IT'S COMPLETELY INTACT, TOO! WHAT A DISCOVERY!
MAYBE THE REST OF THE SKELETON IS NEARBY!
YEAH! IF WE CAN FIND THE WHOLE THING, WE'LL BE WORLD FAMOUS!
WITH THE GRANT MONEY WE'LL GET, WE CAN BUY A PORSCHE!
HOW WILL **THIS** LOOK ON THE COVER OF NATIONAL GEOGRAPHIC?

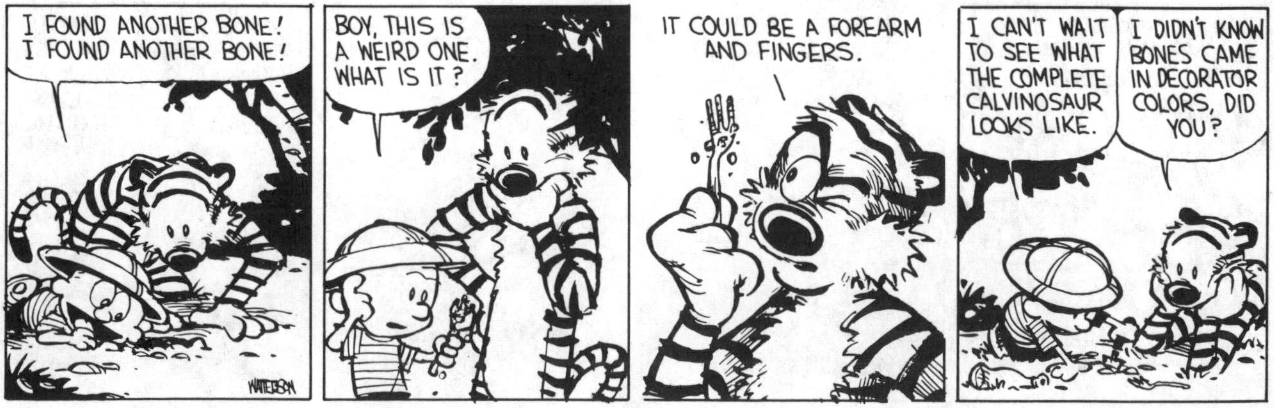
I FOUND ANOTHER BONE! I FOUND ANOTHER BONE!
BOY, THIS IS A WEIRD ONE. WHAT IS IT?
IT COULD BE A FOREARM AND FINGERS.
I CAN'T WAIT TO SEE WHAT THE COMPLETE CALVINOSAUR LOOKS LIKE.
I DIDN'T KNOW BONES CAME IN DECORATOR COLORS, DID YOU?

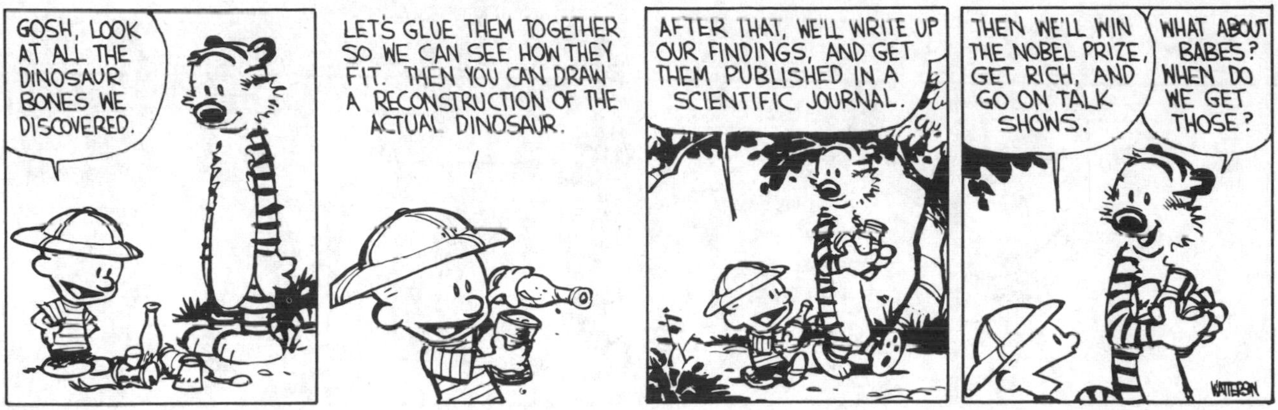
GOSH, LOOK AT ALL THE DINOSAUR BONES WE DISCOVERED.
LET'S GLUE THEM TOGETHER SO WE CAN SEE HOW THEY FIT. THEN YOU CAN DRAW A RECONSTRUCTION OF THE ACTUAL DINOSAUR.
AFTER THAT, WE'LL WRITE UP OUR FINDINGS, AND GET THEM PUBLISHED IN A SCIENTIFIC JOURNAL.
THEN WE'LL WIN THE NOBEL PRIZE, GET RICH, AND GO ON TALK SHOWS.
WHAT ABOUT BABES? WHEN DO WE GET THOSE?
WATTERSON

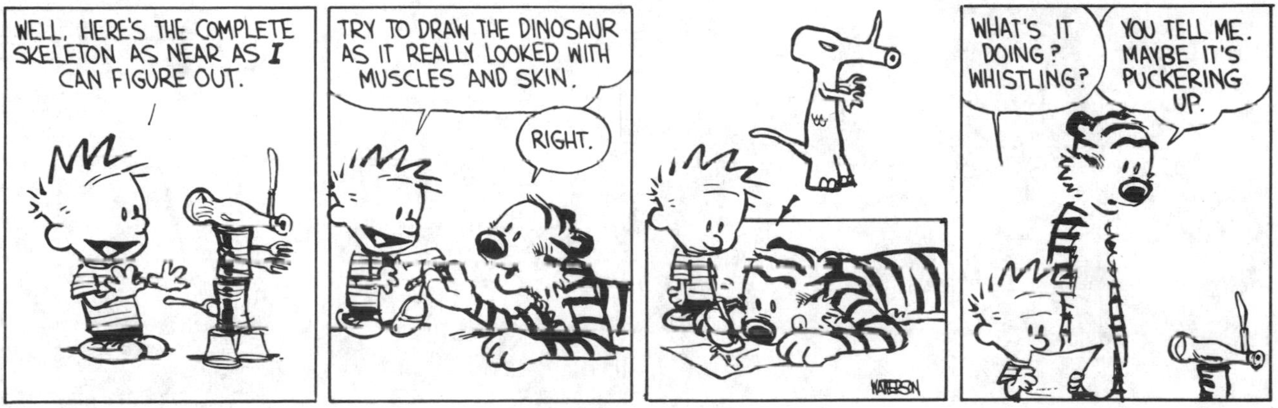
WELL, HERE'S THE COMPLETE SKELETON AS NEAR AS ***I*** CAN FIGURE OUT.
TRY TO DRAW THE DINOSAUR AS IT REALLY LOOKED WITH MUSCLES AND SKIN.
RIGHT.
WATTERSON
WHAT'S IT DOING? WHISTLING?
YOU TELL ME. MAYBE IT'S PUCKERING UP.

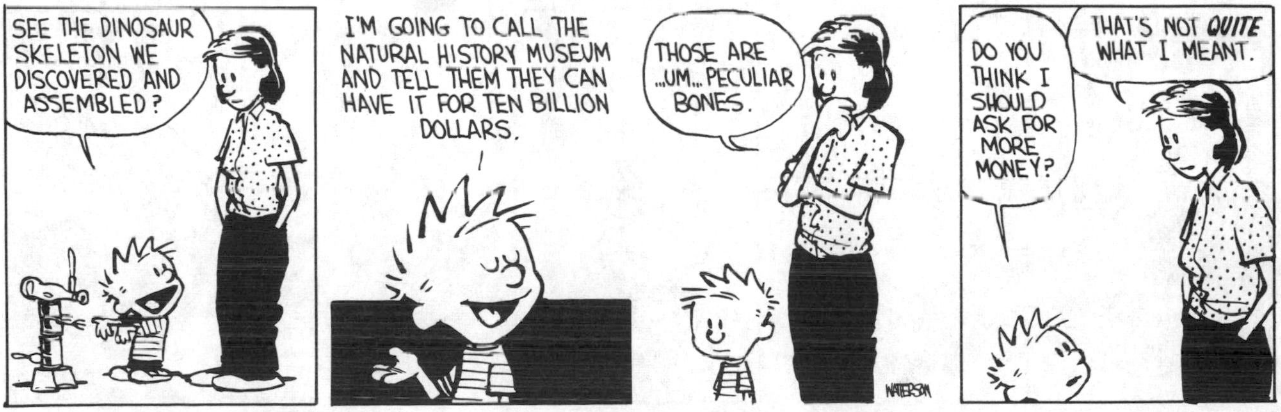
SEE THE DINOSAUR SKELETON WE DISCOVERED AND ASSEMBLED?
I'M GOING TO CALL THE NATURAL HISTORY MUSEUM AND TELL THEM THEY CAN HAVE IT FOR TEN BILLION DOLLARS.
THOSE ARE ...UM... PECULIAR BONES.
WATTERSON
DO YOU THINK I SHOULD ASK FOR MORE MONEY?
THAT'S NOT ***QUITE*** WHAT I MEANT.

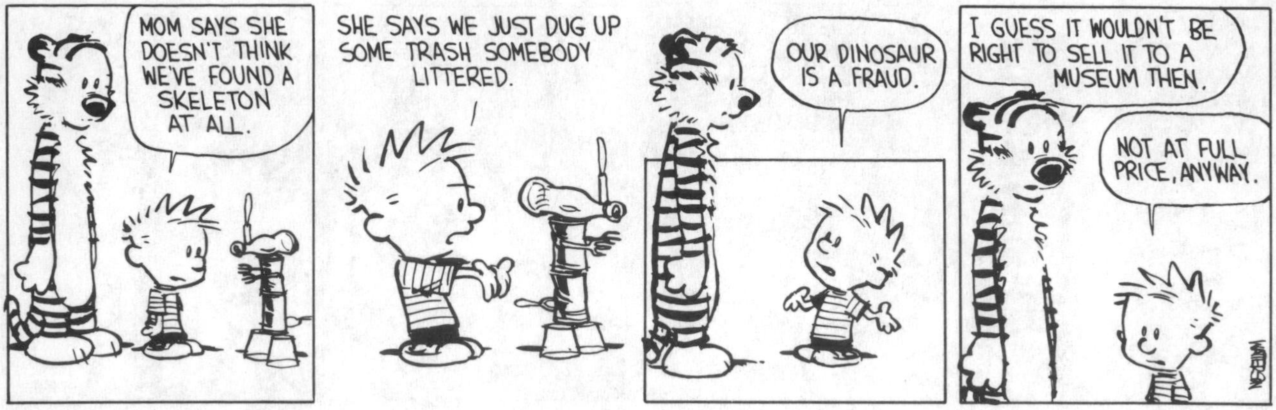
MOM SAYS SHE DOESN'T THINK WE'VE FOUND A SKELETON AT ALL.
SHE SAYS WE JUST DUG UP SOME TRASH SOMEBODY LITTERED.
OUR DINOSAUR IS A FRAUD.
I GUESS IT WOULDN'T BE RIGHT TO SELL IT TO A MUSEUM THEN.
NOT AT FULL PRICE, ANYWAY.

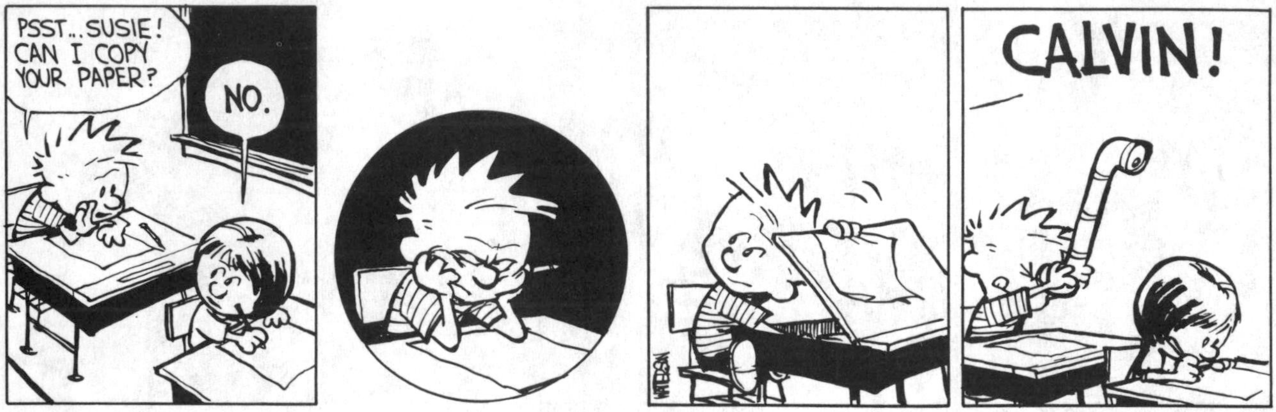
PSST...SUSIE! CAN I COPY YOUR PAPER?
NO.
CALVIN!

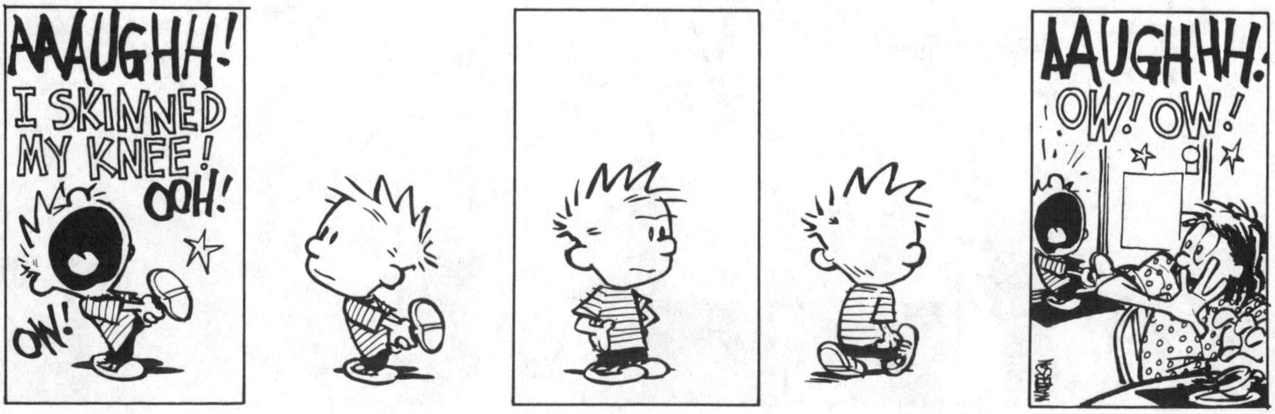
AAAUGHH!
I SKINNED MY KNEE!
OOH!
OW!
AAUGHHH!
OW! OW!

Calvin and Hobbes
by WATTERSON

THE CALL GOES OUT! WE'RE ON THE MOVE!

UP THROUGH THE WINDING MAZE! FASTER! FASTER!

CALVIN SCRAMBLES UP THE GRAINY TUNNEL!

OUT HE POPS INTO THE BLINDING SUN! CALVIN THE ANT RUSHES DOWN THE HILL TO THE BRICK WALK!

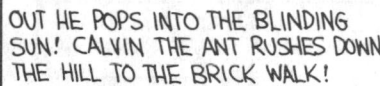

OTHER ANTS RUSH AROUND HIM IN THEIR MAD HURRY! CALVIN TRIES TO KEEP UP!

AT LAST HE REACHES THE MONSTROUS DEAD CATERPILLAR! WITHOUT PAUSING, HE HOISTS IT UP!

THE QUEEN DEMANDS HIS TIRELESS TOIL! CALVIN IS BACK OFF TO THE ANT-HILL AS FAST AS HE CAN GO!

WORK, WORK, WORK! THAT'S ALL I'M GOOD FOR AROUND HERE!

I HARDLY THINK PICKING UP YOUR ROOM ONCE IN A WHILE QUALIFIES YOU AS A SLAVE.

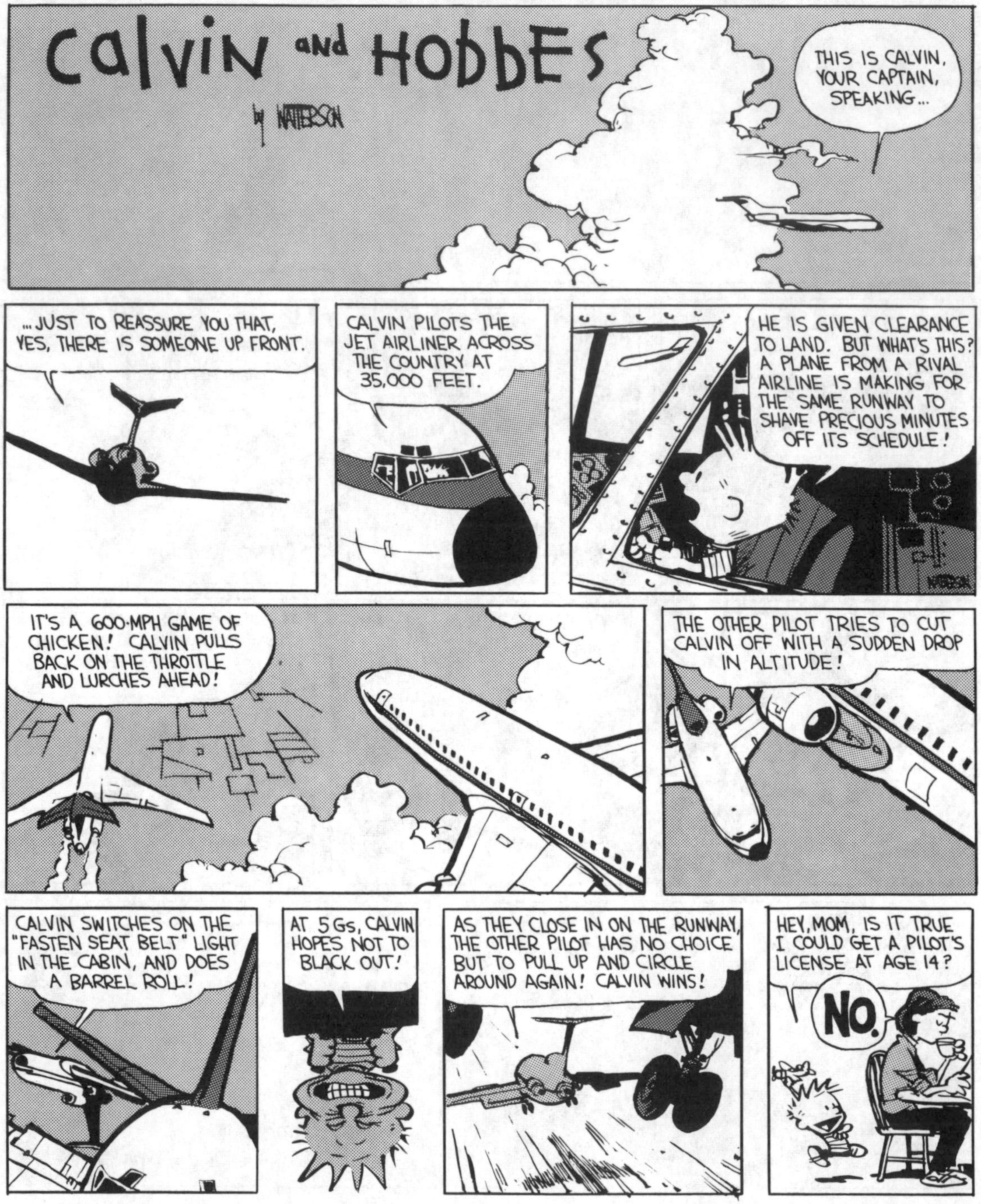
Calvin and HOBBES
by WATTERSON
THIS IS CALVIN, YOUR CAPTAIN, SPEAKING...
...JUST TO REASSURE YOU THAT, YES, THERE IS SOMEONE UP FRONT.
CALVIN PILOTS THE JET AIRLINER ACROSS THE COUNTRY AT 35,000 FEET.
HE IS GIVEN CLEARANCE TO LAND. BUT WHAT'S THIS? A PLANE FROM A RIVAL AIRLINE IS MAKING FOR THE SAME RUNWAY TO SHAVE PRECIOUS MINUTES OFF ITS SCHEDULE!
WATTERSON
IT'S A 600-MPH GAME OF CHICKEN! CALVIN PULLS BACK ON THE THROTTLE AND LURCHES AHEAD!
THE OTHER PILOT TRIES TO CUT CALVIN OFF WITH A SUDDEN DROP IN ALTITUDE!
CALVIN SWITCHES ON THE "FASTEN SEAT BELT" LIGHT IN THE CABIN, AND DOES A BARREL ROLL!
AT 5 Gs, CALVIN HOPES NOT TO BLACK OUT!
AS THEY CLOSE IN ON THE RUNWAY, THE OTHER PILOT HAS NO CHOICE BUT TO PULL UP AND CIRCLE AROUND AGAIN! CALVIN WINS!
HEY, MOM, IS IT TRUE I COULD GET A PILOT'S LICENSE AT AGE 14?
NO.

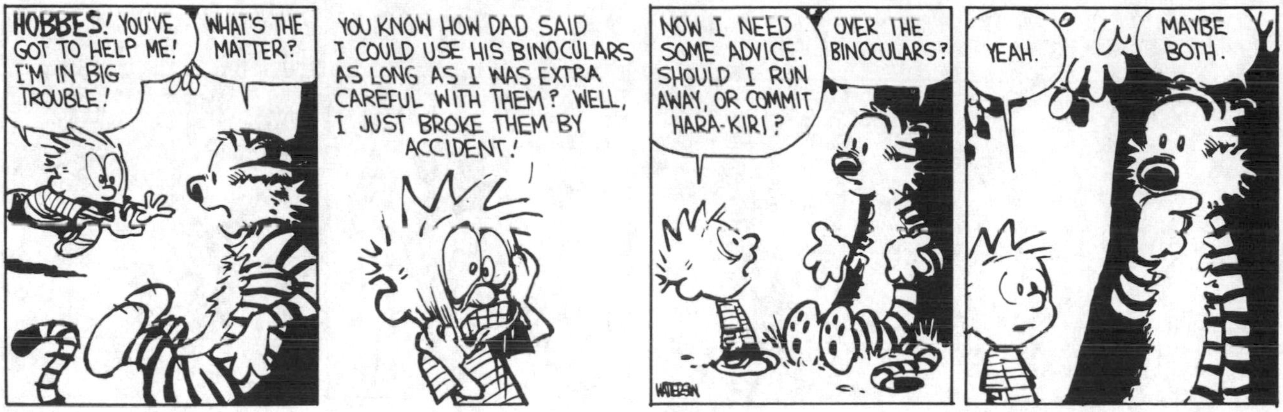
HOBBES! YOU'VE GOT TO HELP ME! I'M IN BIG TROUBLE!
WHAT'S THE MATTER?
YOU KNOW HOW DAD SAID I COULD USE HIS BINOCULARS AS LONG AS I WAS EXTRA CAREFUL WITH THEM? WELL, I JUST BROKE THEM BY ACCIDENT!
NOW I NEED SOME ADVICE. SHOULD I RUN AWAY, OR COMMIT HARA-KIRI?
OVER THE BINOCULARS?
YEAH.
MAYBE BOTH.

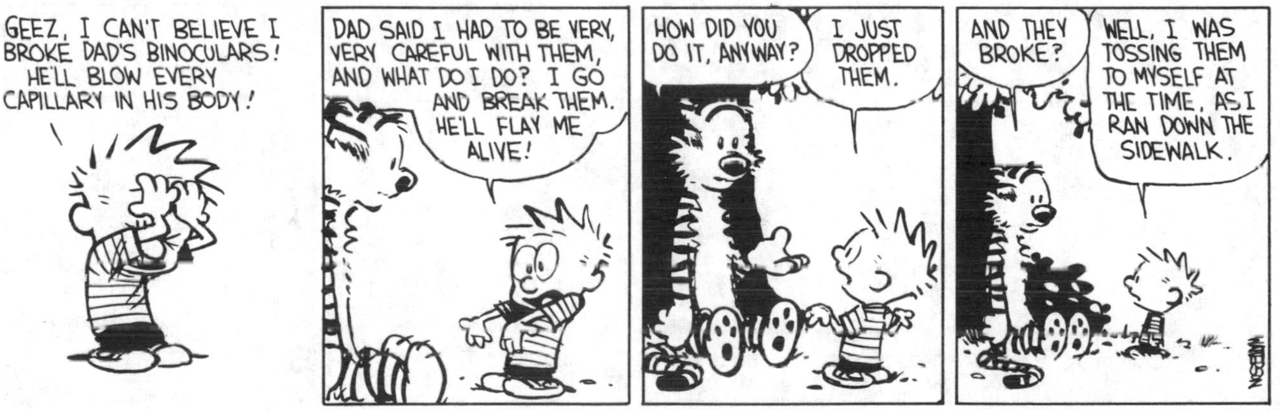
GEEZ, I CAN'T BELIEVE I BROKE DAD'S BINOCULARS! HE'LL BLOW EVERY CAPILLARY IN HIS BODY!
DAD SAID I HAD TO BE VERY, VERY CAREFUL WITH THEM, AND WHAT DO I DO? I GO AND BREAK THEM. HE'LL FLAY ME ALIVE!
HOW DID YOU DO IT, ANYWAY?
I JUST DROPPED THEM.
AND THEY BROKE?
WELL, I WAS TOSSING THEM TO MYSELF AT THE TIME, AS I RAN DOWN THE SIDEWALK.

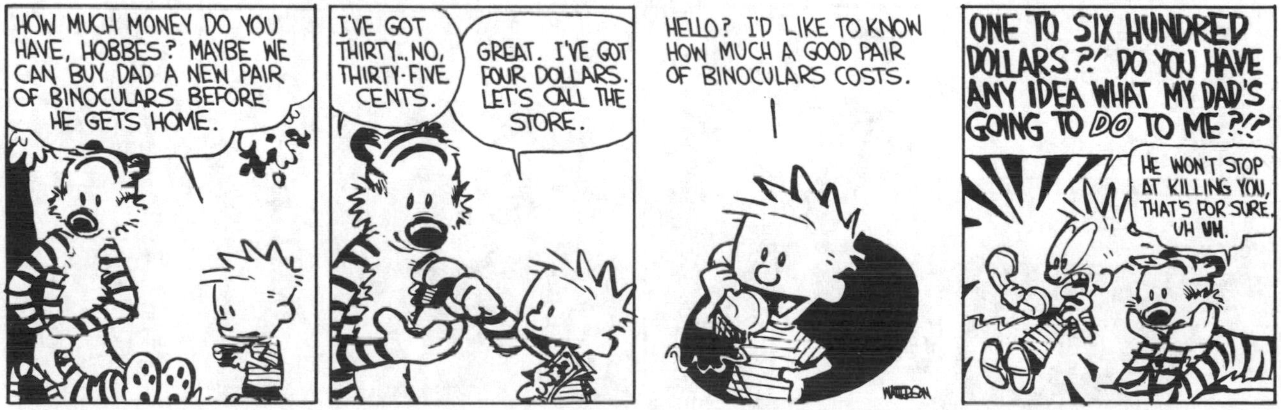
HOW MUCH MONEY DO YOU HAVE, HOBBES? MAYBE WE CAN BUY DAD A NEW PAIR OF BINOCULARS BEFORE HE GETS HOME.
I'VE GOT THIRTY... NO, THIRTY-FIVE CENTS.
GREAT. I'VE GOT FOUR DOLLARS. LET'S CALL THE STORE.
HELLO? I'D LIKE TO KNOW HOW MUCH A GOOD PAIR OF BINOCULARS COSTS.
ONE TO SIX HUNDRED DOLLARS?! DO YOU HAVE ANY IDEA WHAT MY DAD'S GOING TO DO TO ME?!?
HE WON'T STOP AT KILLING YOU, THAT'S FOR SURE. UH UH.

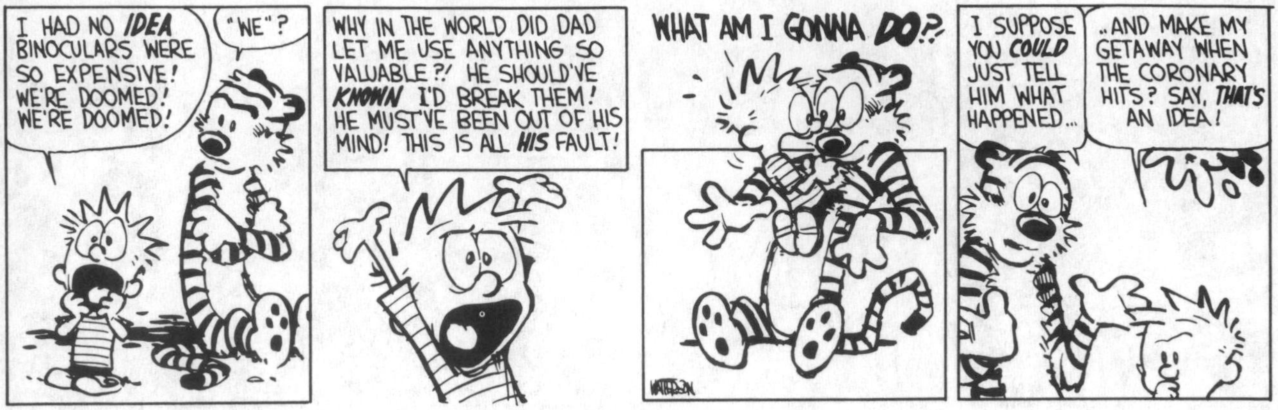
I HAD NO IDEA BINOCULARS WERE SO EXPENSIVE! WE'RE DOOMED! WE'RE DOOMED!
"WE"?
WHY IN THE WORLD DID DAD LET ME USE ANYTHING SO VALUABLE?! HE SHOULD'VE KNOWN I'D BREAK THEM! HE MUST'VE BEEN OUT OF HIS MIND! THIS IS ALL HIS FAULT!
WHAT AM I GONNA DO?!
I SUPPOSE YOU COULD JUST TELL HIM WHAT HAPPENED...
..AND MAKE MY GETAWAY WHEN THE CORONARY HITS? SAY, THAT'S AN IDEA!

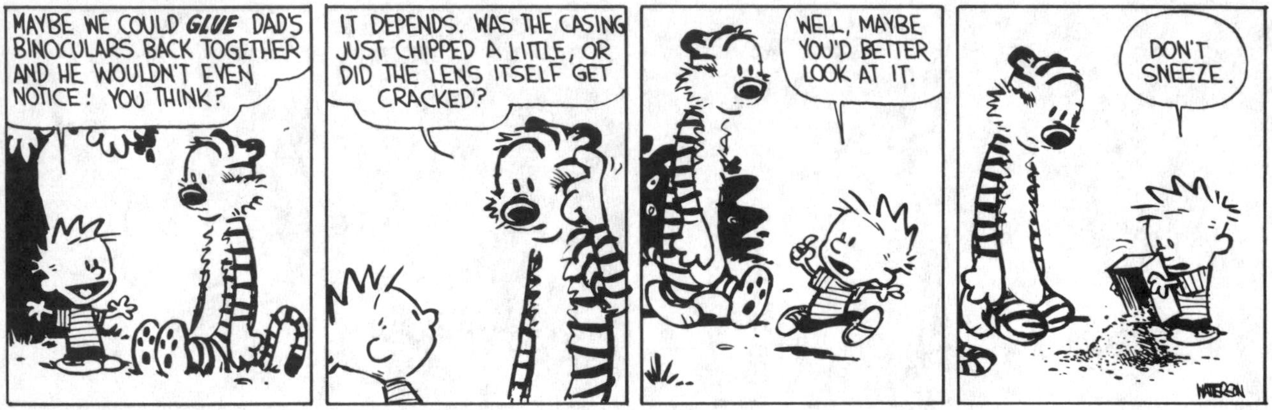
MAYBE WE COULD GLUE DAD'S BINOCULARS BACK TOGETHER AND HE WOULDN'T EVEN NOTICE! YOU THINK?
IT DEPENDS. WAS THE CASING JUST CHIPPED A LITTLE, OR DID THE LENS ITSELF GET CRACKED?
WELL, MAYBE YOU'D BETTER LOOK AT IT.
DON'T SNEEZE.

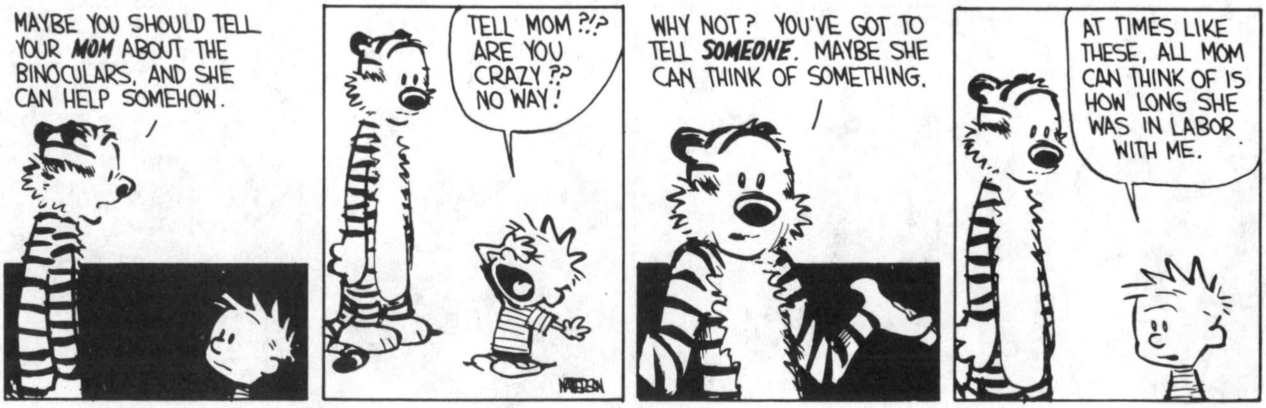
MAYBE YOU SHOULD TELL YOUR MOM ABOUT THE BINOCULARS, AND SHE CAN HELP SOMEHOW.
TELL MOM?!? ARE YOU CRAZY?? NO WAY!
WHY NOT? YOU'VE GOT TO TELL SOMEONE. MAYBE SHE CAN THINK OF SOMETHING.
AT TIMES LIKE THESE, ALL MOM CAN THINK OF IS HOW LONG SHE WAS IN LABOR WITH ME.

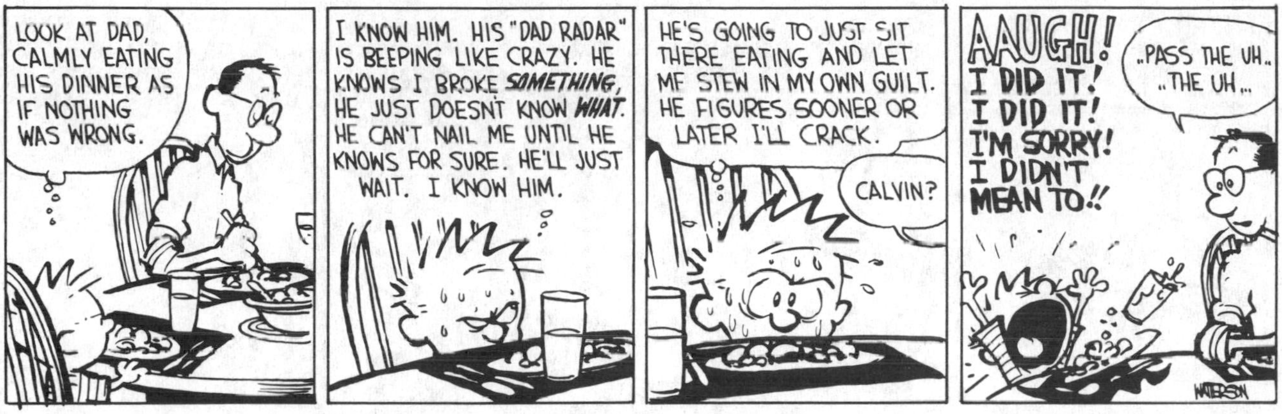
LOOK AT DAD, CALMLY EATING HIS DINNER AS IF NOTHING WAS WRONG.
I KNOW HIM. HIS "DAD RADAR" IS BEEPING LIKE CRAZY. HE KNOWS I BROKE SOMETHING, HE JUST DOESN'T KNOW WHAT. HE CAN'T NAIL ME UNTIL HE KNOWS FOR SURE. HE'LL JUST WAIT. I KNOW HIM.
HE'S GOING TO JUST SIT THERE EATING AND LET ME STEW IN MY OWN GUILT. HE FIGURES SOONER OR LATER I'LL CRACK.
CALVIN?
AAUGH! I DID IT! I DID IT! I'M SORRY! I DIDN'T MEAN TO!!
..PASS THE UH.. ..THE UH...
WATERSON

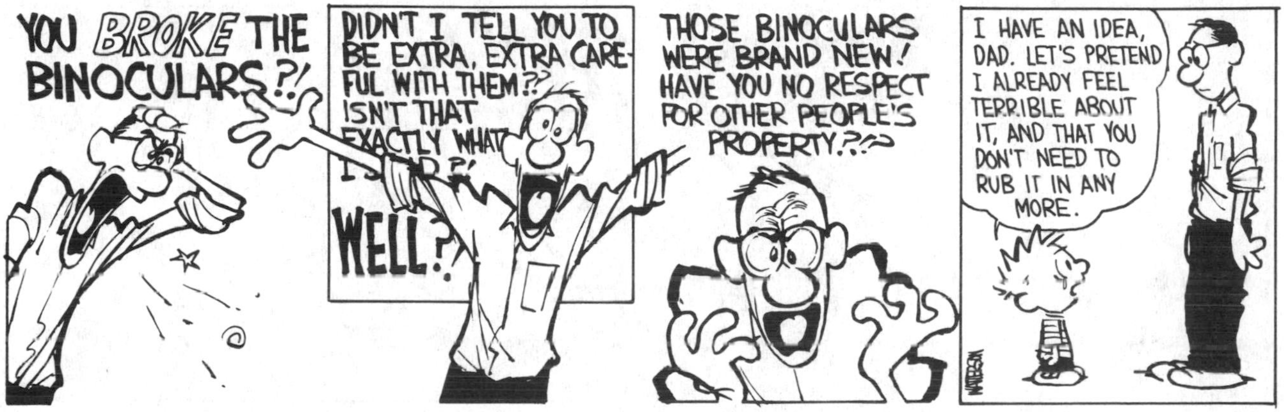
YOU BROKE THE BINOCULARS?!
DIDN'T I TELL YOU TO BE EXTRA, EXTRA CAREFUL WITH THEM?! ISN'T THAT EXACTLY WHAT
WELL?!
THOSE BINOCULARS WERE BRAND NEW! HAVE YOU NO RESPECT FOR OTHER PEOPLE'S PROPERTY?!?!
I HAVE AN IDEA, DAD. LET'S PRETEND I ALREADY FEEL TERRIBLE ABOUT IT, AND THAT YOU DON'T NEED TO RUB IT IN ANY MORE.
WATERSON

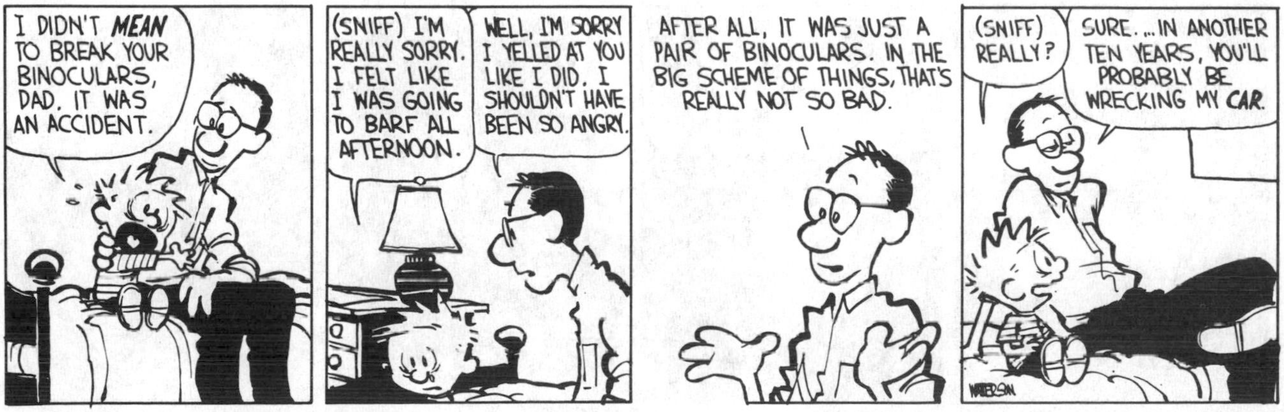
I DIDN'T MEAN TO BREAK YOUR BINOCULARS, DAD. IT WAS AN ACCIDENT.
(SNIFF) I'M REALLY SORRY. I FELT LIKE I WAS GOING TO BARF ALL AFTERNOON.
WELL, I'M SORRY I YELLED AT YOU LIKE I DID. I SHOULDN'T HAVE BEEN SO ANGRY.
AFTER ALL, IT WAS JUST A PAIR OF BINOCULARS. IN THE BIG SCHEME OF THINGS, THAT'S REALLY NOT SO BAD.
(SNIFF) REALLY?
SURE. ...IN ANOTHER TEN YEARS, YOU'LL PROBABLY BE WRECKING MY CAR.
WATERSON

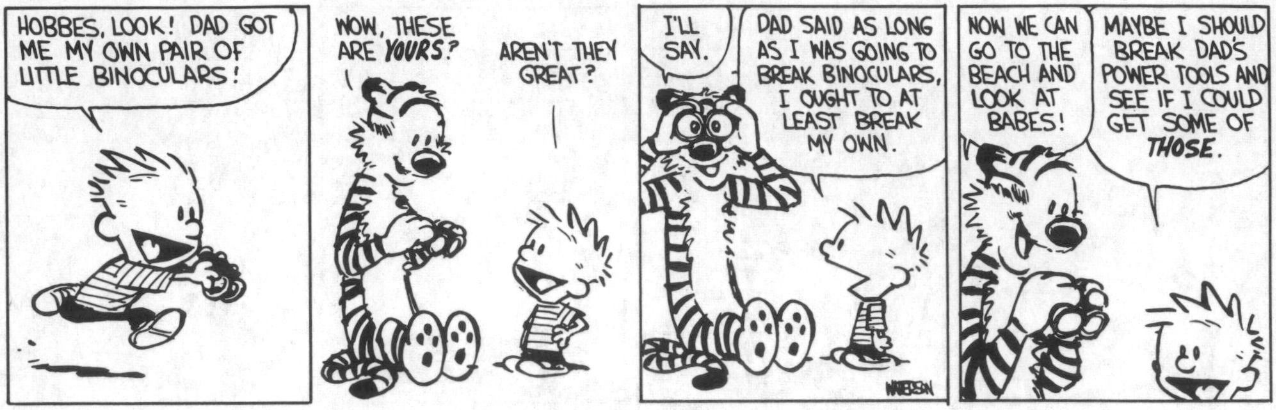
HOBBES, LOOK! DAD GOT ME MY OWN PAIR OF LITTLE BINOCULARS!
WOW, THESE ARE *YOURS*?
AREN'T THEY GREAT?
I'LL SAY.
DAD SAID AS LONG AS I WAS GOING TO BREAK BINOCULARS, I OUGHT TO AT LEAST BREAK MY OWN.
NOW WE CAN GO TO THE BEACH AND LOOK AT BABES!
MAYBE I SHOULD BREAK DAD'S POWER TOOLS AND SEE IF I COULD GET SOME OF *THOSE*.
WATTERSON

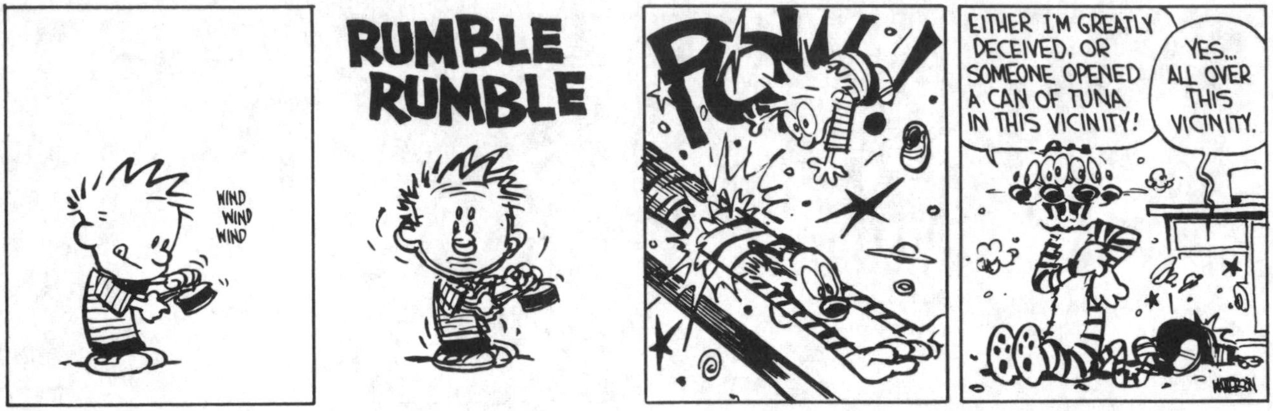
WIND WIND WIND
RUMBLE RUMBLE
POW!
EITHER I'M GREATLY DECEIVED, OR SOMEONE OPENED A CAN OF TUNA IN THIS VICINITY!
YES... ALL OVER THIS VICINITY.
WATTERSON

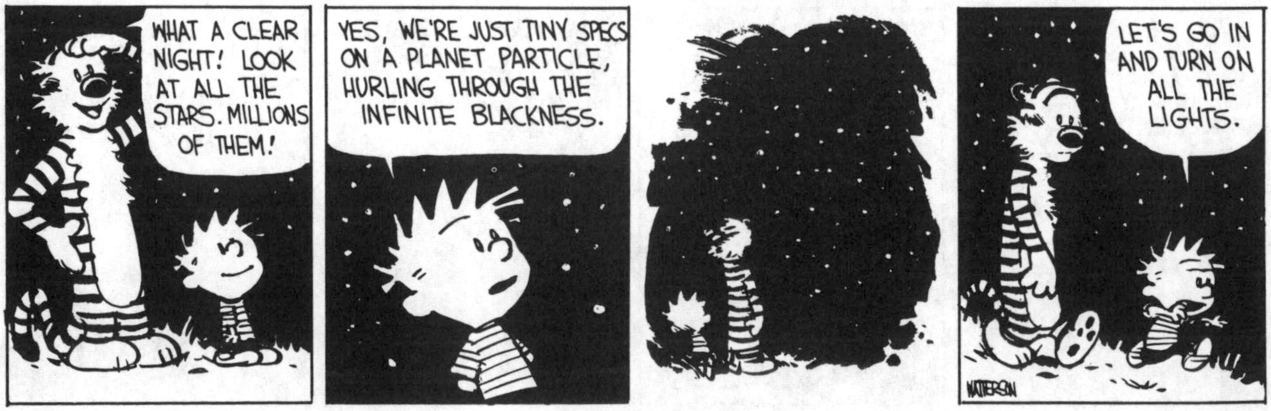
WHAT A CLEAR NIGHT! LOOK AT ALL THE STARS. MILLIONS OF THEM!
YES, WE'RE JUST TINY SPECS ON A PLANET PARTICLE, HURLING THROUGH THE INFINITE BLACKNESS.
LET'S GO IN AND TURN ON ALL THE LIGHTS.
WATTERSON

Calvin and HOBBES
by WATTERSON
I GOT A HIT! I GOT A HIT!
ONLY BECAUSE I LET YOU!
HA HA! A HOME RUN!
YOU DIDN'T TOUCH ALL THE BASES!
I DID, TOO.
NO, YOU DIDN'T. YOU DIDN'T TOUCH SEVENTH BASE.
YES, I DID! I TOUCHED THE WATER BARREL RIGHT AFTER THE FRONT PORCH.
THAT'S NOT SEVENTH BASE. THAT'S TWELFTH BASE!
I THOUGHT THE GARAGE DOOR WAS TWELFTH.
THE GARAGE DOOR IS TWENTY-THIRD BASE. YOU TOUCHED THEM ALL OUT OF ORDER, AND YOU STILL DIDN'T TOUCH THE SECRET BASE.
THE SECRET BASE?? WHAT'S THE SECRET BASE?!
I CAN'T TELL YOU. IT'S A SECRET.
I CAN'T BELIEVE THIS MORONIC SPORT IS OUR NATIONAL PASTIME.
YOU'RE OUT. GIVE ME A DOLLAR.
WATTERSON

CALVIN and HOBBES by WATTERSON

zzzzzzzzzzzzz

FILTH! CONTAMINATION! PESTILENCE! HA HA HA!

OF ALL LIVING CREATURES, FEW ARE MORE REPULSIVE THAN CALVIN THE BUG!

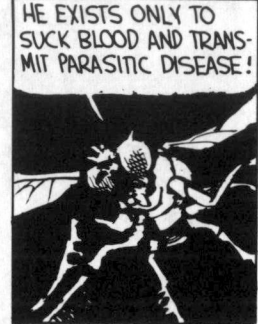

HE EXISTS ONLY TO SUCK BLOOD AND TRANSMIT PARASITIC DISEASE!

SEARCHING FOR SOMEONE TO INFECT, CALVIN FLIES LOW OVER THE PICNIC TABLE!

INGREDIENTS: SALT,

HIS SENSITIVE ANTENNAE PICK UP THE SCENT OF HUMAN FLESH!

TOUCHING DOWN, CALVIN INSERTS HIS NEEDLELIKE PROBOSCIS INTO A VEIN! PROTOZOANS IN HIS SALIVA QUICKLY INDUCE PLAGUE!

WILL YOU STOP THAT AWFUL SLURPING?! YOU'RE MAKING ME SICK!

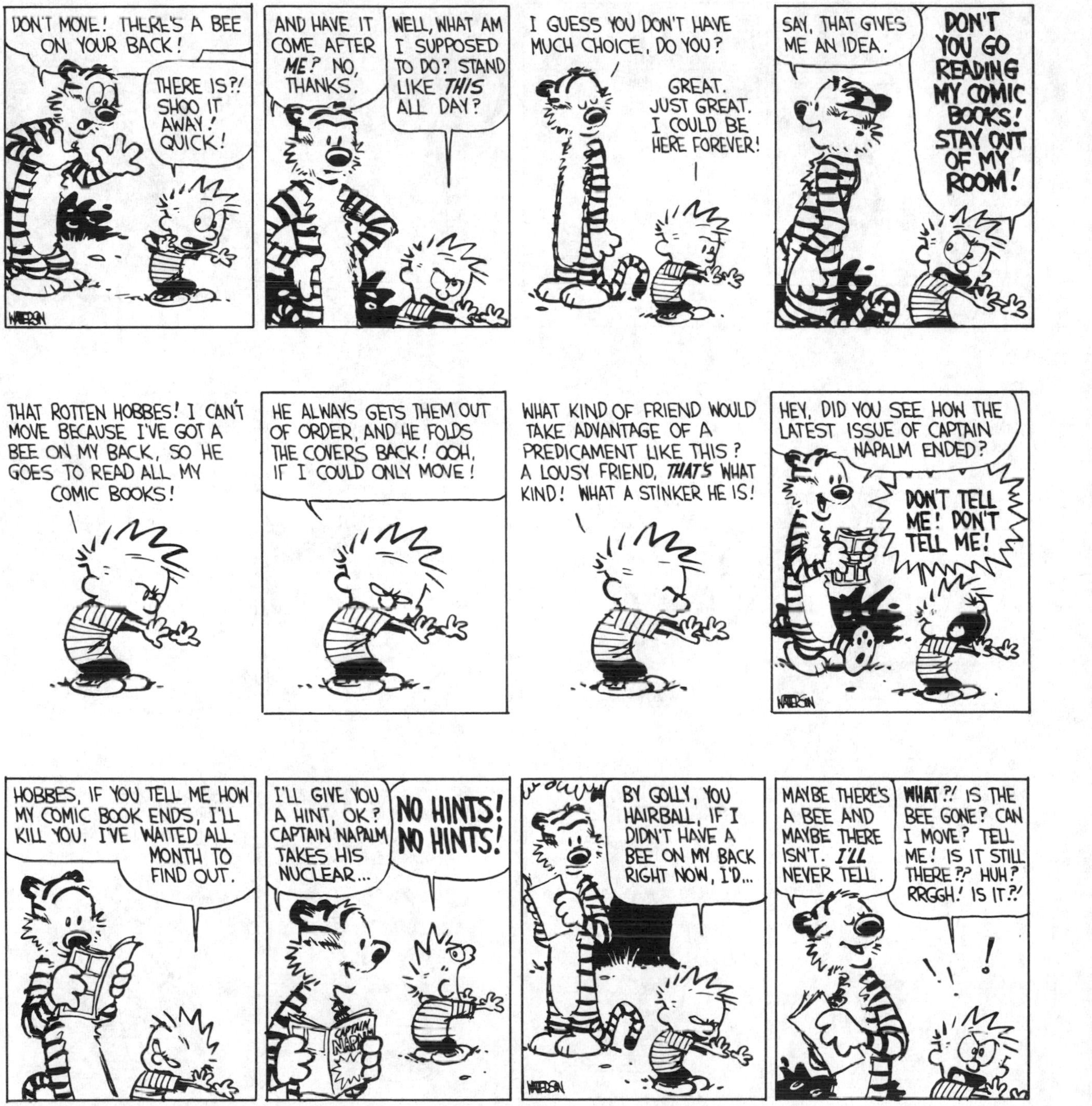
DON'T MOVE! THERE'S A BEE ON YOUR BACK!
THERE IS?! SHOO IT AWAY! QUICK!
WATTERSON
AND HAVE IT COME AFTER ME? NO, THANKS.
WELL, WHAT AM I SUPPOSED TO DO? STAND LIKE THIS ALL DAY?
I GUESS YOU DON'T HAVE MUCH CHOICE, DO YOU?
GREAT. JUST GREAT. I COULD BE HERE FOREVER!
SAY, THAT GIVES ME AN IDEA.
DON'T YOU GO READING MY COMIC BOOKS! STAY OUT OF MY ROOM!
THAT ROTTEN HOBBES! I CAN'T MOVE BECAUSE I'VE GOT A BEE ON MY BACK, SO HE GOES TO READ ALL MY COMIC BOOKS!
HE ALWAYS GETS THEM OUT OF ORDER, AND HE FOLDS THE COVERS BACK! OOH, IF I COULD ONLY MOVE!
WHAT KIND OF FRIEND WOULD TAKE ADVANTAGE OF A PREDICAMENT LIKE THIS? A LOUSY FRIEND, THAT'S WHAT KIND! WHAT A STINKER HE IS!
HEY, DID YOU SEE HOW THE LATEST ISSUE OF CAPTAIN NAPALM ENDED?
DON'T TELL ME! DON'T TELL ME!
WATTERSON
HOBBES, IF YOU TELL ME HOW MY COMIC BOOK ENDS, I'LL KILL YOU. I'VE WAITED ALL MONTH TO FIND OUT.
I'LL GIVE YOU A HINT, OK? CAPTAIN NAPALM TAKES HIS NUCLEAR...
NO HINTS! NO HINTS!
CAPTAIN NAPALM
BY GOLLY, YOU HAIRBALL, IF I DIDN'T HAVE A BEE ON MY BACK RIGHT NOW, I'D...
WATTERSON
MAYBE THERE'S A BEE AND MAYBE THERE ISN'T. I'LL NEVER TELL.
WHAT?! IS THE BEE GONE? CAN I MOVE? TELL ME! IS IT STILL THERE?? HUH? RRGGH! IS IT?!
! ! !

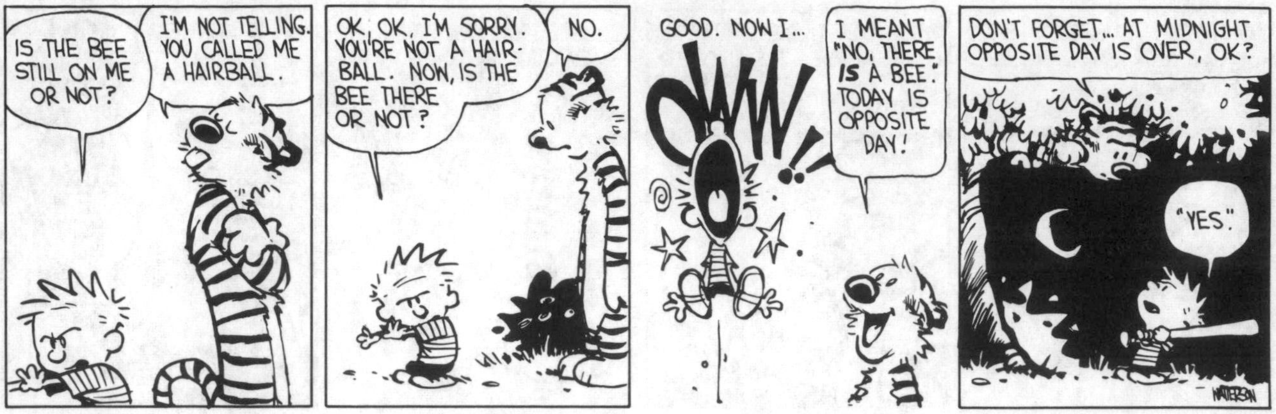
IS THE BEE STILL ON ME OR NOT?
I'M NOT TELLING. YOU CALLED ME A HAIRBALL.
OK, OK, I'M SORRY. YOU'RE NOT A HAIR-BALL. NOW, IS THE BEE THERE OR NOT?
NO.
GOOD. NOW I...
OWW!!
I MEANT "NO, THERE IS A BEE." TODAY IS OPPOSITE DAY!
DON'T FORGET... AT MIDNIGHT OPPOSITE DAY IS OVER, OK?
"YES."

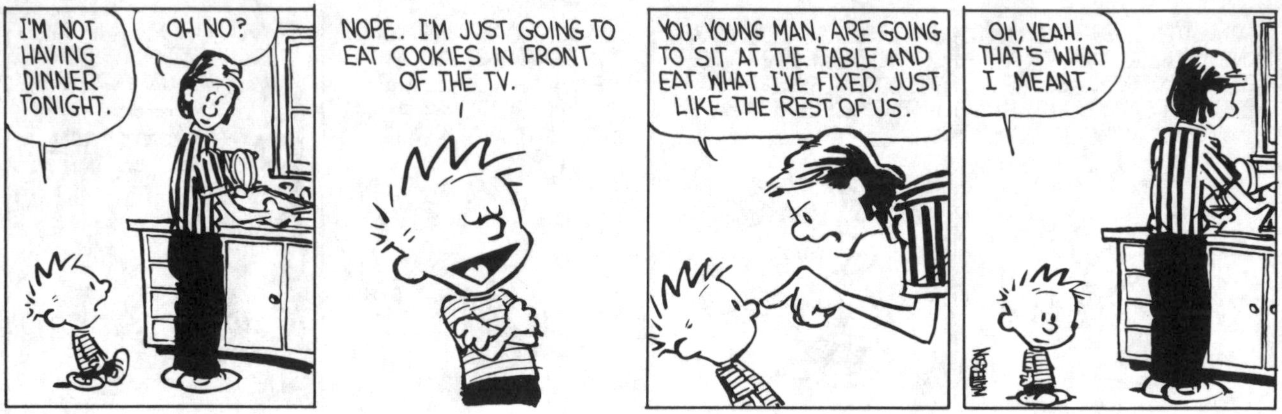
I'M NOT HAVING DINNER TONIGHT.
OH NO?
NOPE. I'M JUST GOING TO EAT COOKIES IN FRONT OF THE TV.
YOU, YOUNG MAN, ARE GOING TO SIT AT THE TABLE AND EAT WHAT I'VE FIXED, JUST LIKE THE REST OF US.
OH, YEAH. THAT'S WHAT I MEANT.

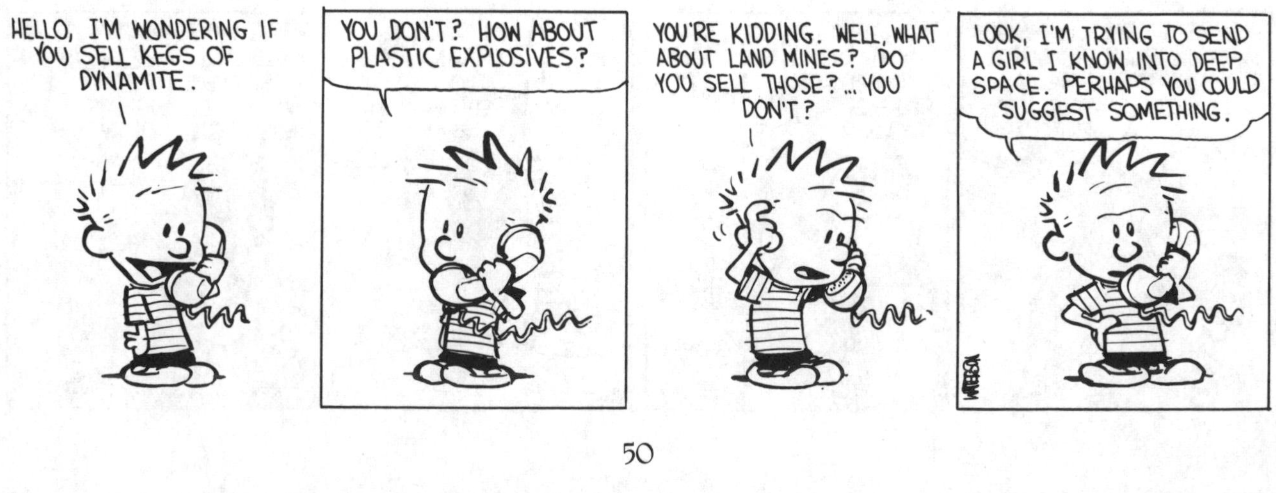
HELLO, I'M WONDERING IF YOU SELL KEGS OF DYNAMITE.
YOU DON'T? HOW ABOUT PLASTIC EXPLOSIVES?
YOU'RE KIDDING. WELL, WHAT ABOUT LAND MINES? DO YOU SELL THOSE? ... YOU DON'T?
LOOK, I'M TRYING TO SEND A GIRL I KNOW INTO DEEP SPACE. PERHAPS YOU COULD SUGGEST SOMETHING.

Calvin and HOBBES
by WATTERSON
FWOOOOSH
AS IF LIFE ISN'T SHORT ENOUGH.
WATTERSON

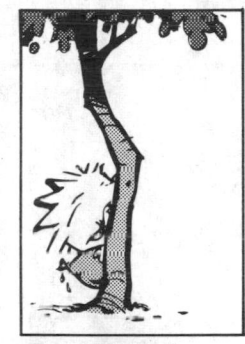

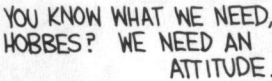

Panel 1:
YOU KNOW WHAT WE NEED, HOBBES? WE NEED AN ATTITUDE.

Panel 2:
AN ATTITUDE?

YEAH. YOU CAN'T BE COOL IF YOU DON'T HAVE AN ATTITUDE.

Panel 3:
REALLY?

SURE. THEY'RE ALL THE RAGE. NOW WHAT KIND OF ATTITUDE COULD *WE* HAVE?

Panel 4:
WE COULD BE COURTEOUSLY DEFERENTIAL.

OH, GOOD. THAT'S *REAL* COOL.

Panel 5:
I'VE DECIDED TO BE A FATALIST.

Panel 6:
ALL EVENTS ARE PREORDAINED AND UNALTERABLE. WHATEVER WILL BE WILL BE. THAT WAY, IF ANYTHING BAD HAPPENS, IT'S NOT MY FAULT. IT'S FATE.

Panel 7:
TRIP

WAUGH!

Panel 8:
TOO BAD YOU WERE FATED TO DO THAT.

THAT WASN'T FATE!

Panel 9:
DO YOU THINK GROWN-UPS WILL HAVE THE WORLD FIXED UP BY THE TIME THEY HAND IT OVER TO US?

Panel 10:
NOT THE WAY THEY'RE GOING.

THAT'S WHAT *I* THOUGHT.

Panel 11:
I GUESS THAT MEANS IT'S UP TO *US* THEN.

Panel 12:
SOMEHOW, I'M NOT REASSURED.

HA! WHEN *I'M* PRESIDENT, I'LL HAVE THINGS WHIPPED INTO SHAPE IN NO TIME.

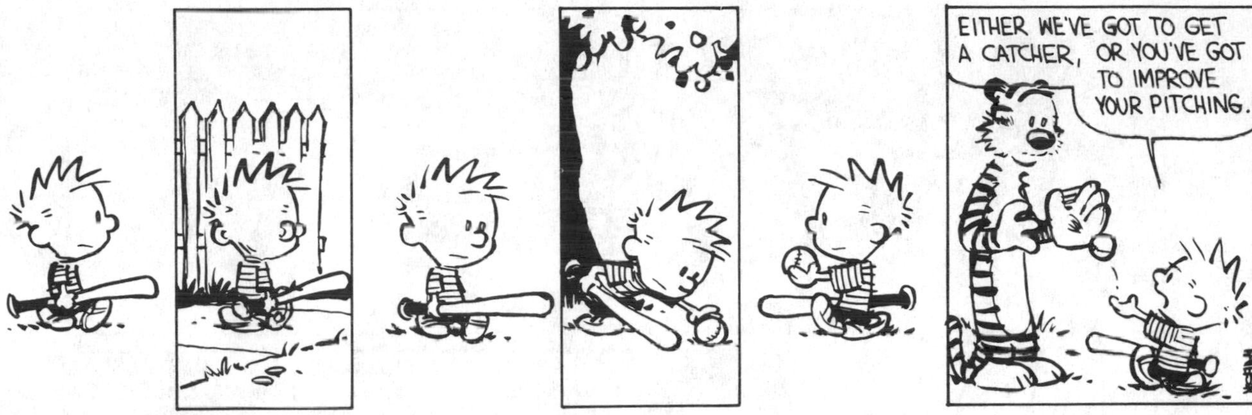
EITHER WE'VE GOT TO GET A CATCHER, OR YOU'VE GOT TO IMPROVE YOUR PITCHING.

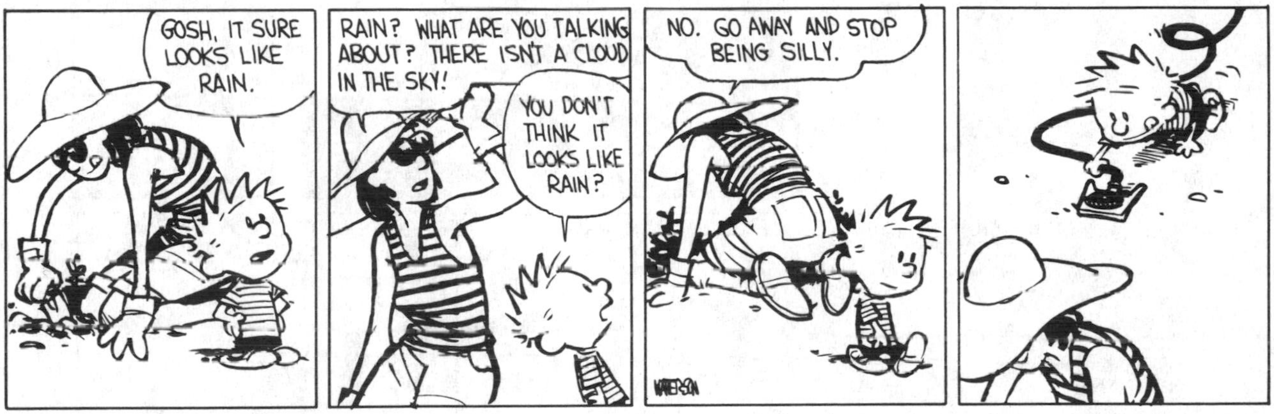
GOSH, IT SURE LOOKS LIKE RAIN.
RAIN? WHAT ARE YOU TALKING ABOUT? THERE ISN'T A CLOUD IN THE SKY!
YOU DON'T THINK IT LOOKS LIKE RAIN?
NO. GO AWAY AND STOP BEING SILLY.

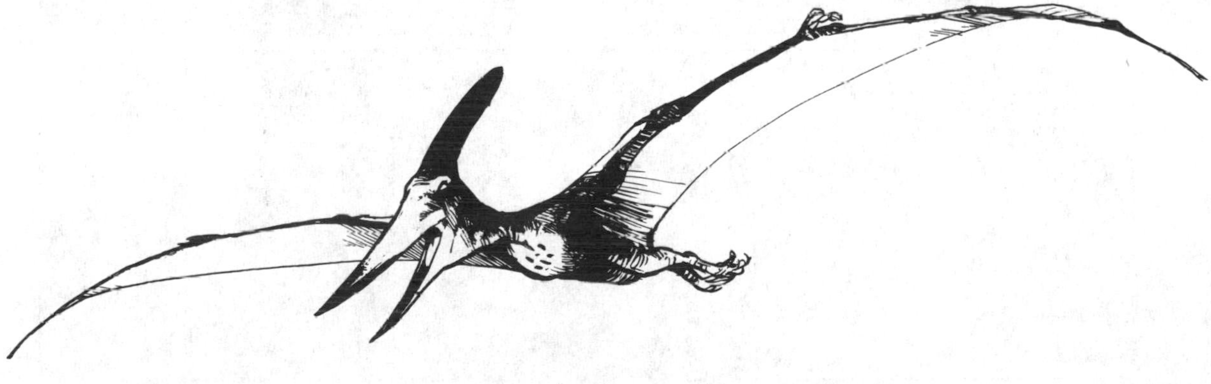

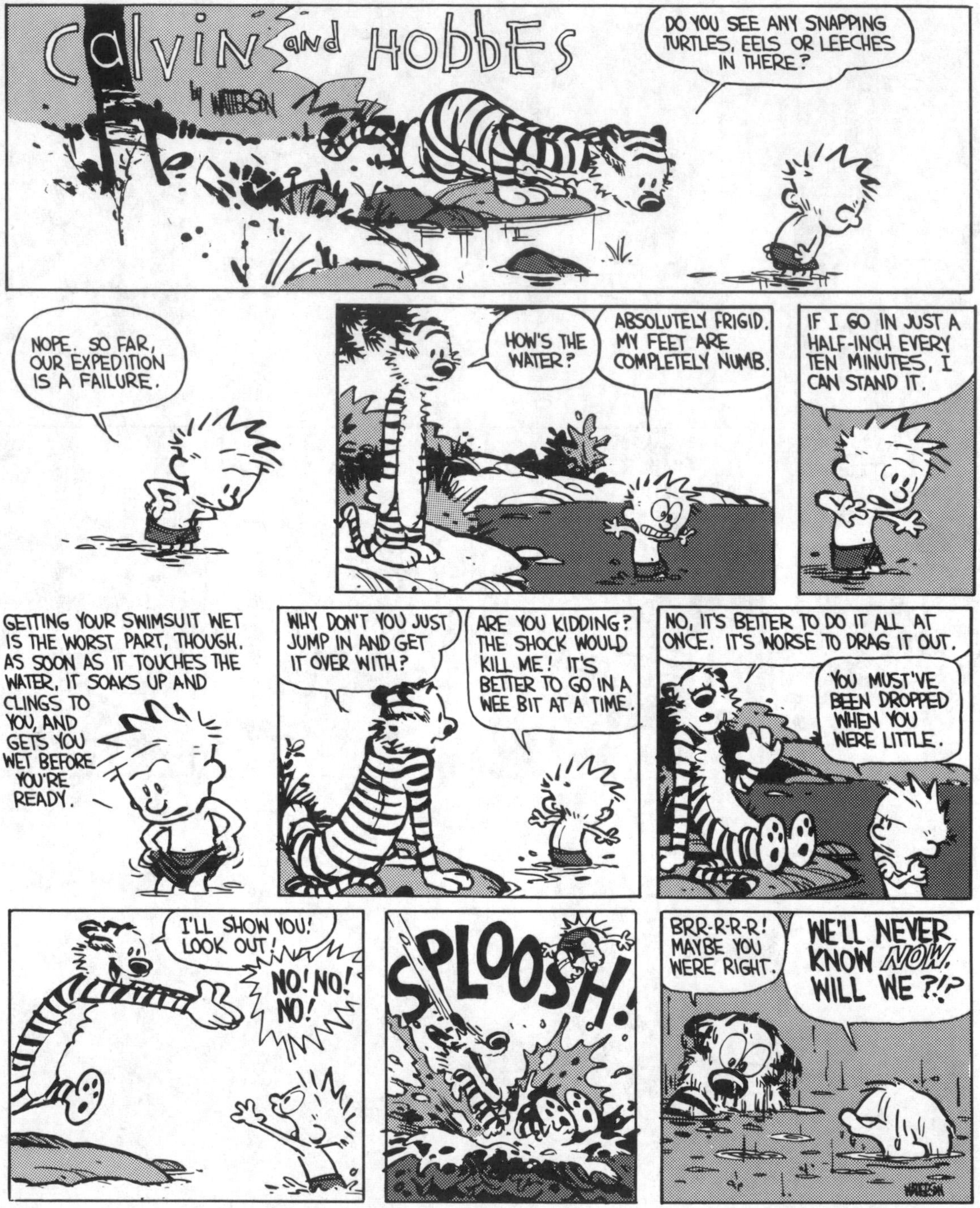
Calvin and HOBBES
by WATTERSON
DO YOU SEE ANY SNAPPING TURTLES, EELS OR LEECHES IN THERE?
NOPE. SO FAR, OUR EXPEDITION IS A FAILURE.
HOW'S THE WATER?
ABSOLUTELY FRIGID. MY FEET ARE COMPLETELY NUMB.
IF I GO IN JUST A HALF-INCH EVERY TEN MINUTES, I CAN STAND IT.
GETTING YOUR SWIMSUIT WET IS THE WORST PART, THOUGH. AS SOON AS IT TOUCHES THE WATER, IT SOAKS UP AND CLINGS TO YOU, AND GETS YOU WET BEFORE YOU'RE READY.
WHY DON'T YOU JUST JUMP IN AND GET IT OVER WITH?
ARE YOU KIDDING? THE SHOCK WOULD KILL ME! IT'S BETTER TO GO IN A WEE BIT AT A TIME.
NO, IT'S BETTER TO DO IT ALL AT ONCE. IT'S WORSE TO DRAG IT OUT.
YOU MUST'VE BEEN DROPPED WHEN YOU WERE LITTLE.
I'LL SHOW YOU! LOOK OUT!
NO! NO! NO!
SPLOOSH!
BRR-R-R-R! MAYBE YOU WERE RIGHT.
WE'LL NEVER KNOW NOW, WILL WE ?!?
WATTERSON

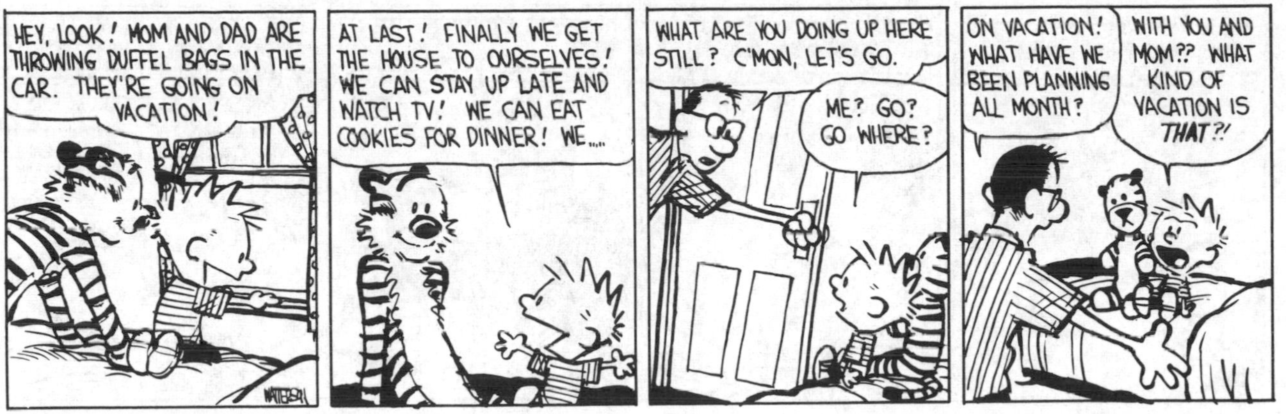
HEY, LOOK! MOM AND DAD ARE THROWING DUFFEL BAGS IN THE CAR. THEY'RE GOING ON VACATION!
AT LAST! FINALLY WE GET THE HOUSE TO OURSELVES! WE CAN STAY UP LATE AND WATCH TV! WE CAN EAT COOKIES FOR DINNER! WE....
WHAT ARE YOU DOING UP HERE STILL? C'MON, LET'S GO.
ME? GO? GO WHERE?
ON VACATION! WHAT HAVE WE BEEN PLANNING ALL MONTH?
WITH YOU AND MOM?? WHAT KIND OF VACATION IS THAT?!

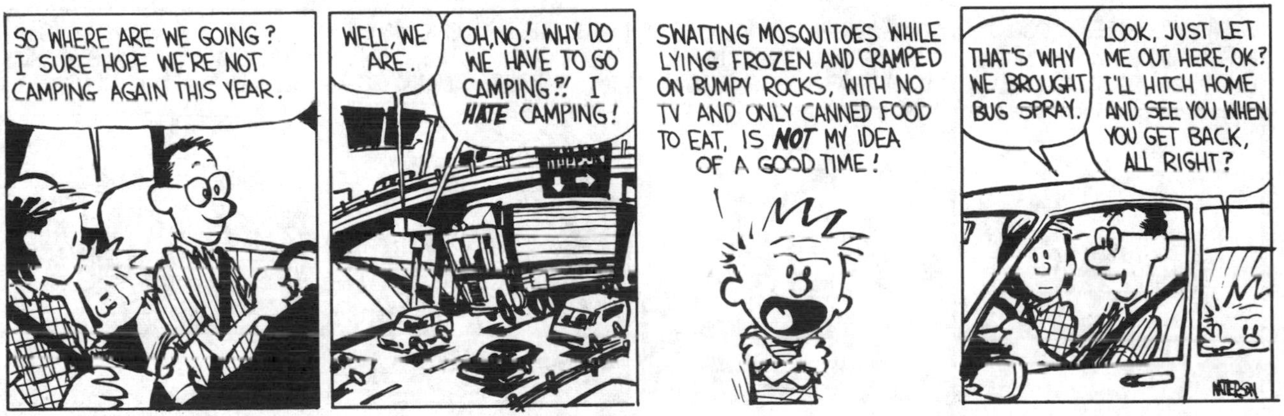
SO WHERE ARE WE GOING? I SURE HOPE WE'RE NOT CAMPING AGAIN THIS YEAR.
WELL, WE ARE.
OH, NO! WHY DO WE HAVE TO GO CAMPING?! I HATE CAMPING!
SWATTING MOSQUITOES WHILE LYING FROZEN AND CRAMPED ON BUMPY ROCKS, WITH NO TV AND ONLY CANNED FOOD TO EAT, IS NOT MY IDEA OF A GOOD TIME!
THAT'S WHY WE BROUGHT BUG SPRAY.
LOOK, JUST LET ME OUT HERE, OK? I'LL HITCH HOME AND SEE YOU WHEN YOU GET BACK, ALL RIGHT?

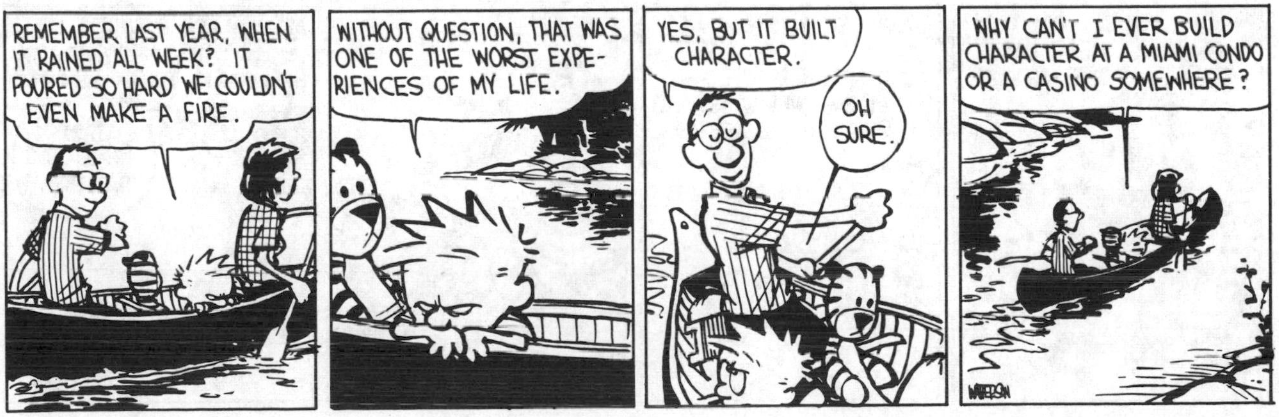
REMEMBER LAST YEAR, WHEN IT RAINED ALL WEEK? IT POURED SO HARD WE COULDN'T EVEN MAKE A FIRE.
WITHOUT QUESTION, THAT WAS ONE OF THE WORST EXPE-RIENCES OF MY LIFE.
YES, BUT IT BUILT CHARACTER.
OH SURE.
WHY CAN'T I EVER BUILD CHARACTER AT A MIAMI CONDO OR A CASINO SOMEWHERE?

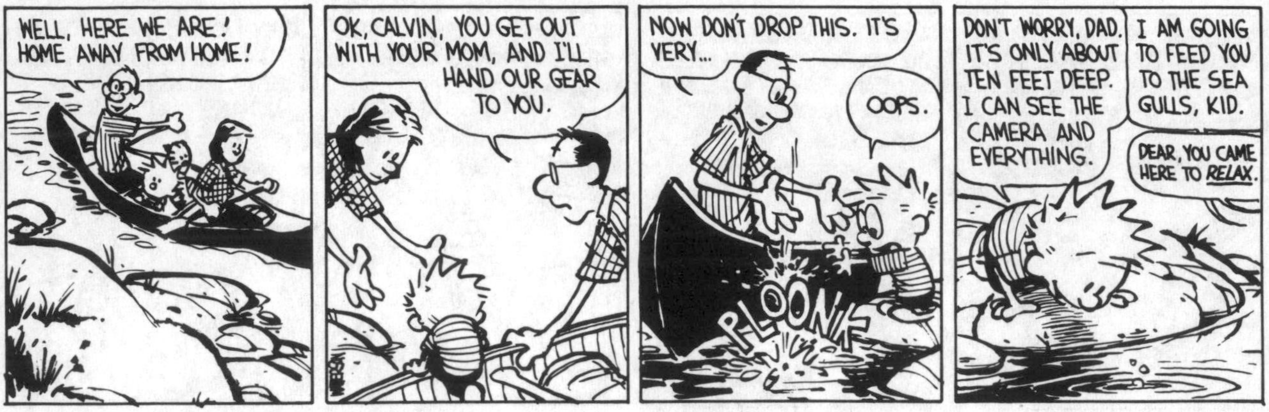
WELL, HERE WE ARE! HOME AWAY FROM HOME!
OK, CALVIN, YOU GET OUT WITH YOUR MOM, AND I'LL HAND OUR GEAR TO YOU.
NOW DON'T DROP THIS. IT'S VERY...
OOPS.
PLOONK
DON'T WORRY, DAD. IT'S ONLY ABOUT TEN FEET DEEP. I CAN SEE THE CAMERA AND EVERYTHING.
I AM GOING TO FEED YOU TO THE SEA GULLS, KID.
DEAR, YOU CAME HERE TO RELAX.

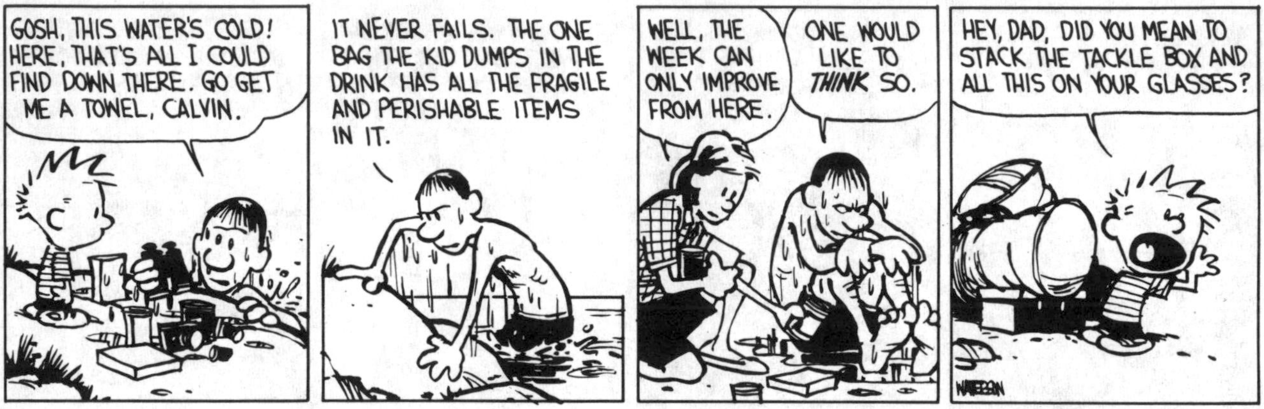
GOSH, THIS WATER'S COLD! HERE, THAT'S ALL I COULD FIND DOWN THERE. GO GET ME A TOWEL, CALVIN.
IT NEVER FAILS. THE ONE BAG THE KID DUMPS IN THE DRINK HAS ALL THE FRAGILE AND PERISHABLE ITEMS IN IT.
WELL, THE WEEK CAN ONLY IMPROVE FROM HERE.
ONE WOULD LIKE TO THINK SO.
HEY, DAD, DID YOU MEAN TO STACK THE TACKLE BOX AND ALL THIS ON YOUR GLASSES?

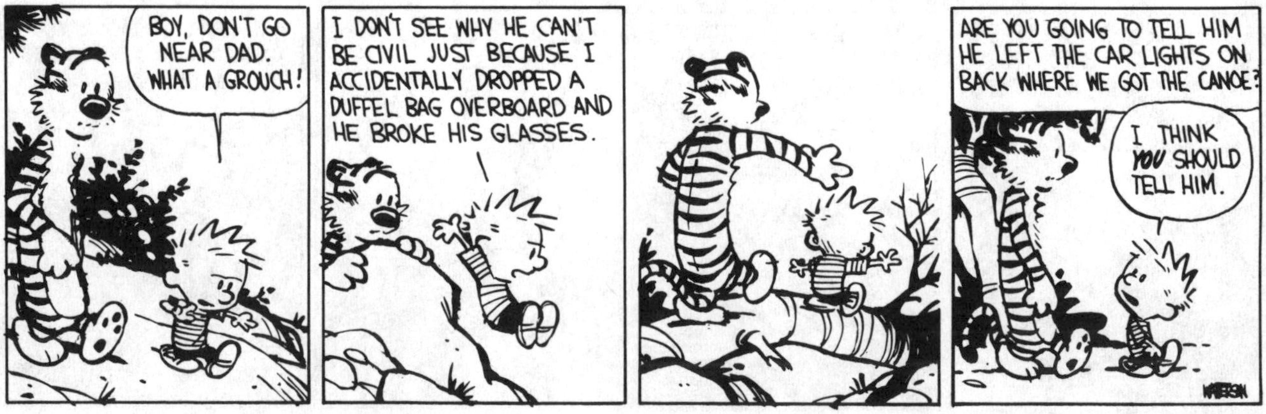
BOY, DON'T GO NEAR DAD. WHAT A GROUCH!
I DON'T SEE WHY HE CAN'T BE CIVIL JUST BECAUSE I ACCIDENTALLY DROPPED A DUFFEL BAG OVERBOARD AND HE BROKE HIS GLASSES.
ARE YOU GOING TO TELL HIM HE LEFT THE CAR LIGHTS ON BACK WHERE WE GOT THE CANOE?
I THINK YOU SHOULD TELL HIM.

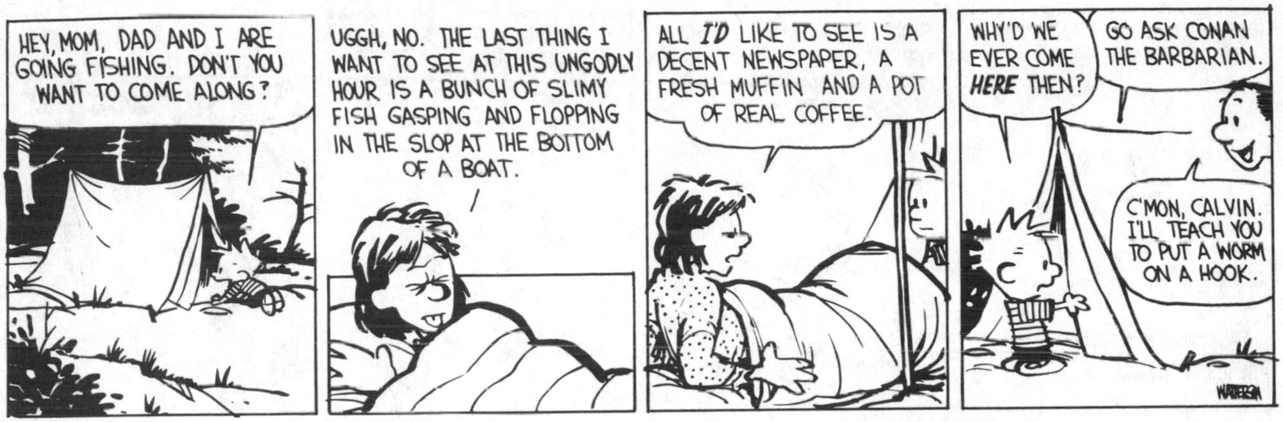
HEY, MOM, DAD AND I ARE GOING FISHING. DON'T YOU WANT TO COME ALONG?
UGGH, NO. THE LAST THING I WANT TO SEE AT THIS UNGODLY HOUR IS A BUNCH OF SLIMY FISH GASPING AND FLOPPING IN THE SLOP AT THE BOTTOM OF A BOAT.
ALL I'D LIKE TO SEE IS A DECENT NEWSPAPER, A FRESH MUFFIN AND A POT OF REAL COFFEE.
WHY'D WE EVER COME HERE THEN?
GO ASK CONAN THE BARBARIAN.
C'MON, CALVIN. I'LL TEACH YOU TO PUT A WORM ON A HOOK.

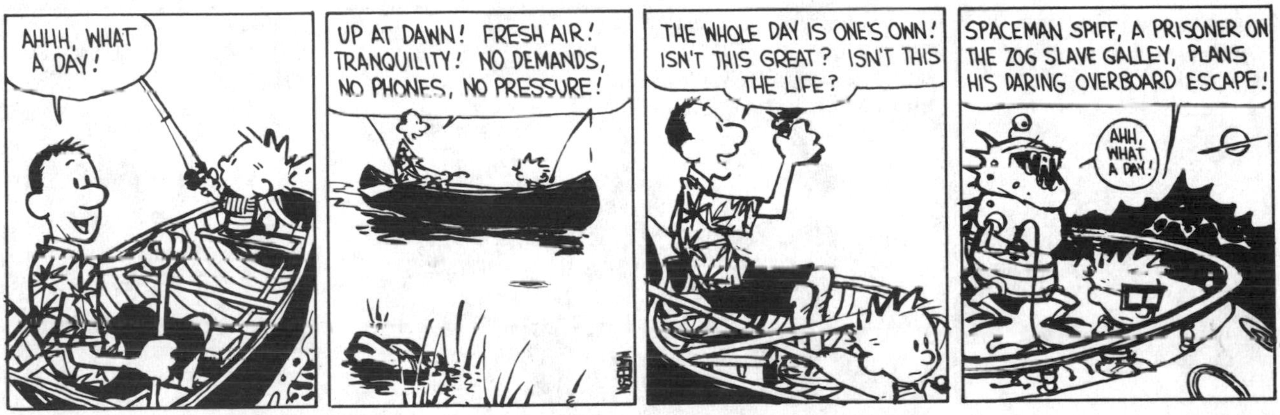
AHHH, WHAT A DAY!
UP AT DAWN! FRESH AIR! TRANQUILITY! NO DEMANDS, NO PHONES, NO PRESSURE!
THE WHOLE DAY IS ONE'S OWN! ISN'T THIS GREAT? ISN'T THIS THE LIFE?
SPACEMAN SPIFF, A PRISONER ON THE ZOG SLAVE GALLEY, PLANS HIS DARING OVERBOARD ESCAPE!
AHH, WHAT A DAY!

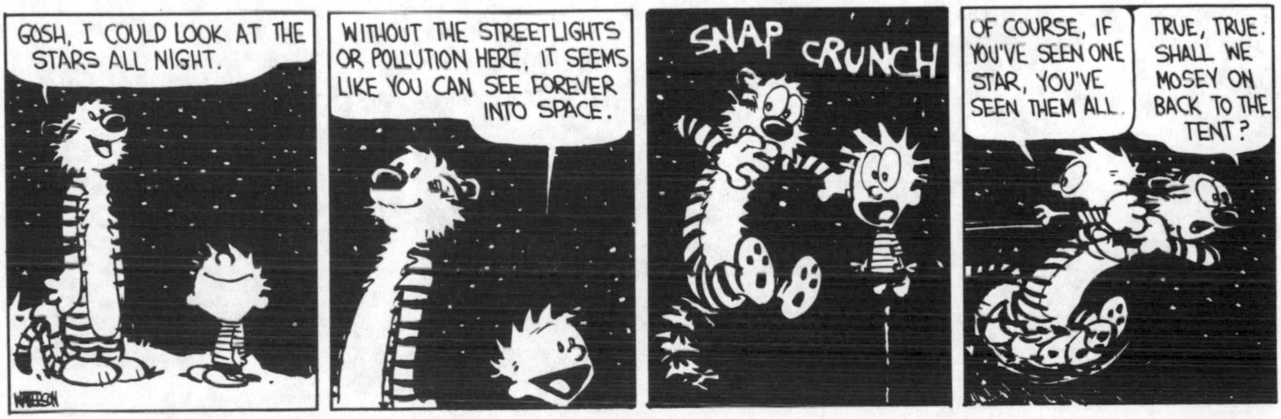
GOSH, I COULD LOOK AT THE STARS ALL NIGHT.
WITHOUT THE STREETLIGHTS OR POLLUTION HERE, IT SEEMS LIKE YOU CAN SEE FOREVER INTO SPACE.
SNAP
CRUNCH
OF COURSE, IF YOU'VE SEEN ONE STAR, YOU'VE SEEN THEM ALL.
TRUE, TRUE. SHALL WE MOSEY ON BACK TO THE TENT?

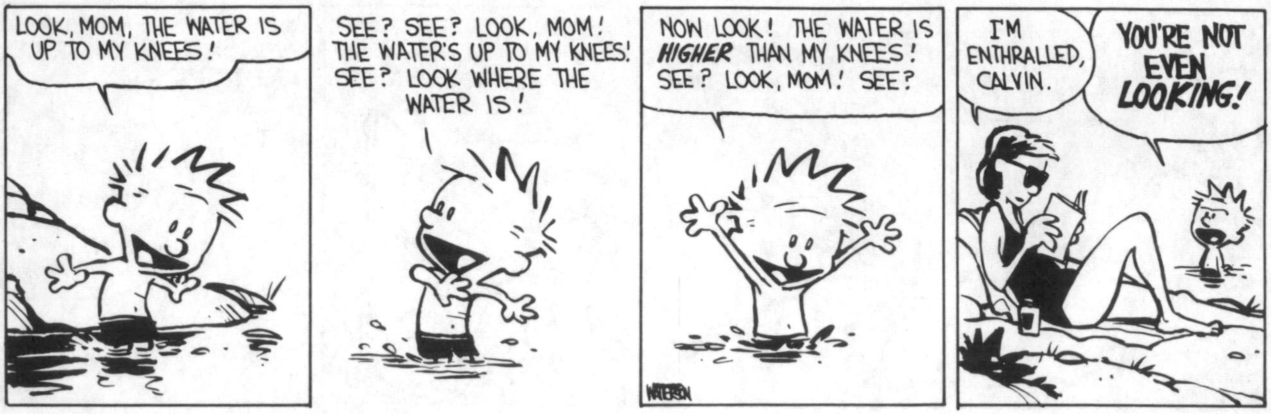
LOOK, MOM, THE WATER IS UP TO MY KNEES!
SEE? SEE? LOOK, MOM! THE WATER'S UP TO MY KNEES! SEE? LOOK WHERE THE WATER IS!
NOW LOOK! THE WATER IS HIGHER THAN MY KNEES! SEE? LOOK, MOM! SEE?
I'M ENTHRALLED, CALVIN.
YOU'RE NOT EVEN LOOKING!

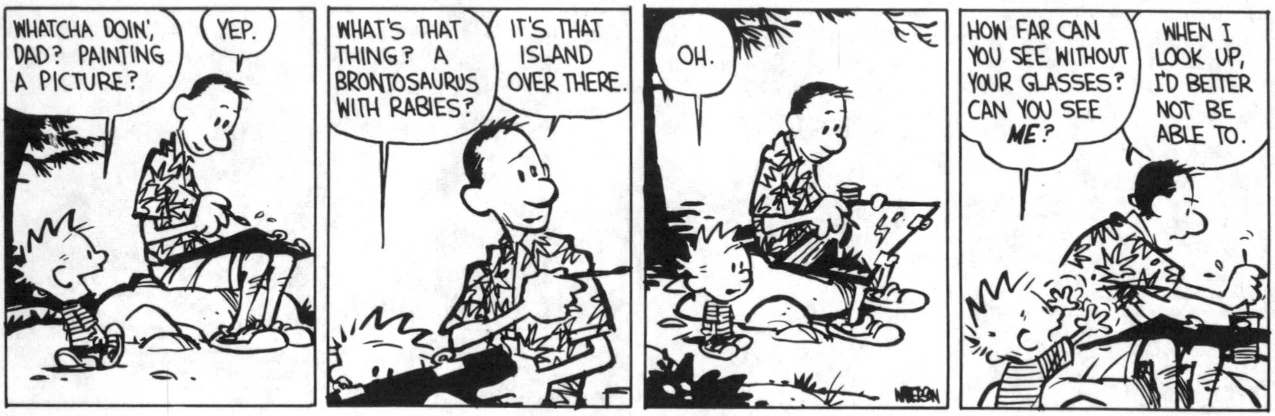
WHATCHA DOIN', DAD? PAINTING A PICTURE?
YEP.
WHAT'S THAT THING? A BRONTOSAURUS WITH RABIES?
IT'S THAT ISLAND OVER THERE.
OH.
HOW FAR CAN YOU SEE WITHOUT YOUR GLASSES? CAN YOU SEE ME?
WHEN I LOOK UP, I'D BETTER NOT BE ABLE TO.

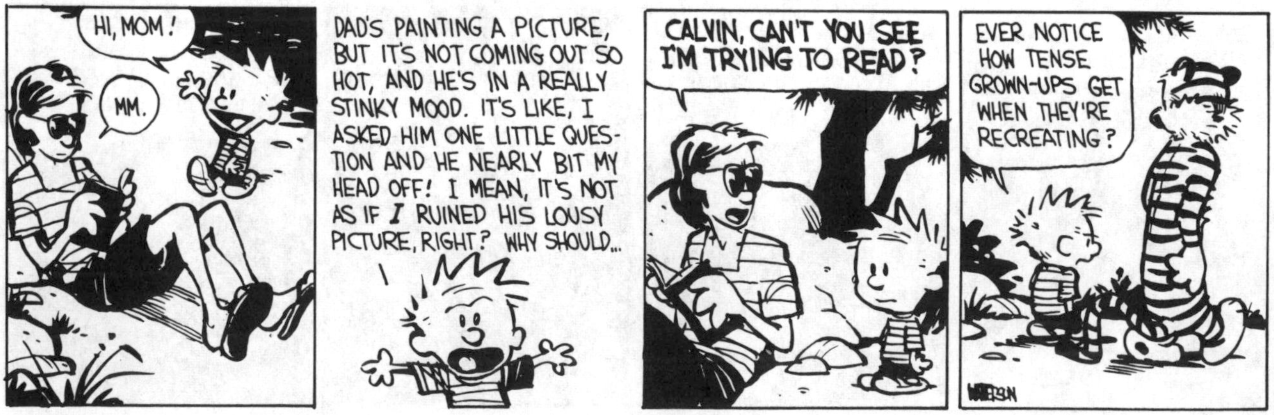
HI, MOM!
MM.
DAD'S PAINTING A PICTURE, BUT IT'S NOT COMING OUT SO HOT, AND HE'S IN A REALLY STINKY MOOD. IT'S LIKE, I ASKED HIM ONE LITTLE QUESTION AND HE NEARLY BIT MY HEAD OFF! I MEAN, IT'S NOT AS IF I RUINED HIS LOUSY PICTURE, RIGHT? WHY SHOULD...
CALVIN, CAN'T YOU SEE I'M TRYING TO READ?
EVER NOTICE HOW TENSE GROWN-UPS GET WHEN THEY'RE RECREATING?

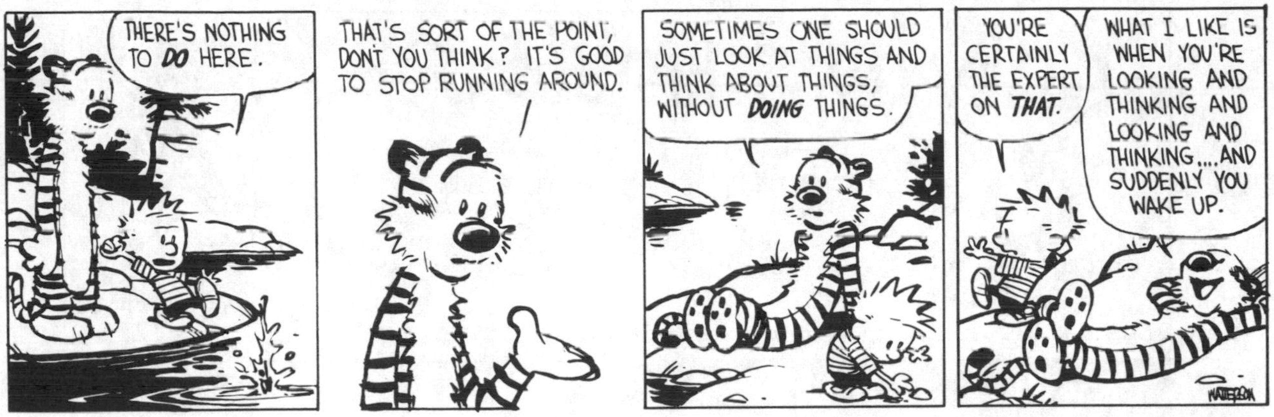
THERE'S NOTHING TO DO HERE.
THAT'S SORT OF THE POINT, DON'T YOU THINK? IT'S GOOD TO STOP RUNNING AROUND.
SOMETIMES ONE SHOULD JUST LOOK AT THINGS AND THINK ABOUT THINGS, WITHOUT DOING THINGS.
YOU'RE CERTAINLY THE EXPERT ON THAT.
WHAT I LIKE IS WHEN YOU'RE LOOKING AND THINKING AND LOOKING AND THINKING....AND SUDDENLY YOU WAKE UP.

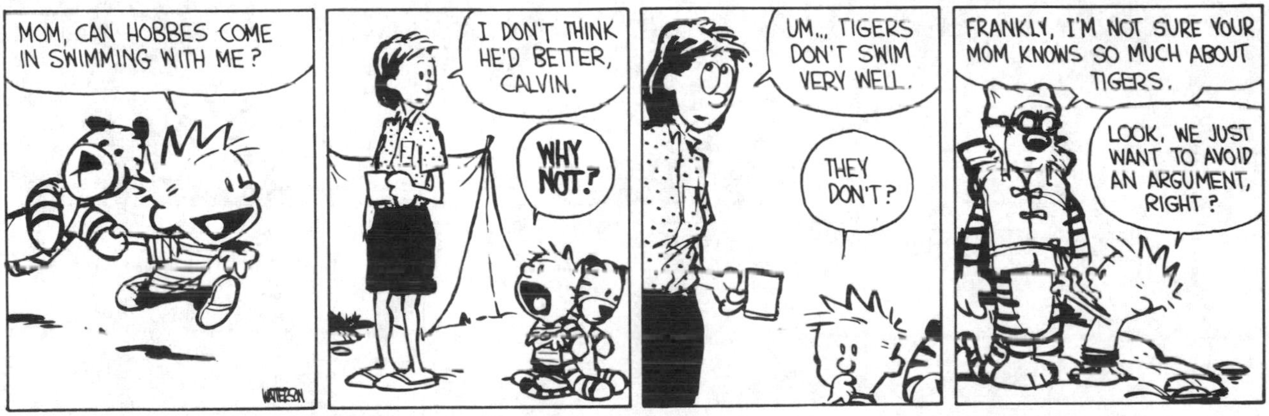
MOM, CAN HOBBES COME IN SWIMMING WITH ME?
I DON'T THINK HE'D BETTER, CALVIN.
WHY NOT?
UM... TIGERS DON'T SWIM VERY WELL.
THEY DON'T?
FRANKLY, I'M NOT SURE YOUR MOM KNOWS SO MUCH ABOUT TIGERS.
LOOK, WE JUST WANT TO AVOID AN ARGUMENT, RIGHT?

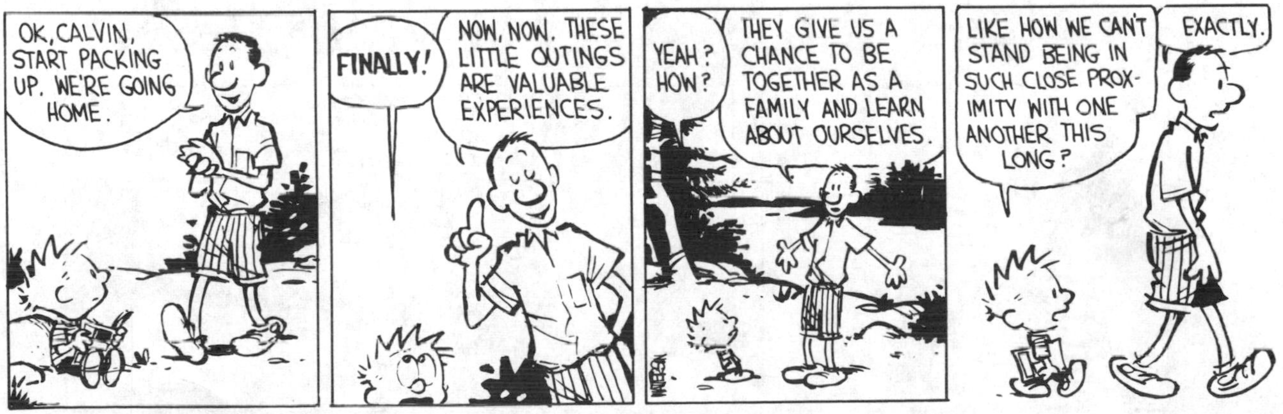
OK, CALVIN, START PACKING UP. WE'RE GOING HOME.
FINALLY!
NOW, NOW. THESE LITTLE OUTINGS ARE VALUABLE EXPERIENCES.
YEAH? HOW?
THEY GIVE US A CHANCE TO BE TOGETHER AS A FAMILY AND LEARN ABOUT OURSELVES.
LIKE HOW WE CAN'T STAND BEING IN SUCH CLOSE PROX-IMITY WITH ONE ANOTHER THIS LONG?
EXACTLY.

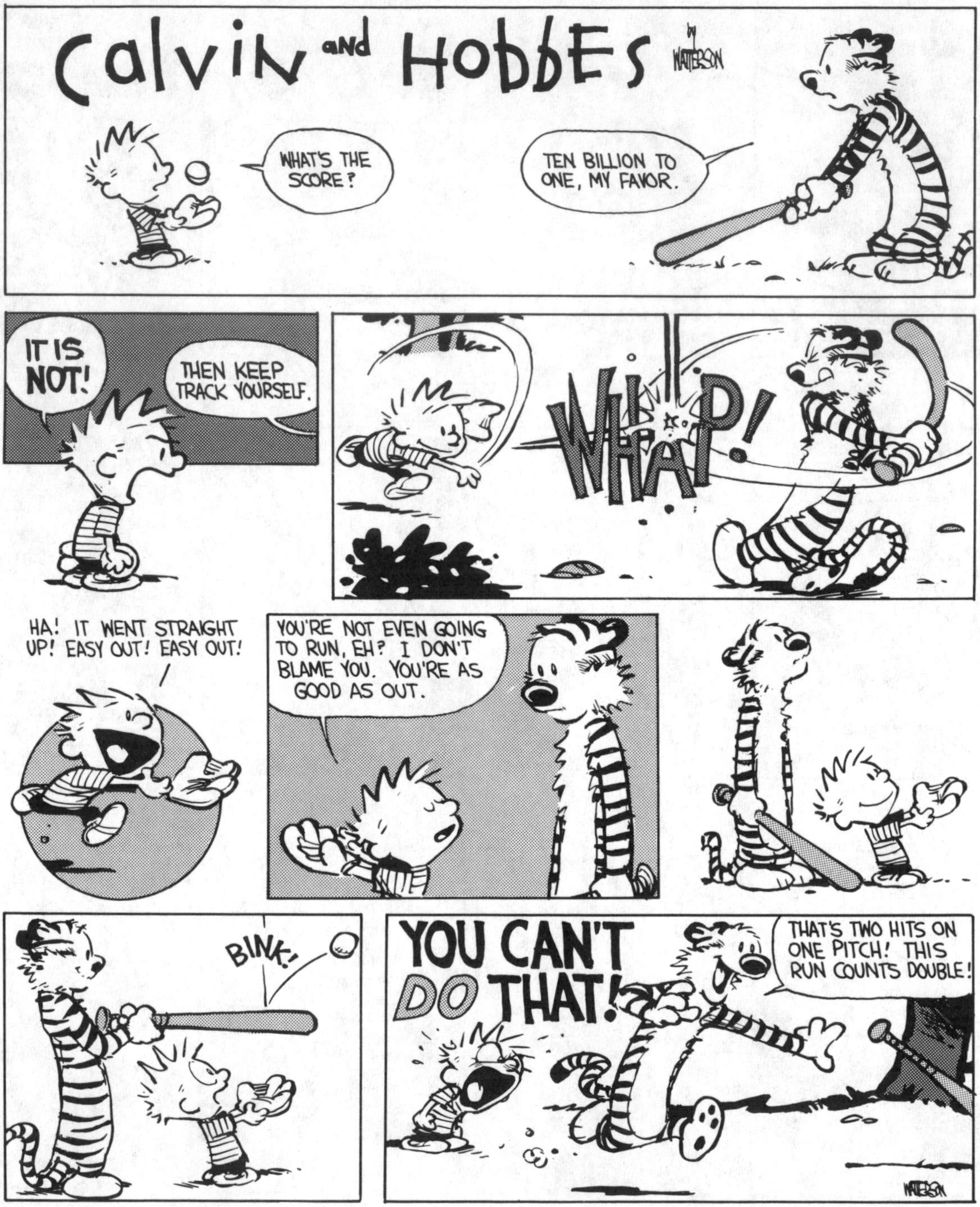
Calvin and Hobbes
by WATTERSON
WHAT'S THE SCORE?
TEN BILLION TO ONE, MY FAVOR.
IT IS NOT!
THEN KEEP TRACK YOURSELF.
WHAP!
HA! IT WENT STRAIGHT UP! EASY OUT! EASY OUT!
YOU'RE NOT EVEN GOING TO RUN, EH? I DON'T BLAME YOU. YOU'RE AS GOOD AS OUT.
BINK!
YOU CAN'T DO THAT!
THAT'S TWO HITS ON ONE PITCH! THIS RUN COUNTS DOUBLE!
WATTERSON

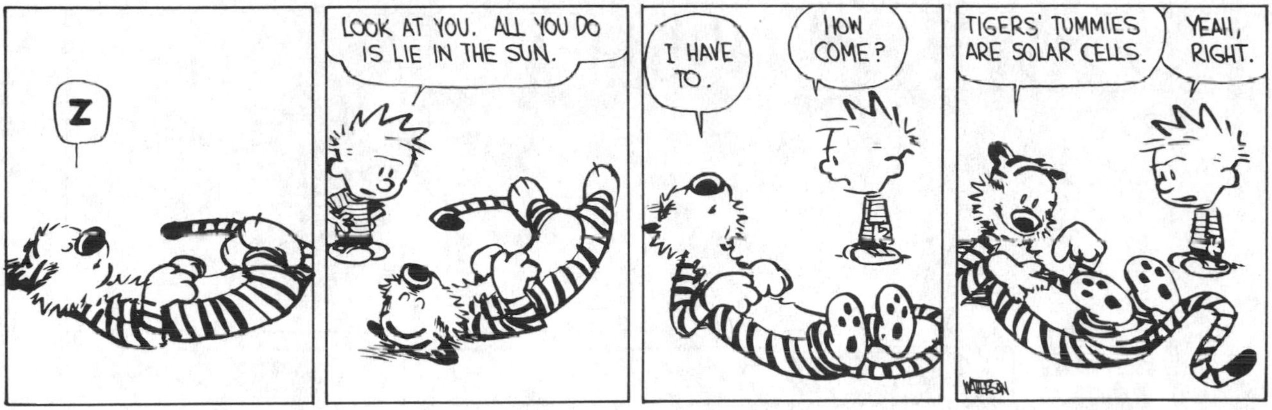
Z
LOOK AT YOU. ALL YOU DO IS LIE IN THE SUN.
I HAVE TO.
HOW COME?
TIGERS' TUMMIES ARE SOLAR CELLS.
YEAH, RIGHT.

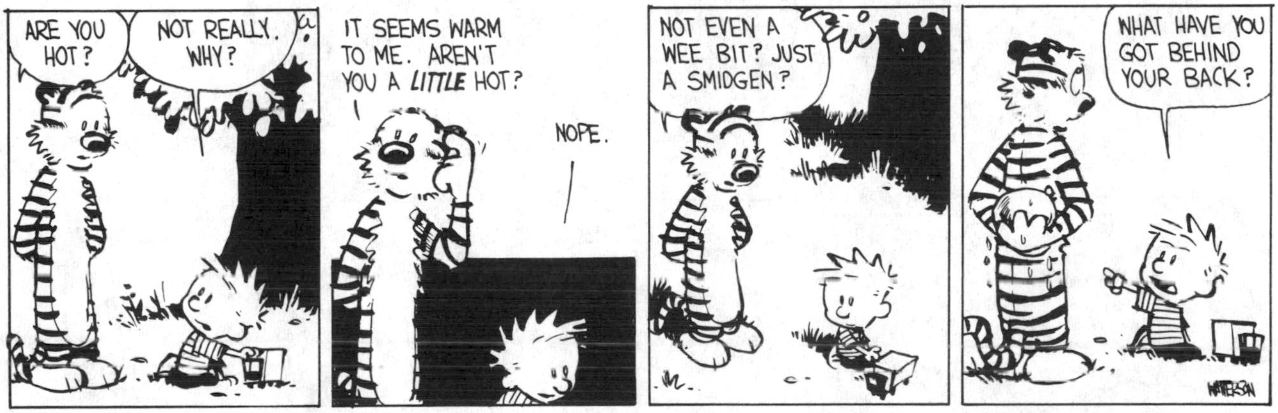
ARE YOU HOT?
NOT REALLY. WHY?
IT SEEMS WARM TO ME. AREN'T YOU A *LITTLE* HOT?
NOPE.
NOT EVEN A WEE BIT? JUST A SMIDGEN?
WHAT HAVE YOU GOT BEHIND YOUR BACK?

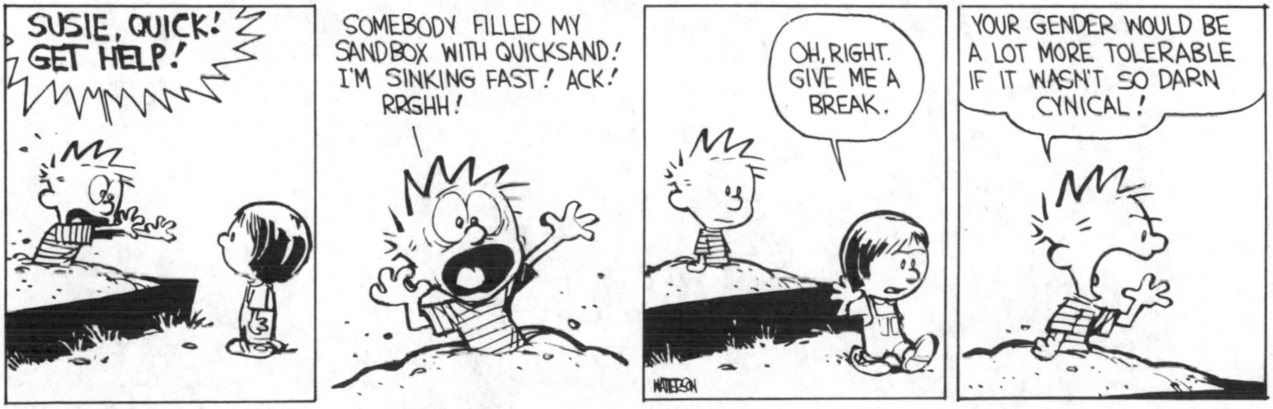
SUSIE, QUICK! GET HELP!
SOMEBODY FILLED MY SANDBOX WITH QUICKSAND! I'M SINKING FAST! ACK! RRGHH!
OH, RIGHT. GIVE ME A BREAK.
YOUR GENDER WOULD BE A LOT MORE TOLERABLE IF IT WASN'T SO DARN CYNICAL!

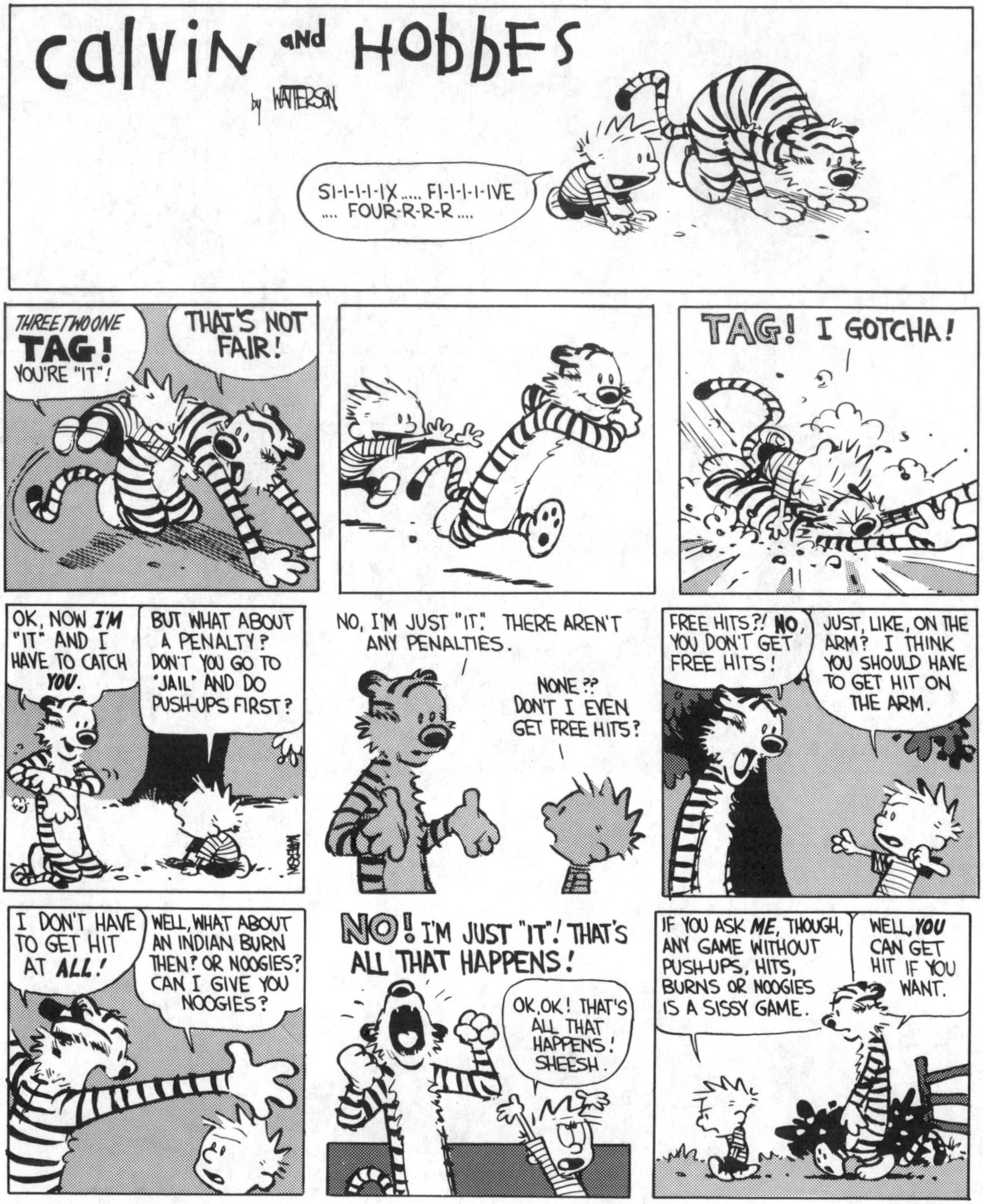

Calvin and HOBBES
by WATTERSON
SI-I-I-I-IX..... FI-I-I-I-IVE .... FOUR-R-R-R....
THREETWOONE TAG! YOU'RE "IT"!
THAT'S NOT FAIR!
TAG! I GOTCHA!
OK, NOW I'M "IT" AND I HAVE TO CATCH YOU.
BUT WHAT ABOUT A PENALTY? DON'T YOU GO TO 'JAIL' AND DO PUSH-UPS FIRST?
NO, I'M JUST "IT". THERE AREN'T ANY PENALTIES.
NONE?? DON'T I EVEN GET FREE HITS?
FREE HITS?! NO, YOU DON'T GET FREE HITS!
JUST, LIKE, ON THE ARM? I THINK YOU SHOULD HAVE TO GET HIT ON THE ARM.
I DON'T HAVE TO GET HIT AT ALL!
WELL, WHAT ABOUT AN INDIAN BURN THEN? OR NOOGIES? CAN I GIVE YOU NOOGIES?
NO! I'M JUST "IT"! THAT'S ALL THAT HAPPENS!
OK, OK! THAT'S ALL THAT HAPPENS! SHEESH.
IF YOU ASK ME, THOUGH, ANY GAME WITHOUT PUSH-UPS, HITS, BURNS OR NOOGIES IS A SISSY GAME.
WELL, YOU CAN GET HIT IF YOU WANT.

THIS PROBABLY JUST GOES TO SHOW SOMETHING, BUT I SURE DON'T KNOW WHAT.
THERE'S QUITE A BREEZE UP HERE. I'M REALLY MOVING. THERE'S THE RIVER AND THE TOWN TRIANGLE.
HEY, DOWN THERE! MY NAME IS CALVIN! TELL MY TIGER, HOBBES, I'M BLOWING AWAY ON A BALLOON!
CAN ANYONE HEAR ME? TELL HOBBES HE CAN'T READ MY COMIC BOOKS JUST 'CAUSE I'M NOT AROUND, OK?
...OH, YEAH, TELL MY PARENTS WHAT HAPPENED, TOO, ALL RIGHT? HELLO? HELLO?
UH OH, I'M HEADING INTO A FLOCK OF DUCKS!
EXCUSE ME! COMING THROUGH!
PARDON ME! GANGWAY! BEEP BEEP!
...BOY, IF LOOKS COULD KILL.

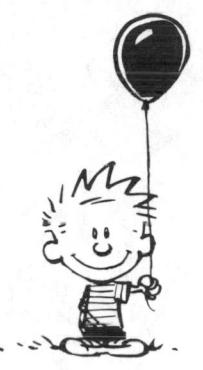

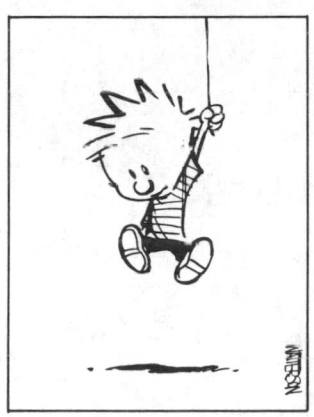

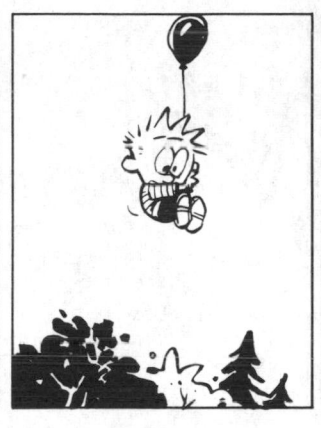

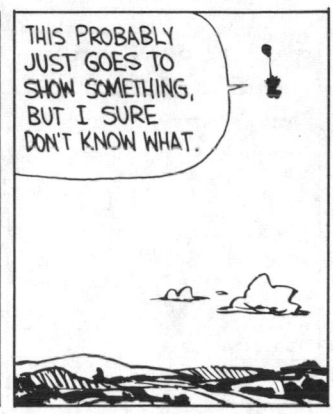

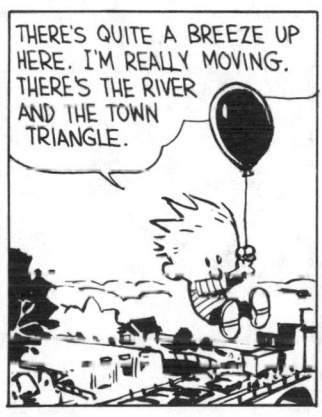

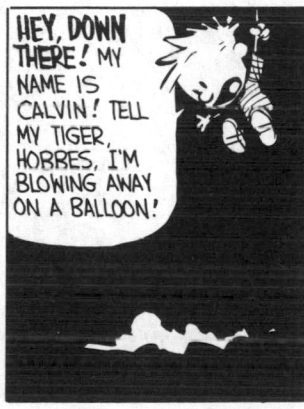

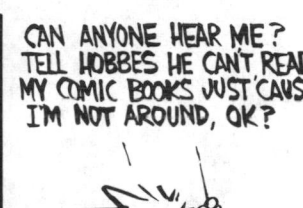

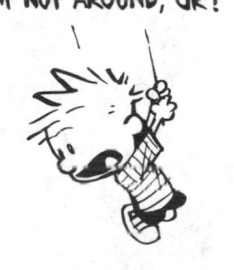

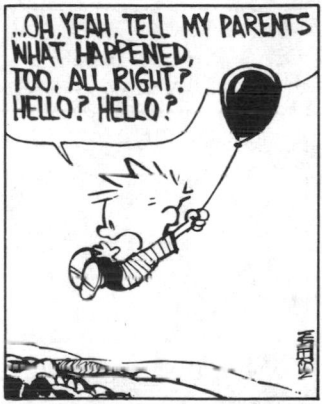

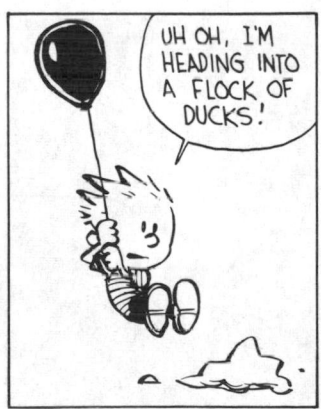

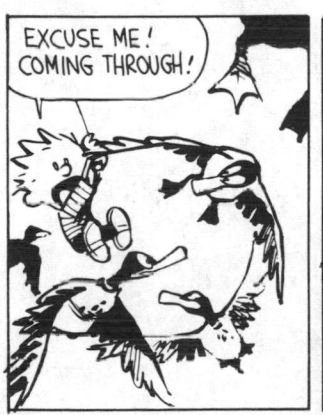

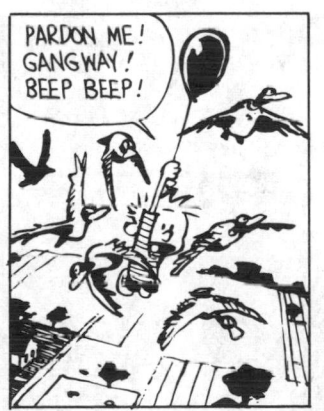

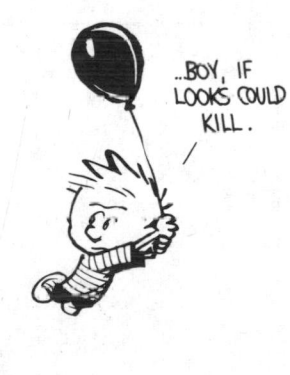

MY HANDS ARE GETTING TIRED. I'LL TIE THE BALLOON STRING ONTO MY BELT LOOP.
THERE...
WHOOP
SHOOF
IF A PLANE COMES ALONG NOW, I'M GONNA DIE.
WATTERSON
WELL, I SUPPOSE THINGS DON'T GET WORSE THAN HANGING FROM A HELIUM BALLOON A MILE ABOVE SOME UNRECOGNIZED STATE.
OF COURSE, MY GRIP COULD WEAKEN, OR I COULD GET SUCKED INTO A JET INTAKE.
THAT'S ONE OF THE REMARKABLE THINGS ABOUT LIFE. IT'S NEVER SO BAD THAT IT CAN'T GET WORSE.
WATTERSON
BOY, I'M JUST GOING HIGHER AND HIGHER.
I SUPPOSE EVENTUALLY THE PRESSURE IN THE BALLOON WILL BE GREATER THAN THE AIR PRESSURE AROUND IT, AND THE BALLOON WILL...
WATTERSON
POP!

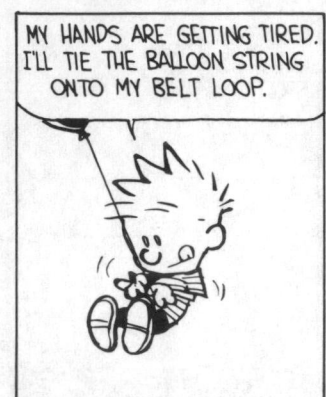

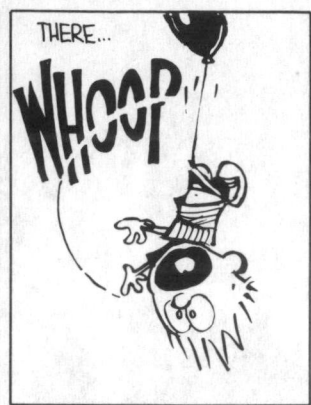

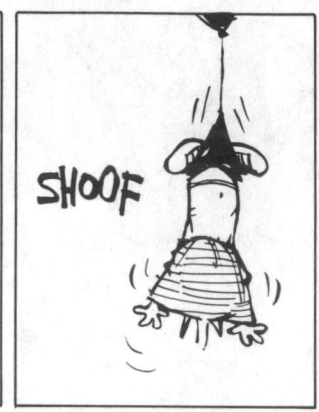

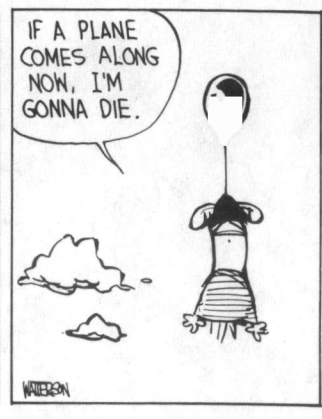

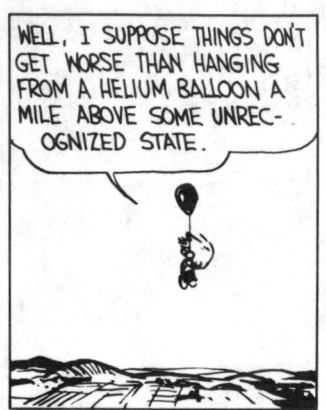

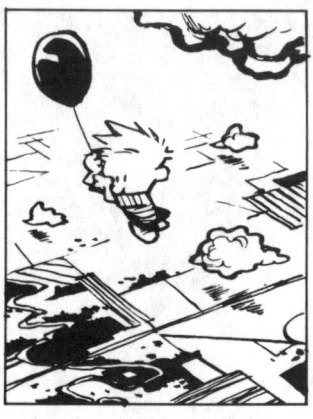

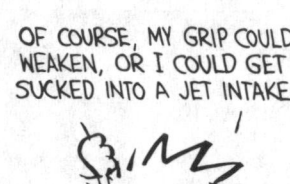

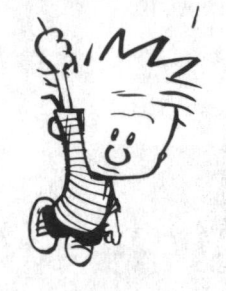

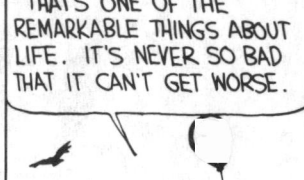

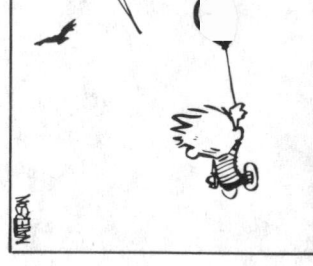

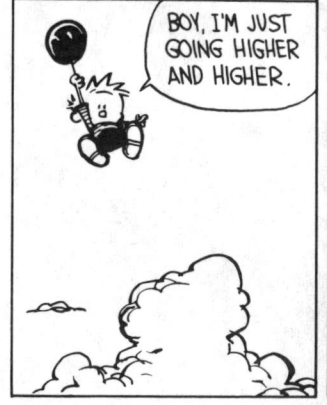

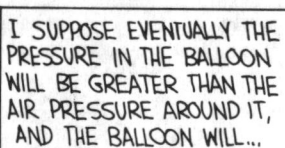

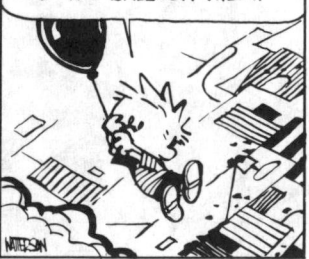

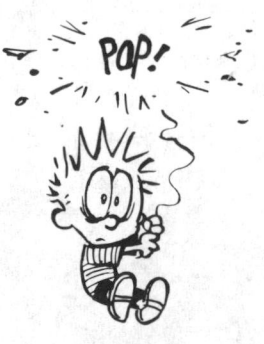

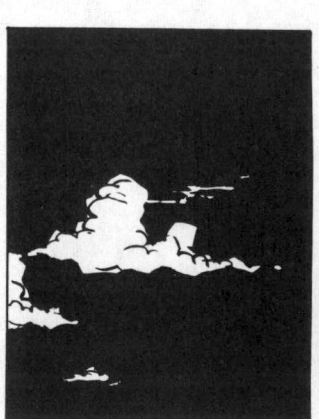

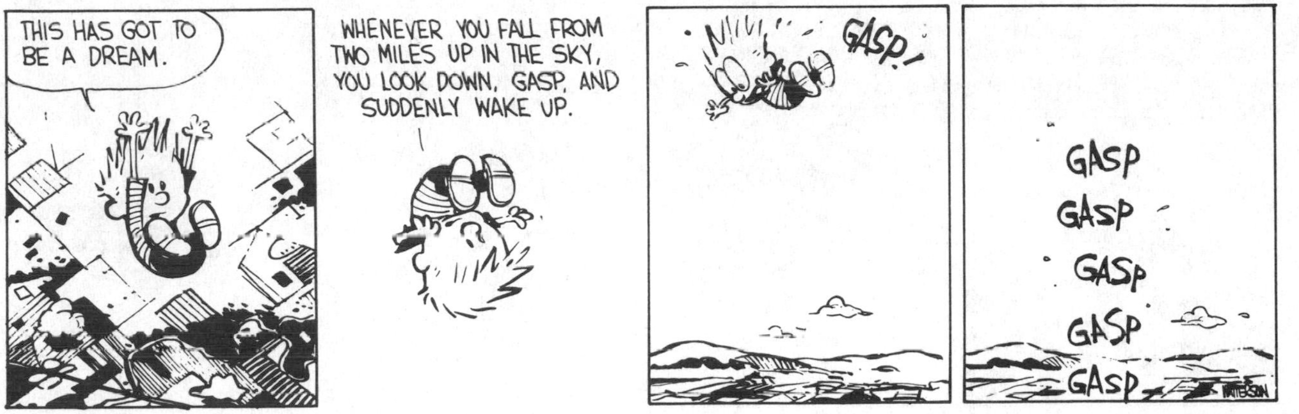
THIS HAS GOT TO BE A DREAM.
WHENEVER YOU FALL FROM TWO MILES UP IN THE SKY, YOU LOOK DOWN, GASP, AND SUDDENLY WAKE UP.
GASP!
GASP
GASP
GASP
GASP
GASP

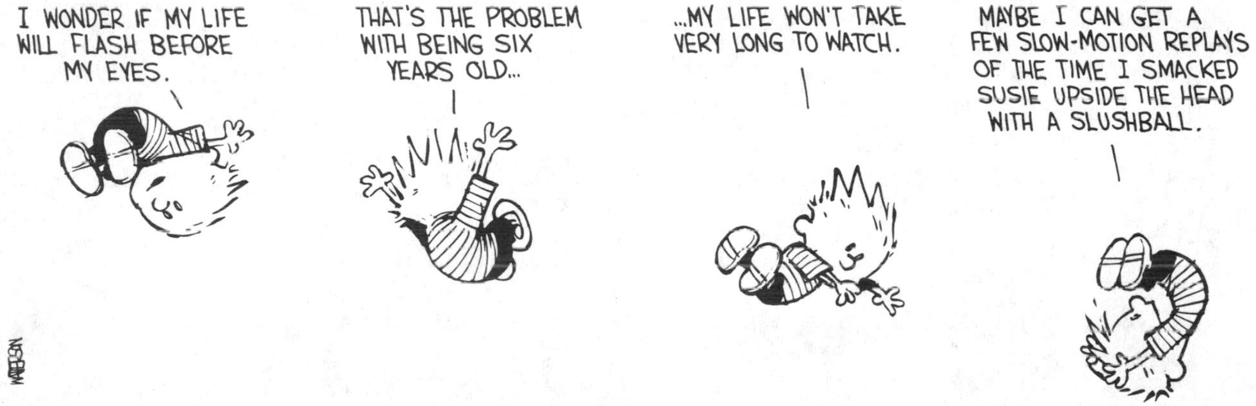
I WONDER IF MY LIFE WILL FLASH BEFORE MY EYES.
THAT'S THE PROBLEM WITH BEING SIX YEARS OLD...
...MY LIFE WON'T TAKE VERY LONG TO WATCH.
MAYBE I CAN GET A FEW SLOW-MOTION REPLAYS OF THE TIME I SMACKED SUSIE UPSIDE THE HEAD WITH A SLUSHBALL.

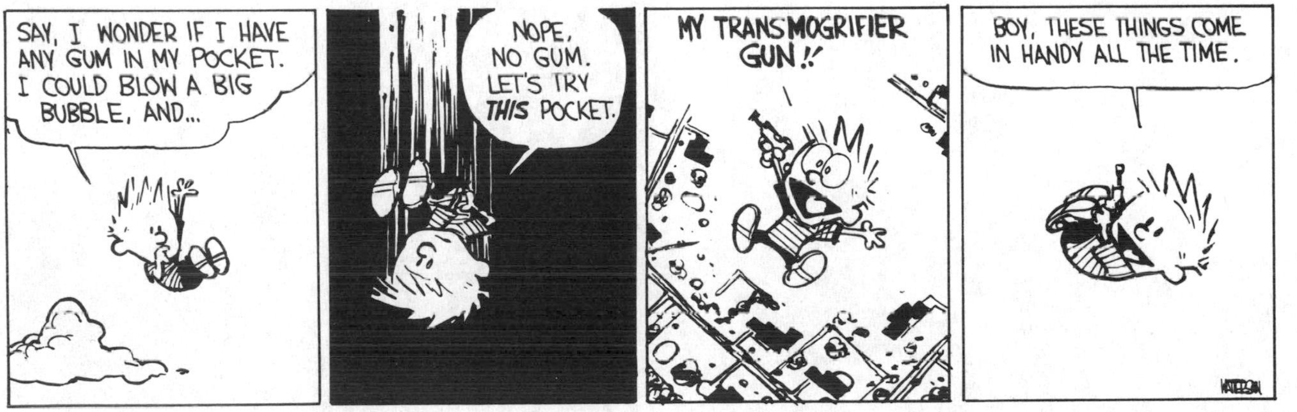
SAY, I WONDER IF I HAVE ANY GUM IN MY POCKET. I COULD BLOW A BIG BUBBLE, AND...
NOPE, NO GUM. LET'S TRY *THIS* POCKET.
MY TRANSMOGRIFIER GUN!!
BOY, THESE THINGS COME IN HANDY ALL THE TIME.

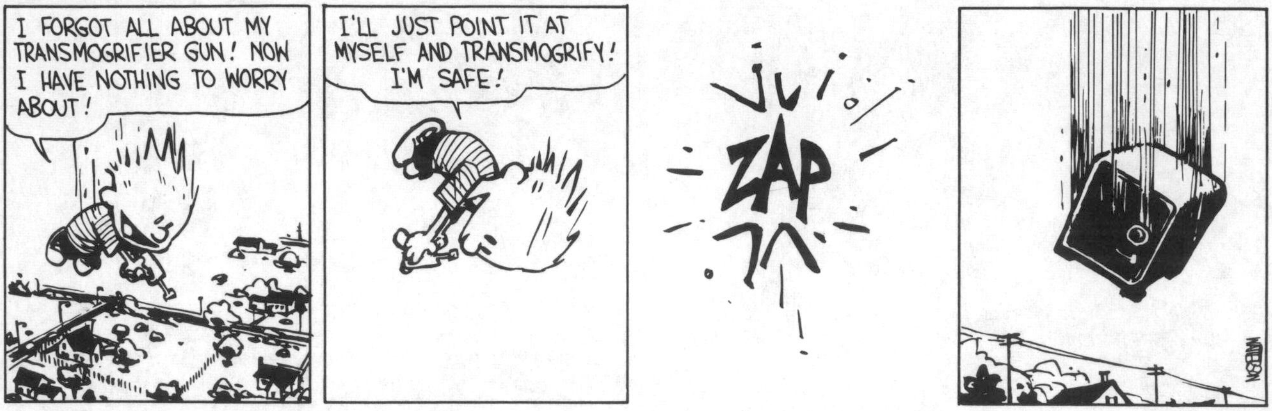
I FORGOT ALL ABOUT MY TRANSMOGRIFIER GUN! NOW I HAVE NOTHING TO WORRY ABOUT!
I'LL JUST POINT IT AT MYSELF AND TRANSMOGRIFY! I'M SAFE!
ZAP

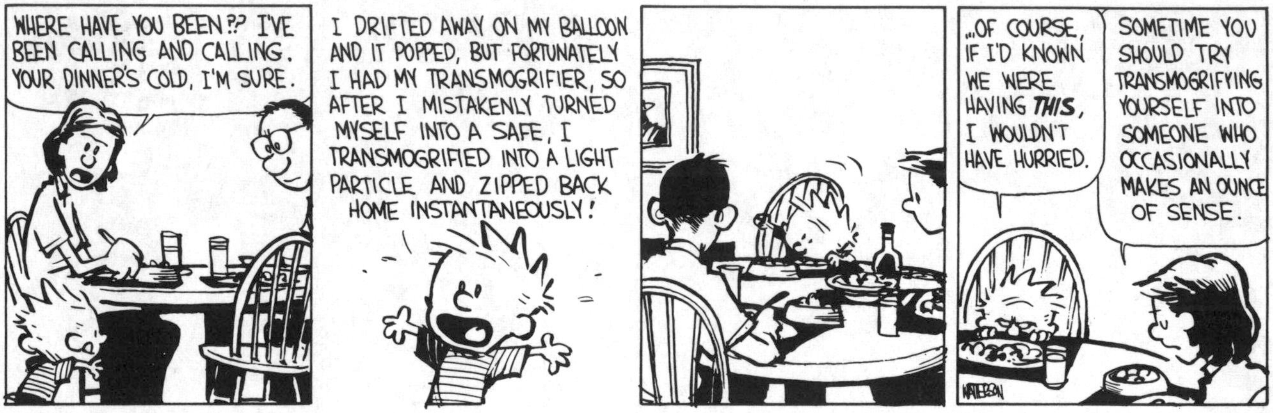
WHERE HAVE YOU BEEN?? I'VE BEEN CALLING AND CALLING. YOUR DINNER'S COLD, I'M SURE.
I DRIFTED AWAY ON MY BALLOON AND IT POPPED, BUT FORTUNATELY I HAD MY TRANSMOGRIFIER, SO AFTER I MISTAKENLY TURNED MYSELF INTO A SAFE, I TRANSMOGRIFIED INTO A LIGHT PARTICLE AND ZIPPED BACK HOME INSTANTANEOUSLY!
...OF COURSE, IF I'D KNOWN WE WERE HAVING **THIS**, I WOULDN'T HAVE HURRIED.
SOMETIME YOU SHOULD TRY TRANSMOGRIFYING YOURSELF INTO SOMEONE WHO OCCASIONALLY MAKES AN OUNCE OF SENSE.

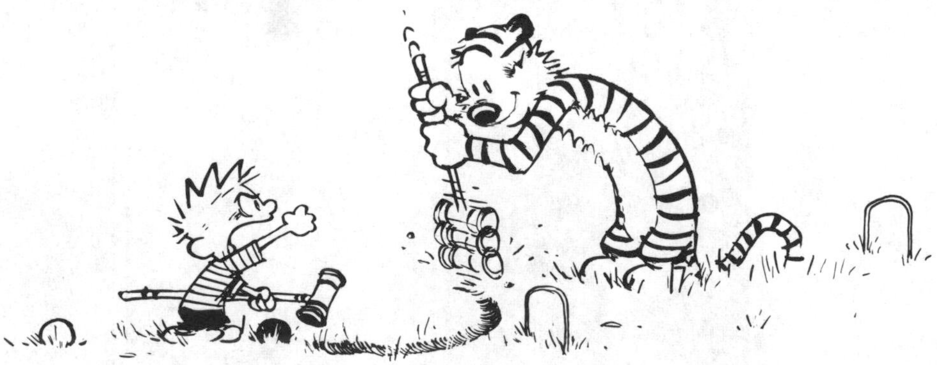

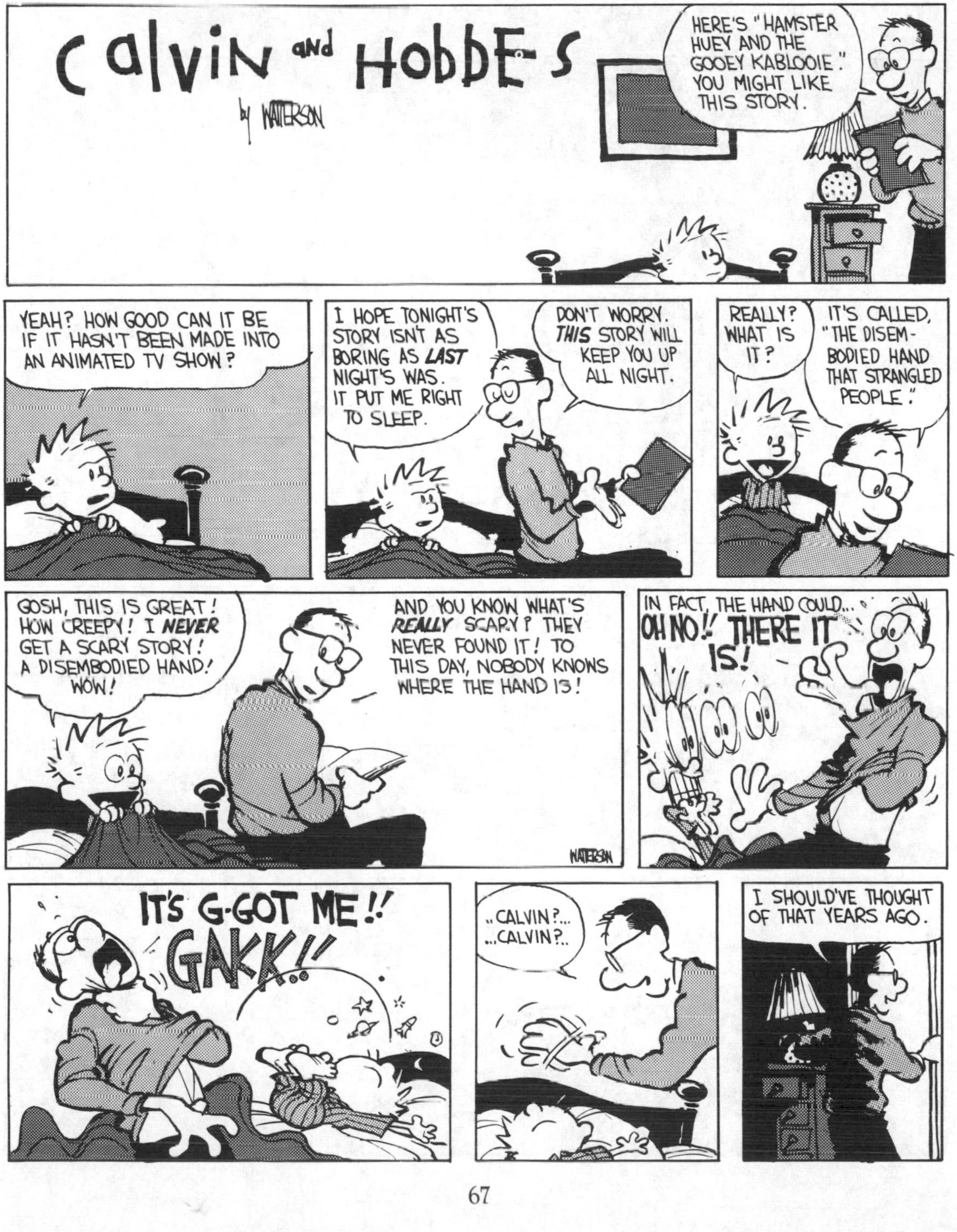
Calvin and HobbeS
by WATTERSON
HERE'S "HAMSTER HUEY AND THE GOOEY KABLOOIE." YOU MIGHT LIKE THIS STORY.
YEAH? HOW GOOD CAN IT BE IF IT HASN'T BEEN MADE INTO AN ANIMATED TV SHOW?
I HOPE TONIGHT'S STORY ISN'T AS BORING AS LAST NIGHT'S WAS. IT PUT ME RIGHT TO SLEEP.
DON'T WORRY. THIS STORY WILL KEEP YOU UP ALL NIGHT.
REALLY? WHAT IS IT?
IT'S CALLED, "THE DISEMBODIED HAND THAT STRANGLED PEOPLE."
GOSH, THIS IS GREAT! HOW CREEPY! I NEVER GET A SCARY STORY! A DISEMBODIED HAND! WOW!
AND YOU KNOW WHAT'S REALLY SCARY? THEY NEVER FOUND IT! TO THIS DAY, NOBODY KNOWS WHERE THE HAND IS!
WATTERSON
IN FACT, THE HAND COULD...
OH NO!! THERE IT IS!
IT'S G-GOT ME!!
GAKK!!
..CALVIN?... ...CALVIN?..
I SHOULD'VE THOUGHT OF THAT YEARS AGO.

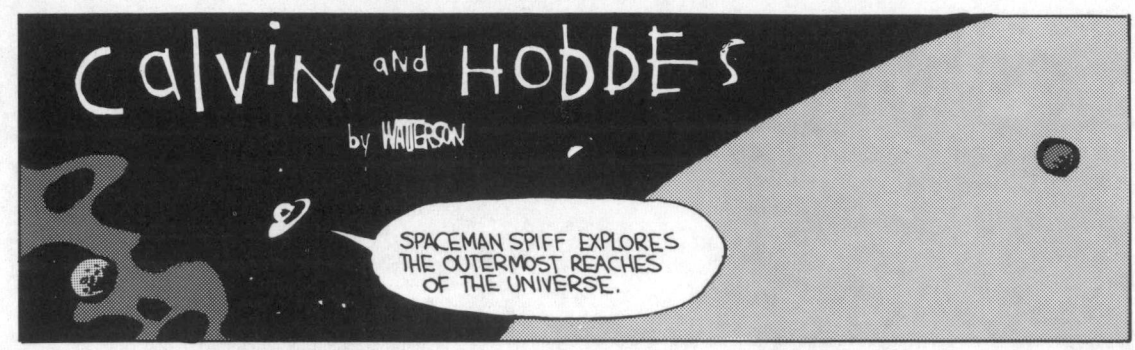

Calvin and HOBBES
by WATTERSON
SPACEMAN SPIFF EXPLORES THE OUTERMOST REACHES OF THE UNIVERSE.
BY POPULAR REQUEST.
INTREPID EXPLORER SPACEMAN SPIFF LANDS ON AN UNCHARTED PLANET. WHAT STRANGE WONDERS WILL HE DISCOVER HERE?
SPIFF SETS OUT IN SEARCH OF SENTIENT LIFE!
WHAT A STRANGE PLANET THIS IS! ITS SURFACE IS SURPRISINGLY SOFT AND POROUS!
AND HERE CURIOUS GEYSERS BLAST HOT AIR!
SUDDENLY IT DAWNS ON HIM! SPIFF IS NOT ON THE PLANET'S SURFACE AT ALL! HE'S WALKING ON A RECLINING ALIEN!!
OUR HERO SETS HIS DEATH RAY BLASTER.
ZZ.. MMF HM?

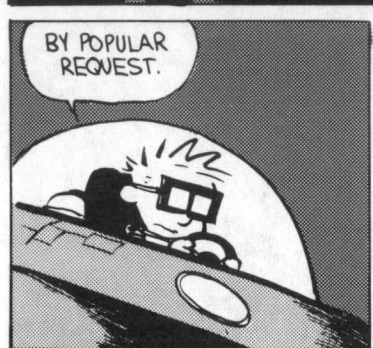

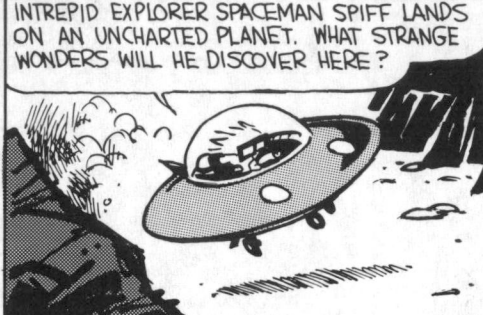

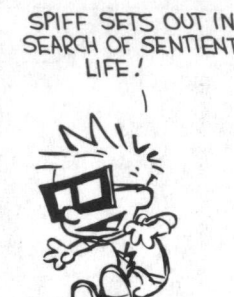

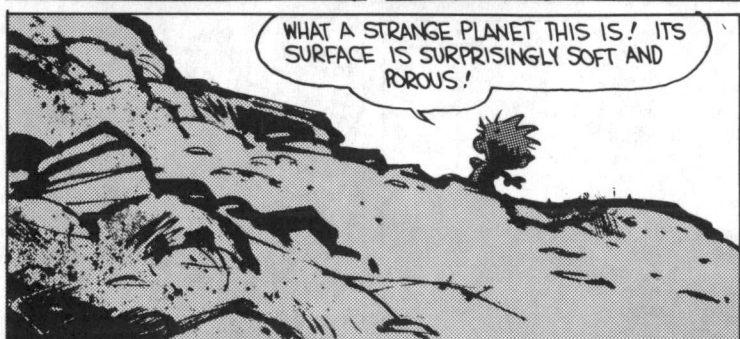

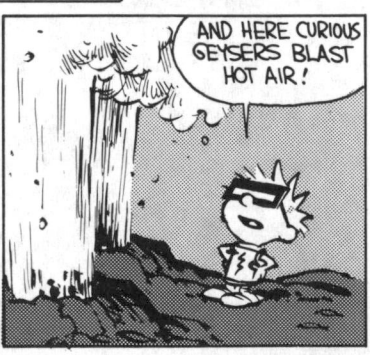

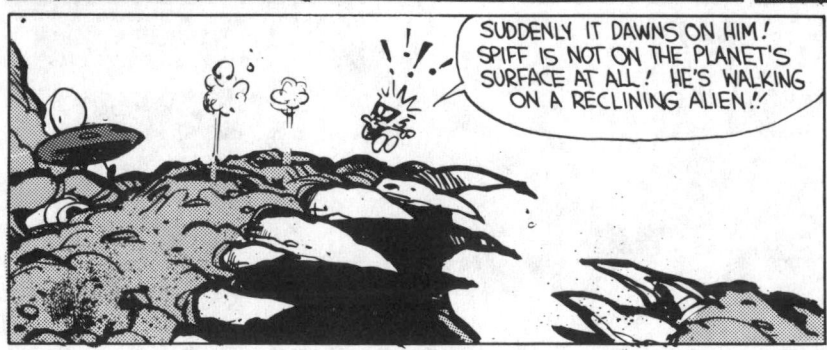

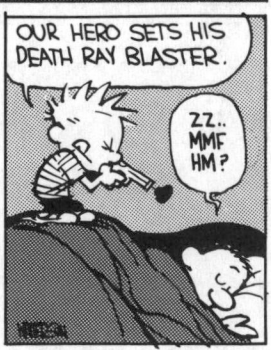

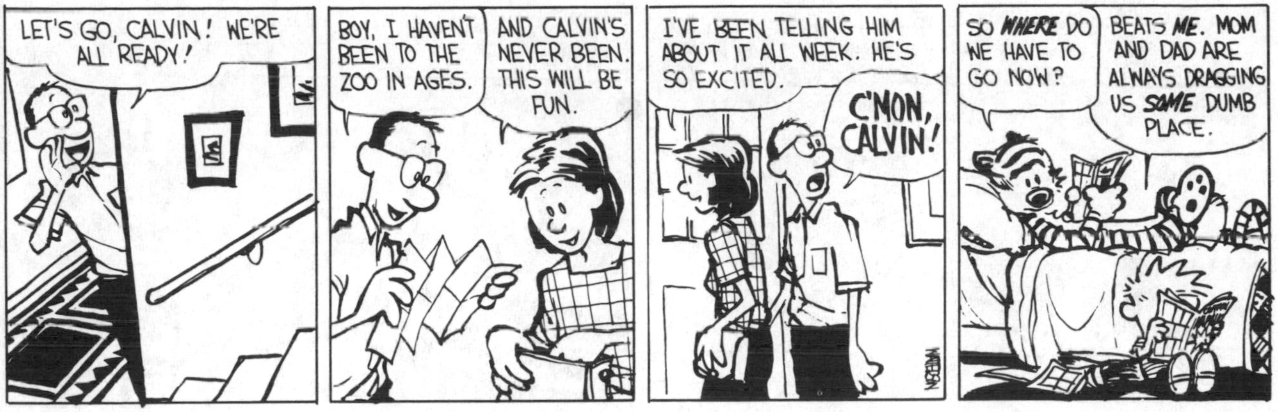
LET'S GO, CALVIN! WE'RE ALL READY!
BOY, I HAVEN'T BEEN TO THE ZOO IN AGES.
AND CALVIN'S NEVER BEEN. THIS WILL BE FUN.
I'VE BEEN TELLING HIM ABOUT IT ALL WEEK. HE'S SO EXCITED.
C'MON, CALVIN!
SO WHERE DO WE HAVE TO GO NOW?
BEATS ME. MOM AND DAD ARE ALWAYS DRAGGING US SOME DUMB PLACE.

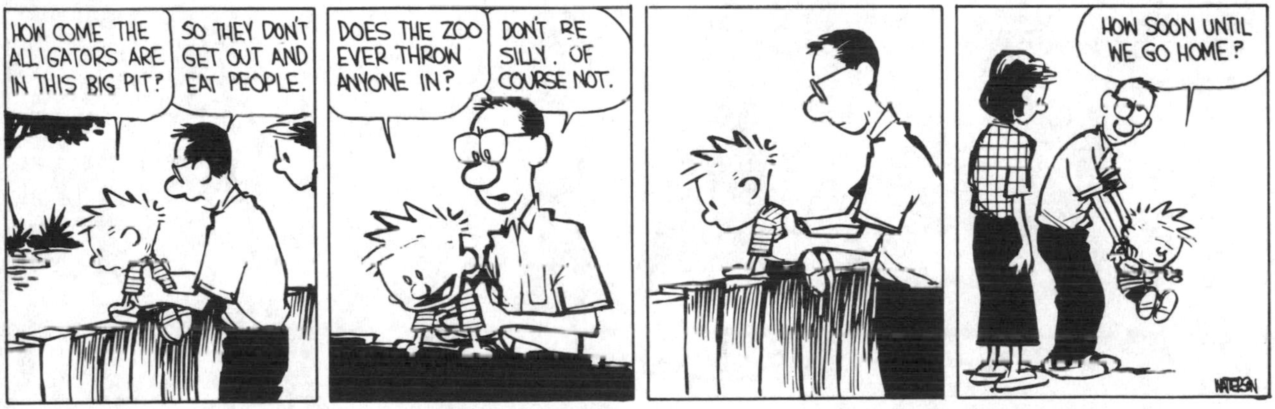
HOW COME THE ALLIGATORS ARE IN THIS BIG PIT?
SO THEY DON'T GET OUT AND EAT PEOPLE.
DOES THE ZOO EVER THROW ANYONE IN?
DON'T BE SILLY. OF COURSE NOT.
HOW SOON UNTIL WE GO HOME?

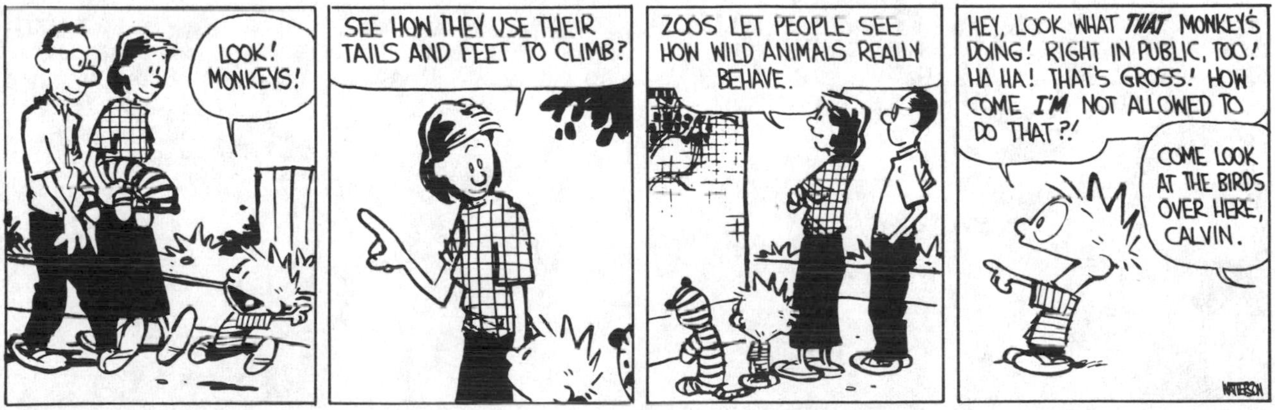
LOOK! MONKEYS!
SEE HOW THEY USE THEIR TAILS AND FEET TO CLIMB?
ZOOS LET PEOPLE SEE HOW WILD ANIMALS REALLY BEHAVE.
HEY, LOOK WHAT THAT MONKEY'S DOING! RIGHT IN PUBLIC, TOO! HA HA! THAT'S GROSS! HOW COME I'M NOT ALLOWED TO DO THAT?!
COME LOOK AT THE BIRDS OVER HERE, CALVIN.

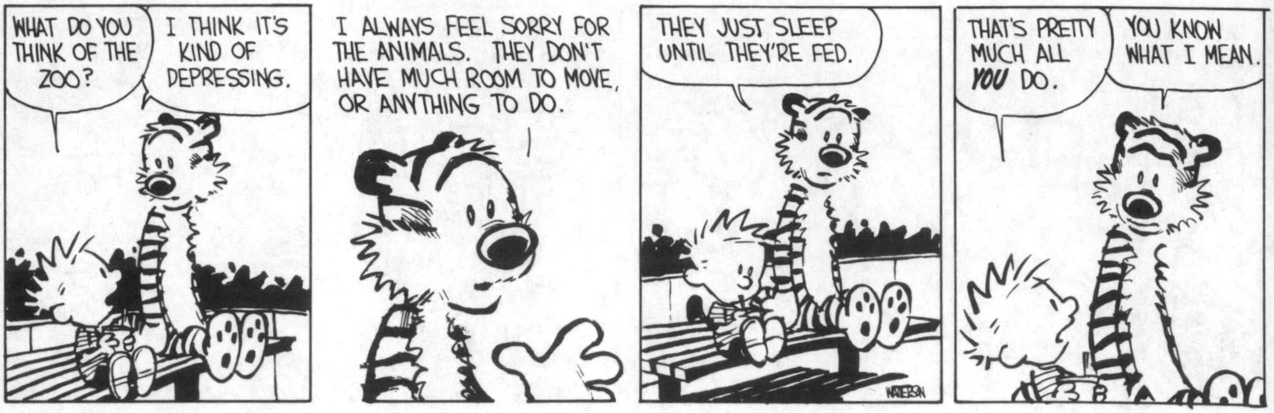
WHAT DO YOU THINK OF THE ZOO?
I THINK IT'S KIND OF DEPRESSING.
I ALWAYS FEEL SORRY FOR THE ANIMALS. THEY DON'T HAVE MUCH ROOM TO MOVE, OR ANYTHING TO DO.
THEY JUST SLEEP UNTIL THEY'RE FED.
THAT'S PRETTY MUCH ALL *YOU* DO.
YOU KNOW WHAT I MEAN.

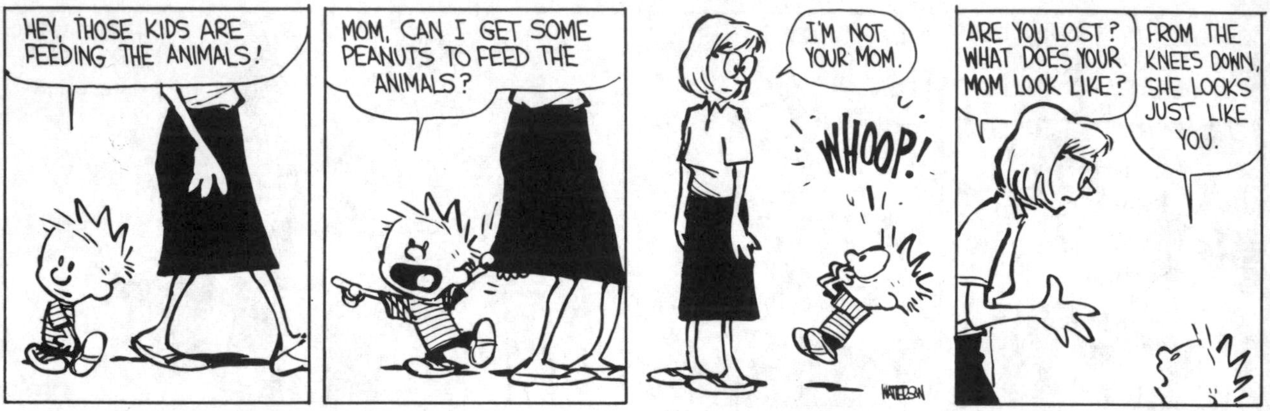
HEY, THOSE KIDS ARE FEEDING THE ANIMALS!
MOM, CAN I GET SOME PEANUTS TO FEED THE ANIMALS?
I'M NOT YOUR MOM.
WHOOP!
ARE YOU LOST? WHAT DOES YOUR MOM LOOK LIKE?
FROM THE KNEES DOWN, SHE LOOKS JUST LIKE YOU.

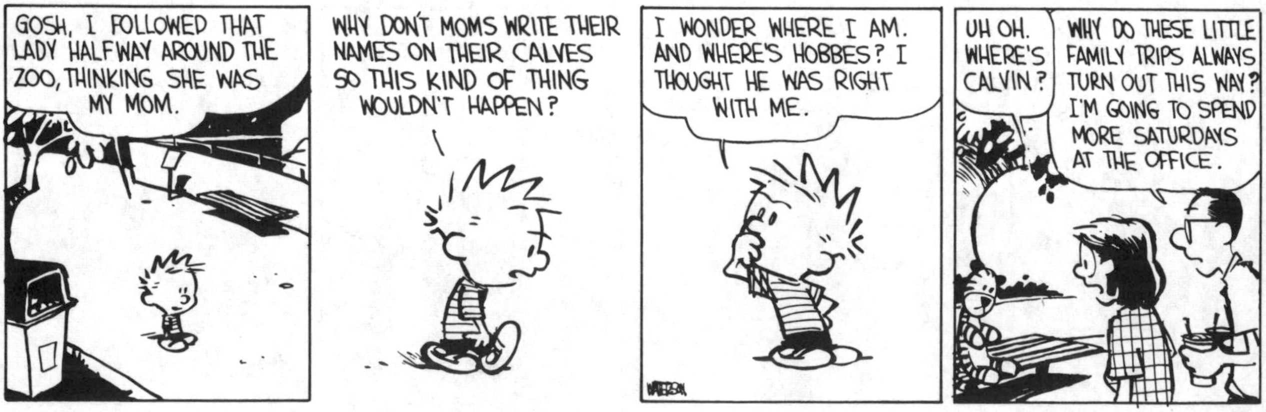
GOSH, I FOLLOWED THAT LADY HALFWAY AROUND THE ZOO, THINKING SHE WAS MY MOM.
WHY DON'T MOMS WRITE THEIR NAMES ON THEIR CALVES SO THIS KIND OF THING WOULDN'T HAPPEN?
I WONDER WHERE I AM. AND WHERE'S HOBBES? I THOUGHT HE WAS RIGHT WITH ME.
UH OH. WHERE'S CALVIN?
WHY DO THESE LITTLE FAMILY TRIPS ALWAYS TURN OUT THIS WAY? I'M GOING TO SPEND MORE SATURDAYS AT THE OFFICE.

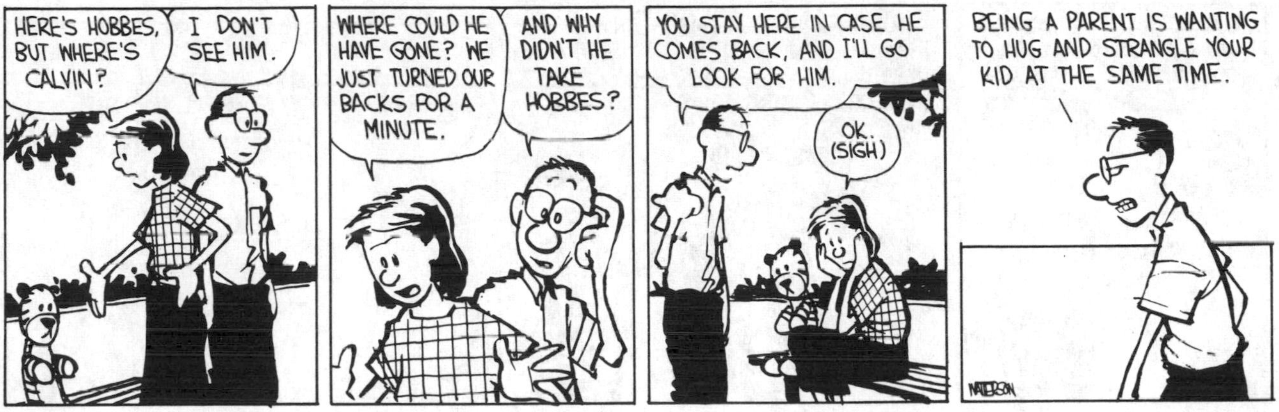
HERE'S HOBBES, BUT WHERE'S CALVIN?
I DON'T SEE HIM.
WHERE COULD HE HAVE GONE? WE JUST TURNED OUR BACKS FOR A MINUTE.
AND WHY DIDN'T HE TAKE HOBBES?
YOU STAY HERE IN CASE HE COMES BACK, AND I'LL GO LOOK FOR HIM.
OK. (SIGH)
BEING A PARENT IS WANTING TO HUG AND STRANGLE YOUR KID AT THE SAME TIME.
WATTERSON

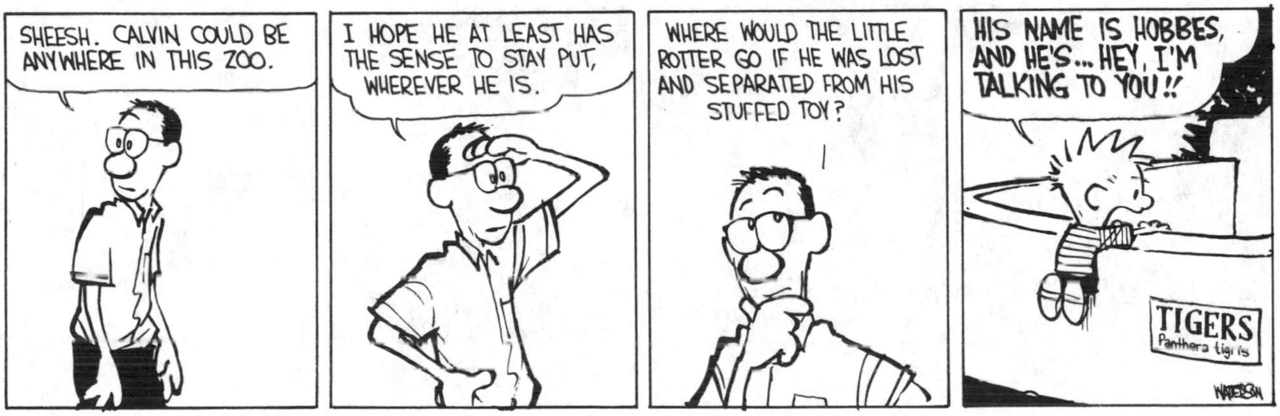
SHEESH. CALVIN COULD BE ANYWHERE IN THIS ZOO.
I HOPE HE AT LEAST HAS THE SENSE TO STAY PUT, WHEREVER HE IS.
WHERE WOULD THE LITTLE ROTTER GO IF HE WAS LOST AND SEPARATED FROM HIS STUFFED TOY?
HIS NAME IS HOBBES, AND HE'S... HEY, I'M TALKING TO YOU!!
TIGERS
Panthera tigris
WATTERSON

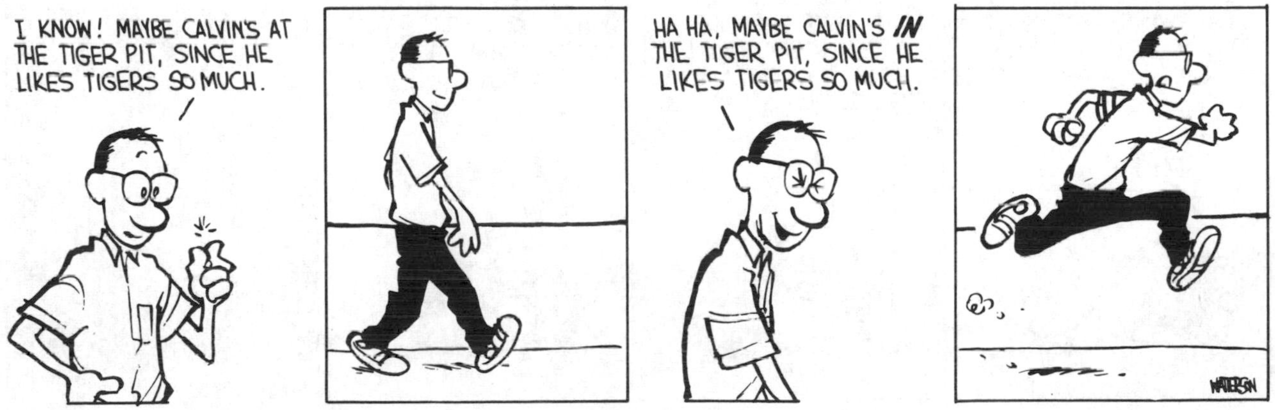
I KNOW! MAYBE CALVIN'S AT THE TIGER PIT, SINCE HE LIKES TIGERS SO MUCH.
HA HA, MAYBE CALVIN'S *IN* THE TIGER PIT, SINCE HE LIKES TIGERS SO MUCH.
WATTERSON

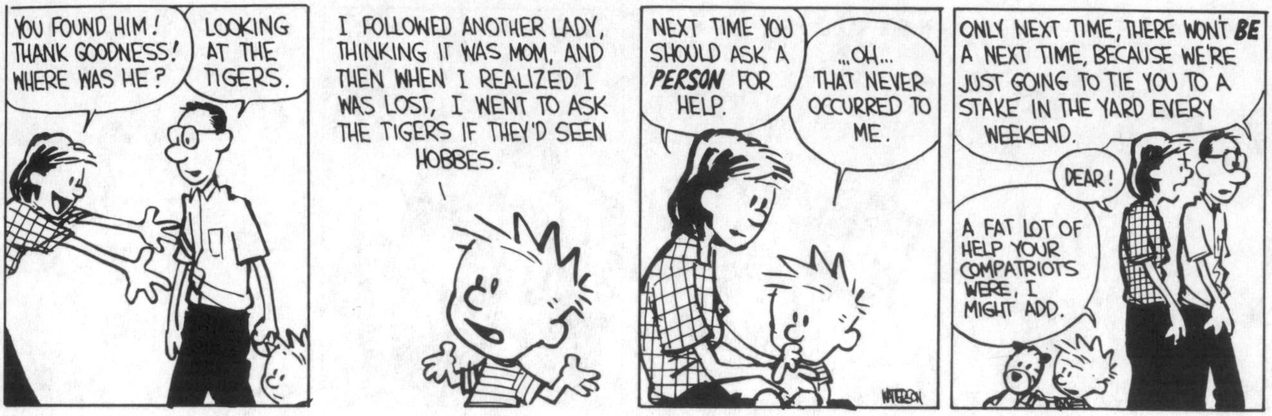
YOU FOUND HIM! THANK GOODNESS! WHERE WAS HE?
LOOKING AT THE TIGERS.
I FOLLOWED ANOTHER LADY, THINKING IT WAS MOM, AND THEN WHEN I REALIZED I WAS LOST, I WENT TO ASK THE TIGERS IF THEY'D SEEN HOBBES.
NEXT TIME YOU SHOULD ASK A **PERSON** FOR HELP.
...OH... THAT NEVER OCCURRED TO ME.
ONLY NEXT TIME, THERE WON'T **BE** A NEXT TIME, BECAUSE WE'RE JUST GOING TO TIE YOU TO A STAKE IN THE YARD EVERY WEEKEND.
DEAR!
A FAT LOT OF HELP YOUR COMPATRIOTS WERE, I MIGHT ADD.

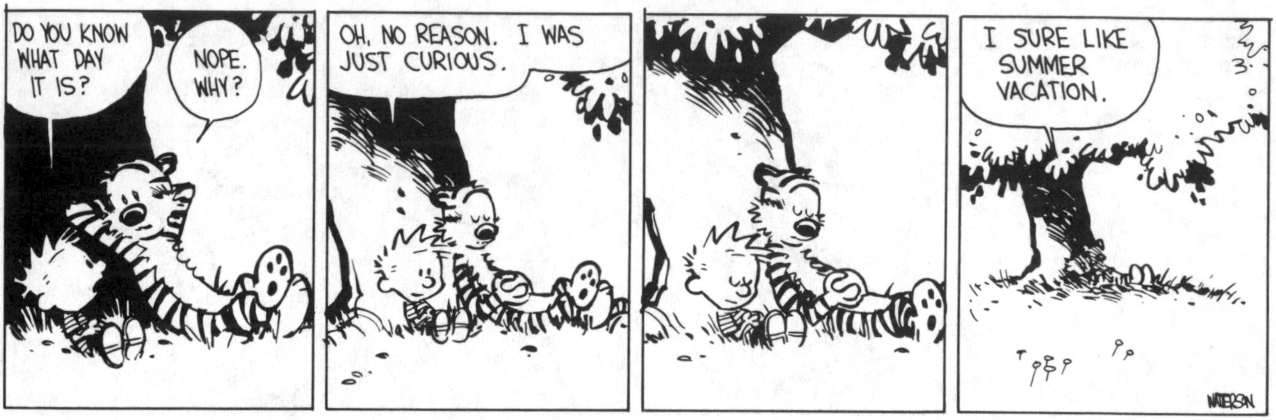
DO YOU KNOW WHAT DAY IT IS?
NOPE. WHY?
OH, NO REASON. I WAS JUST CURIOUS.
I SURE LIKE SUMMER VACATION.

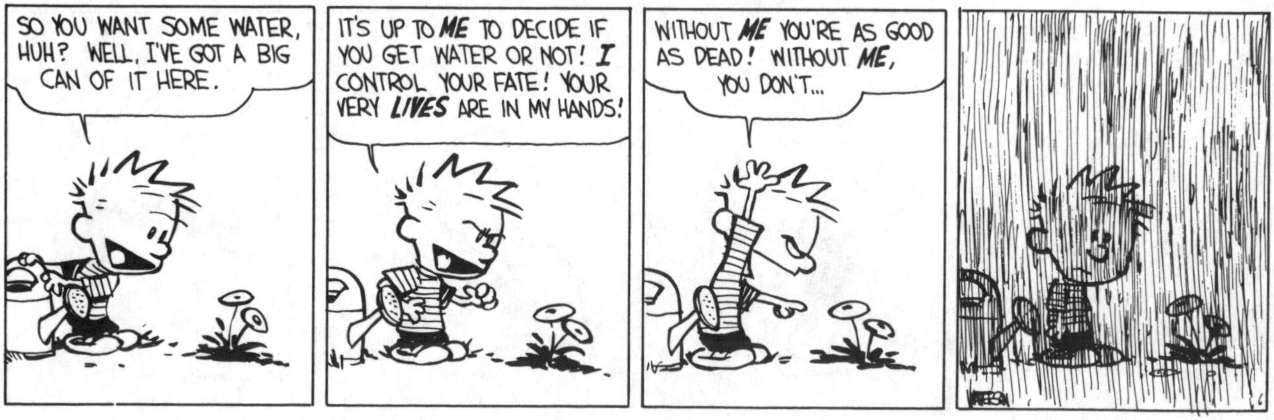
SO YOU WANT SOME WATER, HUH? WELL, I'VE GOT A BIG CAN OF IT HERE.
IT'S UP TO **ME** TO DECIDE IF YOU GET WATER OR NOT! ***I*** CONTROL YOUR FATE! YOUR VERY ***LIVES*** ARE IN MY HANDS!
WITHOUT **ME** YOU'RE AS GOOD AS DEAD! WITHOUT **ME**, YOU DON'T...

Calvin and HOBBES
by WATTERSON
I GOT A HIT!
SAFE!
OK, THAT WAS A SINGLE. I HAVE A GHOST RUNNER HERE NOW, SO I CAN BAT AGAIN.
AND MY GHOST RUNNERS WHO WERE ON FIRST AND SECOND BASE ARE NOW ON SECOND AND THIRD, RIGHT?
NOPE. THEY'RE BOTH OUT.
OUT?!
MY GHOST OUTFIELDER TAGGED YOUR GHOST GOING TO THIRD, AND THREW TO MY GHOST SECOND BASEMAN. IT WAS A BRILLIANT DOUBLE PLAY.
THAT NEVER HAPPENED!
YOU'VE GOT TWO OUTS.
WELL, MY GHOST ON FIRST JUST STOLE HOME, SO I'VE GOT ANOTHER RUN! HA HA, SMARTY!
YEAH, WELL, ALL MY OUTFIELD GHOSTS JUST RAN IN AND BEAT THE TOBACCO JUICE OUT OF HIM.
HA! THE GHOST UMPIRE JUST SUSPENDED ALL YOUR GHOSTS FOR ETERNITY. THEY'RE OUT OF THE GAME.
HMPH! IF MY GHOSTS DON'T PLAY, I DON'T PLAY.
YOU FORFEIT THE GAME THEN! YOU LOSE AUTOMATICALLY IF YOU QUIT!
THE GHOST CROWD SUPPORTS ME. THEY'RE "BOO"-ING YOU!
SOMETIMES I WISH I LIVED IN A NEIGHBORHOOD WITH MORE KIDS.
WATTERSON

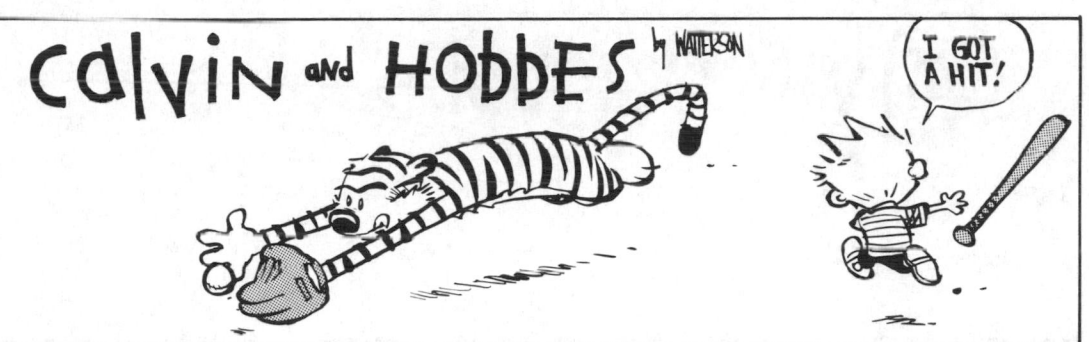

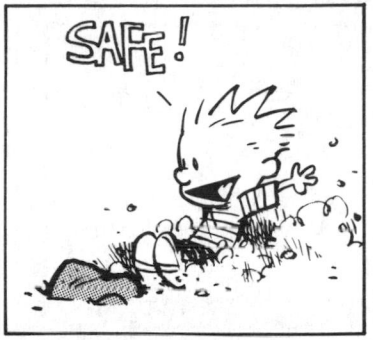

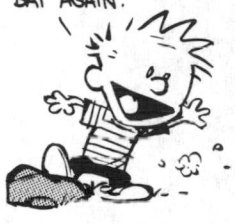

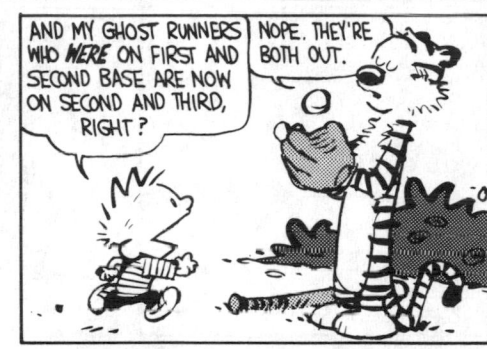

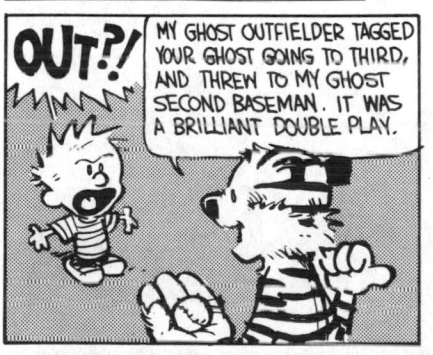

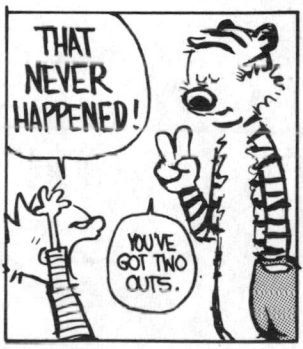

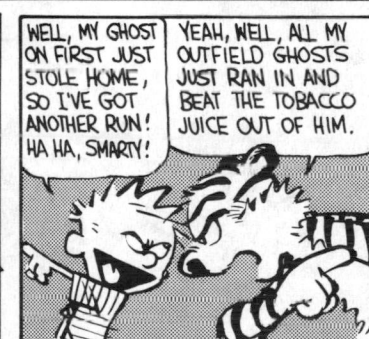

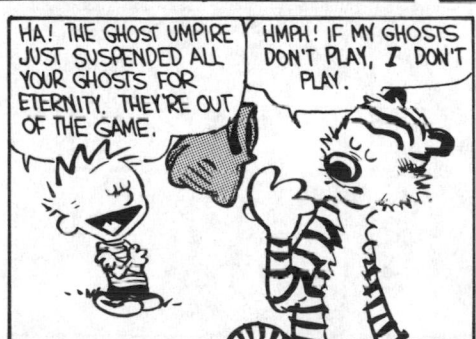

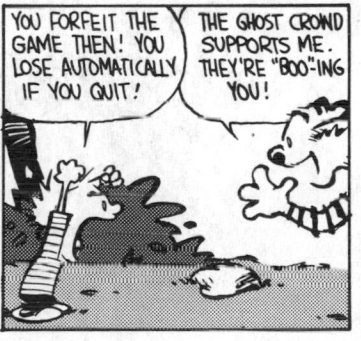

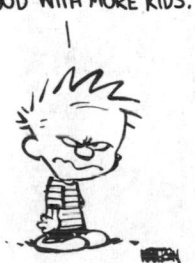

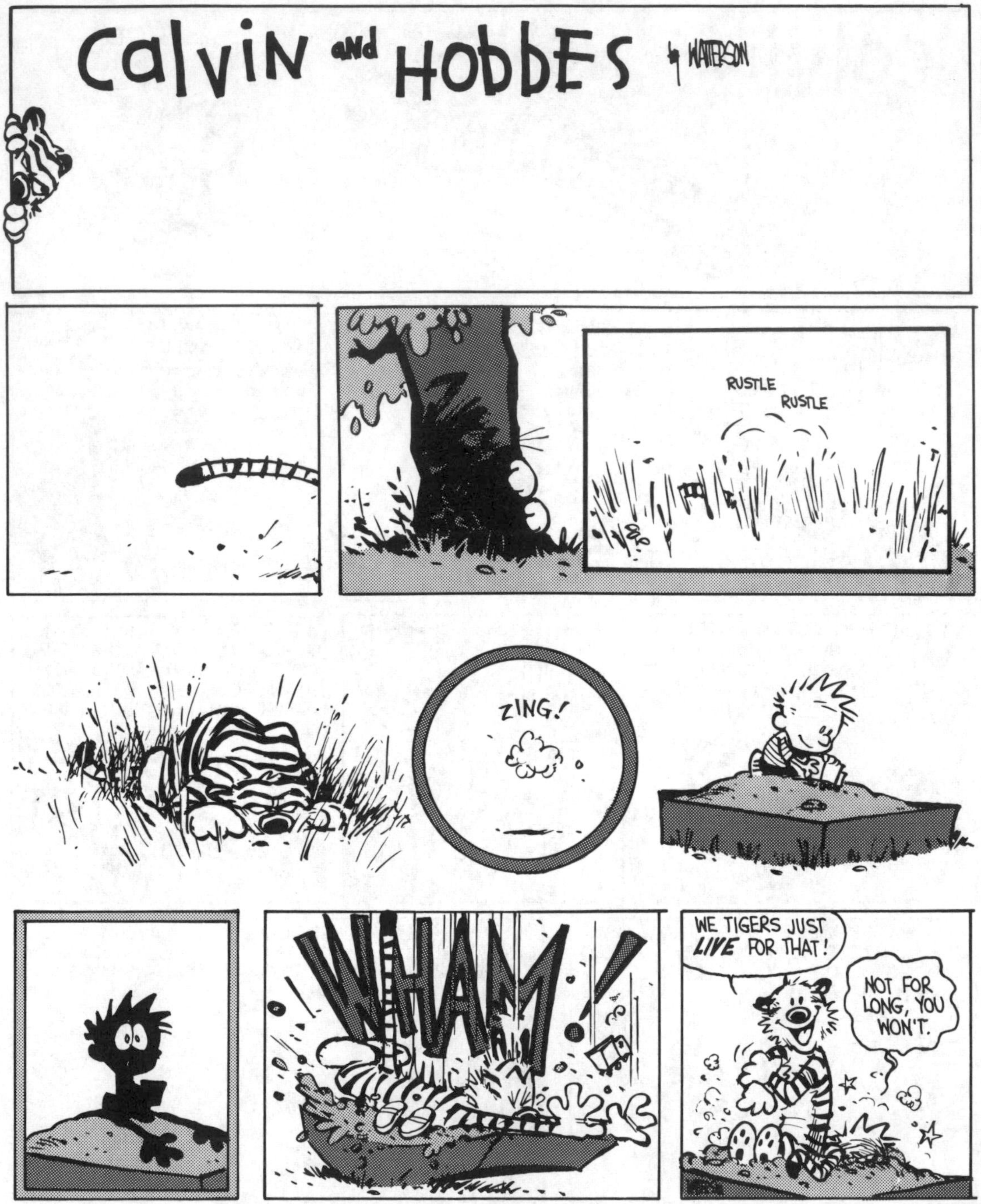
Calvin and HOBBES
by WATTERSON
RUSTLE
RUSTLE
ZING!
WHAM!
WE TIGERS JUST LIVE FOR THAT!
NOT FOR LONG, YOU WON'T.

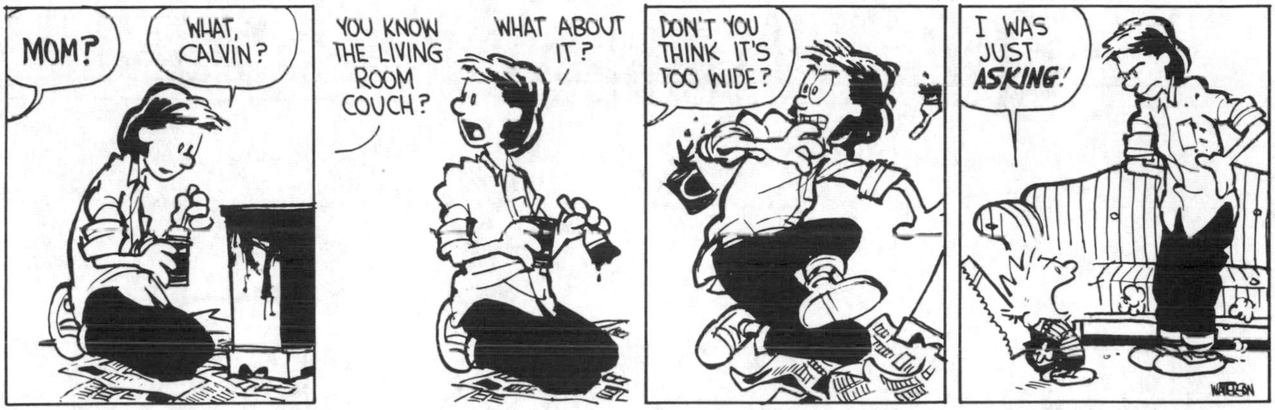
MOM?
WHAT, CALVIN?
YOU KNOW THE LIVING ROOM COUCH?
WHAT ABOUT IT?
DON'T YOU THINK IT'S TOO WIDE?
I WAS JUST *ASKING*!

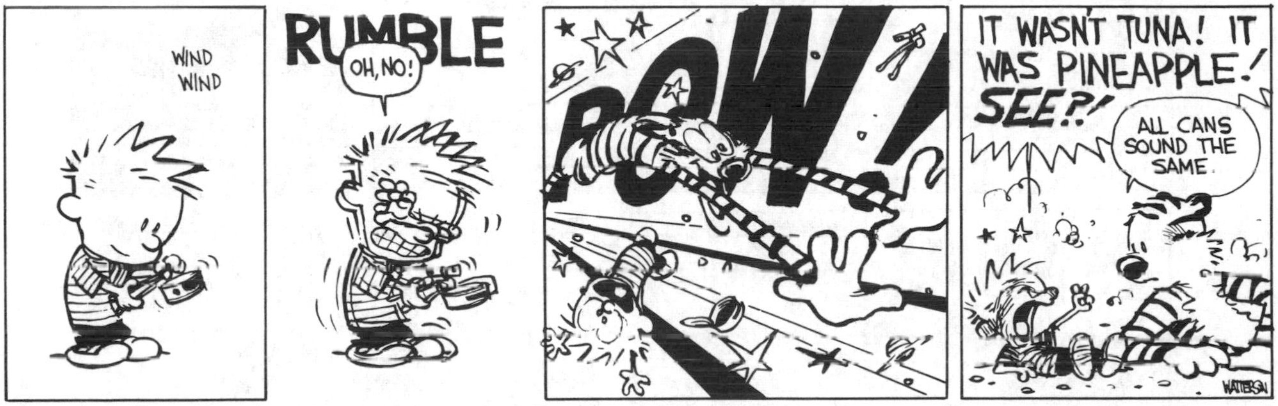
WIND WIND
RUMBLE
OH, NO!
POW!
IT WASN'T TUNA! IT WAS PINEAPPLE! *SEE?!*
ALL CANS SOUND THE SAME.

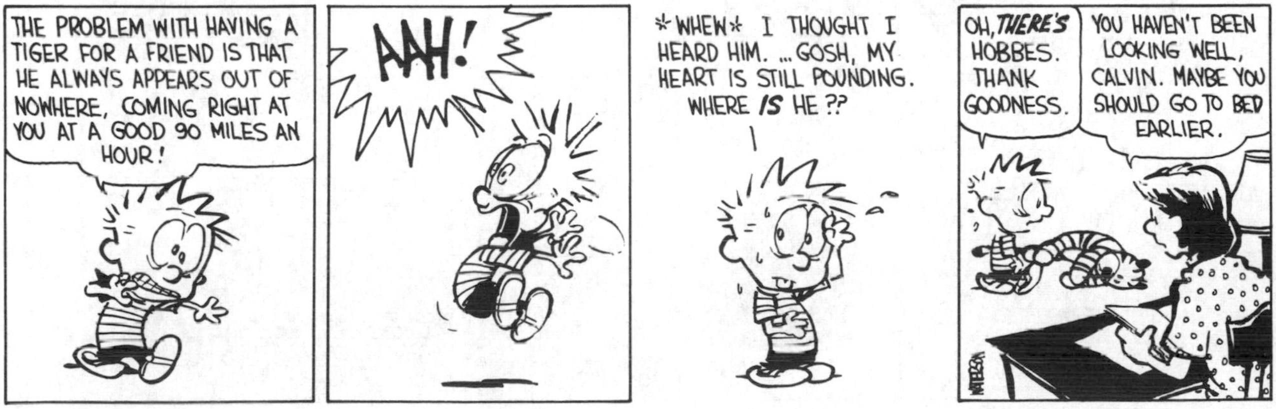
THE PROBLEM WITH HAVING A TIGER FOR A FRIEND IS THAT HE ALWAYS APPEARS OUT OF NOWHERE, COMING RIGHT AT YOU AT A GOOD 90 MILES AN HOUR!
AAH!
WHEW I THOUGHT I HEARD HIM. ...GOSH, MY HEART IS STILL POUNDING. WHERE *IS* HE??
OH, *THERE'S* HOBBES. THANK GOODNESS.
YOU HAVEN'T BEEN LOOKING WELL, CALVIN. MAYBE YOU SHOULD GO TO BED EARLIER.

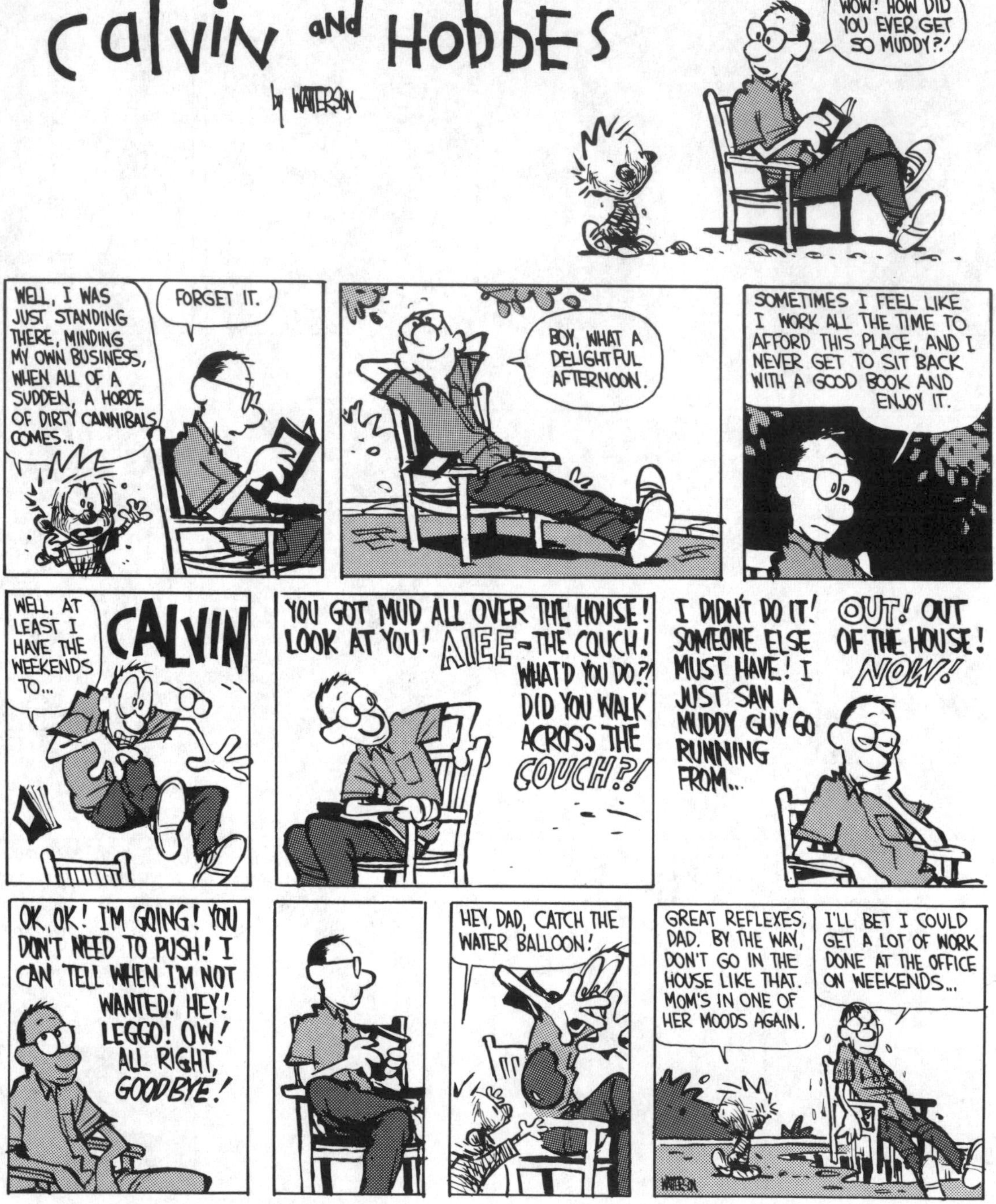
Calvin and HOBBES
by WATTERSON
WOW! HOW DID YOU EVER GET SO MUDDY?!
WELL, I WAS JUST STANDING THERE, MINDING MY OWN BUSINESS, WHEN ALL OF A SUDDEN, A HORDE OF DIRTY CANNIBALS COMES...
FORGET IT.
BOY, WHAT A DELIGHTFUL AFTERNOON.
SOMETIMES I FEEL LIKE I WORK ALL THE TIME TO AFFORD THIS PLACE, AND I NEVER GET TO SIT BACK WITH A GOOD BOOK AND ENJOY IT.
WELL, AT LEAST I HAVE THE WEEKENDS TO...
CALVIN
YOU GOT MUD ALL OVER THE HOUSE! LOOK AT YOU! AIEE - THE COUCH! WHAT'D YOU DO?! DID YOU WALK ACROSS THE COUCH?!
I DIDN'T DO IT! SOMEONE ELSE MUST HAVE! I JUST SAW A MUDDY GUY GO RUNNING FROM...
OUT! OUT OF THE HOUSE! NOW!
OK, OK! I'M GOING! YOU DON'T NEED TO PUSH! I CAN TELL WHEN I'M NOT WANTED! HEY! LEGGO! OW! ALL RIGHT, GOODBYE!
HEY, DAD, CATCH THE WATER BALLOON!
GREAT REFLEXES, DAD. BY THE WAY, DON'T GO IN THE HOUSE LIKE THAT. MOM'S IN ONE OF HER MOODS AGAIN.
I'LL BET I COULD GET A LOT OF WORK DONE AT THE OFFICE ON WEEKENDS...
WATTERSON

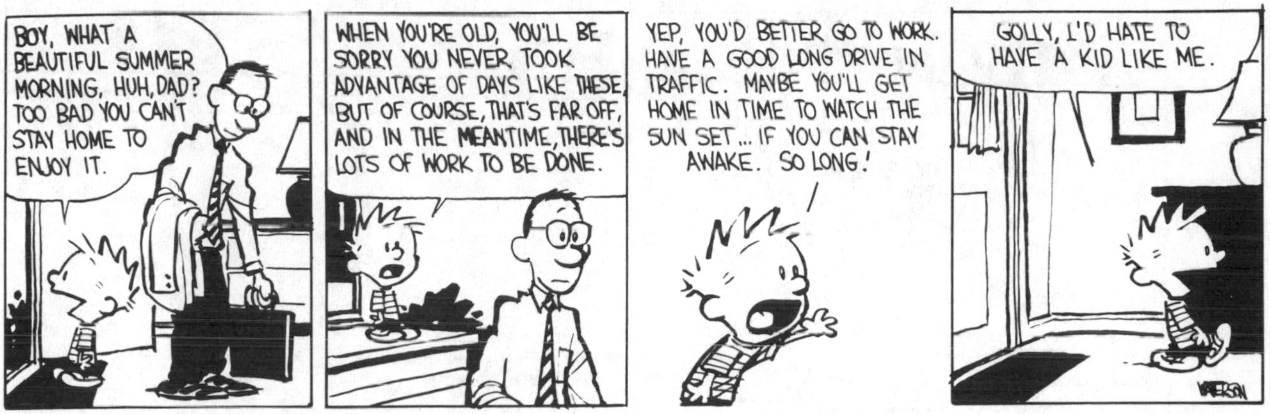
BOY, WHAT A BEAUTIFUL SUMMER MORNING, HUH, DAD? TOO BAD YOU CAN'T STAY HOME TO ENJOY IT.
WHEN YOU'RE OLD, YOU'LL BE SORRY YOU NEVER TOOK ADVANTAGE OF DAYS LIKE THESE, BUT OF COURSE, THAT'S FAR OFF, AND IN THE MEANTIME, THERE'S LOTS OF WORK TO BE DONE.
YEP, YOU'D BETTER GO TO WORK. HAVE A GOOD LONG DRIVE IN TRAFFIC. MAYBE YOU'LL GET HOME IN TIME TO WATCH THE SUN SET... IF YOU CAN STAY AWAKE. SO LONG!
GOLLY, I'D HATE TO HAVE A KID LIKE ME.
WATERSON

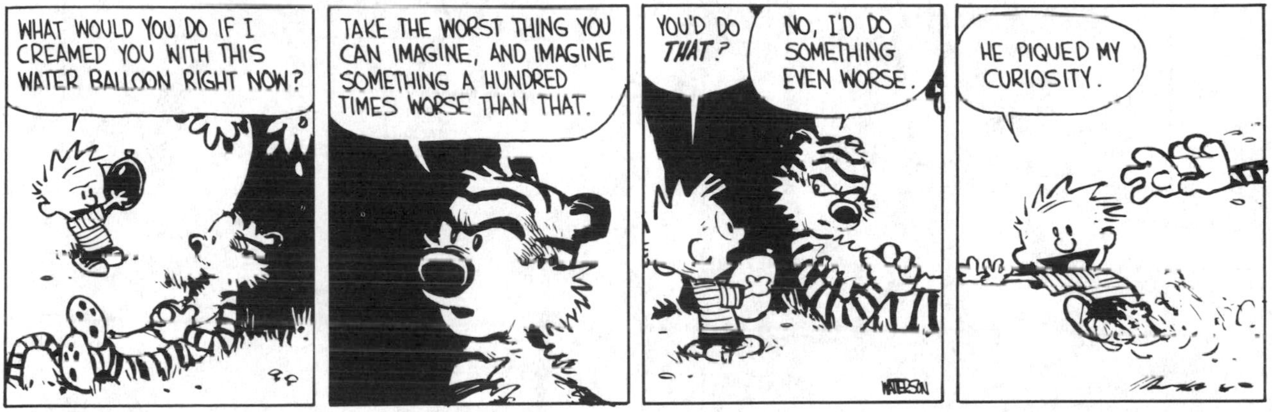
WHAT WOULD YOU DO IF I CREAMED YOU WITH THIS WATER BALLOON RIGHT NOW?
TAKE THE WORST THING YOU CAN IMAGINE, AND IMAGINE SOMETHING A HUNDRED TIMES WORSE THAN THAT.
YOU'D DO *THAT*?
NO, I'D DO SOMETHING EVEN WORSE.
WATERSON
HE PIQUED MY CURIOSITY.

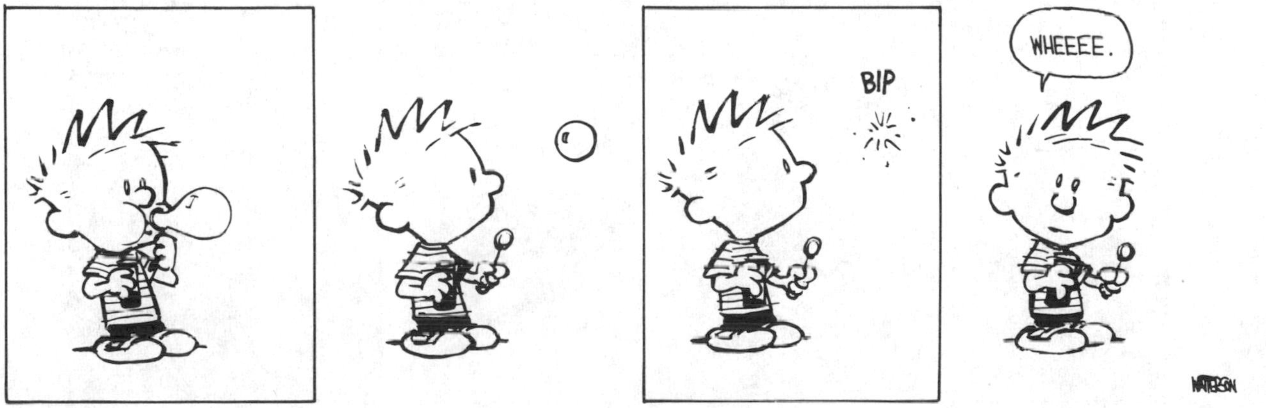
BIP
WHEEEE.
WATERSON

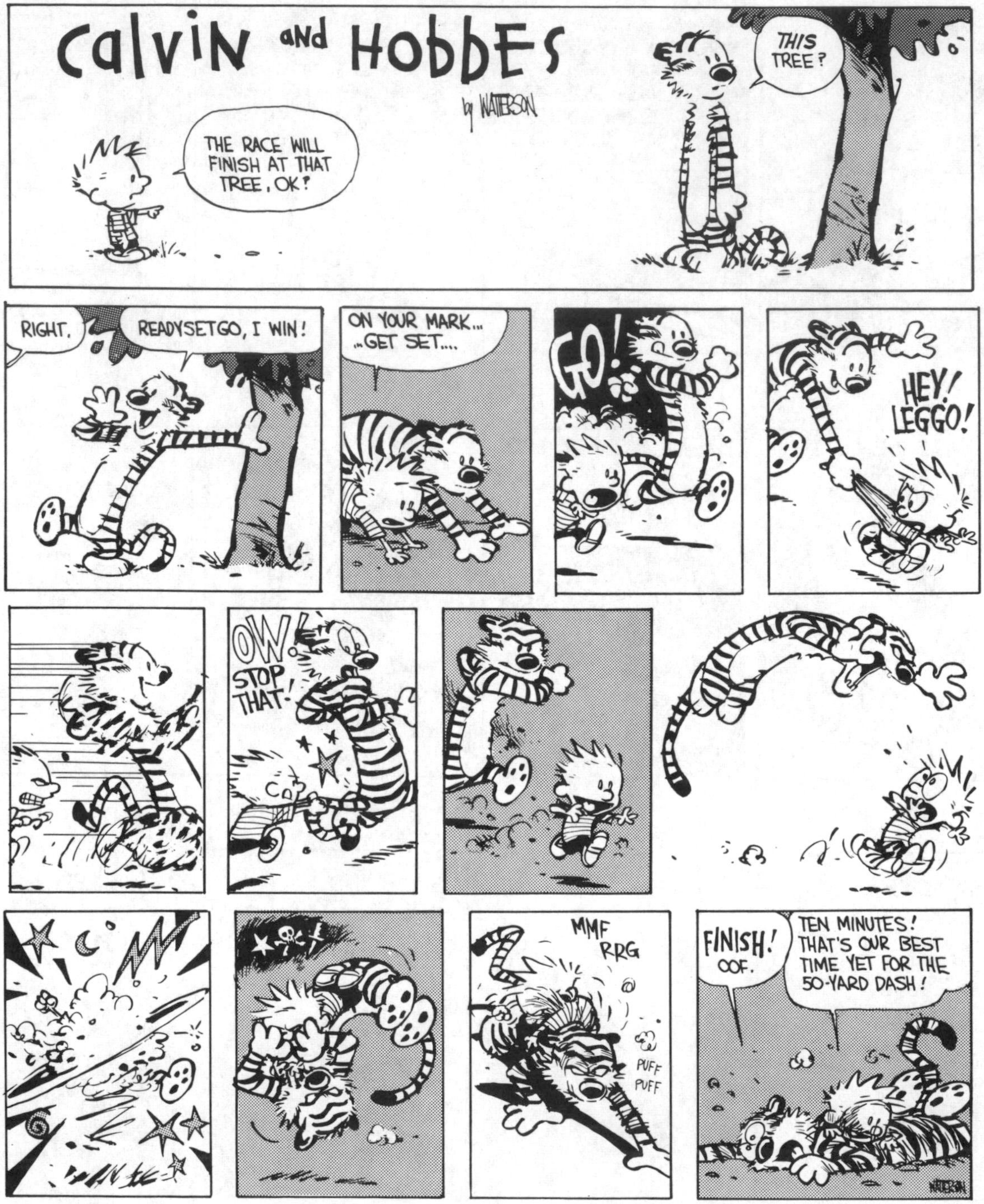
Calvin and Hobbes
by WATTERSON
THE RACE WILL FINISH AT THAT TREE, OK?
THIS TREE?
RIGHT.
READYSETGO, I WIN!
ON YOUR MARK... ...GET SET....
GO!
HEY! LEGGO!
OW!
STOP THAT!
MMF
RRG
PUFF
PUFF
FINISH!
OOF.
TEN MINUTES! THAT'S OUR BEST TIME YET FOR THE 50-YARD DASH!
WATTERSON

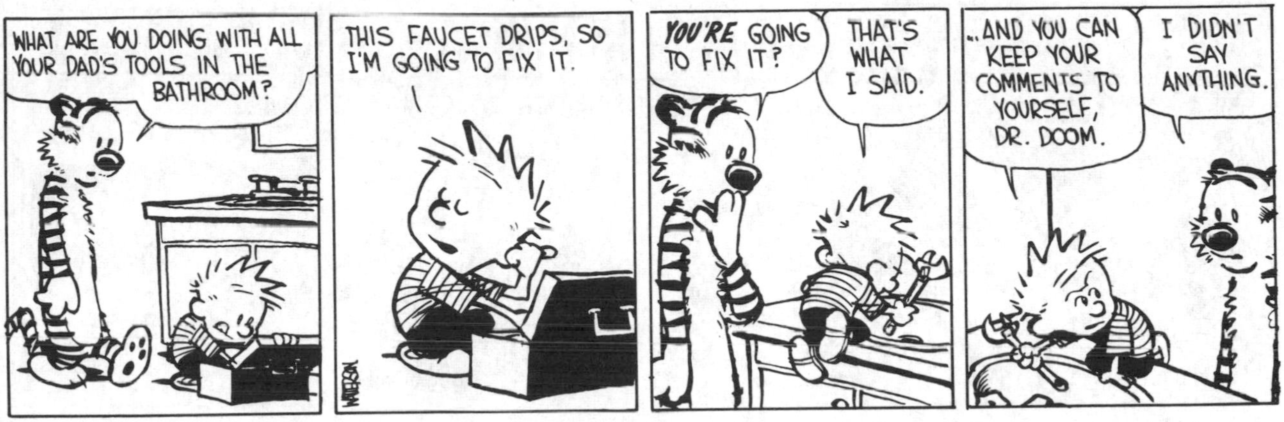
WHAT ARE YOU DOING WITH ALL YOUR DAD'S TOOLS IN THE BATHROOM?
THIS FAUCET DRIPS, SO I'M GOING TO FIX IT.
YOU'RE GOING TO FIX IT?
THAT'S WHAT I SAID.
..AND YOU CAN KEEP YOUR COMMENTS TO YOURSELF, DR. DOOM.
I DIDN'T SAY ANYTHING.

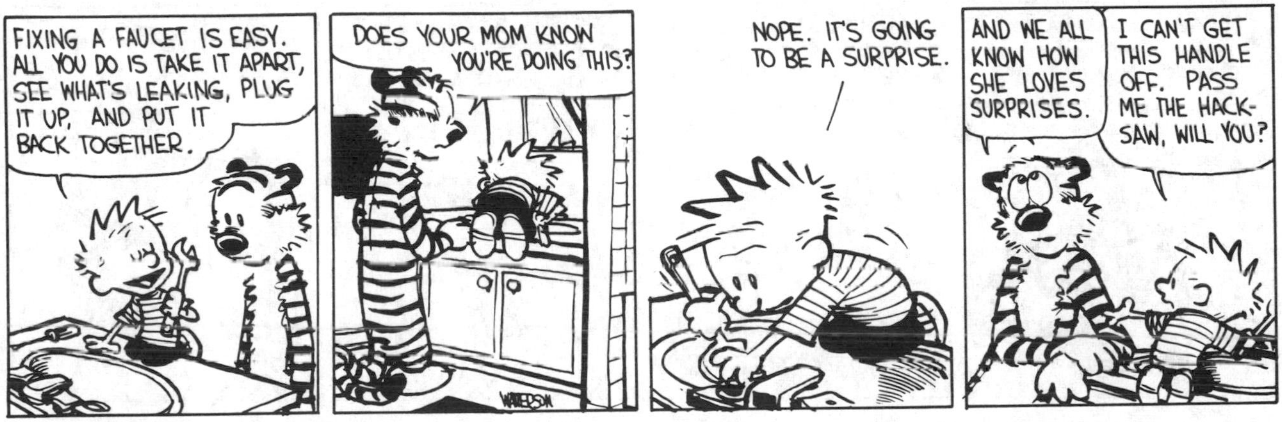
FIXING A FAUCET IS EASY. ALL YOU DO IS TAKE IT APART, SEE WHAT'S LEAKING, PLUG IT UP, AND PUT IT BACK TOGETHER.
DOES YOUR MOM KNOW YOU'RE DOING THIS?
NOPE. IT'S GOING TO BE A SURPRISE.
AND WE ALL KNOW HOW SHE LOVES SURPRISES.
I CAN'T GET THIS HANDLE OFF. PASS ME THE HACK-SAW, WILL YOU?

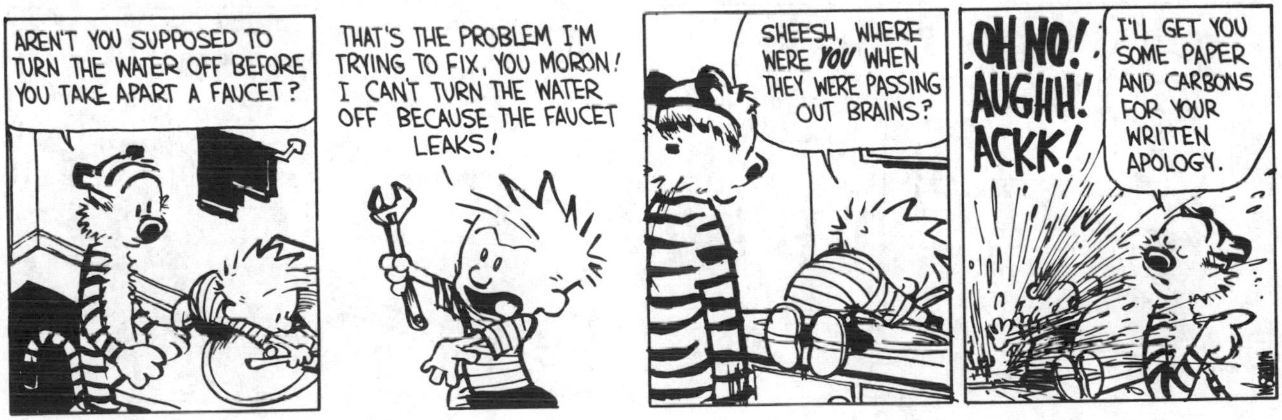
AREN'T YOU SUPPOSED TO TURN THE WATER OFF BEFORE YOU TAKE APART A FAUCET?
THAT'S THE PROBLEM I'M TRYING TO FIX, YOU MORON! I CAN'T TURN THE WATER OFF BECAUSE THE FAUCET LEAKS!
SHEESH, WHERE WERE YOU WHEN THEY WERE PASSING OUT BRAINS?
OH NO! AUGHH! ACKK!
I'LL GET YOU SOME PAPER AND CARBONS FOR YOUR WRITTEN APOLOGY.

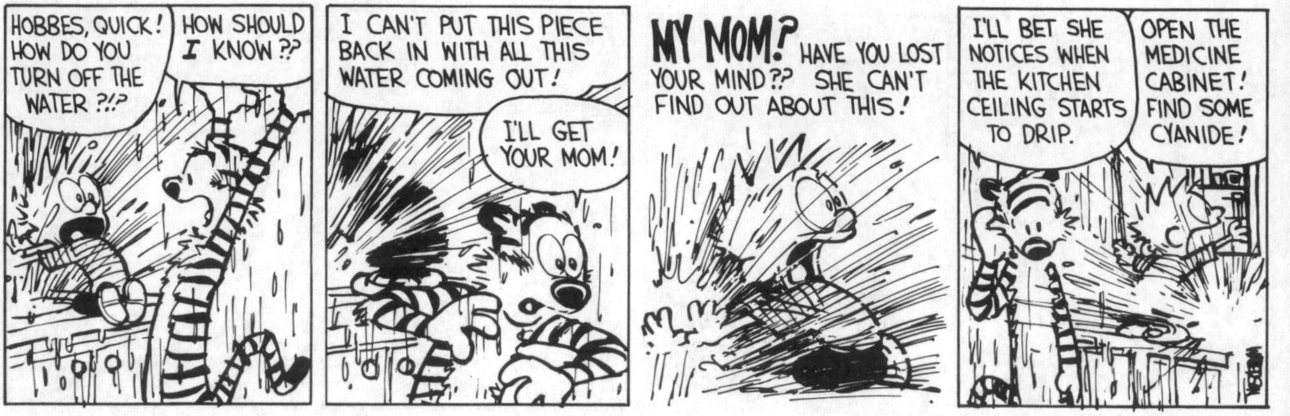
HOBBES, QUICK! HOW DO YOU TURN OFF THE WATER ?!?
HOW SHOULD I KNOW ??
I CAN'T PUT THIS PIECE BACK IN WITH ALL THIS WATER COMING OUT!
I'LL GET YOUR MOM!
MY MOM? HAVE YOU LOST YOUR MIND?? SHE CAN'T FIND OUT ABOUT THIS!
I'LL BET SHE NOTICES WHEN THE KITCHEN CEILING STARTS TO DRIP.
OPEN THE MEDICINE CABINET! FIND SOME CYANIDE!

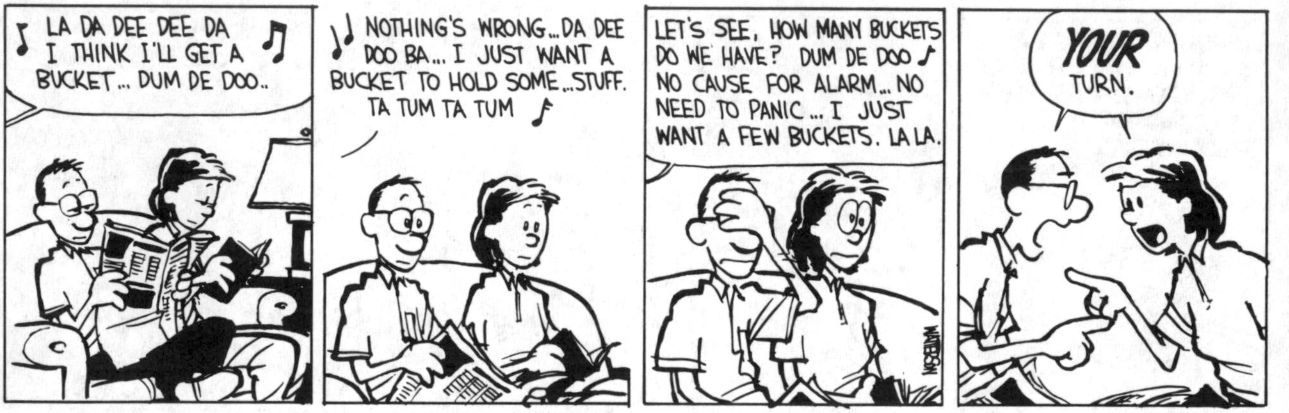
LA DA DEE DEE DA I THINK I'LL GET A BUCKET... DUM DE DOO..
NOTHING'S WRONG...DA DEE DOO BA... I JUST WANT A BUCKET TO HOLD SOME...STUFF. TA TUM TA TUM
LET'S SEE, HOW MANY BUCKETS DO WE HAVE? DUM DE DOO NO CAUSE FOR ALARM... NO NEED TO PANIC ... I JUST WANT A FEW BUCKETS. LA LA.
YOUR TURN.

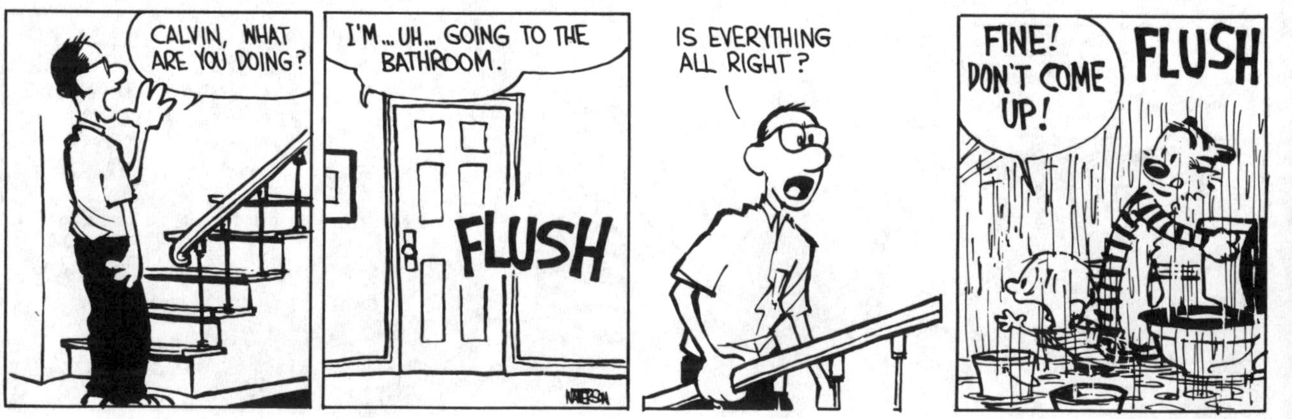
CALVIN, WHAT ARE YOU DOING?
I'M... UH... GOING TO THE BATHROOM.
FLUSH
IS EVERYTHING ALL RIGHT?
FINE! DON'T COME UP!
FLUSH

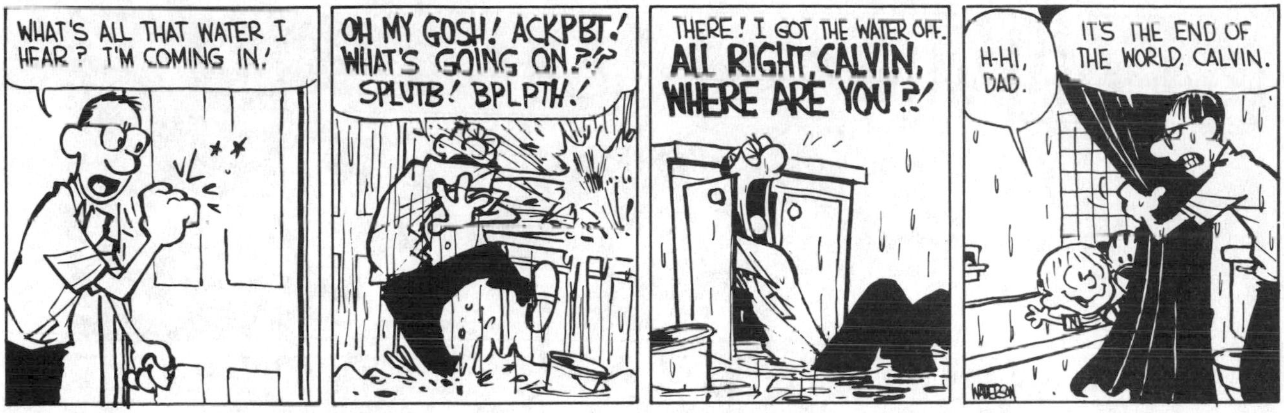
WHAT'S ALL THAT WATER I HEAR? I'M COMING IN!
OH MY GOSH! ACKPBT! WHAT'S GOING ON?!? SPLUTB! BPLPTH!
THERE! I GOT THE WATER OFF. ALL RIGHT, CALVIN, WHERE ARE YOU?!
H-HI, DAD.
IT'S THE END OF THE WORLD, CALVIN.

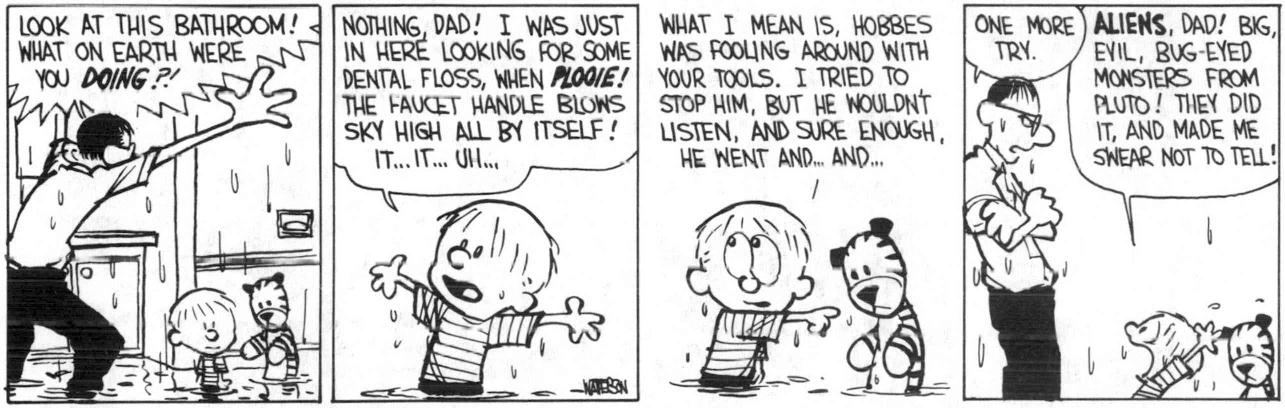
LOOK AT THIS BATHROOM! WHAT ON EARTH WERE YOU DOING?!
NOTHING, DAD! I WAS JUST IN HERE LOOKING FOR SOME DENTAL FLOSS, WHEN PLOOIE! THE FAUCET HANDLE BLOWS SKY HIGH ALL BY ITSELF! IT... IT... UH...
WHAT I MEAN IS, HOBBES WAS FOOLING AROUND WITH YOUR TOOLS. I TRIED TO STOP HIM, BUT HE WOULDN'T LISTEN, AND SURE ENOUGH, HE WENT AND... AND...
ONE MORE TRY.
ALIENS, DAD! BIG, EVIL, BUG-EYED MONSTERS FROM PLUTO! THEY DID IT, AND MADE ME SWEAR NOT TO TELL!

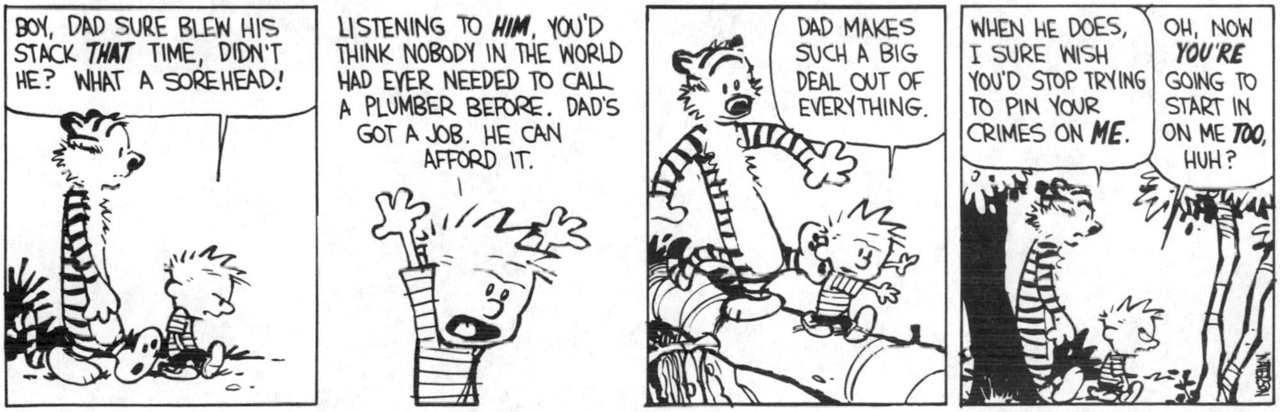
BOY, DAD SURE BLEW HIS STACK THAT TIME, DIDN'T HE? WHAT A SOREHEAD!
LISTENING TO HIM, YOU'D THINK NOBODY IN THE WORLD HAD EVER NEEDED TO CALL A PLUMBER BEFORE. DAD'S GOT A JOB. HE CAN AFFORD IT.
DAD MAKES SUCH A BIG DEAL OUT OF EVERYTHING.
WHEN HE DOES, I SURE WISH YOU'D STOP TRYING TO PIN YOUR CRIMES ON ME.
OH, NOW YOU'RE GOING TO START IN ON ME TOO, HUH?

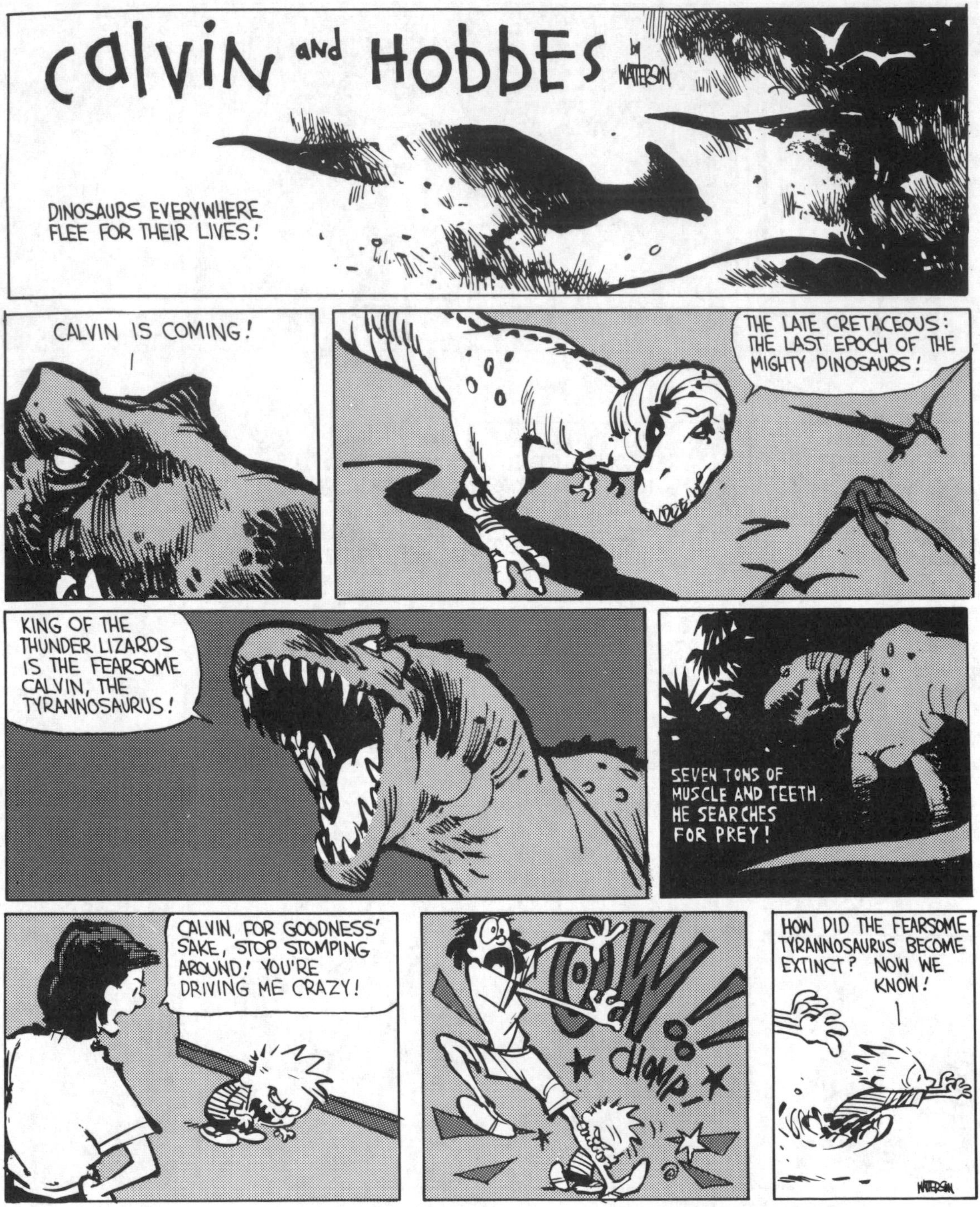
Calvin and Hobbes
by WATTERSON
DINOSAURS EVERYWHERE FLEE FOR THEIR LIVES!
CALVIN IS COMING!
THE LATE CRETACEOUS: THE LAST EPOCH OF THE MIGHTY DINOSAURS!
KING OF THE THUNDER LIZARDS IS THE FEARSOME CALVIN, THE TYRANNOSAURUS!
SEVEN TONS OF MUSCLE AND TEETH. HE SEARCHES FOR PREY!
CALVIN, FOR GOODNESS' SAKE, STOP STOMPING AROUND! YOU'RE DRIVING ME CRAZY!
OW!!
CHOMP!
HOW DID THE FEARSOME TYRANNOSAURUS BECOME EXTINCT? NOW WE KNOW!
WATTERSON

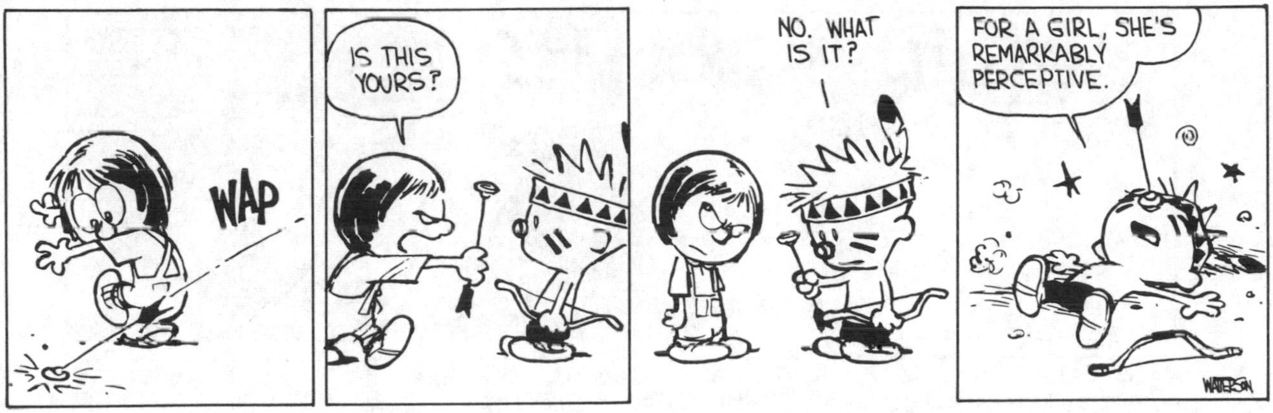

WAP
IS THIS YOURS?
NO. WHAT IS IT?
FOR A GIRL, SHE'S REMARKABLY PERCEPTIVE.
WATTERSON

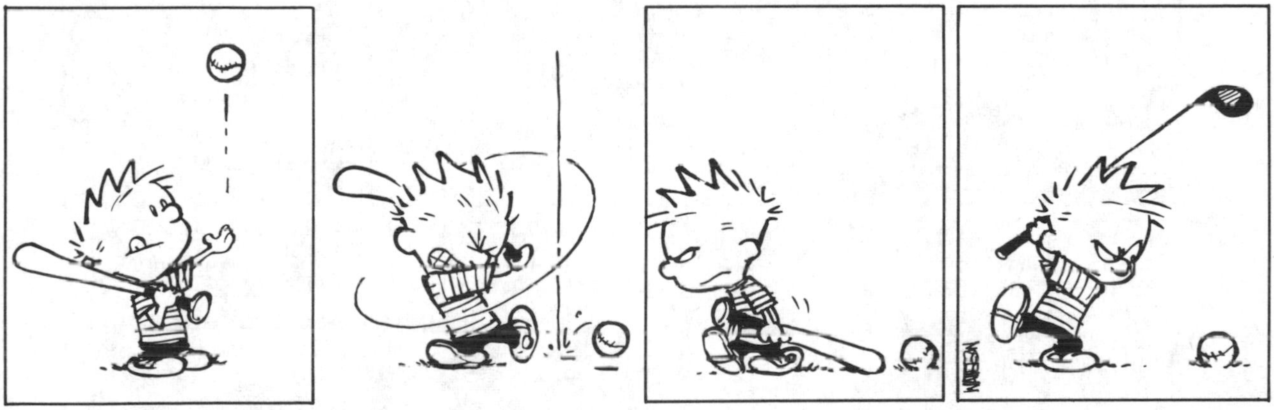

WATTERSON

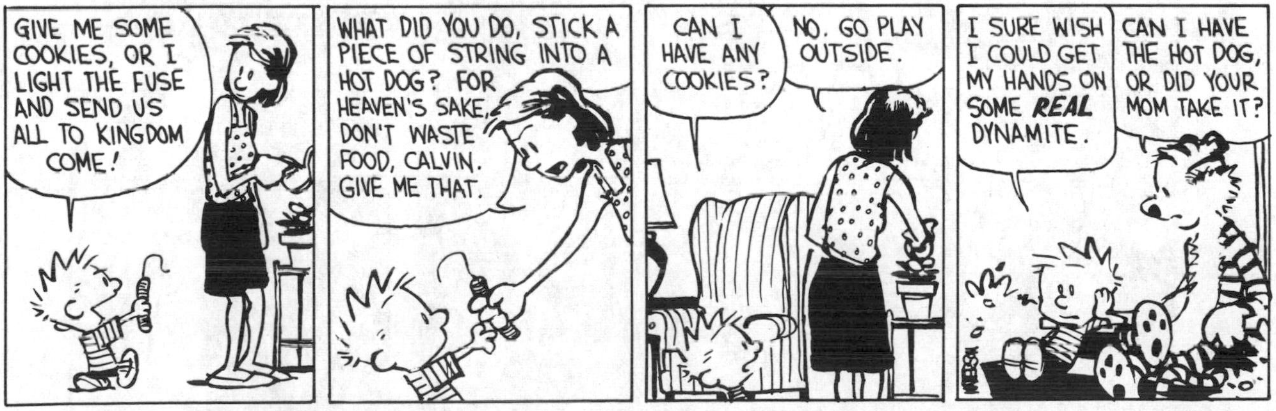

GIVE ME SOME COOKIES, OR I LIGHT THE FUSE AND SEND US ALL TO KINGDOM COME!
WHAT DID YOU DO, STICK A PIECE OF STRING INTO A HOT DOG? FOR HEAVEN'S SAKE, DON'T WASTE FOOD, CALVIN. GIVE ME THAT.
CAN I HAVE ANY COOKIES?
NO. GO PLAY OUTSIDE.
I SURE WISH I COULD GET MY HANDS ON SOME REAL DYNAMITE.
CAN I HAVE THE HOT DOG, OR DID YOUR MOM TAKE IT?
WATTERSON

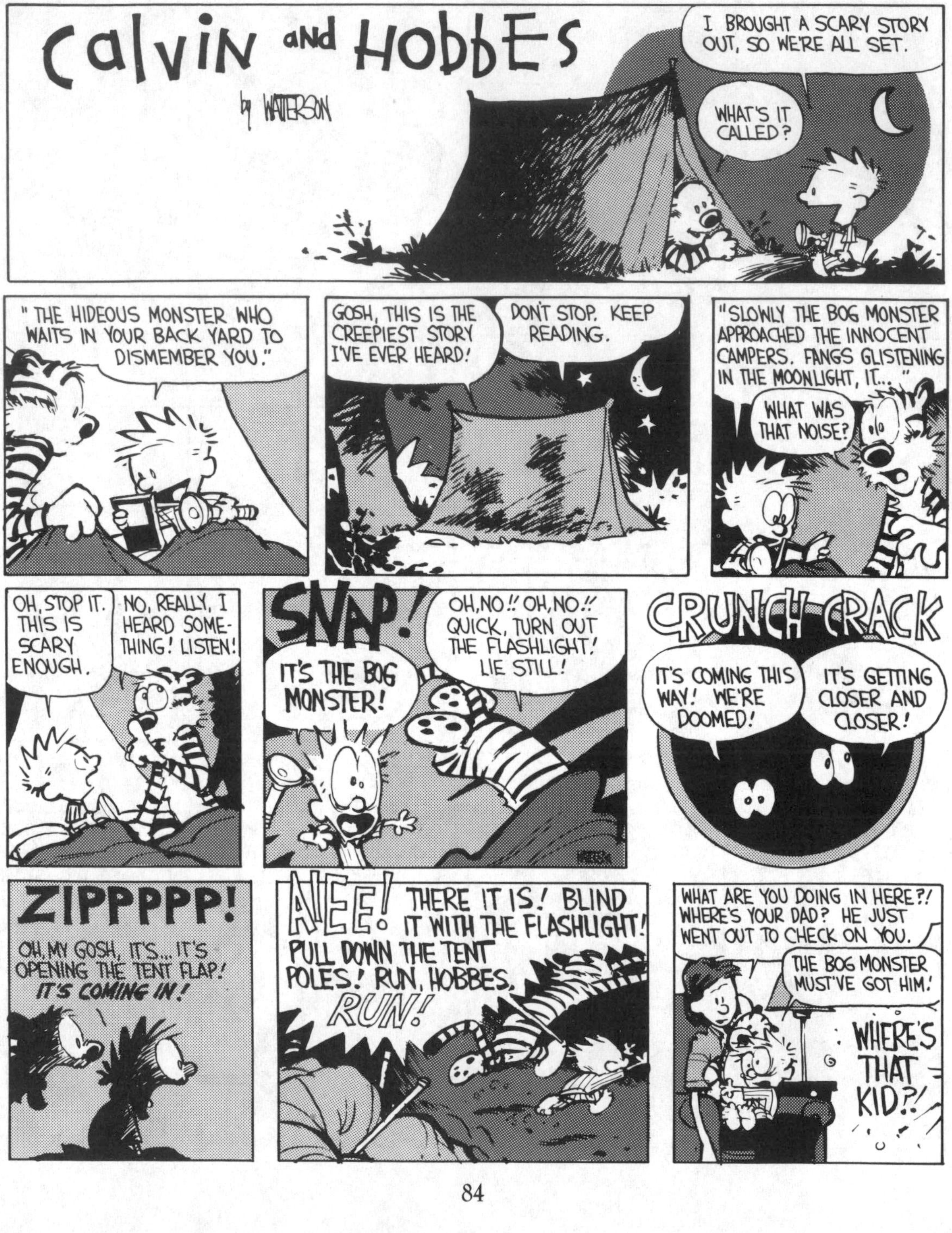
Calvin and HOBBES
by WATTERSON
I BROUGHT A SCARY STORY OUT, SO WE'RE ALL SET.
WHAT'S IT CALLED?
"THE HIDEOUS MONSTER WHO WAITS IN YOUR BACK YARD TO DISMEMBER YOU."
GOSH, THIS IS THE CREEPIEST STORY I'VE EVER HEARD!
DON'T STOP. KEEP READING.
"SLOWLY THE BOG MONSTER APPROACHED THE INNOCENT CAMPERS. FANGS GLISTENING IN THE MOONLIGHT, IT..."
WHAT WAS THAT NOISE?
OH, STOP IT. THIS IS SCARY ENOUGH.
NO, REALLY, I HEARD SOMETHING! LISTEN!
SNAP!
IT'S THE BOG MONSTER!
OH, NO!! OH, NO!! QUICK, TURN OUT THE FLASHLIGHT! LIE STILL!
CRUNCH CRACK
IT'S COMING THIS WAY! WE'RE DOOMED!
IT'S GETTING CLOSER AND CLOSER!
ZIPPPPPP!
OH, MY GOSH, IT'S... IT'S OPENING THE TENT FLAP! IT'S COMING IN!
AIEE!
THERE IT IS! BLIND IT WITH THE FLASHLIGHT! PULL DOWN THE TENT POLES! RUN, HOBBES. RUN!
WHAT ARE YOU DOING IN HERE?! WHERE'S YOUR DAD? HE JUST WENT OUT TO CHECK ON YOU.
THE BOG MONSTER MUST'VE GOT HIM!
WHERE'S THAT KID?!

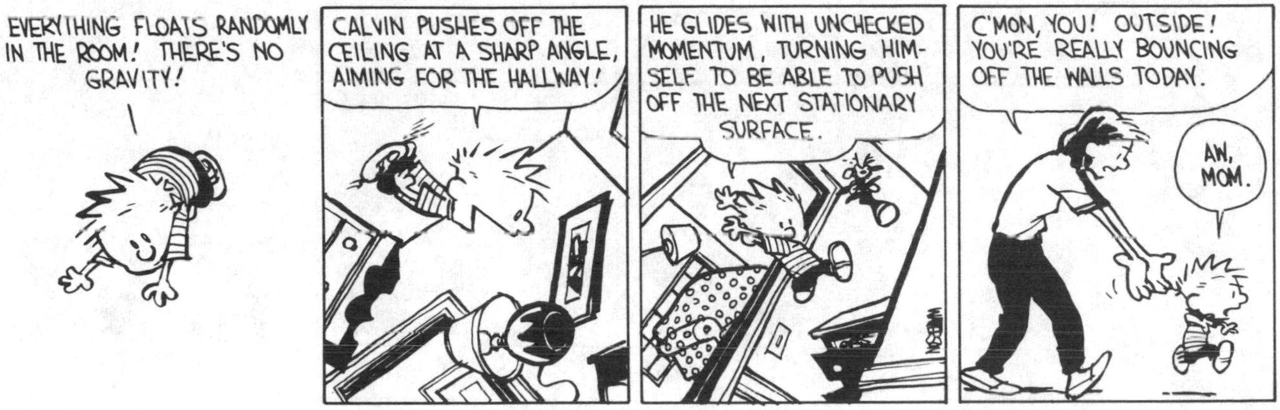
EVERYTHING FLOATS RANDOMLY IN THE ROOM! THERE'S NO GRAVITY!
CALVIN PUSHES OFF THE CEILING AT A SHARP ANGLE, AIMING FOR THE HALLWAY!
HE GLIDES WITH UNCHECKED MOMENTUM, TURNING HIMSELF TO BE ABLE TO PUSH OFF THE NEXT STATIONARY SURFACE.
C'MON, YOU! OUTSIDE! YOU'RE REALLY BOUNCING OFF THE WALLS TODAY.
AW, MOM.

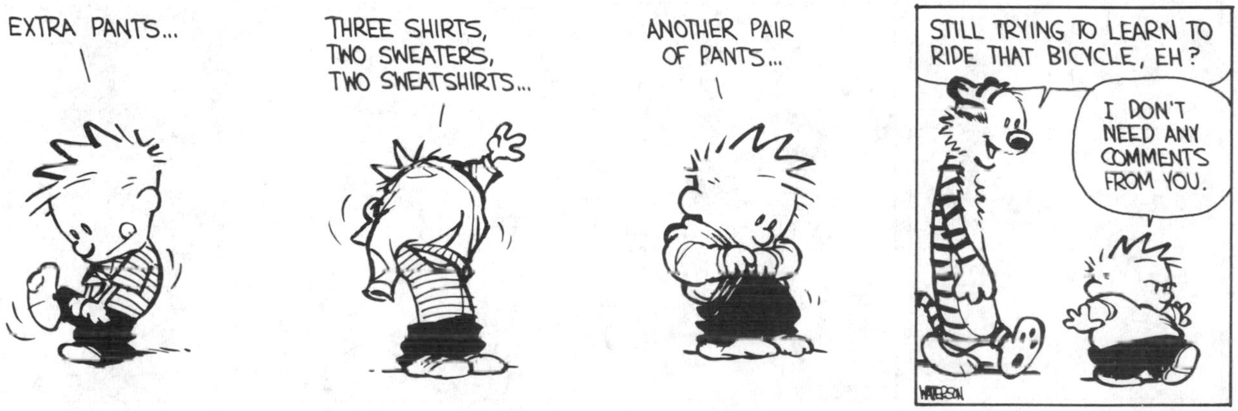
EXTRA PANTS...
THREE SHIRTS, TWO SWEATERS, TWO SWEATSHIRTS...
ANOTHER PAIR OF PANTS...
STILL TRYING TO LEARN TO RIDE THAT BICYCLE, EH?
I DON'T NEED ANY COMMENTS FROM YOU.

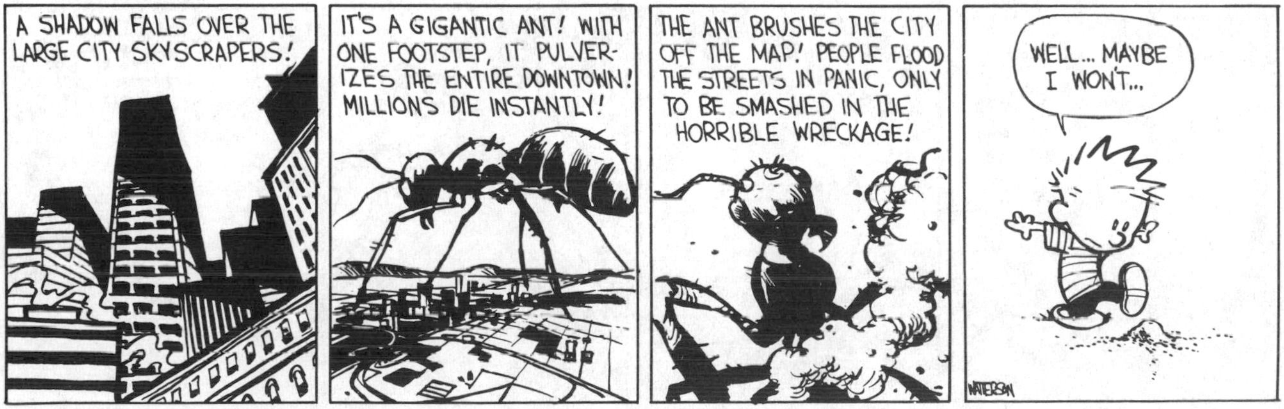
A SHADOW FALLS OVER THE LARGE CITY SKYSCRAPERS!
IT'S A GIGANTIC ANT! WITH ONE FOOTSTEP, IT PULVERIZES THE ENTIRE DOWNTOWN! MILLIONS DIE INSTANTLY!
THE ANT BRUSHES THE CITY OFF THE MAP! PEOPLE FLOOD THE STREETS IN PANIC, ONLY TO BE SMASHED IN THE HORRIBLE WRECKAGE!
WELL... MAYBE I WON'T...

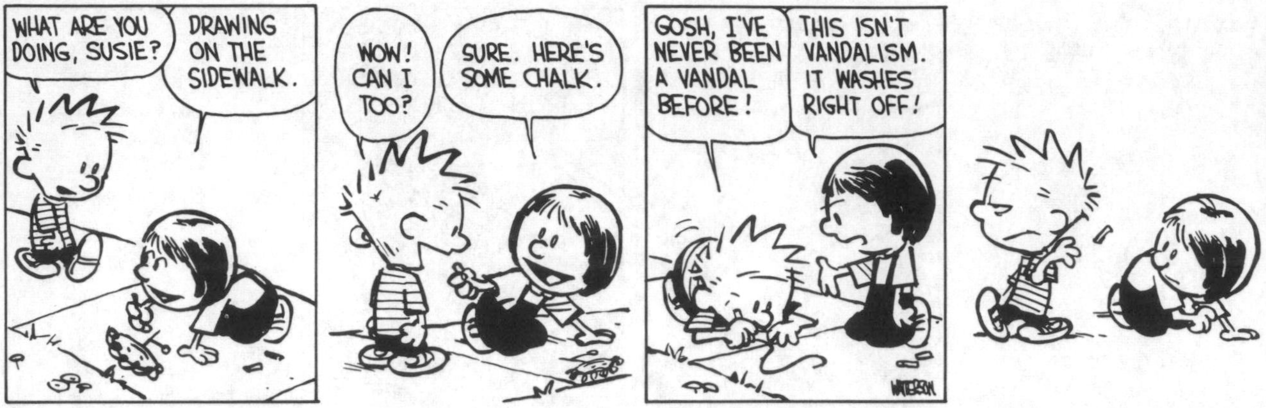
WHAT ARE YOU DOING, SUSIE?
DRAWING ON THE SIDEWALK.
WOW! CAN I TOO?
SURE. HERE'S SOME CHALK.
GOSH, I'VE NEVER BEEN A VANDAL BEFORE!
THIS ISN'T VANDALISM. IT WASHES RIGHT OFF!

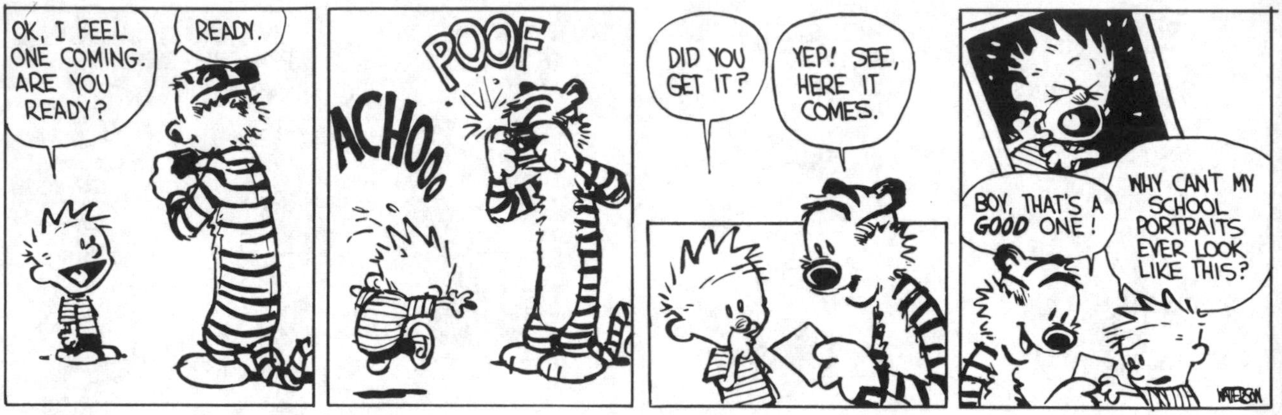
OK, I FEEL ONE COMING. ARE YOU READY?
READY.
POOF
ACHOOO
DID YOU GET IT?
YEP! SEE, HERE IT COMES.
BOY, THAT'S A **GOOD** ONE!
WHY CAN'T MY SCHOOL PORTRAITS EVER LOOK LIKE THIS?

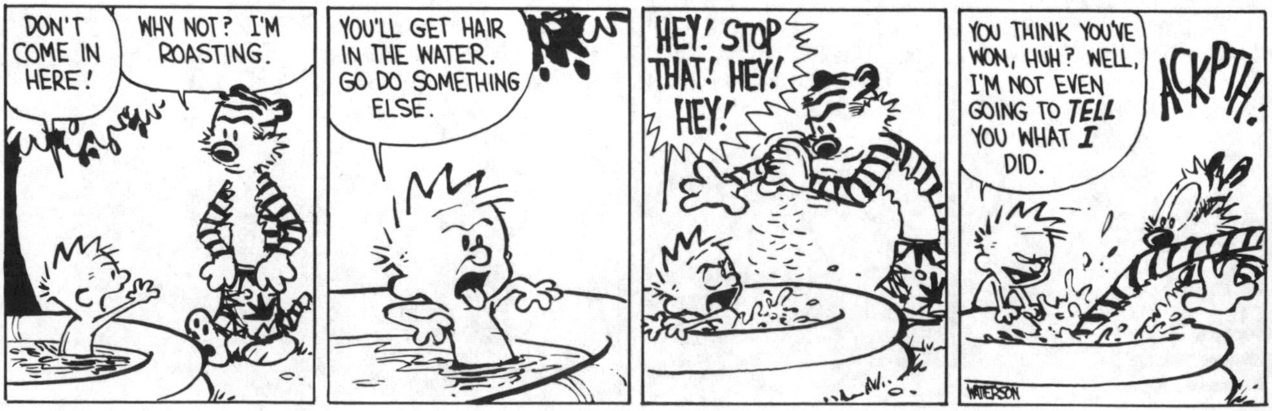
DON'T COME IN HERE!
WHY NOT? I'M ROASTING.
YOU'LL GET HAIR IN THE WATER. GO DO SOMETHING ELSE.
HEY! STOP THAT! HEY! HEY!
YOU THINK YOU'VE WON, HUH? WELL, I'M NOT EVEN GOING TO ***TELL*** YOU WHAT ***I*** DID.
ACKPTH!

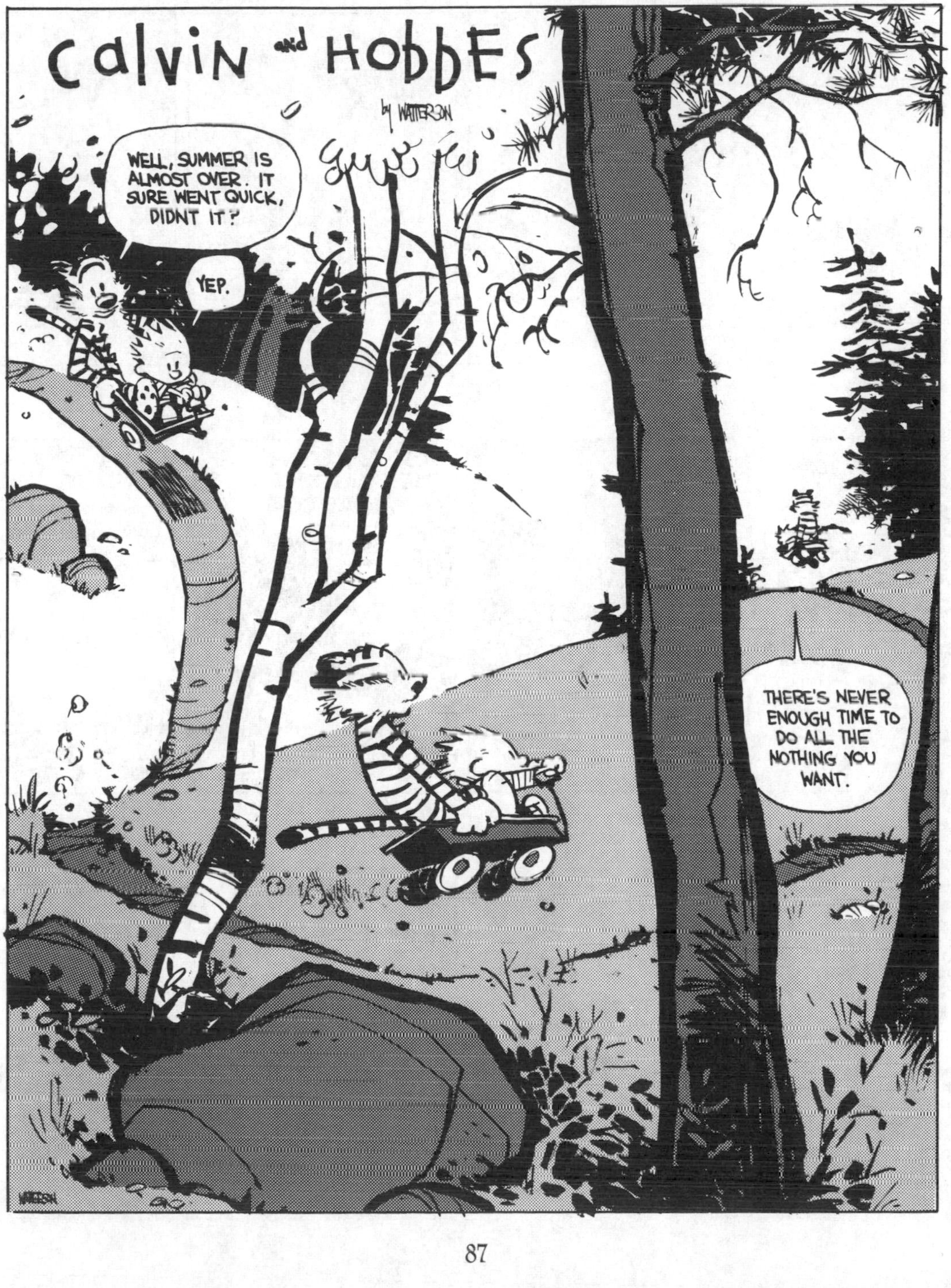
Calvin and HOBBES
by WATTERSON
WELL, SUMMER IS ALMOST OVER. IT SURE WENT QUICK, DIDNT IT?
YEP.
THERE'S NEVER ENOUGH TIME TO DO ALL THE NOTHING YOU WANT.

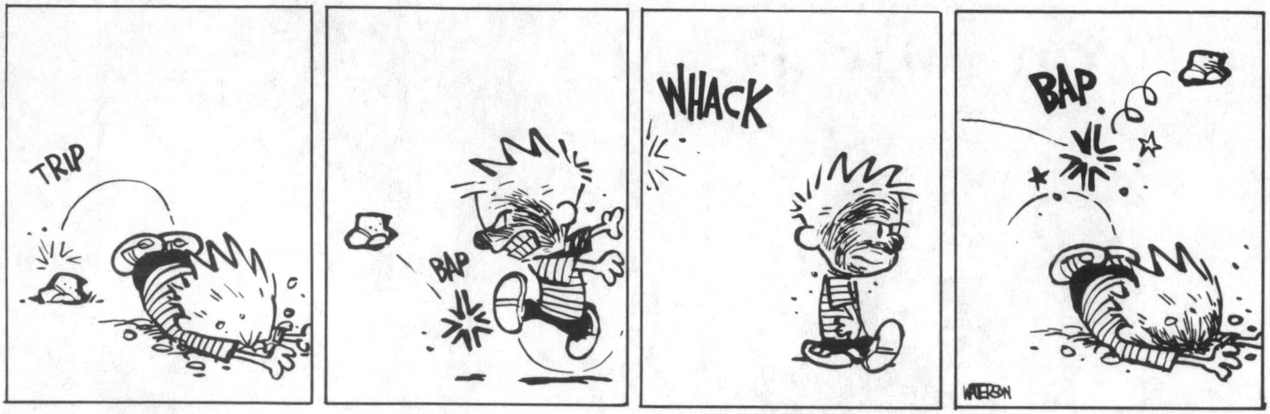
TRIP
BAP
WHACK
BAP

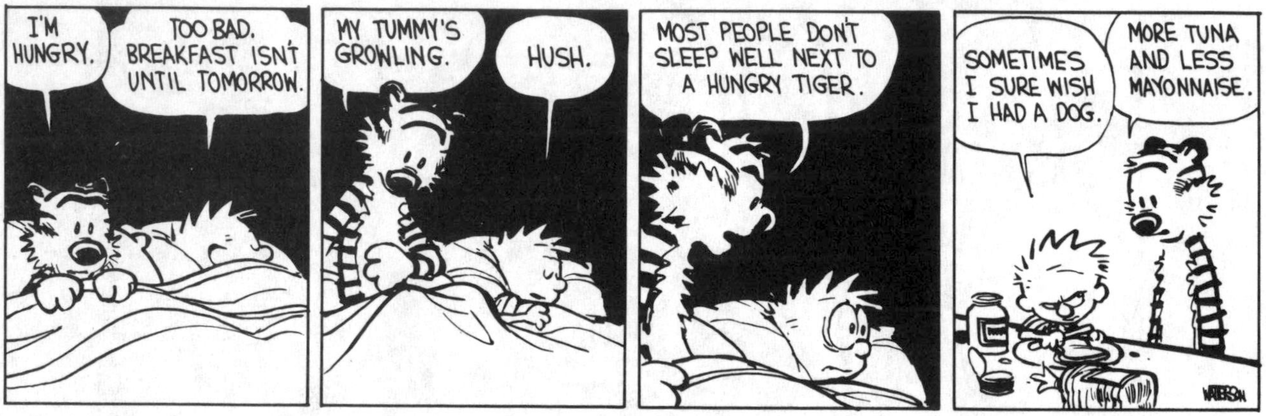
I'M HUNGRY.
TOO BAD. BREAKFAST ISN'T UNTIL TOMORROW.
MY TUMMY'S GROWLING.
HUSH.
MOST PEOPLE DON'T SLEEP WELL NEXT TO A HUNGRY TIGER.
SOMETIMES I SURE WISH I HAD A DOG.
MORE TUNA AND LESS MAYONNAISE.

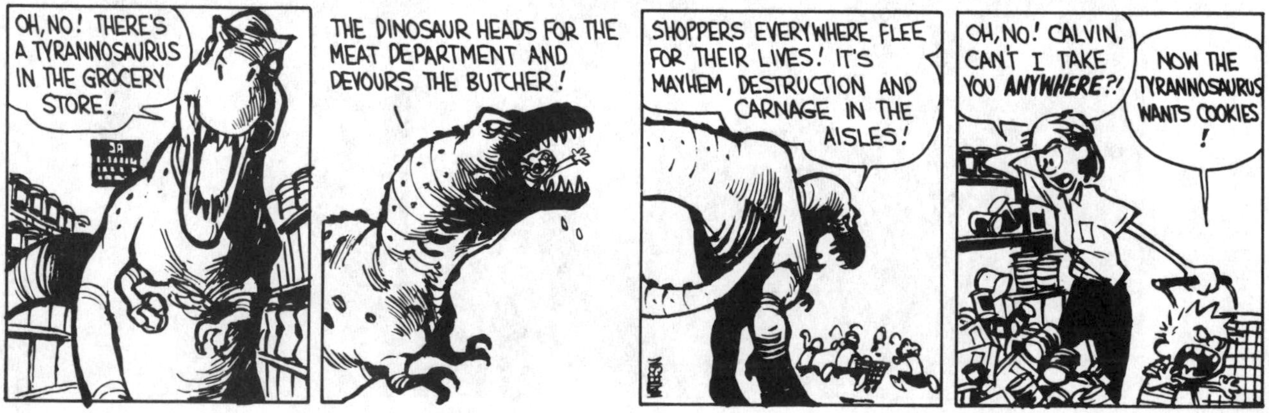
OH, NO! THERE'S A TYRANNOSAURUS IN THE GROCERY STORE!
THE DINOSAUR HEADS FOR THE MEAT DEPARTMENT AND DEVOURS THE BUTCHER!
SHOPPERS EVERYWHERE FLEE FOR THEIR LIVES! IT'S MAYHEM, DESTRUCTION AND CARNAGE IN THE AISLES!
OH, NO! CALVIN, CAN'T I TAKE YOU ANYWHERE?!
NOW THE TYRANNOSAURUS WANTS COOKIES!

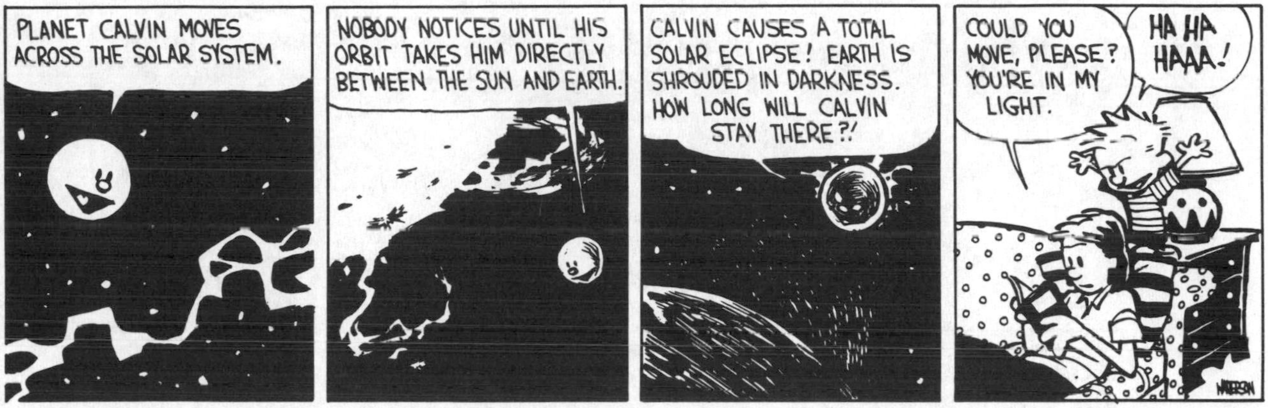
PLANET CALVIN MOVES ACROSS THE SOLAR SYSTEM.
NOBODY NOTICES UNTIL HIS ORBIT TAKES HIM DIRECTLY BETWEEN THE SUN AND EARTH.
CALVIN CAUSES A TOTAL SOLAR ECLIPSE! EARTH IS SHROUDED IN DARKNESS. HOW LONG WILL CALVIN STAY THERE?!
COULD YOU MOVE, PLEASE? YOU'RE IN MY LIGHT.
HA HA HAAA!

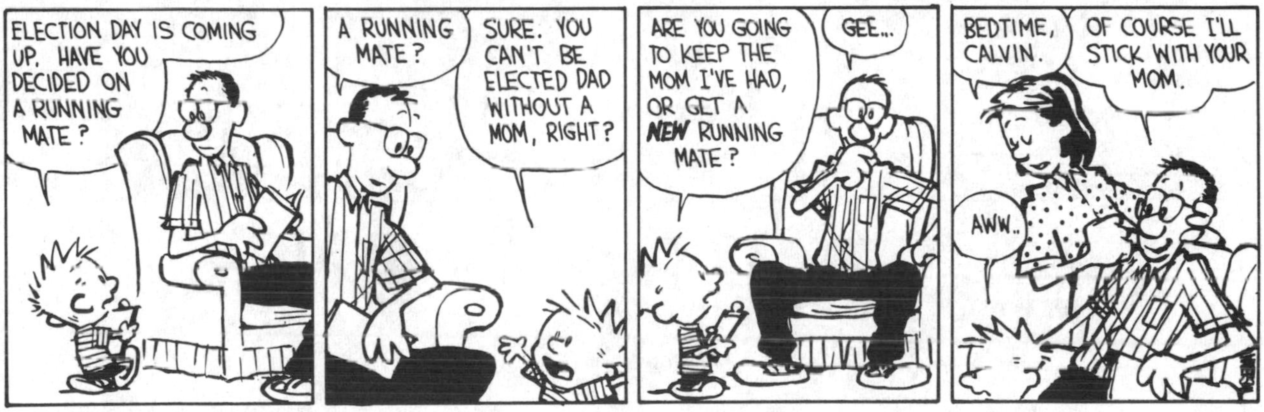
ELECTION DAY IS COMING UP. HAVE YOU DECIDED ON A RUNNING MATE?
A RUNNING MATE?
SURE. YOU CAN'T BE ELECTED DAD WITHOUT A MOM, RIGHT?
ARE YOU GOING TO KEEP THE MOM I'VE HAD, OR GET A NEW RUNNING MATE?
GEE...
BEDTIME, CALVIN.
OF COURSE I'LL STICK WITH YOUR MOM.
AWW..

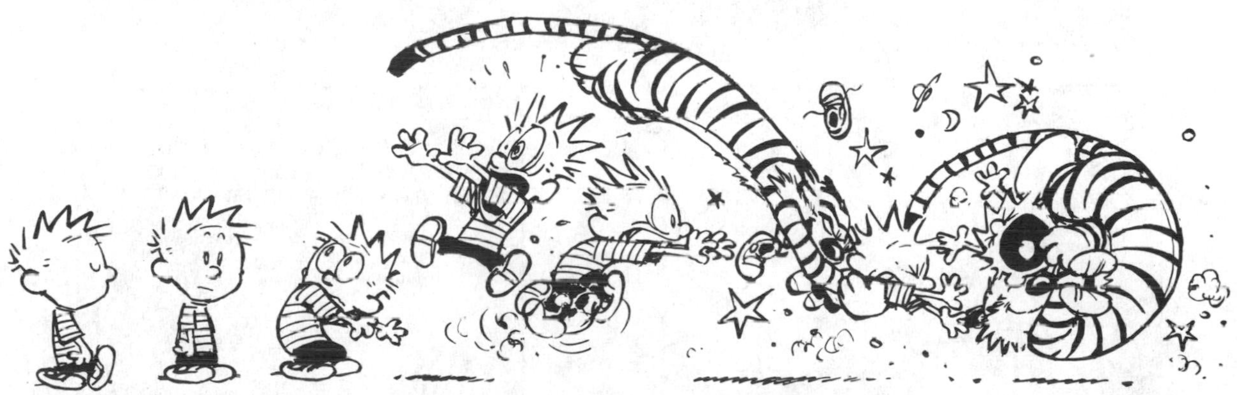

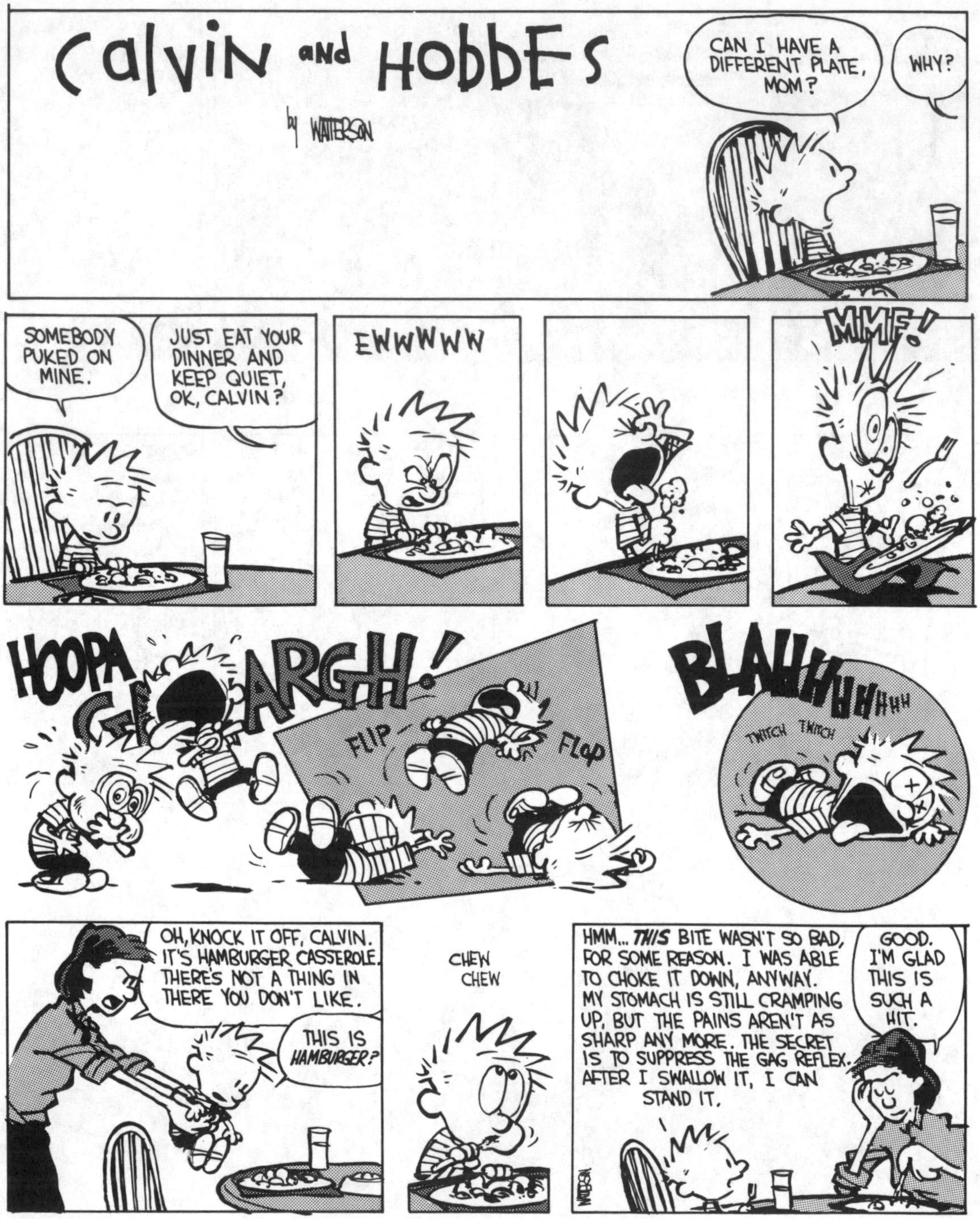
Calvin and HOBBES
by WATTERSON
CAN I HAVE A DIFFERENT PLATE, MOM?
WHY?
SOMEBODY PUKED ON MINE.
JUST EAT YOUR DINNER AND KEEP QUIET, OK, CALVIN?
EWWWWW
MMF!
HOOPA
ARGH!
FLIP
FLOP
BLAHHHHHHH
TWITCH TWITCH
OH, KNOCK IT OFF, CALVIN. IT'S HAMBURGER CASSEROLE. THERE'S NOT A THING IN THERE YOU DON'T LIKE.
THIS IS HAMBURGER?
CHEW CHEW
HMM... THIS BITE WASN'T SO BAD, FOR SOME REASON. I WAS ABLE TO CHOKE IT DOWN, ANYWAY. MY STOMACH IS STILL CRAMPING UP, BUT THE PAINS AREN'T AS SHARP ANY MORE. THE SECRET IS TO SUPPRESS THE GAG REFLEX. AFTER I SWALLOW IT, I CAN STAND IT.
GOOD. I'M GLAD THIS IS SUCH A HIT.
WATTERSON

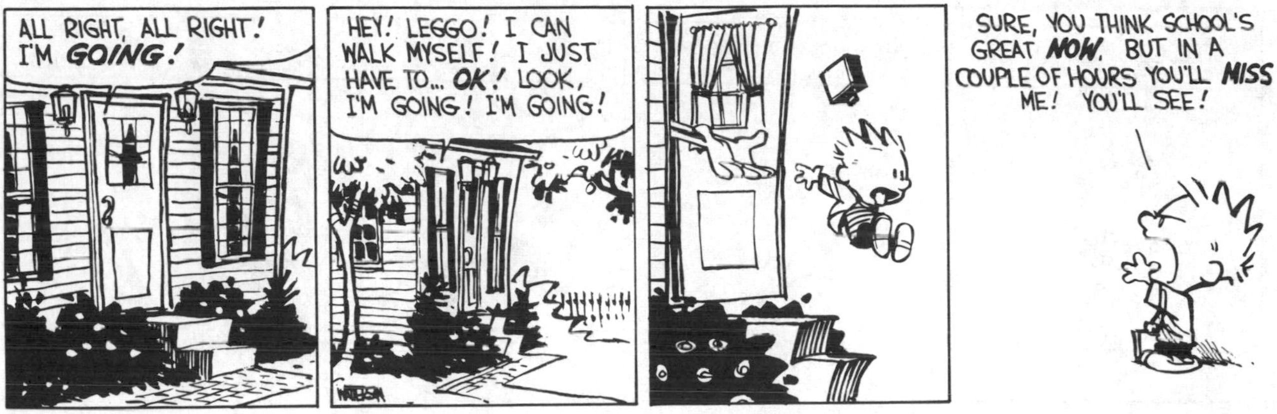
ALL RIGHT, ALL RIGHT! I'M GOING!
HEY! LEGGO! I CAN WALK MYSELF! I JUST HAVE TO... OK! LOOK, I'M GOING! I'M GOING!
SURE, YOU THINK SCHOOL'S GREAT NOW, BUT IN A COUPLE OF HOURS YOU'LL MISS ME! YOU'LL SEE!

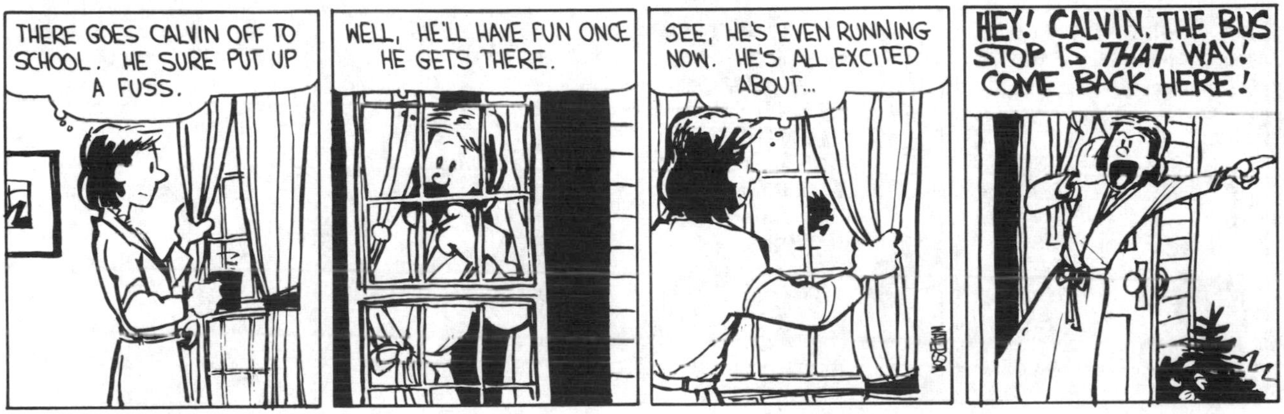
THERE GOES CALVIN OFF TO SCHOOL. HE SURE PUT UP A FUSS.
WELL, HE'LL HAVE FUN ONCE HE GETS THERE.
SEE, HE'S EVEN RUNNING NOW. HE'S ALL EXCITED ABOUT...
HEY! CALVIN, THE BUS STOP IS THAT WAY! COME BACK HERE!

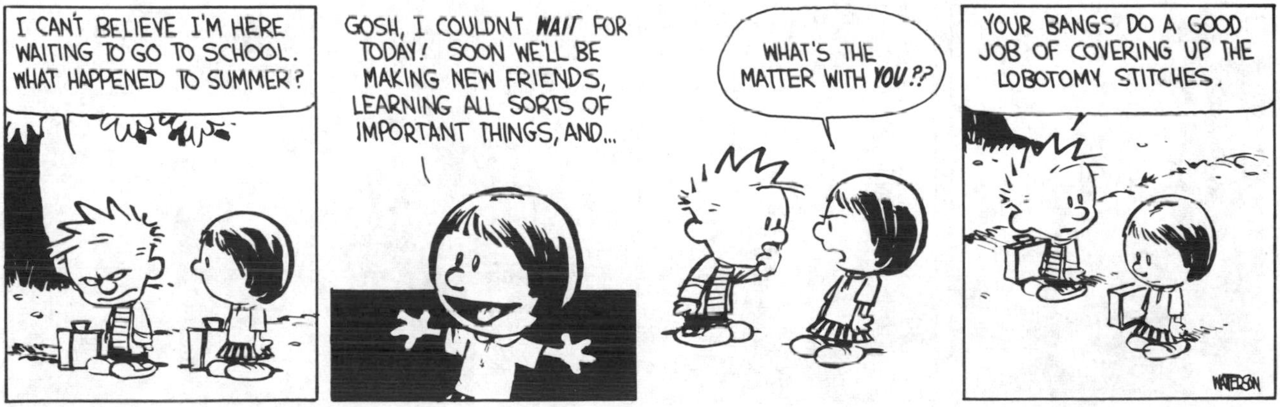
I CAN'T BELIEVE I'M HERE WAITING TO GO TO SCHOOL. WHAT HAPPENED TO SUMMER?
GOSH, I COULDN'T WAIT FOR TODAY! SOON WE'LL BE MAKING NEW FRIENDS, LEARNING ALL SORTS OF IMPORTANT THINGS, AND...
WHAT'S THE MATTER WITH YOU?!?
YOUR BANGS DO A GOOD JOB OF COVERING UP THE LOBOTOMY STITCHES.

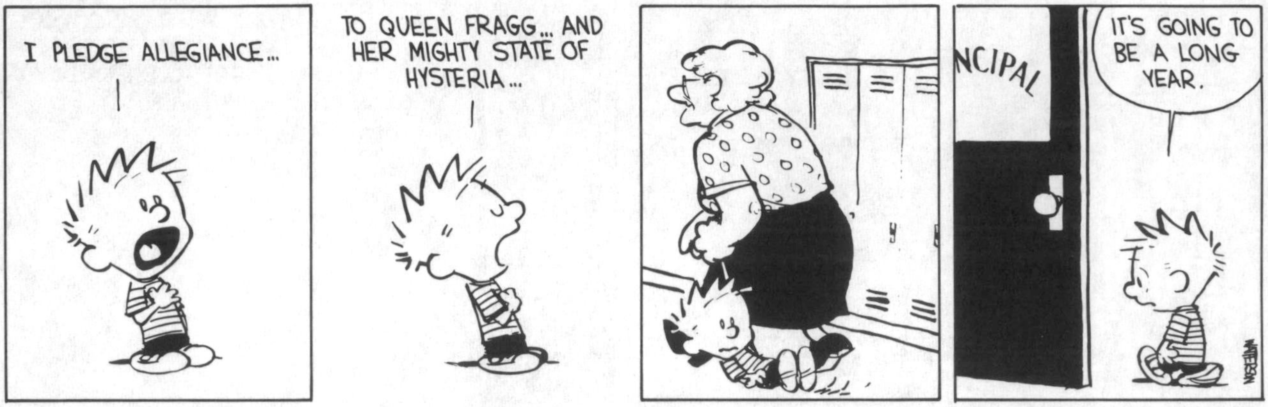
I PLEDGE ALLEGIANCE...
TO QUEEN FRAGG... AND HER MIGHTY STATE OF HYSTERIA...
NCIPAL
IT'S GOING TO BE A LONG YEAR.

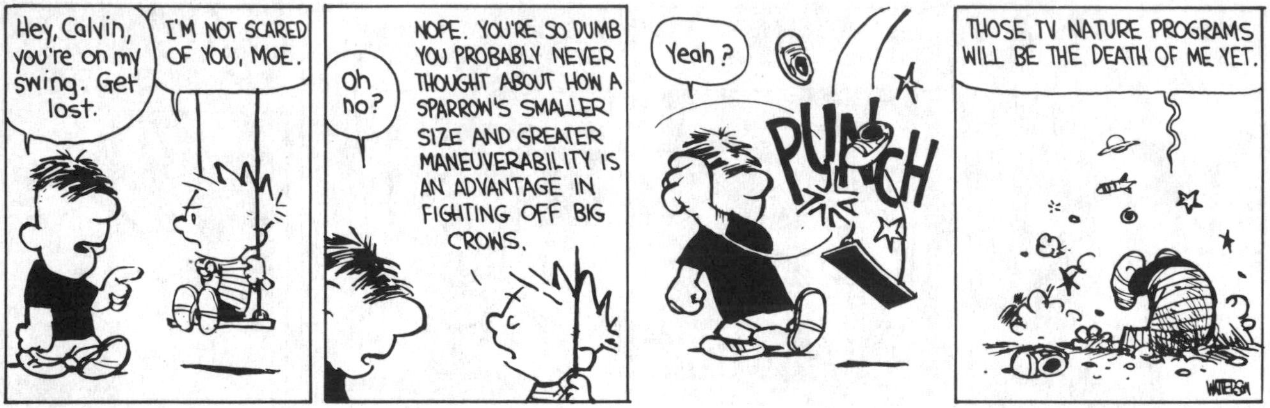
Hey, Calvin, you're on my swing. Get lost.
I'M NOT SCARED OF YOU, MOE.
Oh no?
NOPE. YOU'RE SO DUMB YOU PROBABLY NEVER THOUGHT ABOUT HOW A SPARROW'S SMALLER SIZE AND GREATER MANEUVERABILITY IS AN ADVANTAGE IN FIGHTING OFF BIG CROWS.
Yeah?
PUNCH
THOSE TV NATURE PROGRAMS WILL BE THE DEATH OF ME YET.

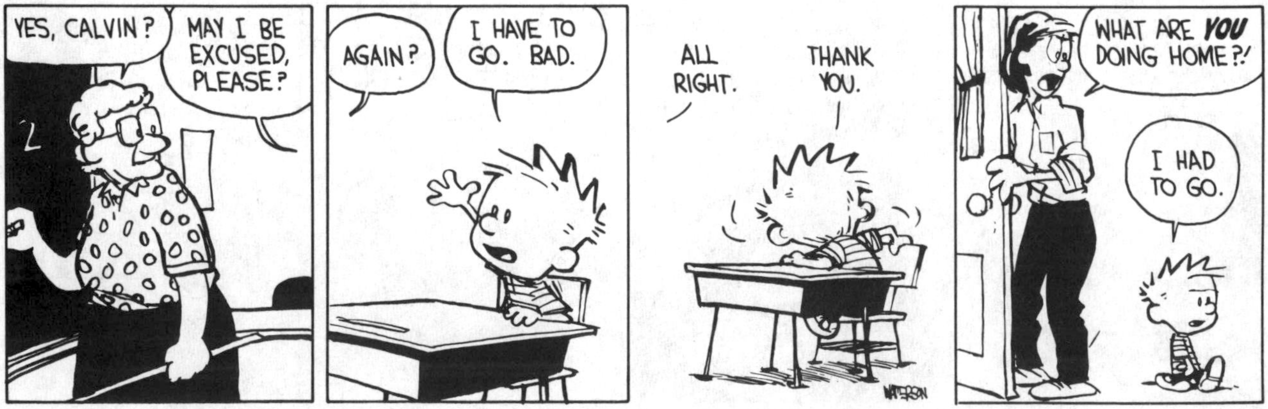
YES, CALVIN?
MAY I BE EXCUSED, PLEASE?
AGAIN?
I HAVE TO GO. BAD.
ALL RIGHT.
THANK YOU.
WHAT ARE YOU DOING HOME?!
I HAD TO GO.

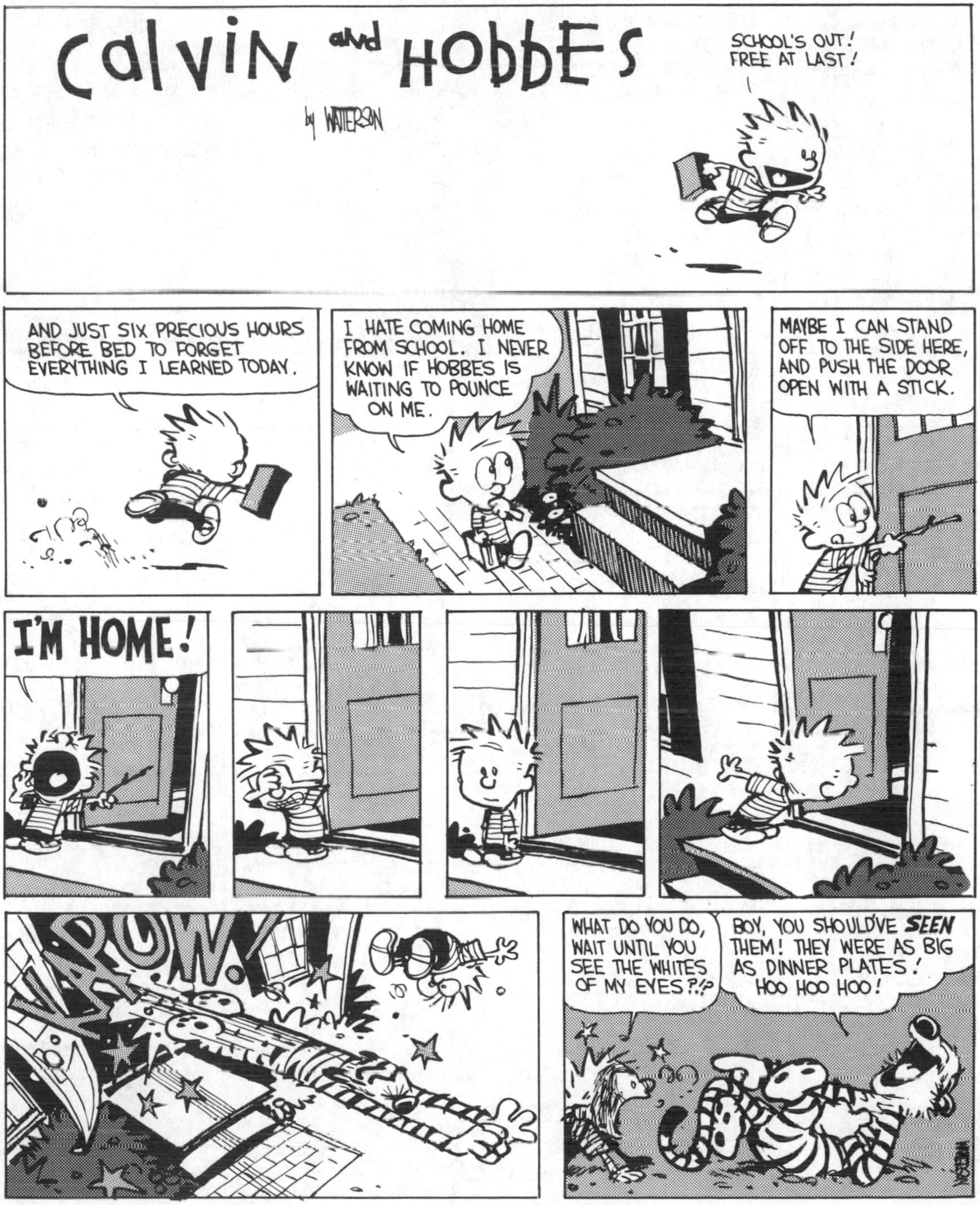
Calvin and HOBBES
by WATTERSON
SCHOOL'S OUT! FREE AT LAST!
AND JUST SIX PRECIOUS HOURS BEFORE BED TO FORGET EVERYTHING I LEARNED TODAY.
I HATE COMING HOME FROM SCHOOL. I NEVER KNOW IF HOBBES IS WAITING TO POUNCE ON ME.
MAYBE I CAN STAND OFF TO THE SIDE HERE, AND PUSH THE DOOR OPEN WITH A STICK.
I'M HOME!
POW!
WHAT DO YOU DO, WAIT UNTIL YOU SEE THE WHITES OF MY EYES?!?
BOY, YOU SHOULD'VE SEEN THEM! THEY WERE AS BIG AS DINNER PLATES! HOO HOO HOO!

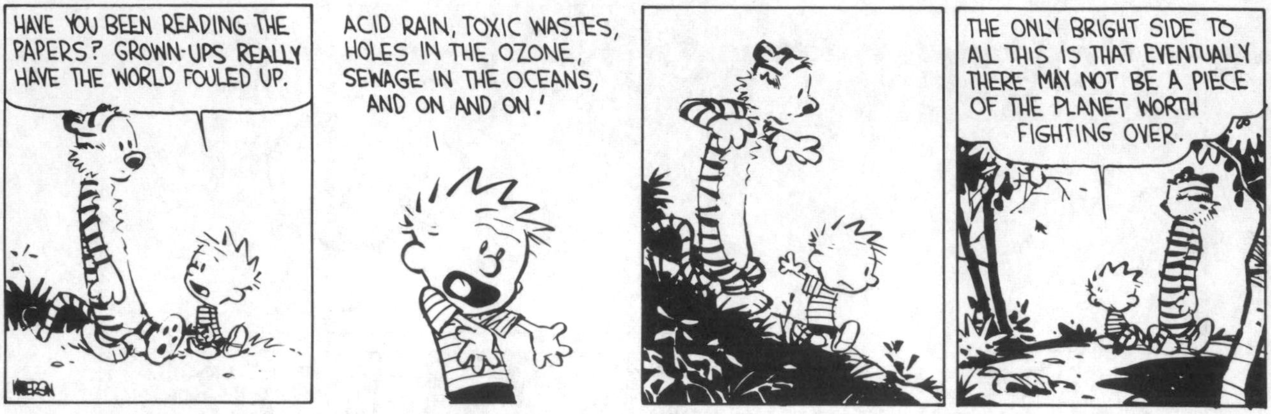
HAVE YOU BEEN READING THE PAPERS? GROWN-UPS REALLY HAVE THE WORLD FOULED UP.
ACID RAIN, TOXIC WASTES, HOLES IN THE OZONE, SEWAGE IN THE OCEANS, AND ON AND ON!
THE ONLY BRIGHT SIDE TO ALL THIS IS THAT EVENTUALLY THERE MAY NOT BE A PIECE OF THE PLANET WORTH FIGHTING OVER.

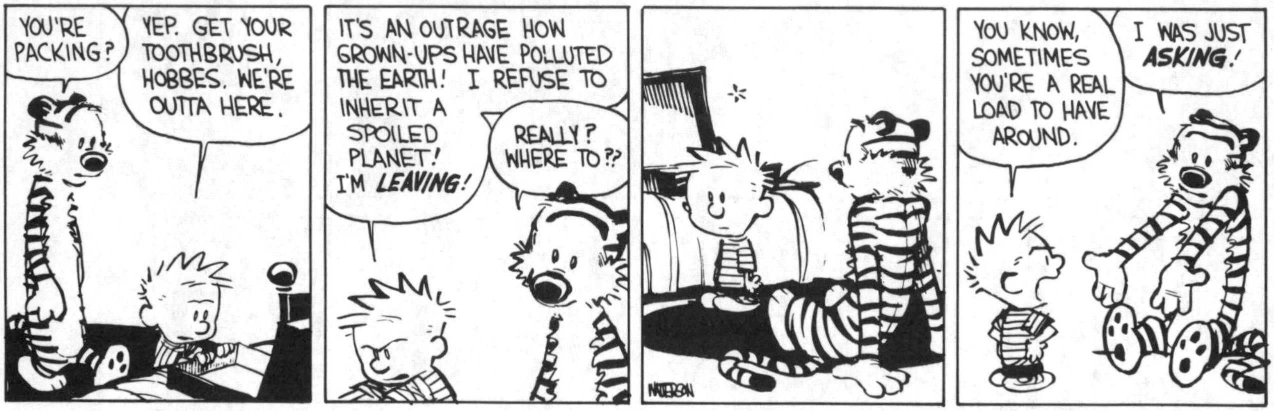
YOU'RE PACKING?
YEP. GET YOUR TOOTHBRUSH, HOBBES. WE'RE OUTTA HERE.
IT'S AN OUTRAGE HOW GROWN-UPS HAVE POLLUTED THE EARTH! I REFUSE TO INHERIT A SPOILED PLANET! I'M LEAVING!
REALLY? WHERE TO?!
YOU KNOW, SOMETIMES YOU'RE A REAL LOAD TO HAVE AROUND.
I WAS JUST ASKING!

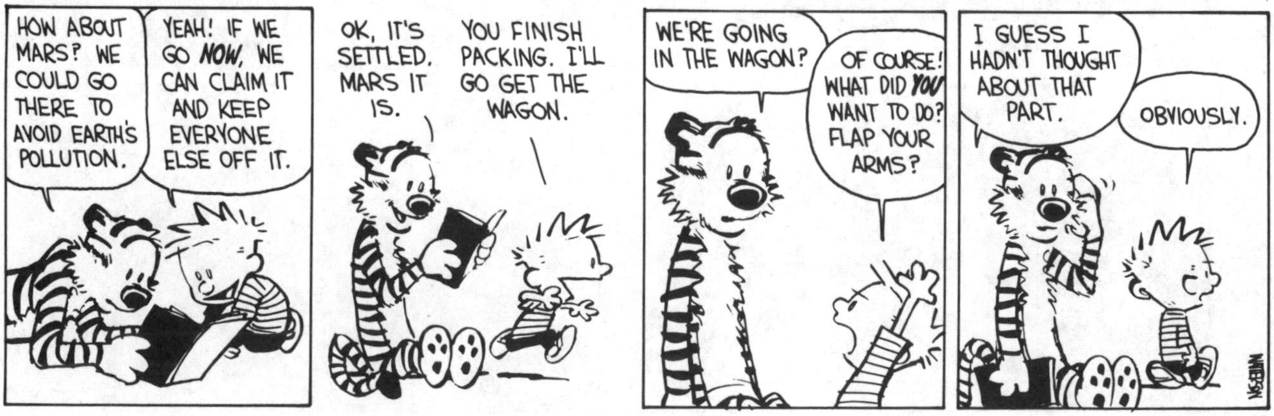
HOW ABOUT MARS? WE COULD GO THERE TO AVOID EARTH'S POLLUTION.
YEAH! IF WE GO NOW, WE CAN CLAIM IT AND KEEP EVERYONE ELSE OFF IT.
OK, IT'S SETTLED. MARS IT IS.
YOU FINISH PACKING. I'LL GO GET THE WAGON.
WE'RE GOING IN THE WAGON?
OF COURSE! WHAT DID YOU WANT TO DO? FLAP YOUR ARMS?
I GUESS I HADN'T THOUGHT ABOUT THAT PART.
OBVIOUSLY.

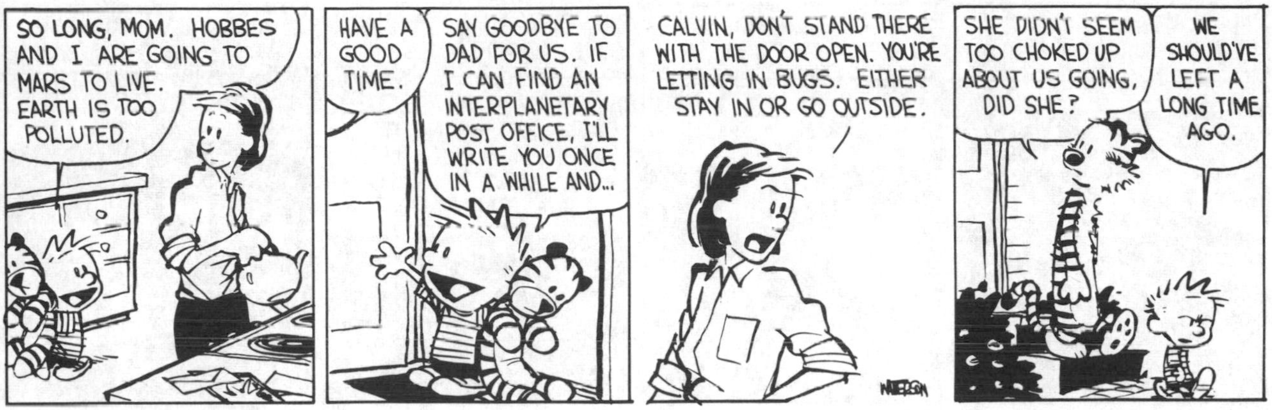
SO LONG, MOM. HOBBES AND I ARE GOING TO MARS TO LIVE. EARTH IS TOO POLLUTED.
HAVE A GOOD TIME.
SAY GOODBYE TO DAD FOR US. IF I CAN FIND AN INTERPLANETARY POST OFFICE, I'LL WRITE YOU ONCE IN A WHILE AND...
CALVIN, DON'T STAND THERE WITH THE DOOR OPEN. YOU'RE LETTING IN BUGS. EITHER STAY IN OR GO OUTSIDE.
SHE DIDN'T SEEM TOO CHOKED UP ABOUT US GOING, DID SHE?
WE SHOULD'VE LEFT A LONG TIME AGO.

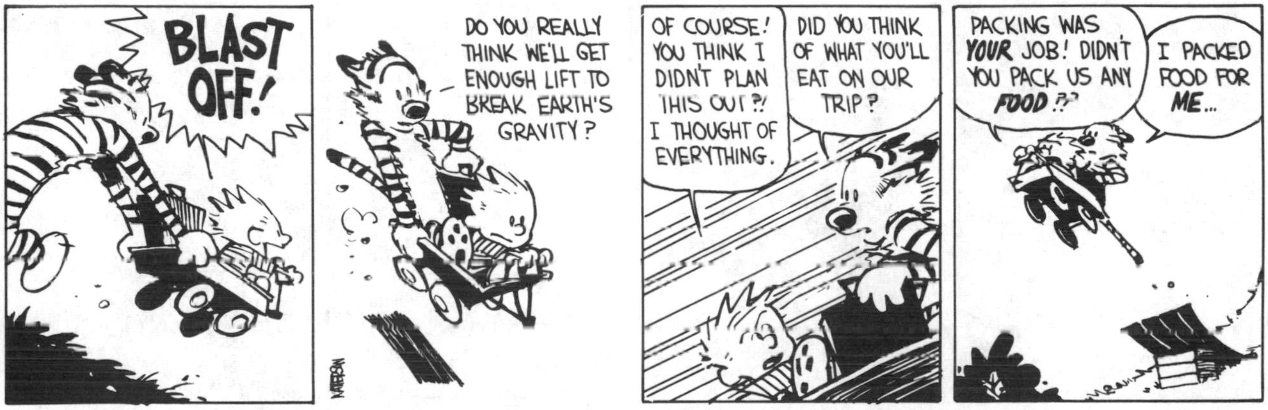
BLAST OFF!
DO YOU REALLY THINK WE'LL GET ENOUGH LIFT TO BREAK EARTH'S GRAVITY?
OF COURSE! YOU THINK I DIDN'T PLAN THIS OUT?! I THOUGHT OF EVERYTHING.
DID YOU THINK OF WHAT YOU'LL EAT ON OUR TRIP?
PACKING WAS YOUR JOB! DIDN'T YOU PACK US ANY FOOD?!?
I PACKED FOOD FOR ME...

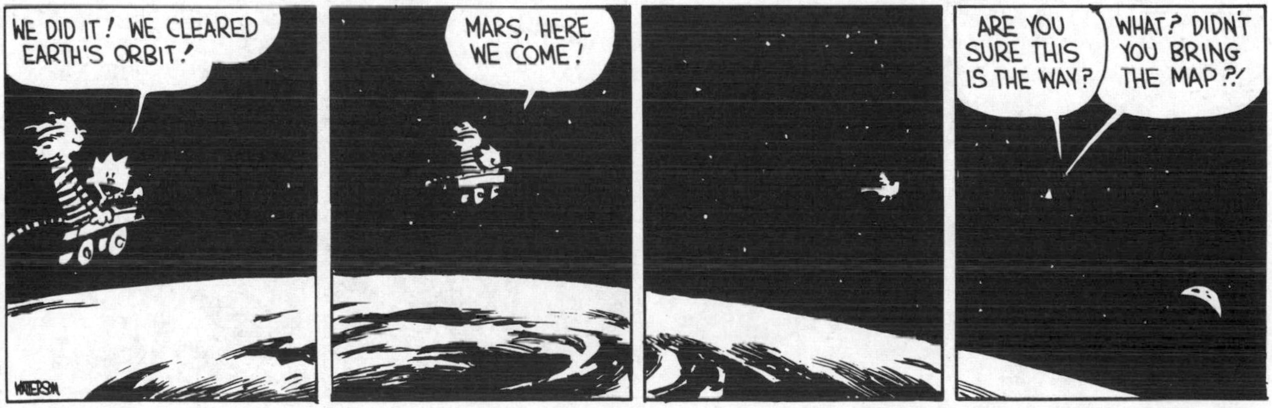
WE DID IT! WE CLEARED EARTH'S ORBIT!
MARS, HERE WE COME!
ARE YOU SURE THIS IS THE WAY?
WHAT? DIDN'T YOU BRING THE MAP?!

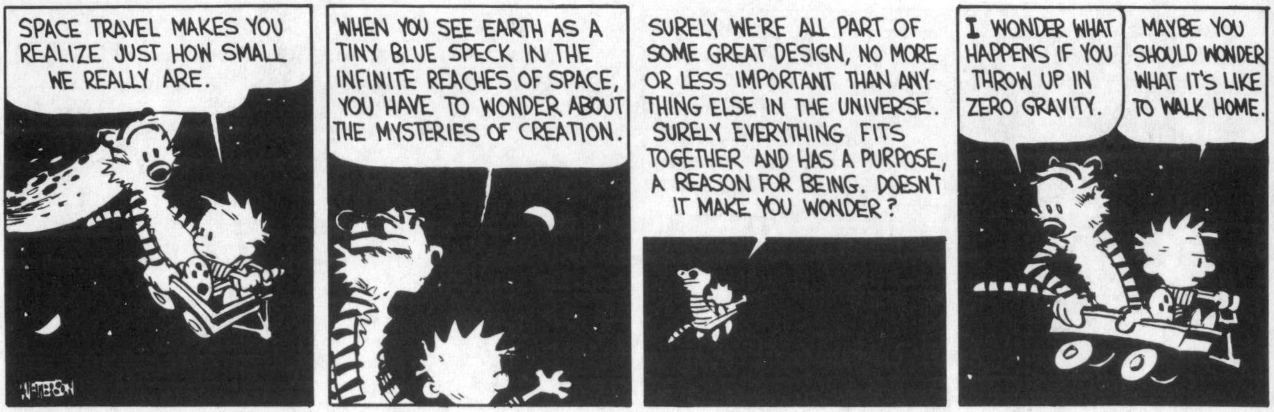
SPACE TRAVEL MAKES YOU REALIZE JUST HOW SMALL WE REALLY ARE.
WHEN YOU SEE EARTH AS A TINY BLUE SPECK IN THE INFINITE REACHES OF SPACE, YOU HAVE TO WONDER ABOUT THE MYSTERIES OF CREATION.
SURELY WE'RE ALL PART OF SOME GREAT DESIGN, NO MORE OR LESS IMPORTANT THAN ANYTHING ELSE IN THE UNIVERSE. SURELY EVERYTHING FITS TOGETHER AND HAS A PURPOSE, A REASON FOR BEING. DOESN'T IT MAKE YOU WONDER?
I WONDER WHAT HAPPENS IF YOU THROW UP IN ZERO GRAVITY.
MAYBE YOU SHOULD WONDER WHAT IT'S LIKE TO WALK HOME.

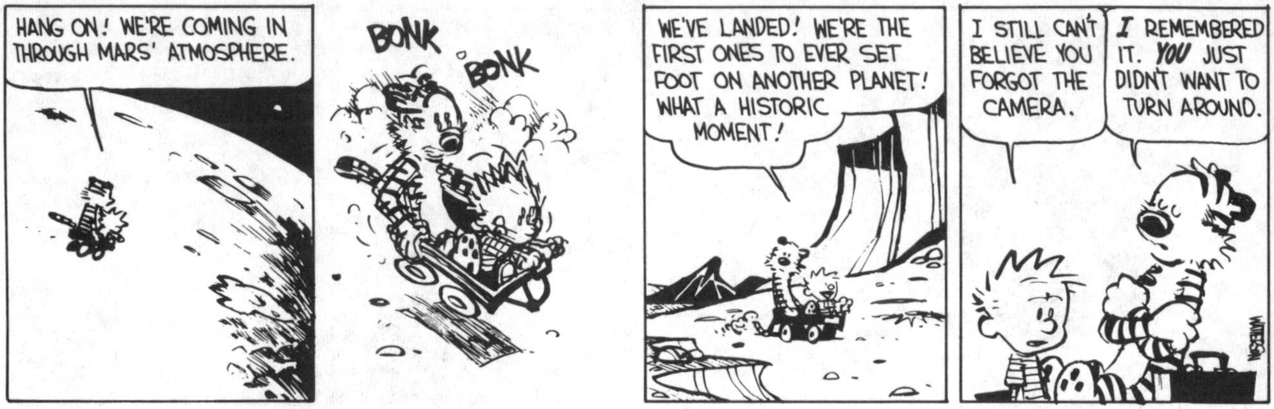
HANG ON! WE'RE COMING IN THROUGH MARS' ATMOSPHERE.
BONK
BONK
WE'VE LANDED! WE'RE THE FIRST ONES TO EVER SET FOOT ON ANOTHER PLANET! WHAT A HISTORIC MOMENT!
I STILL CAN'T BELIEVE YOU FORGOT THE CAMERA.
I REMEMBERED IT. YOU JUST DIDN'T WANT TO TURN AROUND.

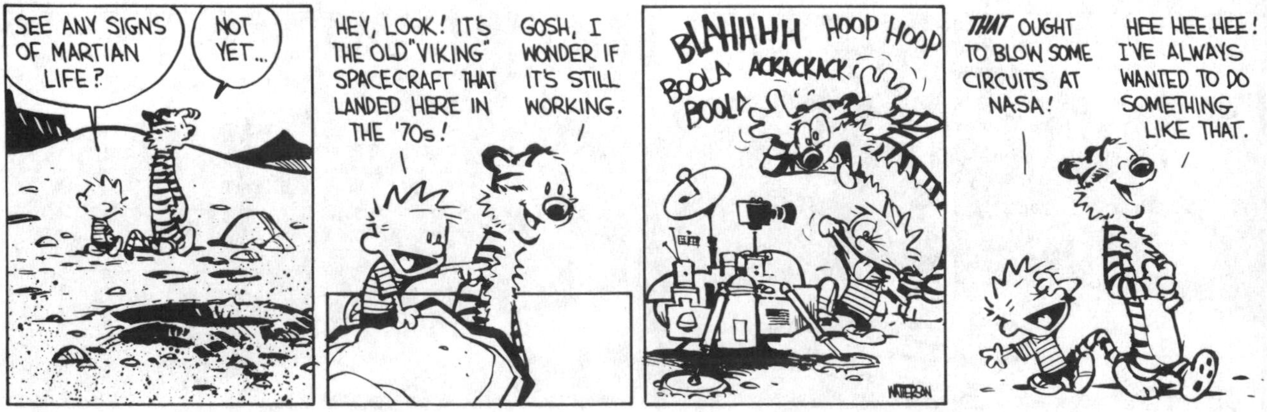
SEE ANY SIGNS OF MARTIAN LIFE?
NOT YET...
HEY, LOOK! IT'S THE OLD "VIKING" SPACECRAFT THAT LANDED HERE IN THE '70s!
GOSH, I WONDER IF IT'S STILL WORKING.
BLAHHHH
HOOP HOOP
BOOLA
ACKACKACK!
BOOLA
THAT OUGHT TO BLOW SOME CIRCUITS AT NASA!
HEE HEE HEE! I'VE ALWAYS WANTED TO DO SOMETHING LIKE THAT.

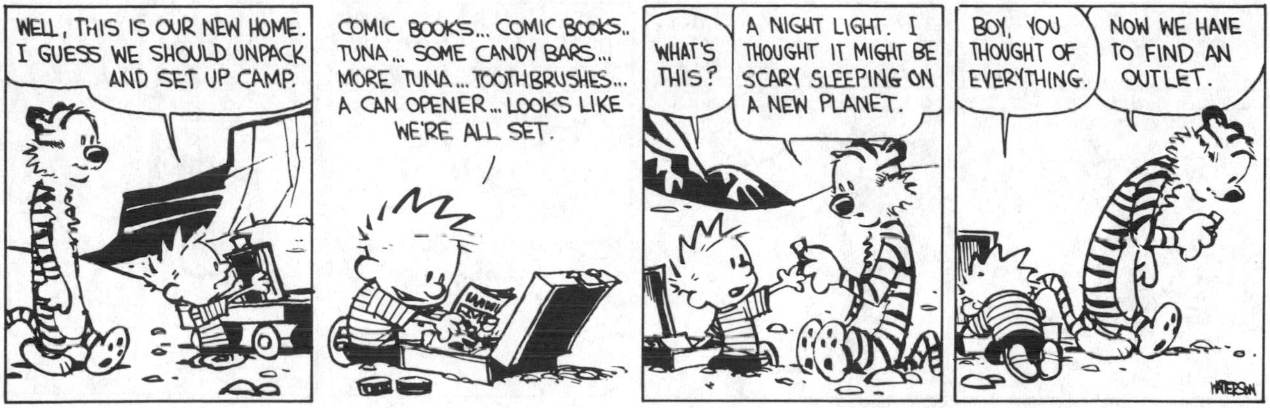
WELL, THIS IS OUR NEW HOME. I GUESS WE SHOULD UNPACK AND SET UP CAMP.
COMIC BOOKS... COMIC BOOKS.. TUNA... SOME CANDY BARS... MORE TUNA... TOOTHBRUSHES... A CAN OPENER... LOOKS LIKE WE'RE ALL SET.
WHAT'S THIS?
A NIGHT LIGHT. I THOUGHT IT MIGHT BE SCARY SLEEPING ON A NEW PLANET.
BOY, YOU THOUGHT OF EVERYTHING.
NOW WE HAVE TO FIND AN OUTLET.
WATERSON

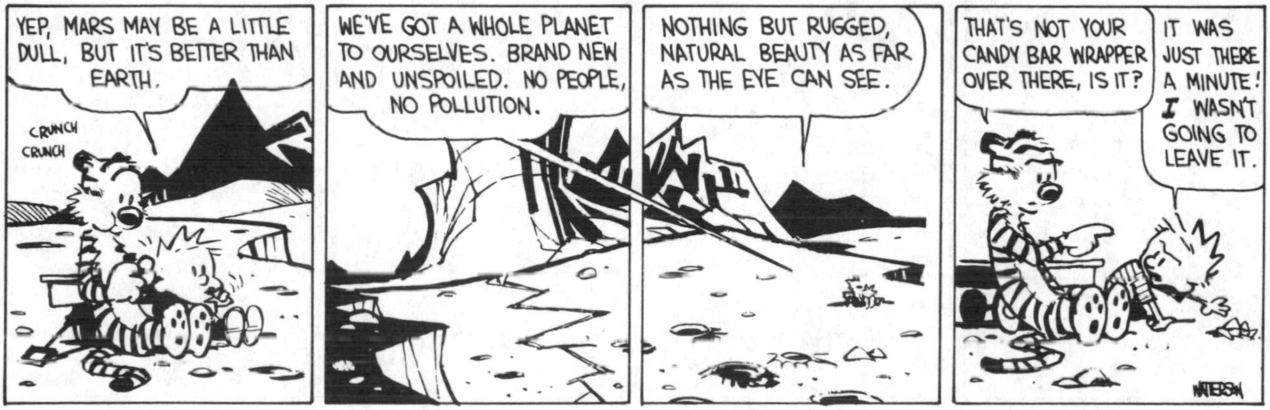
YEP, MARS MAY BE A LITTLE DULL, BUT IT'S BETTER THAN EARTH.
CRUNCH CRUNCH
WE'VE GOT A WHOLE PLANET TO OURSELVES. BRAND NEW AND UNSPOILED. NO PEOPLE, NO POLLUTION.
NOTHING BUT RUGGED, NATURAL BEAUTY AS FAR AS THE EYE CAN SEE.
THAT'S NOT YOUR CANDY BAR WRAPPER OVER THERE, IS IT?
IT WAS JUST THERE A MINUTE! I WASN'T GOING TO LEAVE IT.
WATERSON

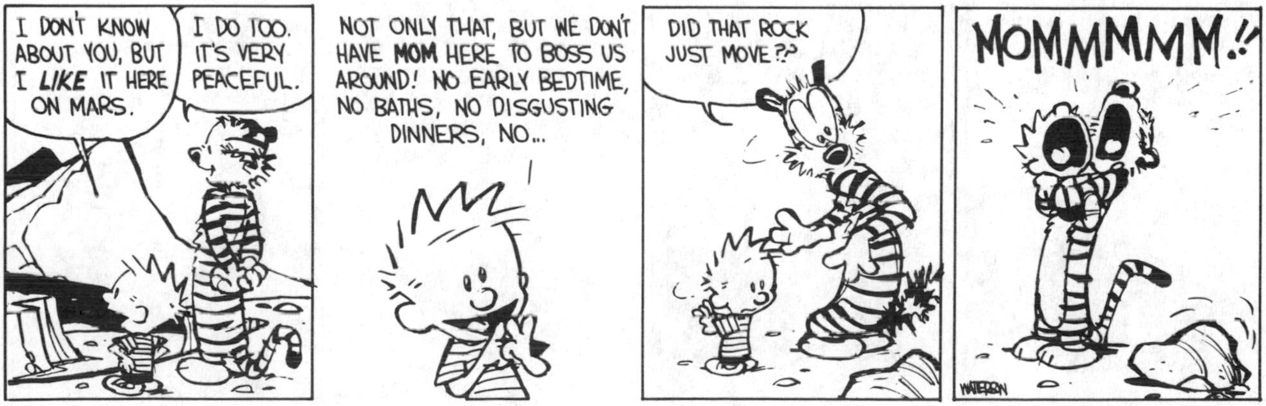
I DON'T KNOW ABOUT YOU, BUT I LIKE IT HERE ON MARS.
I DO TOO. IT'S VERY PEACEFUL.
NOT ONLY THAT, BUT WE DON'T HAVE MOM HERE TO BOSS US AROUND! NO EARLY BEDTIME, NO BATHS, NO DISGUSTING DINNERS, NO...
DID THAT ROCK JUST MOVE??
MOMMMMM!!
WATERSON

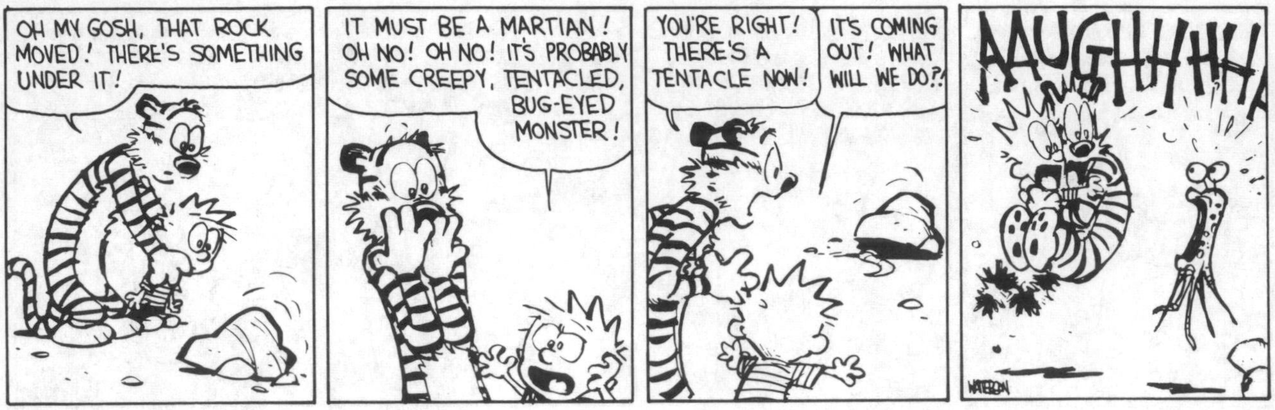
OH MY GOSH, THAT ROCK MOVED! THERE'S SOMETHING UNDER IT!
IT MUST BE A MARTIAN! OH NO! OH NO! IT'S PROBABLY SOME CREEPY, TENTACLED, BUG-EYED MONSTER!
YOU'RE RIGHT! THERE'S A TENTACLE NOW!
IT'S COMING OUT! WHAT WILL WE DO?!
AAUGHHHHA

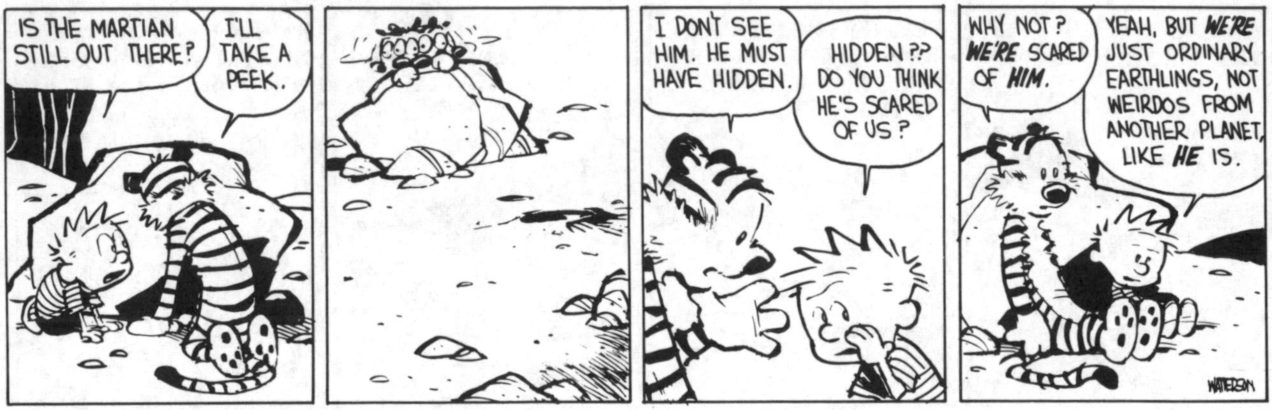
IS THE MARTIAN STILL OUT THERE?
I'LL TAKE A PEEK.
I DON'T SEE HIM. HE MUST HAVE HIDDEN.
HIDDEN?? DO YOU THINK HE'S SCARED OF US?
WHY NOT? WE'RE SCARED OF HIM.
YEAH, BUT WE'RE JUST ORDINARY EARTHLINGS, NOT WEIRDOS FROM ANOTHER PLANET, LIKE HE IS.

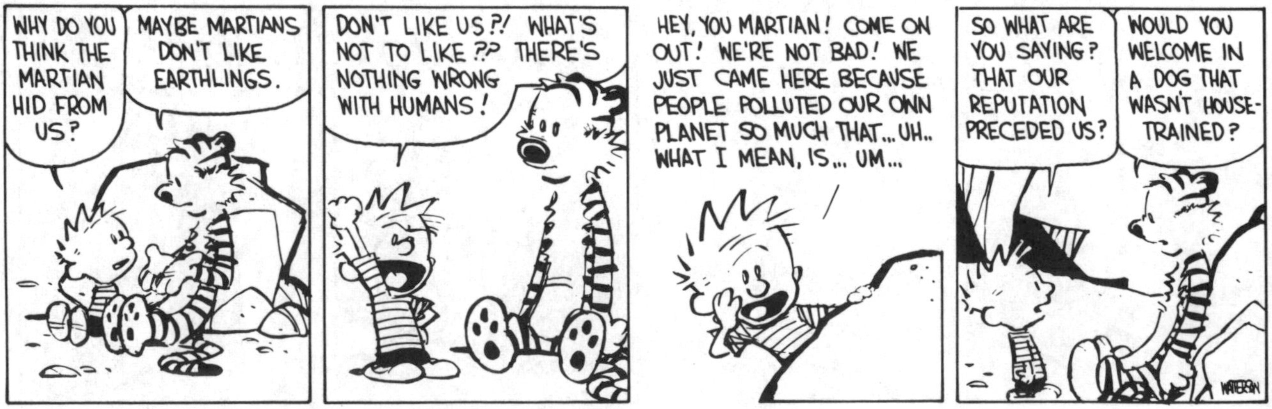
WHY DO YOU THINK THE MARTIAN HID FROM US?
MAYBE MARTIANS DON'T LIKE EARTHLINGS.
DON'T LIKE US?! WHAT'S NOT TO LIKE?? THERE'S NOTHING WRONG WITH HUMANS!
HEY, YOU MARTIAN! COME ON OUT! WE'RE NOT BAD! WE JUST CAME HERE BECAUSE PEOPLE POLLUTED OUR OWN PLANET SO MUCH THAT... UH.. WHAT I MEAN, IS... UM...
SO WHAT ARE YOU SAYING? THAT OUR REPUTATION PRECEDED US?
WOULD YOU WELCOME IN A DOG THAT WASN'T HOUSE-TRAINED?

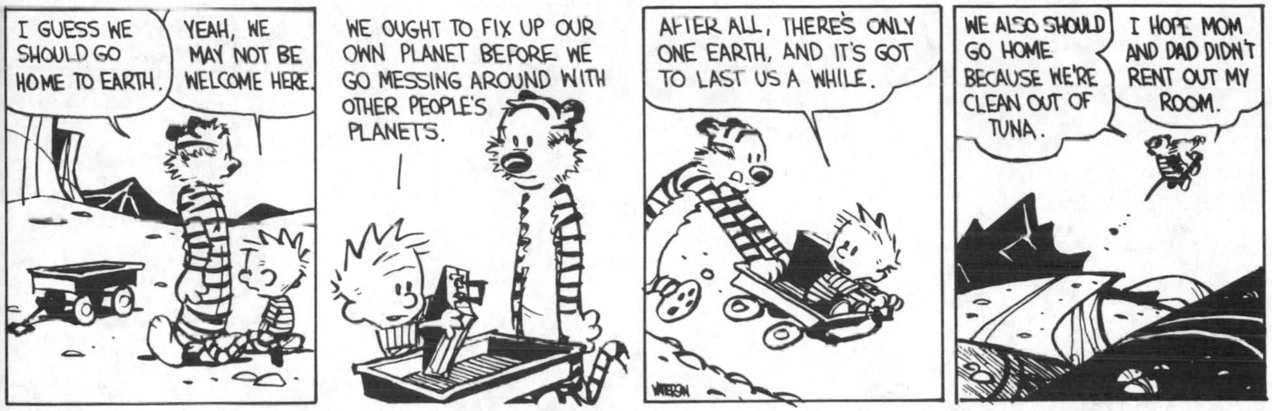
I GUESS WE SHOULD GO HOME TO EARTH.
YEAH, WE MAY NOT BE WELCOME HERE.
WE OUGHT TO FIX UP OUR OWN PLANET BEFORE WE GO MESSING AROUND WITH OTHER PEOPLE'S PLANETS.
AFTER ALL, THERE'S ONLY ONE EARTH, AND IT'S GOT TO LAST US A WHILE.
WE ALSO SHOULD GO HOME BECAUSE WE'RE CLEAN OUT OF TUNA.
I HOPE MOM AND DAD DIDN'T RENT OUT MY ROOM.

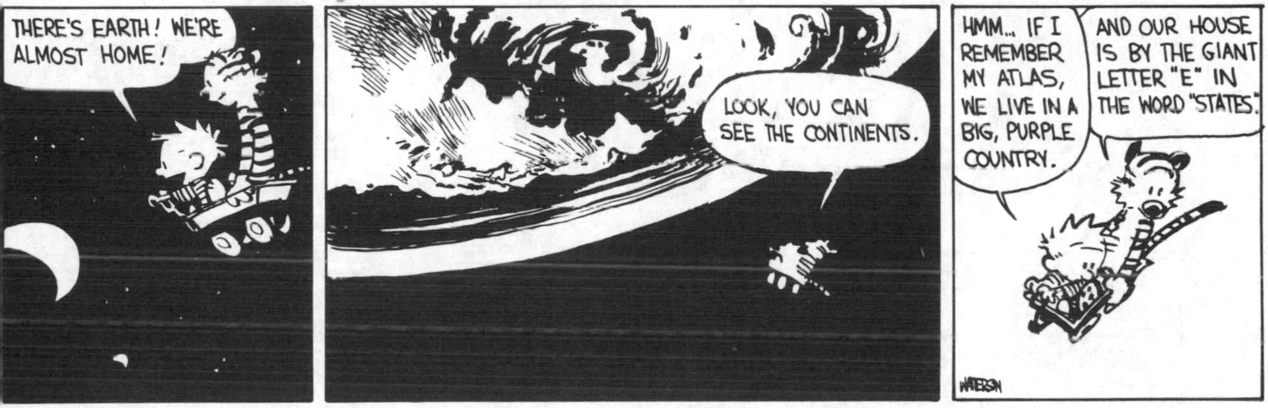
THERE'S EARTH! WE'RE ALMOST HOME!
LOOK, YOU CAN SEE THE CONTINENTS.
HMM... IF I REMEMBER MY ATLAS, WE LIVE IN A BIG, PURPLE COUNTRY.
AND OUR HOUSE IS BY THE GIANT LETTER "E" IN THE WORD "STATES."

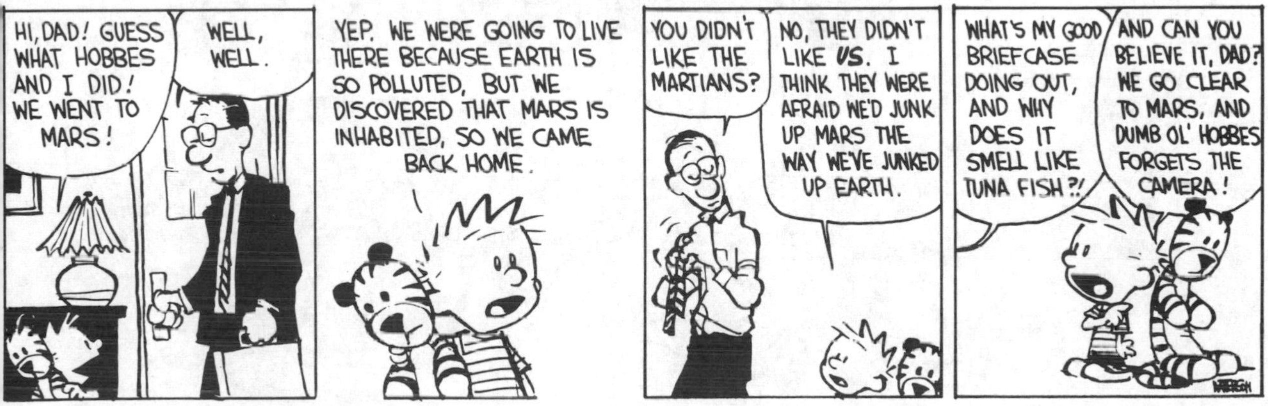
HI, DAD! GUESS WHAT HOBBES AND I DID! WE WENT TO MARS!
WELL, WELL.
YEP. WE WERE GOING TO LIVE THERE BECAUSE EARTH IS SO POLLUTED, BUT WE DISCOVERED THAT MARS IS INHABITED, SO WE CAME BACK HOME.
YOU DIDN'T LIKE THE MARTIANS?
NO, THEY DIDN'T LIKE US. I THINK THEY WERE AFRAID WE'D JUNK UP MARS THE WAY WE'VE JUNKED UP EARTH.
WHAT'S MY GOOD BRIEFCASE DOING OUT, AND WHY DOES IT SMELL LIKE TUNA FISH?!
AND CAN YOU BELIEVE IT, DAD? WE GO CLEAR TO MARS, AND DUMB OL' HOBBES FORGETS THE CAMERA!

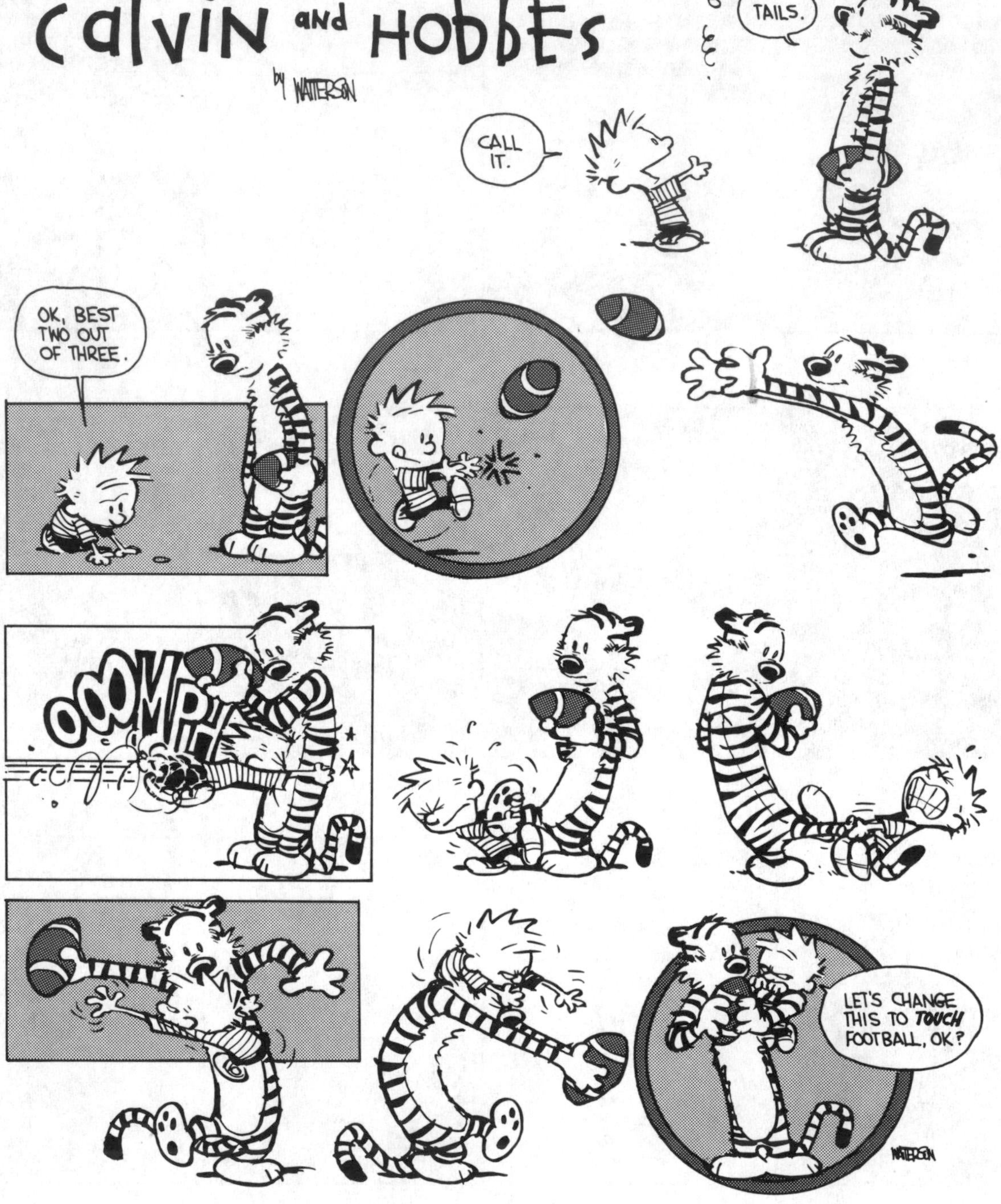
CALVIN and HOBBES
by WATTERSON
TAILS.
CALL IT.
OK, BEST TWO OUT OF THREE.
OOOMPH
LET'S CHANGE THIS TO TOUCH FOOTBALL, OK?
WATTERSON

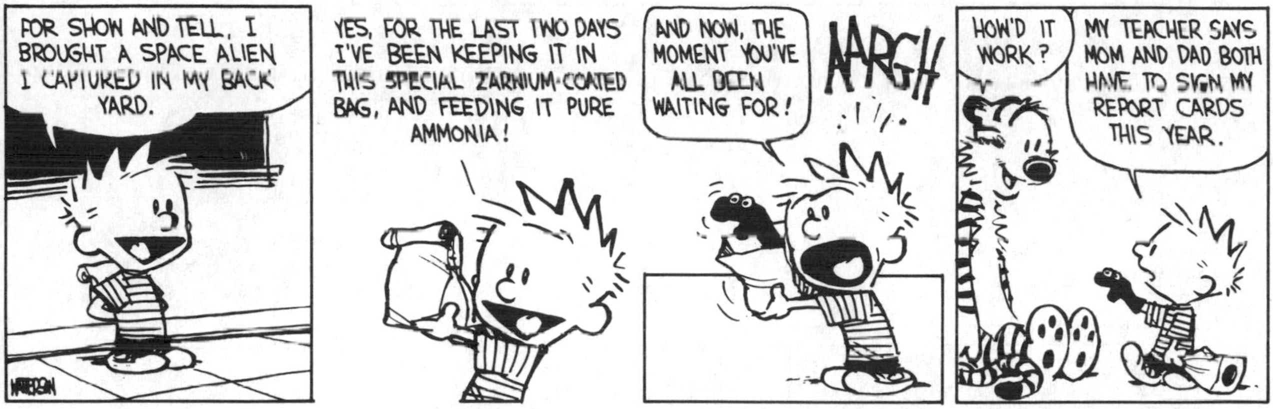

FOR SHOW AND TELL, I BROUGHT A SPACE ALIEN I CAPTURED IN MY BACK YARD.
YES, FOR THE LAST TWO DAYS I'VE BEEN KEEPING IT IN THIS SPECIAL ZARHIUM-COATED BAG, AND FEEDING IT PURE AMMONIA!
AND NOW, THE MOMENT YOU'VE ALL BEEN WAITING FOR!
AARGH
HOW'D IT WORK?
MY TEACHER SAYS MOM AND DAD BOTH HAVE TO SIGN MY REPORT CARDS THIS YEAR.

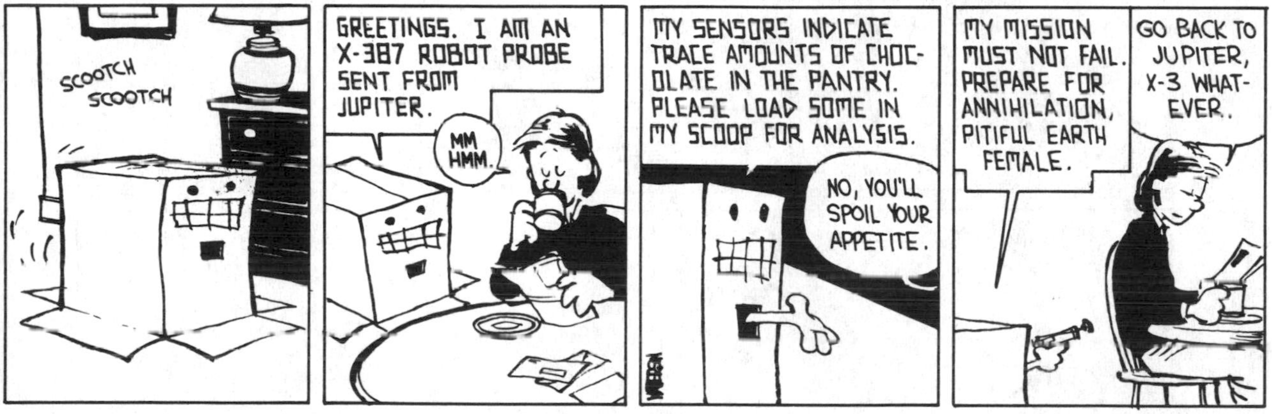

SCOOTCH SCOOTCH
GREETINGS. I AM AN X-387 ROBOT PROBE SENT FROM JUPITER.
MM HMM.
MY SENSORS INDICATE TRACE AMOUNTS OF CHOC-OLATE IN THE PANTRY. PLEASE LOAD SOME IN MY SCOOP FOR ANALYSIS.
NO, YOU'LL SPOIL YOUR APPETITE.
MY MISSION MUST NOT FAIL. PREPARE FOR ANNIHILATION, PITIFUL EARTH FEMALE.
GO BACK TO JUPITER, X-3 WHAT-EVER.

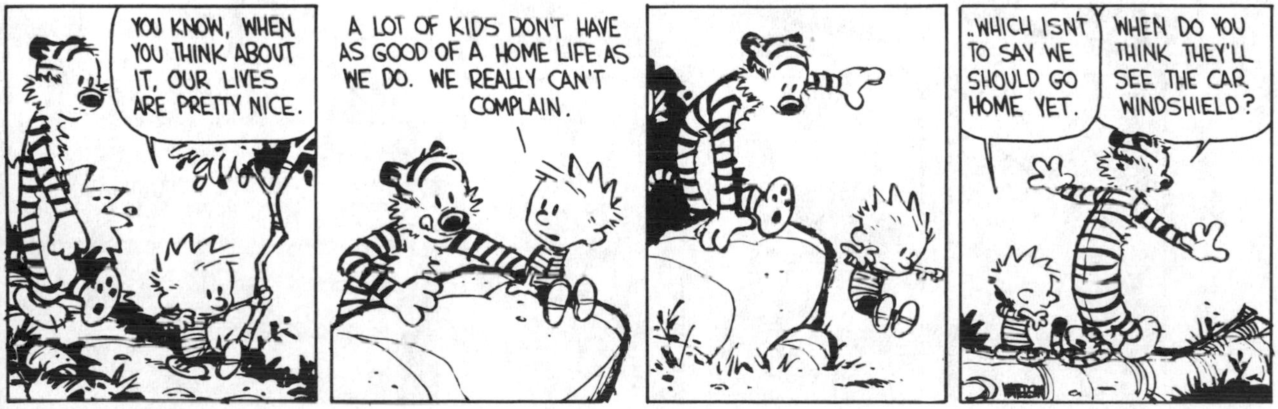

YOU KNOW, WHEN YOU THINK ABOUT IT, OUR LIVES ARE PRETTY NICE.
A LOT OF KIDS DON'T HAVE AS GOOD OF A HOME LIFE AS WE DO. WE REALLY CAN'T COMPLAIN.
..WHICH ISN'T TO SAY WE SHOULD GO HOME YET.
WHEN DO YOU THINK THEY'LL SEE THE CAR WINDSHIELD?

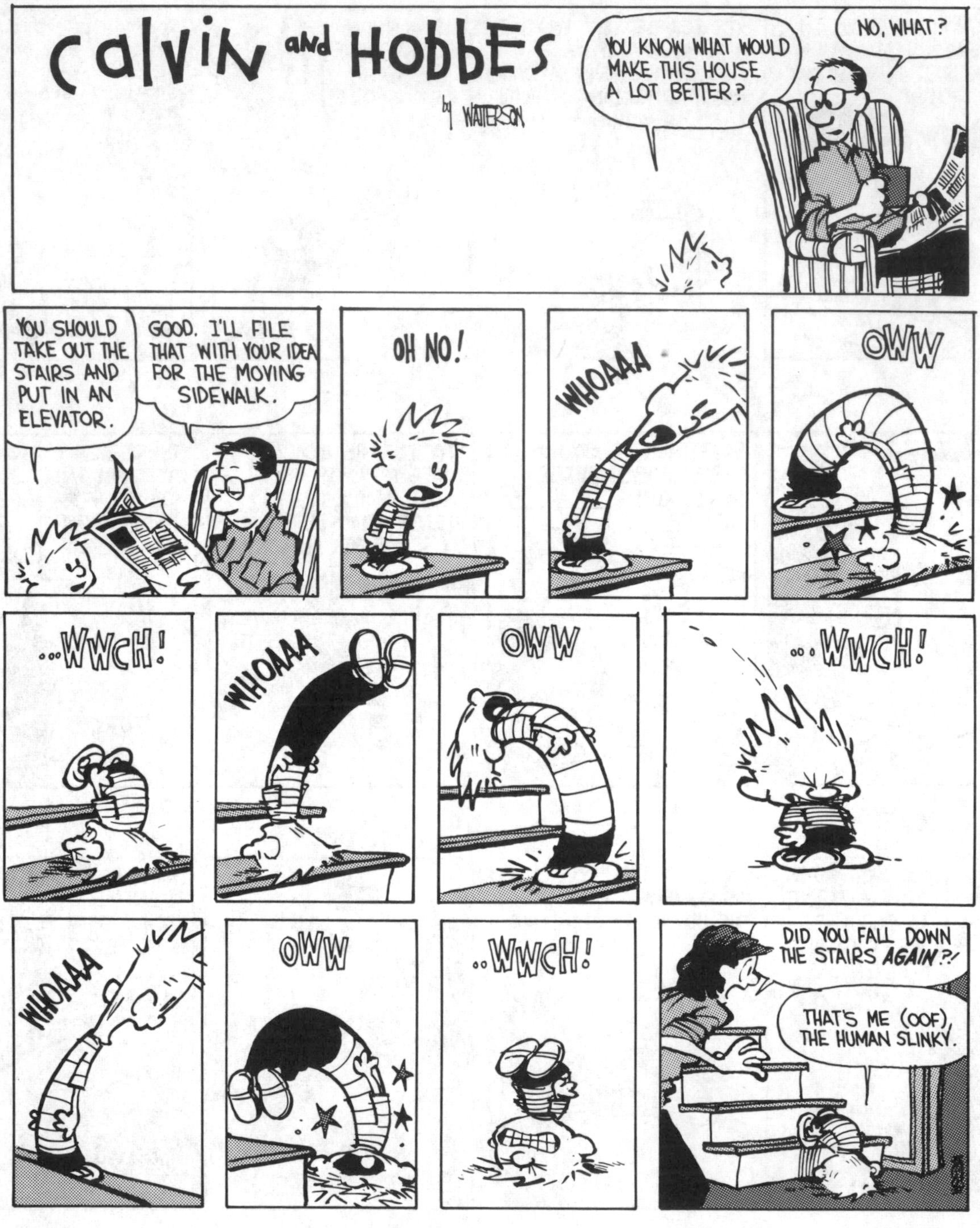
CALVIN AND HOBBES
by WATTERSON
YOU KNOW WHAT WOULD MAKE THIS HOUSE A LOT BETTER?
NO, WHAT?
YOU SHOULD TAKE OUT THE STAIRS AND PUT IN AN ELEVATOR.
GOOD. I'LL FILE THAT WITH YOUR IDEA FOR THE MOVING SIDEWALK.
OH NO!
WHOAAA
OWW
...WWCH!
WHOAAA
OWW
...WWCH!
WHOAAA
OWW
..WWCH!
DID YOU FALL DOWN THE STAIRS AGAIN?!
THAT'S ME (OOF), THE HUMAN SLINKY.

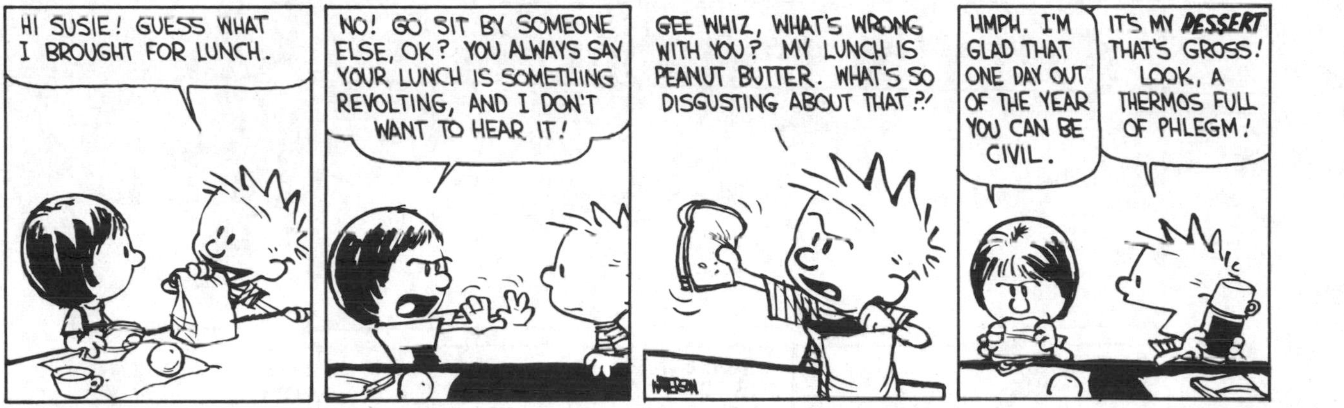
HI SUSIE! GUESS WHAT I BROUGHT FOR LUNCH.
NO! GO SIT BY SOMEONE ELSE, OK? YOU ALWAYS SAY YOUR LUNCH IS SOMETHING REVOLTING, AND I DON'T WANT TO HEAR IT!
GEE WHIZ, WHAT'S WRONG WITH YOU? MY LUNCH IS PEANUT BUTTER. WHAT'S SO DISGUSTING ABOUT THAT?!
HMPH. I'M GLAD THAT ONE DAY OUT OF THE YEAR YOU CAN BE CIVIL.
IT'S MY DESSERT THAT'S GROSS! LOOK, A THERMOS FULL OF PHLEGM!

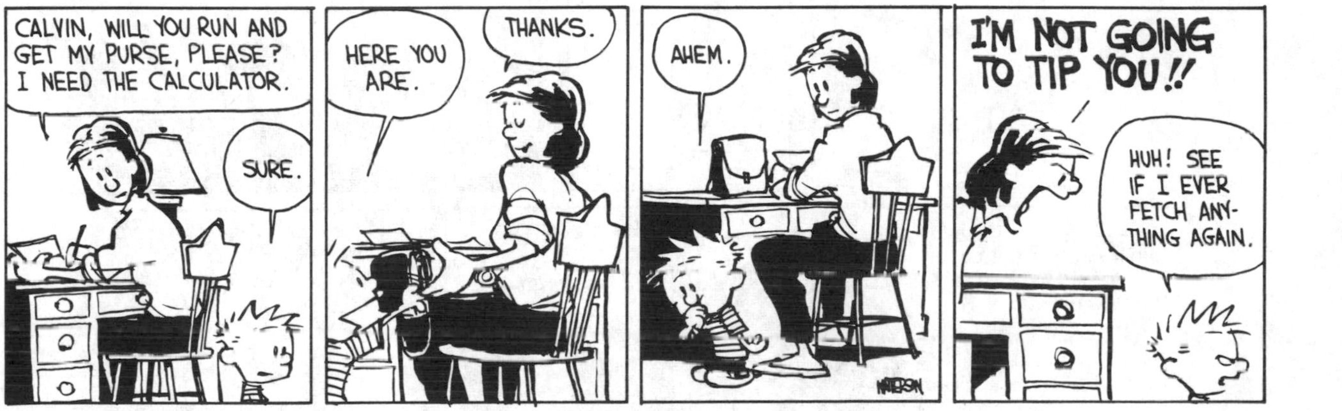
CALVIN, WILL YOU RUN AND GET MY PURSE, PLEASE? I NEED THE CALCULATOR.
SURE.
HERE YOU ARE.
THANKS.
AHEM.
I'M NOT GOING TO TIP YOU!!
HUH! SEE IF I EVER FETCH ANYTHING AGAIN.

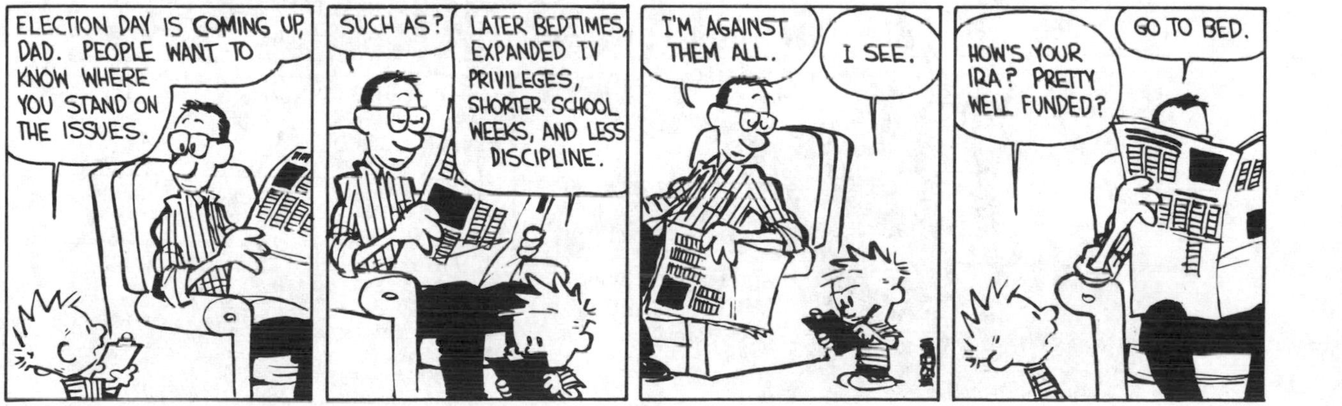
ELECTION DAY IS COMING UP, DAD. PEOPLE WANT TO KNOW WHERE YOU STAND ON THE ISSUES.
SUCH AS?
LATER BEDTIMES, EXPANDED TV PRIVILEGES, SHORTER SCHOOL WEEKS, AND LESS DISCIPLINE.
I'M AGAINST THEM ALL.
I SEE.
HOW'S YOUR IRA? PRETTY WELL FUNDED?
GO TO BED.

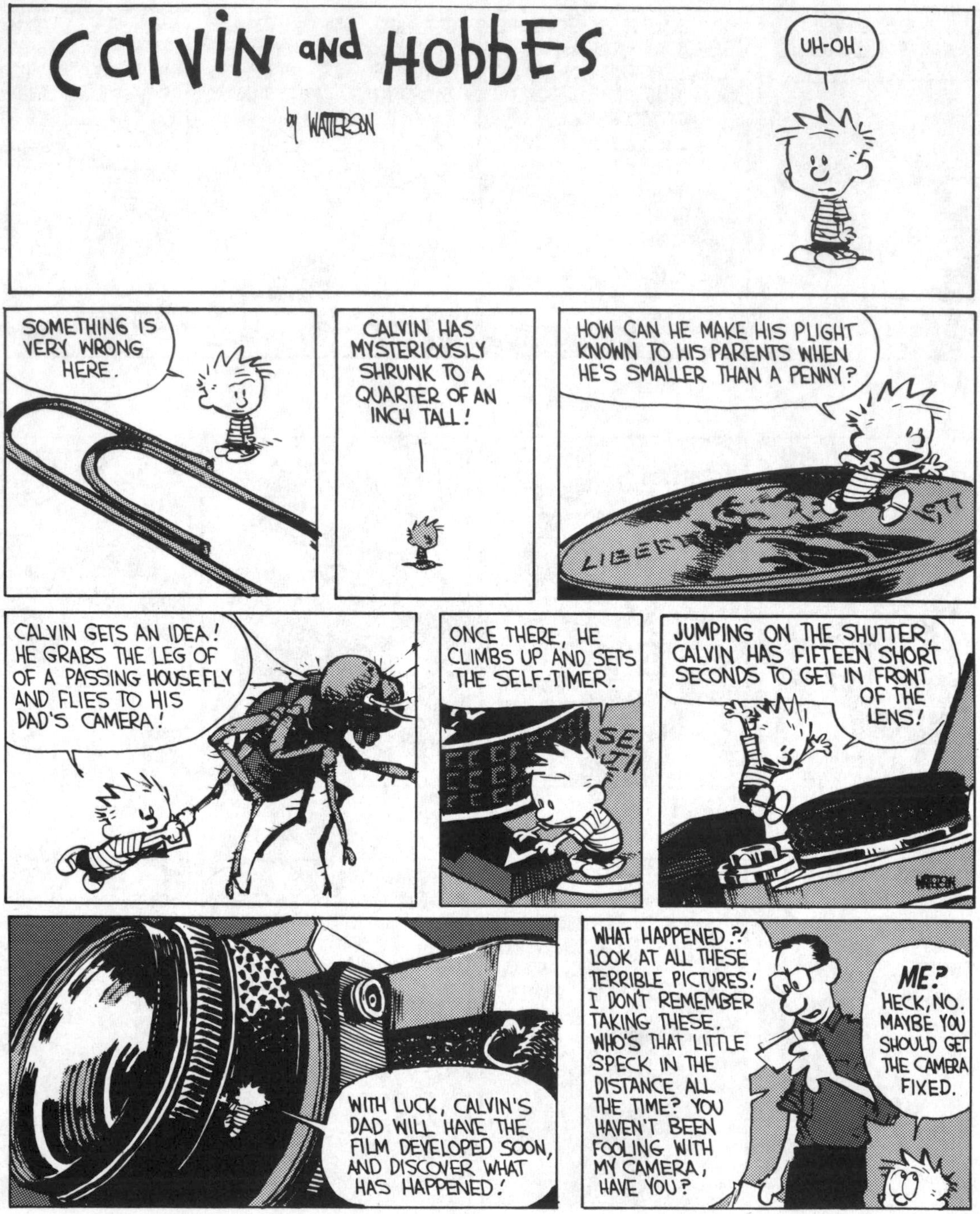
Calvin and HOBBES
by WATTERSON
UH-OH.
SOMETHING IS VERY WRONG HERE.
CALVIN HAS MYSTERIOUSLY SHRUNK TO A QUARTER OF AN INCH TALL!
HOW CAN HE MAKE HIS PLIGHT KNOWN TO HIS PARENTS WHEN HE'S SMALLER THAN A PENNY?
LIBERTY
CALVIN GETS AN IDEA! HE GRABS THE LEG OF OF A PASSING HOUSEFLY AND FLIES TO HIS DAD'S CAMERA!
ONCE THERE, HE CLIMBS UP AND SETS THE SELF-TIMER.
JUMPING ON THE SHUTTER, CALVIN HAS FIFTEEN SHORT SECONDS TO GET IN FRONT OF THE LENS!
WITH LUCK, CALVIN'S DAD WILL HAVE THE FILM DEVELOPED SOON, AND DISCOVER WHAT HAS HAPPENED!
WHAT HAPPENED?! LOOK AT ALL THESE TERRIBLE PICTURES! I DON'T REMEMBER TAKING THESE. WHO'S THAT LITTLE SPECK IN THE DISTANCE ALL THE TIME? YOU HAVEN'T BEEN FOOLING WITH MY CAMERA, HAVE YOU?
ME? HECK, NO. MAYBE YOU SHOULD GET THE CAMERA FIXED.

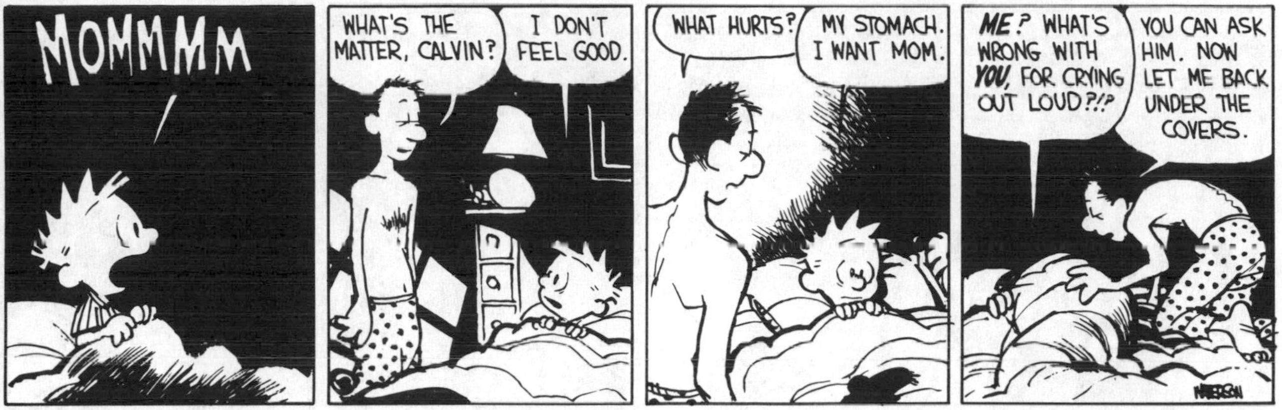
MOMMMM
WHAT'S THE MATTER, CALVIN?
I DON'T FEEL GOOD.
WHAT HURTS?
MY STOMACH. I WANT MOM.
ME? WHAT'S WRONG WITH YOU, FOR CRYING OUT LOUD?!?
YOU CAN ASK HIM. NOW LET ME BACK UNDER THE COVERS.
WATTERSON

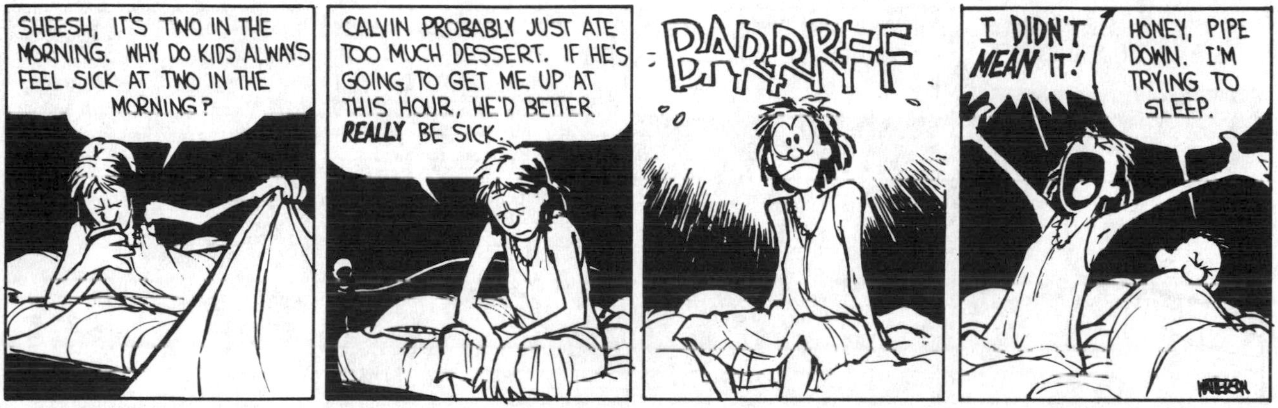
SHEESH, IT'S TWO IN THE MORNING. WHY DO KIDS ALWAYS FEEL SICK AT TWO IN THE MORNING?
CALVIN PROBABLY JUST ATE TOO MUCH DESSERT. IF HE'S GOING TO GET ME UP AT THIS HOUR, HE'D BETTER REALLY BE SICK.
BARRRFF
I DIDN'T MEAN IT!
HONEY, PIPE DOWN. I'M TRYING TO SLEEP.
WATTERSON

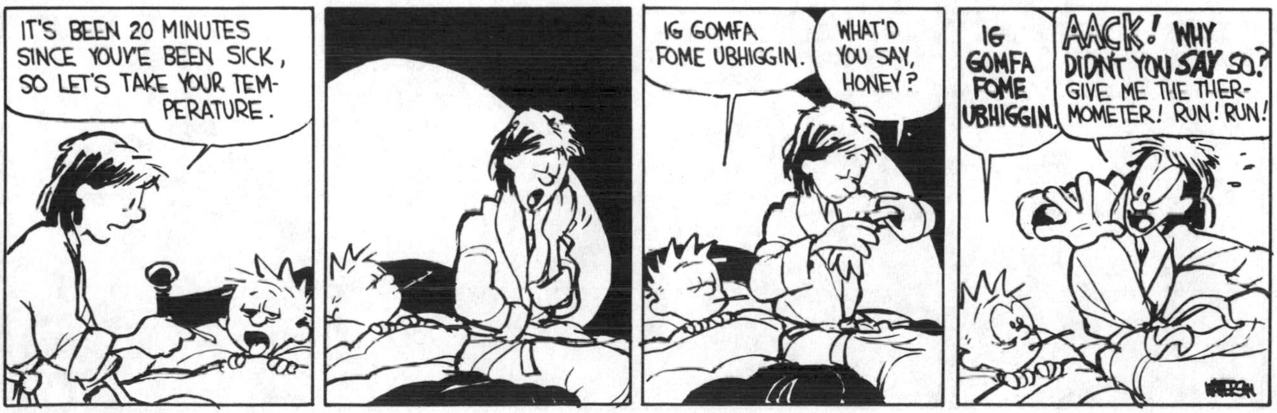
IT'S BEEN 20 MINUTES SINCE YOU'VE BEEN SICK, SO LET'S TAKE YOUR TEMPERATURE.
IG GOMFA FOME UBHIGGIN.
WHAT'D YOU SAY, HONEY?
IG GOMFA FOME UBHIGGIN.
AACK! WHY DIDN'T YOU SAY SO? GIVE ME THE THERMOMETER! RUN! RUN!
WATTERSON

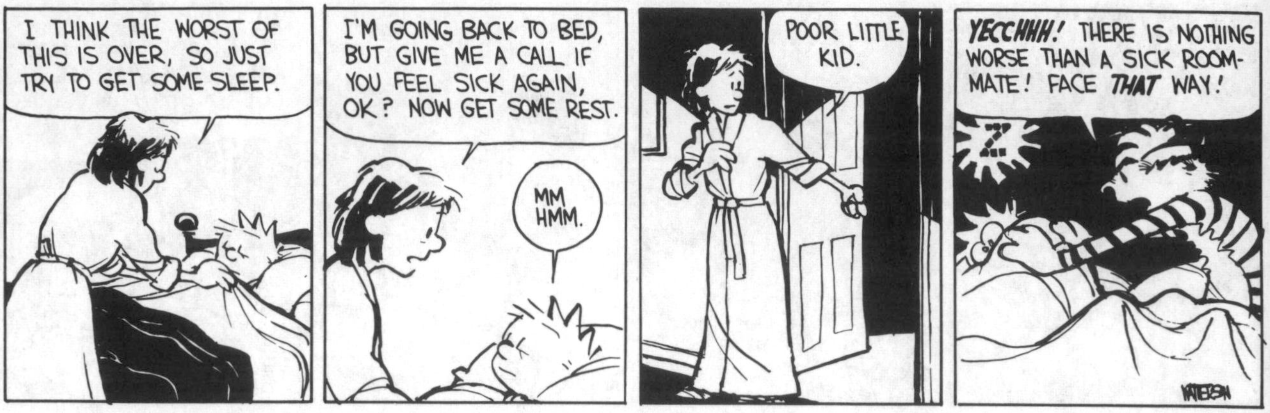
I THINK THE WORST OF THIS IS OVER, SO JUST TRY TO GET SOME SLEEP.
I'M GOING BACK TO BED, BUT GIVE ME A CALL IF YOU FEEL SICK AGAIN, OK? NOW GET SOME REST.
MM HMM.
POOR LITTLE KID.
YECCHHH! THERE IS NOTHING WORSE THAN A SICK ROOM-MATE! FACE THAT WAY!

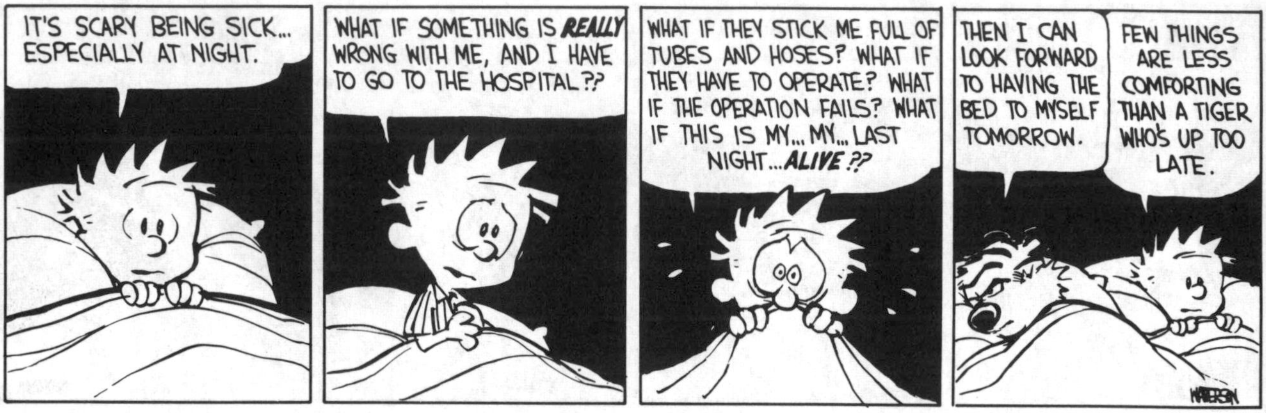
IT'S SCARY BEING SICK... ESPECIALLY AT NIGHT.
WHAT IF SOMETHING IS REALLY WRONG WITH ME, AND I HAVE TO GO TO THE HOSPITAL??
WHAT IF THEY STICK ME FULL OF TUBES AND HOSES? WHAT IF THEY HAVE TO OPERATE? WHAT IF THE OPERATION FAILS? WHAT IF THIS IS MY... MY... LAST NIGHT... ALIVE??
THEN I CAN LOOK FORWARD TO HAVING THE BED TO MYSELF TOMORROW.
FEW THINGS ARE LESS COMFORTING THAN A TIGER WHO'S UP TOO LATE.

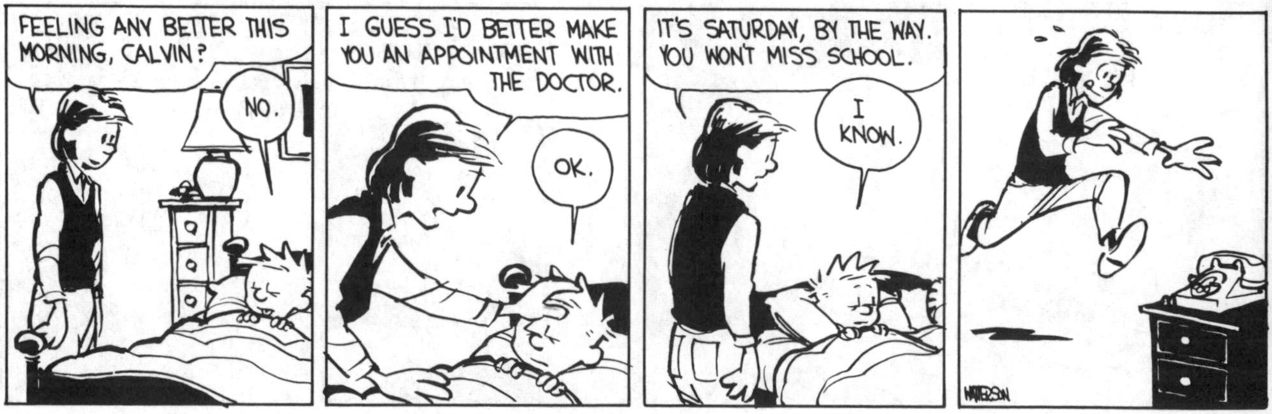
FEELING ANY BETTER THIS MORNING, CALVIN?
NO.
I GUESS I'D BETTER MAKE YOU AN APPOINTMENT WITH THE DOCTOR.
OK.
IT'S SATURDAY, BY THE WAY. YOU WON'T MISS SCHOOL.
I KNOW.

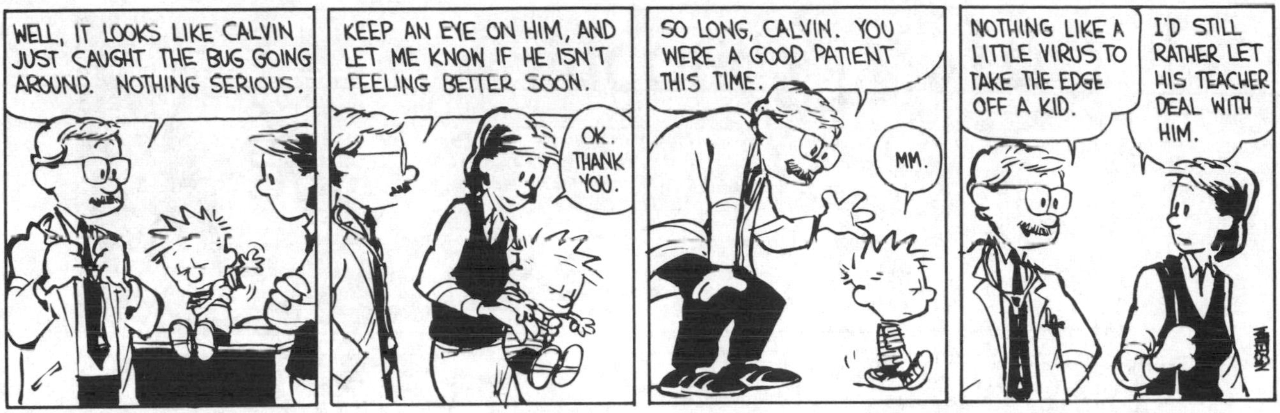
WELL, IT LOOKS LIKE CALVIN JUST CAUGHT THE BUG GOING AROUND. NOTHING SERIOUS.
KEEP AN EYE ON HIM, AND LET ME KNOW IF HE ISN'T FEELING BETTER SOON.
OK. THANK YOU.
SO LONG, CALVIN. YOU WERE A GOOD PATIENT THIS TIME.
MM.
NOTHING LIKE A LITTLE VIRUS TO TAKE THE EDGE OFF A KID.
I'D STILL RATHER LET HIS TEACHER DEAL WITH HIM.

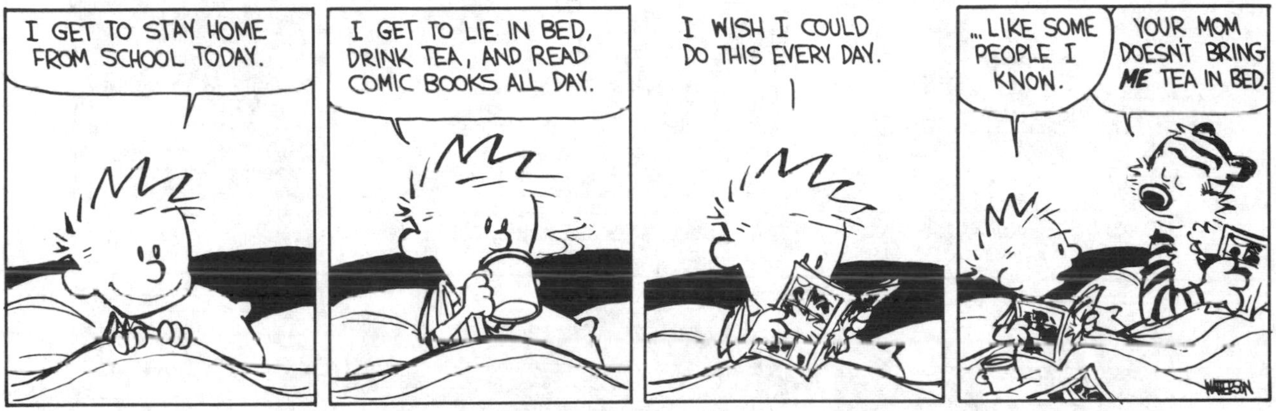
I GET TO STAY HOME FROM SCHOOL TODAY.
I GET TO LIE IN BED, DRINK TEA, AND READ COMIC BOOKS ALL DAY.
I WISH I COULD DO THIS EVERY DAY.
...LIKE SOME PEOPLE I KNOW.
YOUR MOM DOESN'T BRING *ME* TEA IN BED.

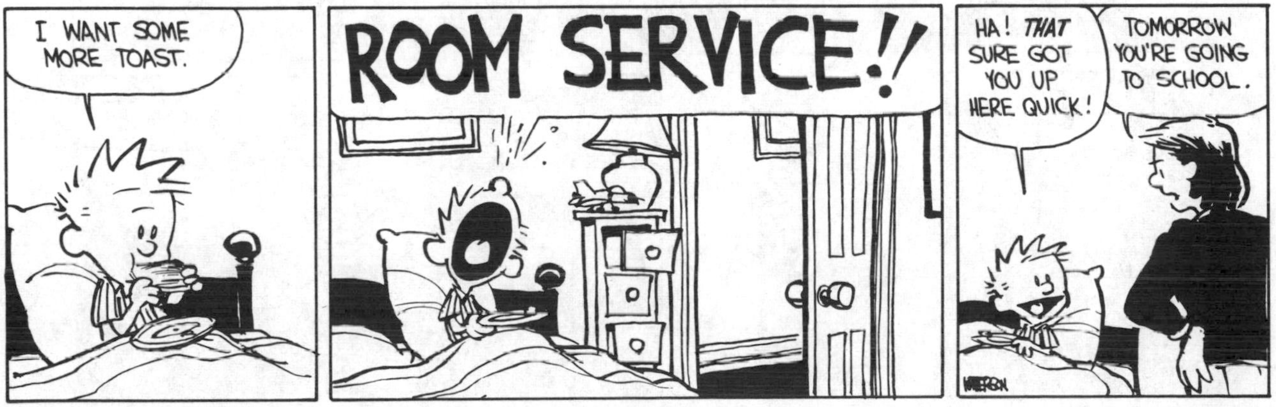
I WANT SOME MORE TOAST.
ROOM SERVICE!!
HA! *THAT* SURE GOT YOU UP HERE QUICK!
TOMORROW YOU'RE GOING TO SCHOOL.

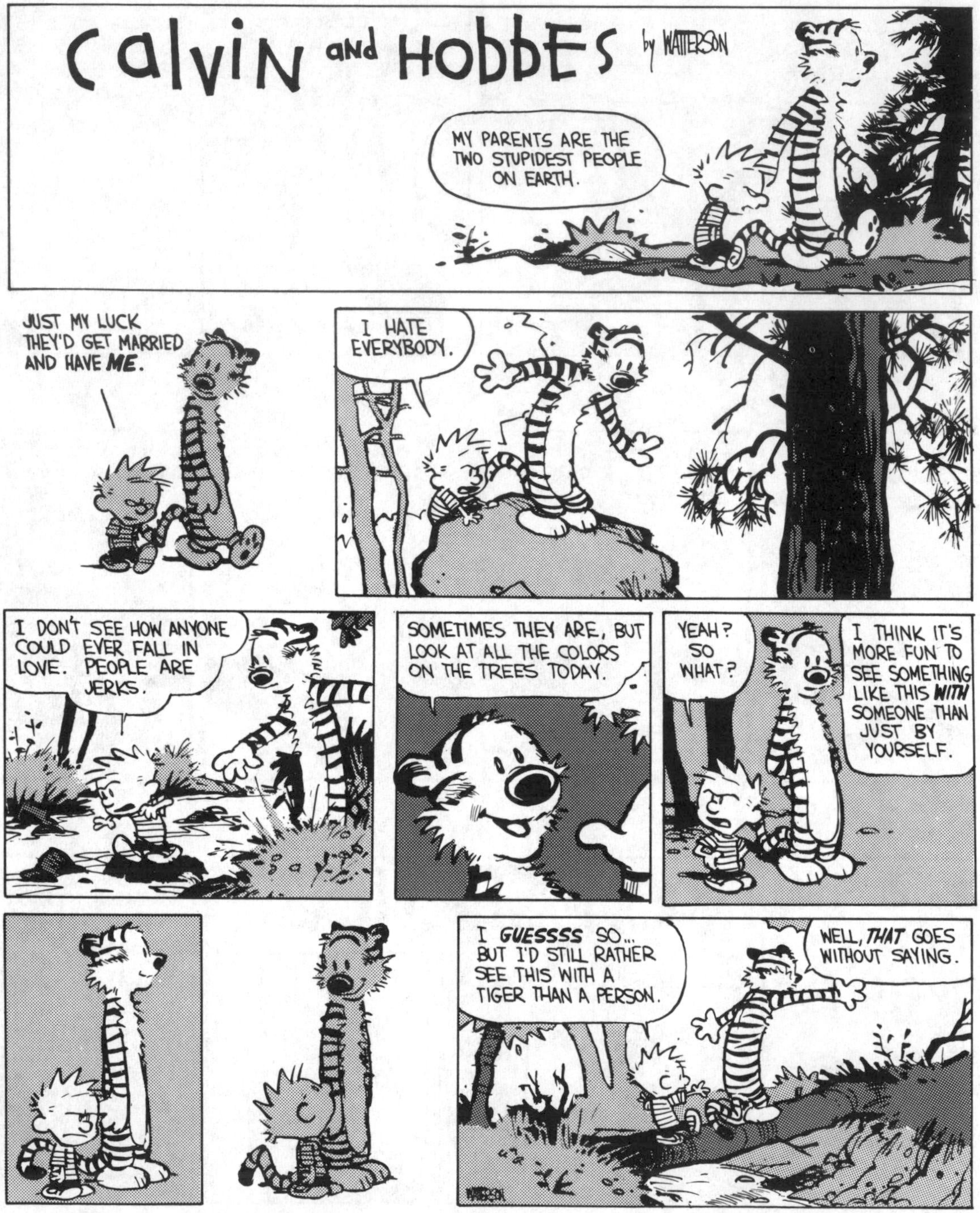
Calvin and HOBBES
by WATTERSON
MY PARENTS ARE THE TWO STUPIDEST PEOPLE ON EARTH.
JUST MY LUCK THEY'D GET MARRIED AND HAVE ME.
I HATE EVERYBODY.
I DON'T SEE HOW ANYONE COULD EVER FALL IN LOVE. PEOPLE ARE JERKS.
SOMETIMES THEY ARE, BUT LOOK AT ALL THE COLORS ON THE TREES TODAY.
YEAH? SO WHAT?
I THINK IT'S MORE FUN TO SEE SOMETHING LIKE THIS WITH SOMEONE THAN JUST BY YOURSELF.
I GUESSSS SO... BUT I'D STILL RATHER SEE THIS WITH A TIGER THAN A PERSON.
WELL, THAT GOES WITHOUT SAYING.

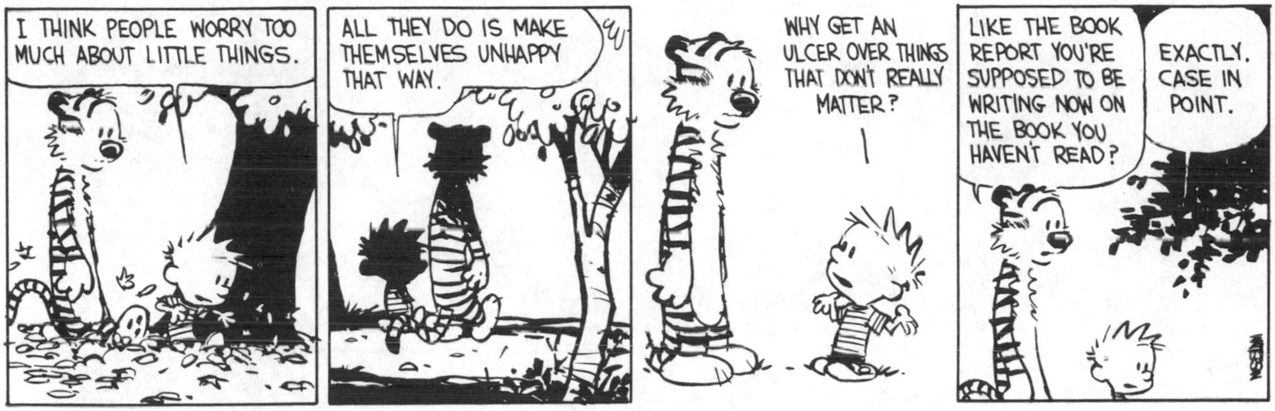
I THINK PEOPLE WORRY TOO MUCH ABOUT LITTLE THINGS.
ALL THEY DO IS MAKE THEMSELVES UNHAPPY THAT WAY.
WHY GET AN ULCER OVER THINGS THAT DON'T REALLY MATTER?
LIKE THE BOOK REPORT YOU'RE SUPPOSED TO BE WRITING NOW ON THE BOOK YOU HAVEN'T READ?
EXACTLY. CASE IN POINT.

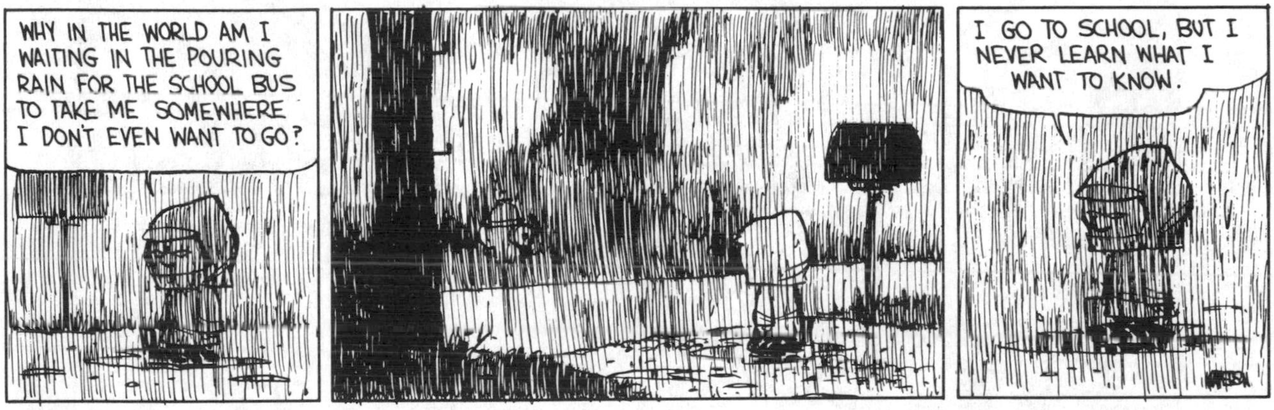
WHY IN THE WORLD AM I WAITING IN THE POURING RAIN FOR THE SCHOOL BUS TO TAKE ME SOMEWHERE I DON'T EVEN WANT TO GO?
I GO TO SCHOOL, BUT I NEVER LEARN WHAT I WANT TO KNOW.

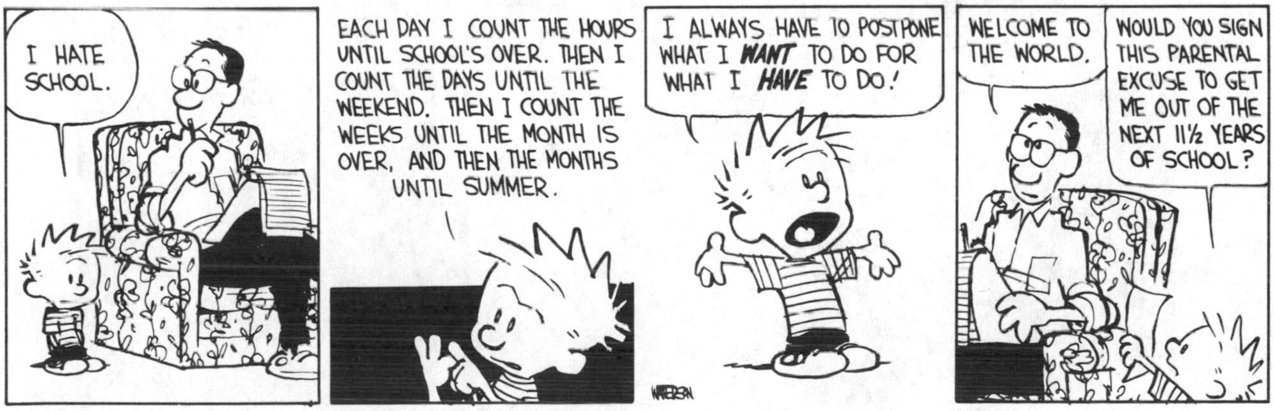
I HATE SCHOOL.
EACH DAY I COUNT THE HOURS UNTIL SCHOOL'S OVER. THEN I COUNT THE DAYS UNTIL THE WEEKEND. THEN I COUNT THE WEEKS UNTIL THE MONTH IS OVER, AND THEN THE MONTHS UNTIL SUMMER.
I ALWAYS HAVE TO POSTPONE WHAT I WANT TO DO FOR WHAT I HAVE TO DO!
WELCOME TO THE WORLD.
WOULD YOU SIGN THIS PARENTAL EXCUSE TO GET ME OUT OF THE NEXT 11½ YEARS OF SCHOOL?

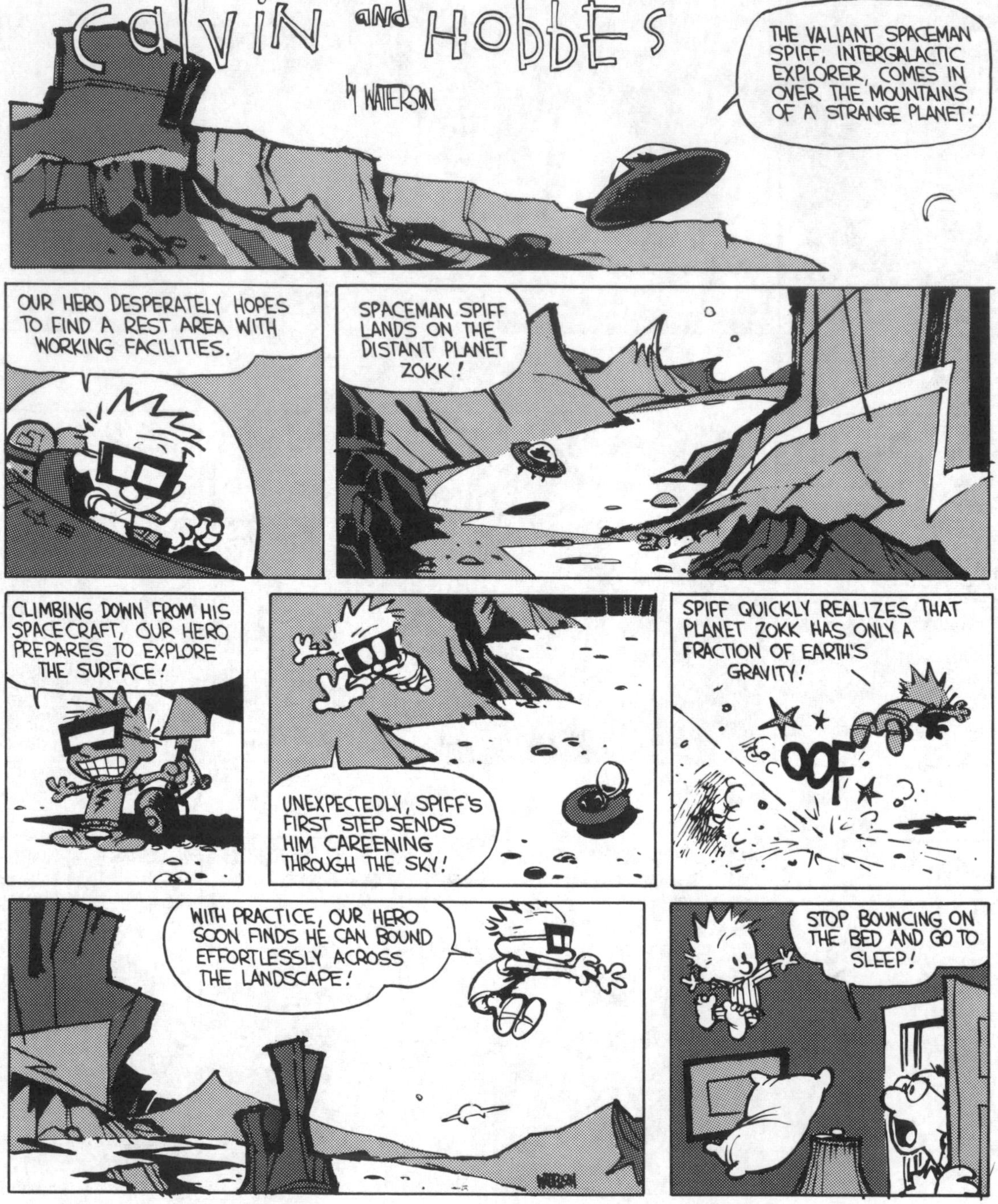
Calvin and HOBBES
by WATTERSON
THE VALIANT SPACEMAN SPIFF, INTERGALACTIC EXPLORER, COMES IN OVER THE MOUNTAINS OF A STRANGE PLANET!
OUR HERO DESPERATELY HOPES TO FIND A REST AREA WITH WORKING FACILITIES.
SPACEMAN SPIFF LANDS ON THE DISTANT PLANET ZOKK!
CLIMBING DOWN FROM HIS SPACECRAFT, OUR HERO PREPARES TO EXPLORE THE SURFACE!
UNEXPECTEDLY, SPIFF'S FIRST STEP SENDS HIM CAREENING THROUGH THE SKY!
SPIFF QUICKLY REALIZES THAT PLANET ZOKK HAS ONLY A FRACTION OF EARTH'S GRAVITY!
OOF
WITH PRACTICE, OUR HERO SOON FINDS HE CAN BOUND EFFORTLESSLY ACROSS THE LANDSCAPE!
STOP BOUNCING ON THE BED AND GO TO SLEEP!

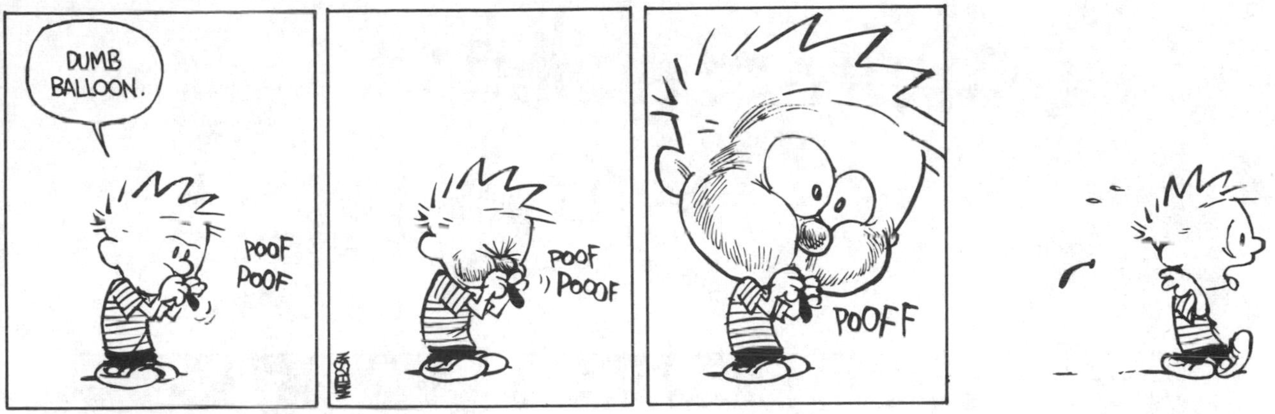
DUMB BALLOON.
POOF POOF
POOF POOOF
POOFF
WATTERSON

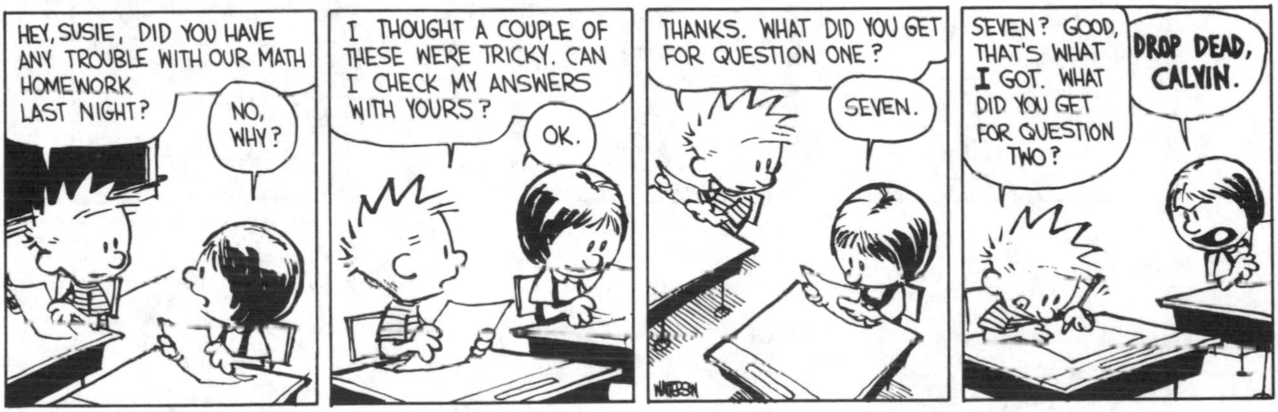
HEY, SUSIE, DID YOU HAVE ANY TROUBLE WITH OUR MATH HOMEWORK LAST NIGHT?
NO, WHY?
I THOUGHT A COUPLE OF THESE WERE TRICKY. CAN I CHECK MY ANSWERS WITH YOURS?
OK.
THANKS. WHAT DID YOU GET FOR QUESTION ONE?
SEVEN.
SEVEN? GOOD, THAT'S WHAT I GOT. WHAT DID YOU GET FOR QUESTION TWO?
DROP DEAD, CALVIN.
WATTERSON

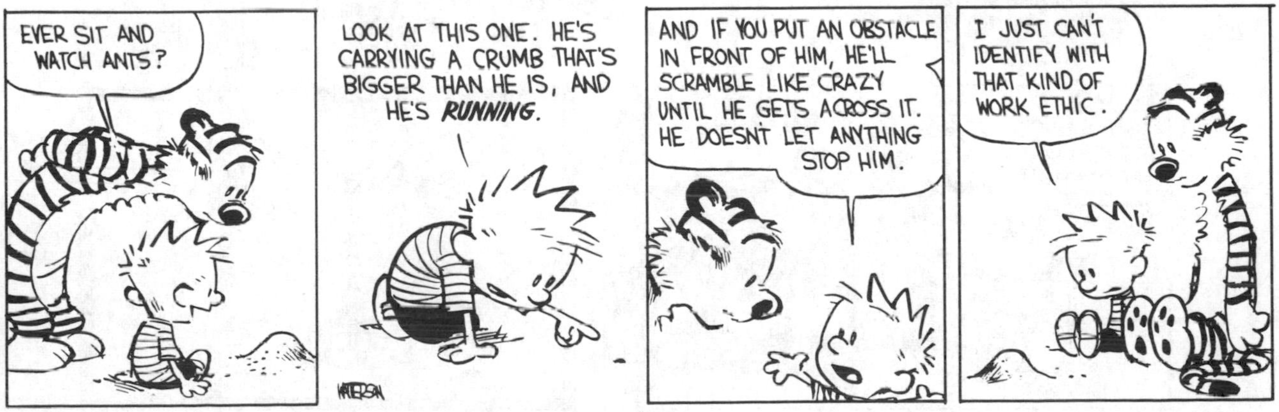
EVER SIT AND WATCH ANTS?
LOOK AT THIS ONE. HE'S CARRYING A CRUMB THAT'S BIGGER THAN HE IS, AND HE'S RUNNING.
AND IF YOU PUT AN OBSTACLE IN FRONT OF HIM, HE'LL SCRAMBLE LIKE CRAZY UNTIL HE GETS ACROSS IT. HE DOESN'T LET ANYTHING STOP HIM.
I JUST CAN'T IDENTIFY WITH THAT KIND OF WORK ETHIC.
WATTERSON

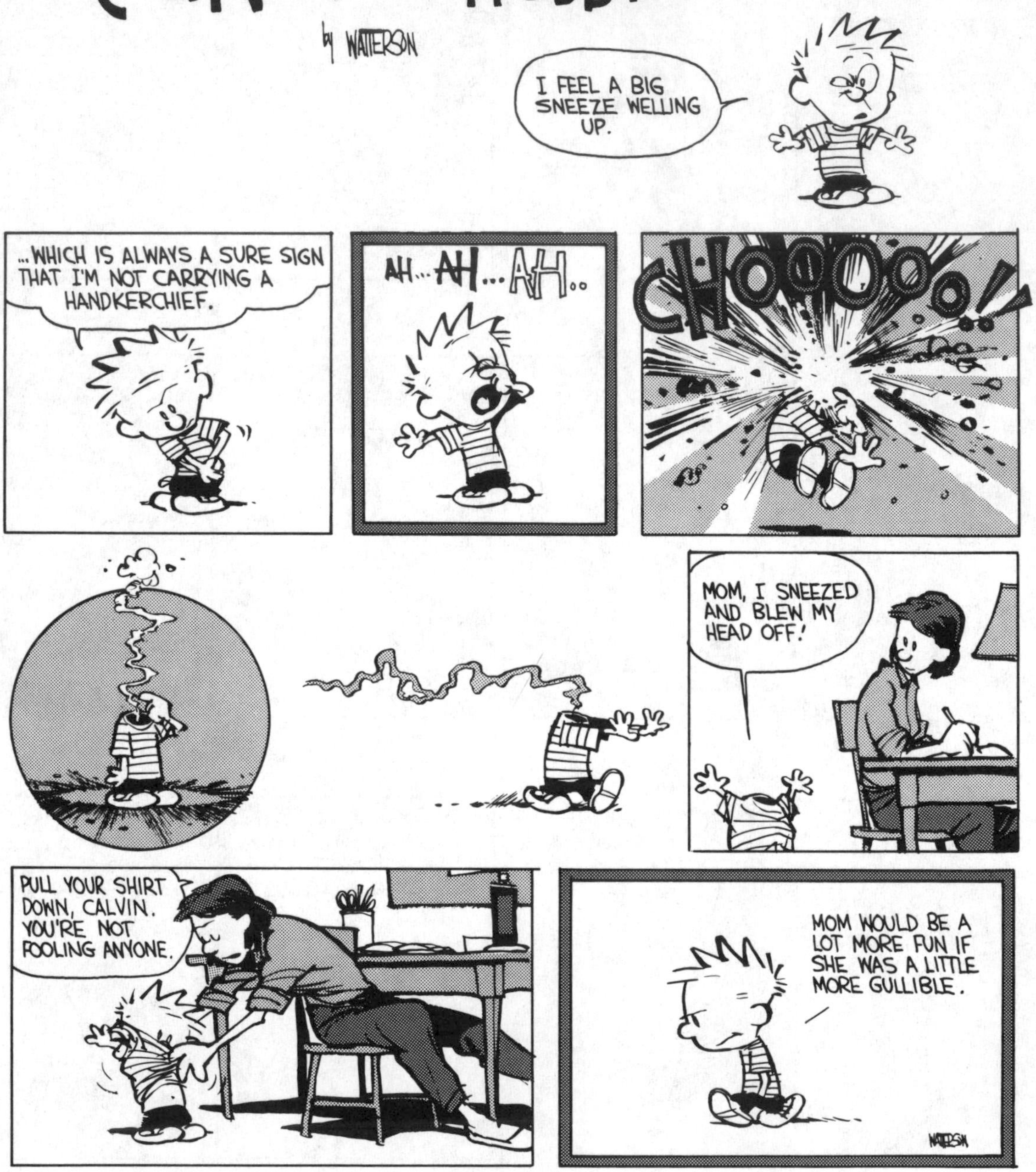
Calvin and HOBBES
by WATTERSON
I FEEL A BIG SNEEZE WELLING UP.
...WHICH IS ALWAYS A SURE SIGN THAT I'M NOT CARRYING A HANDKERCHIEF.
AH... AH... AH..
CHOOOOO!!
MOM, I SNEEZED AND BLEW MY HEAD OFF!
PULL YOUR SHIRT DOWN, CALVIN. YOU'RE NOT FOOLING ANYONE.
MOM WOULD BE A LOT MORE FUN IF SHE WAS A LITTLE MORE GULLIBLE.
WATTERSON

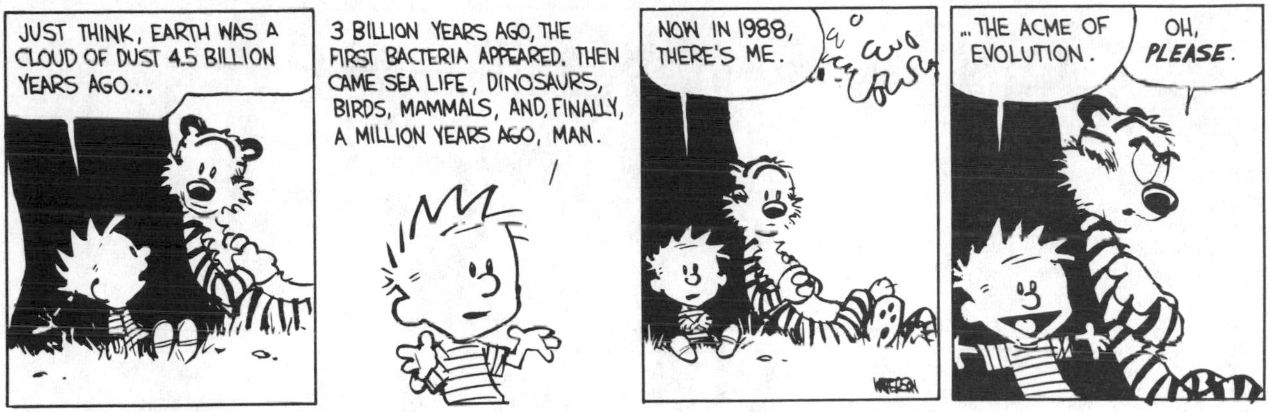
JUST THINK, EARTH WAS A CLOUD OF DUST 4.5 BILLION YEARS AGO...
3 BILLION YEARS AGO, THE FIRST BACTERIA APPEARED. THEN CAME SEA LIFE, DINOSAURS, BIRDS, MAMMALS, AND, FINALLY, A MILLION YEARS AGO, MAN.
NOW IN 1988, THERE'S ME.
...THE ACME OF EVOLUTION.
OH, PLEASE.

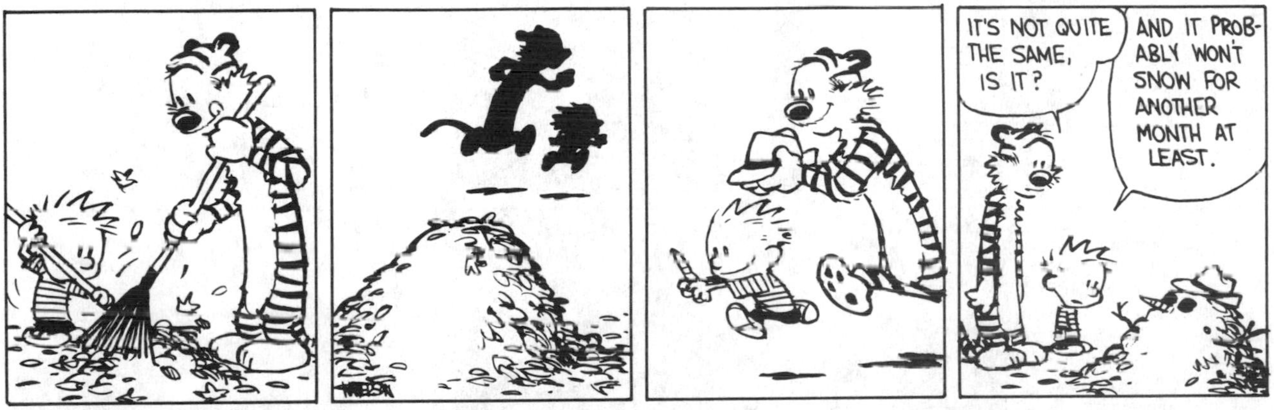
IT'S NOT QUITE THE SAME, IS IT?
AND IT PROBABLY WON'T SNOW FOR ANOTHER MONTH AT LEAST.

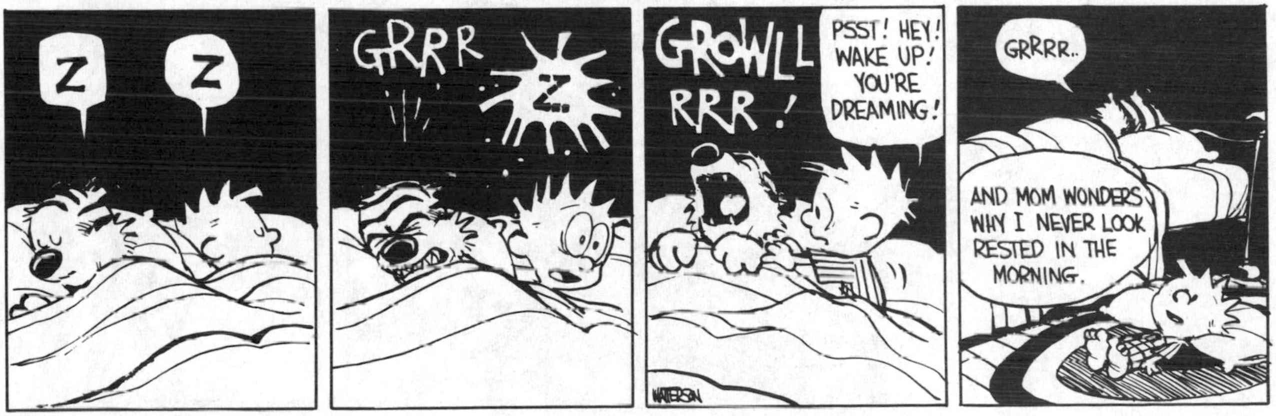
Z
Z
GRRR
Z
GROWLL RRR!
PSST! HEY! WAKE UP! YOU'RE DREAMING!
GRRRR..
AND MOM WONDERS WHY I NEVER LOOK RESTED IN THE MORNING.

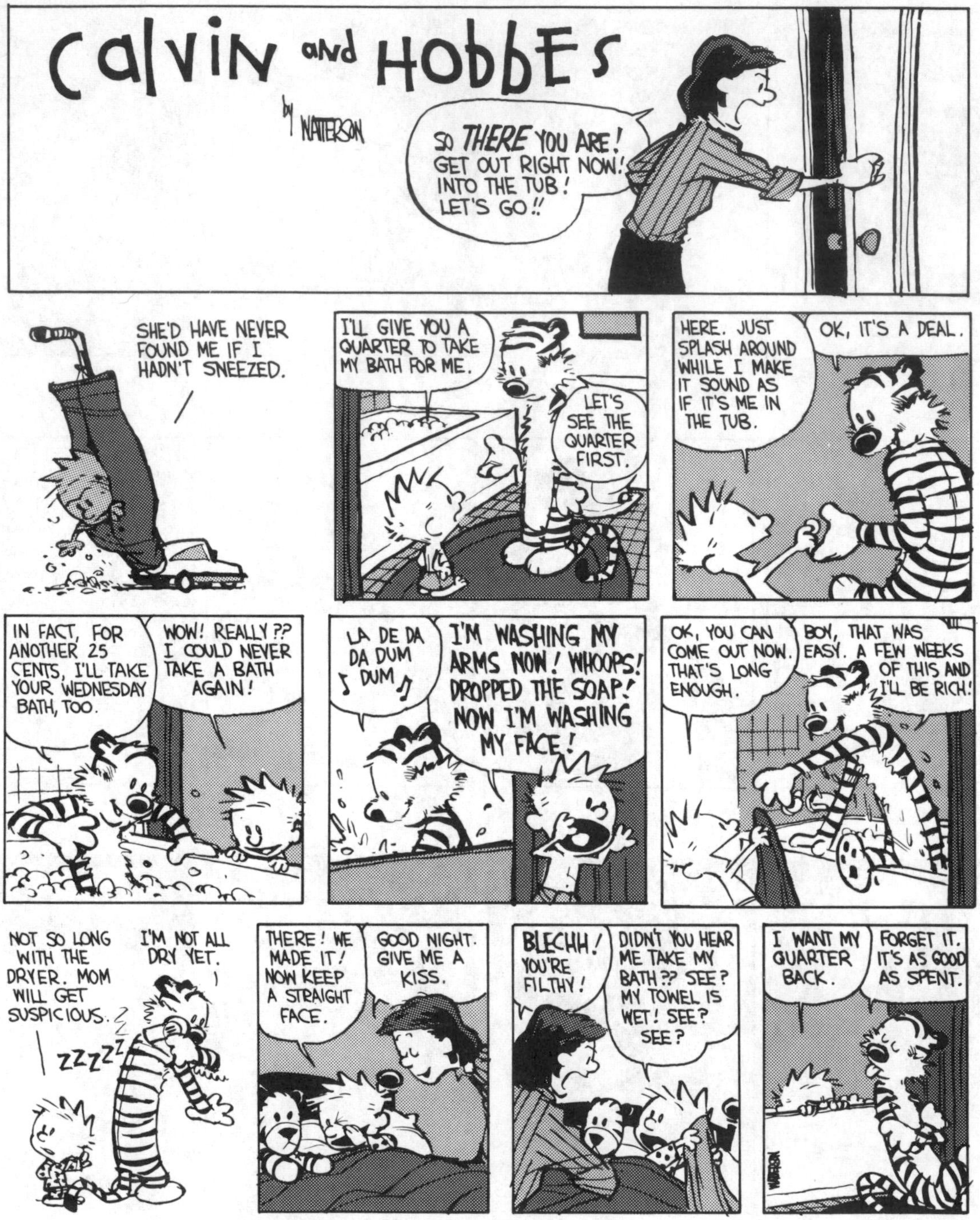
Calvin and HOBBES
by WATTERSON
SO THERE YOU ARE! GET OUT RIGHT NOW! INTO THE TUB! LET'S GO!!
SHE'D HAVE NEVER FOUND ME IF I HADN'T SNEEZED.
I'LL GIVE YOU A QUARTER TO TAKE MY BATH FOR ME.
LET'S SEE THE QUARTER FIRST.
HERE. JUST SPLASH AROUND WHILE I MAKE IT SOUND AS IF IT'S ME IN THE TUB.
OK, IT'S A DEAL.
IN FACT, FOR ANOTHER 25 CENTS, I'LL TAKE YOUR WEDNESDAY BATH, TOO.
WOW! REALLY?? I COULD NEVER TAKE A BATH AGAIN!
LA DE DA DA DUM DUM
I'M WASHING MY ARMS NOW! WHOOPS! DROPPED THE SOAP! NOW I'M WASHING MY FACE!
OK, YOU CAN COME OUT NOW. THAT'S LONG ENOUGH.
BOY, THAT WAS EASY. A FEW WEEKS OF THIS AND I'LL BE RICH!
NOT SO LONG WITH THE DRYER. MOM WILL GET SUSPICIOUS.
I'M NOT ALL DRY YET.
ZZZZZ
THERE! WE MADE IT! NOW KEEP A STRAIGHT FACE.
GOOD NIGHT. GIVE ME A KISS.
BLECHH! YOU'RE FILTHY!
DIDN'T YOU HEAR ME TAKE MY BATH?? SEE? MY TOWEL IS WET! SEE? SEE?
I WANT MY QUARTER BACK.
FORGET IT. IT'S AS GOOD AS SPENT.
WATTERSON

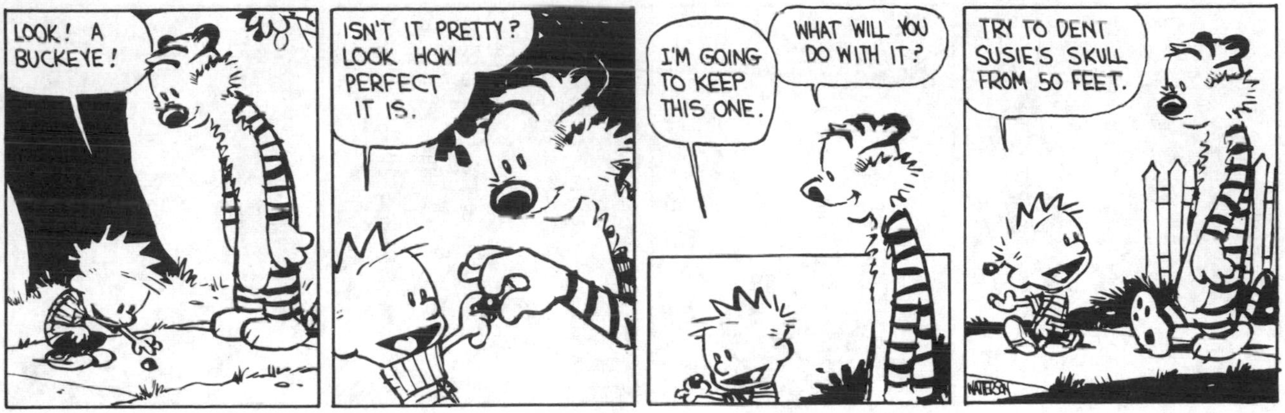
LOOK! A BUCKEYE!
ISN'T IT PRETTY? LOOK HOW PERFECT IT IS.
WHAT WILL YOU DO WITH IT?
I'M GOING TO KEEP THIS ONE.
TRY TO DENT SUSIE'S SKULL FROM 50 FEET.
WATTERSON

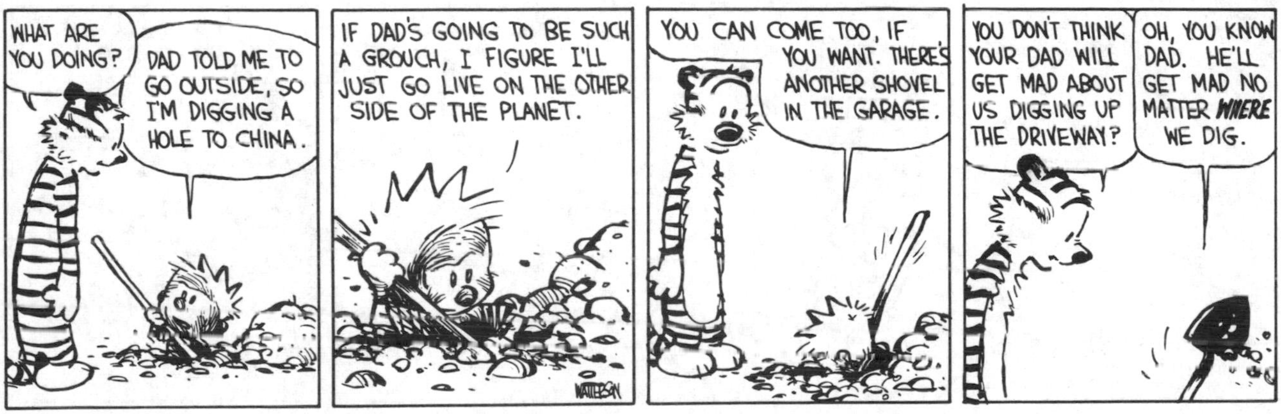
WHAT ARE YOU DOING?
DAD TOLD ME TO GO OUTSIDE, SO I'M DIGGING A HOLE TO CHINA.
IF DAD'S GOING TO BE SUCH A GROUCH, I FIGURE I'LL JUST GO LIVE ON THE OTHER SIDE OF THE PLANET.
WATTERSON
YOU CAN COME TOO, IF YOU WANT. THERE'S ANOTHER SHOVEL IN THE GARAGE.
YOU DON'T THINK YOUR DAD WILL GET MAD ABOUT US DIGGING UP THE DRIVEWAY?
OH, YOU KNOW DAD. HE'LL GET MAD NO MATTER WHERE WE DIG.

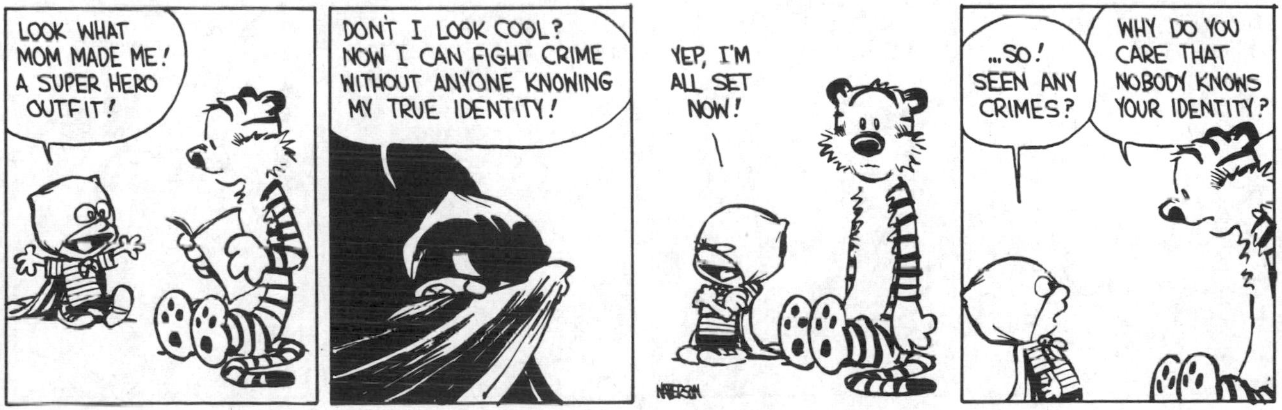
LOOK WHAT MOM MADE ME! A SUPER HERO OUTFIT!
DON'T I LOOK COOL? NOW I CAN FIGHT CRIME WITHOUT ANYONE KNOWING MY TRUE IDENTITY!
YEP, I'M ALL SET NOW!
WATTERSON
...SO! SEEN ANY CRIMES?
WHY DO YOU CARE THAT NOBODY KNOWS YOUR IDENTITY?

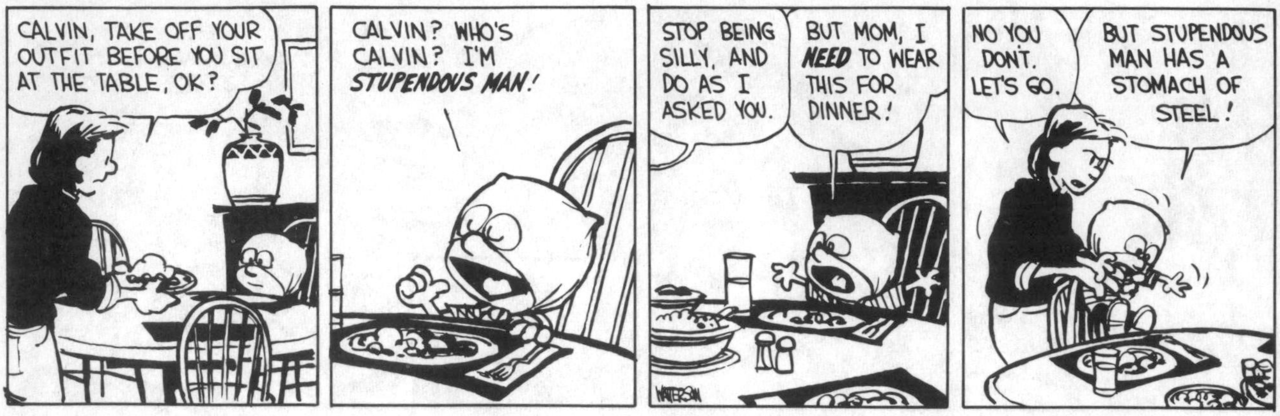
CALVIN, TAKE OFF YOUR OUTFIT BEFORE YOU SIT AT THE TABLE, OK?
CALVIN? WHO'S CALVIN? I'M *STUPENDOUS MAN*!
STOP BEING SILLY, AND DO AS I ASKED YOU.
BUT MOM, I *NEED* TO WEAR THIS FOR DINNER!
NO YOU DON'T. LET'S GO.
BUT STUPENDOUS MAN HAS A STOMACH OF STEEL!
WATERSON

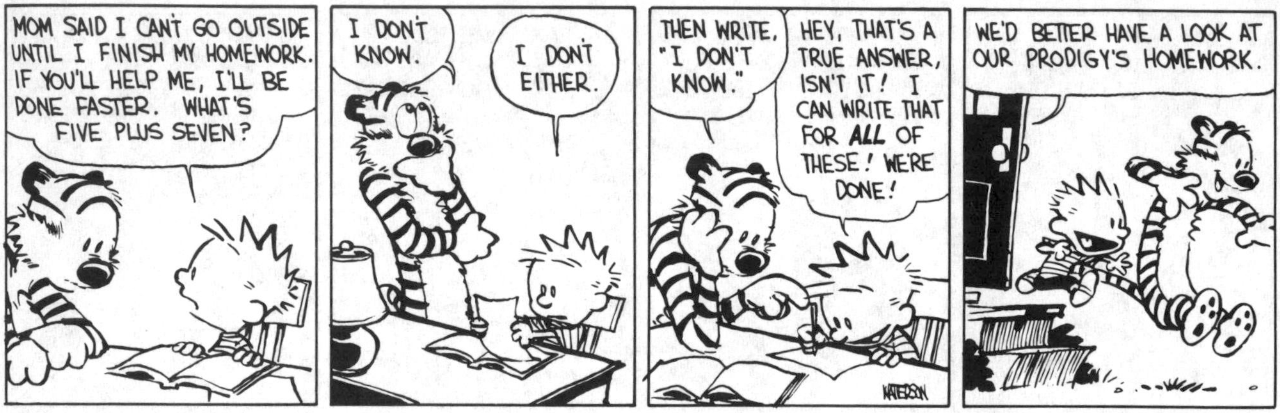
MOM SAID I CAN'T GO OUTSIDE UNTIL I FINISH MY HOMEWORK. IF YOU'LL HELP ME, I'LL BE DONE FASTER. WHAT'S FIVE PLUS SEVEN?
I DON'T KNOW.
I DON'T EITHER.
THEN WRITE, "I DON'T KNOW."
HEY, THAT'S A TRUE ANSWER, ISN'T IT! I CAN WRITE THAT FOR *ALL* OF THESE! WE'RE DONE!
WATERSON
WE'D BETTER HAVE A LOOK AT OUR PRODIGY'S HOMEWORK.

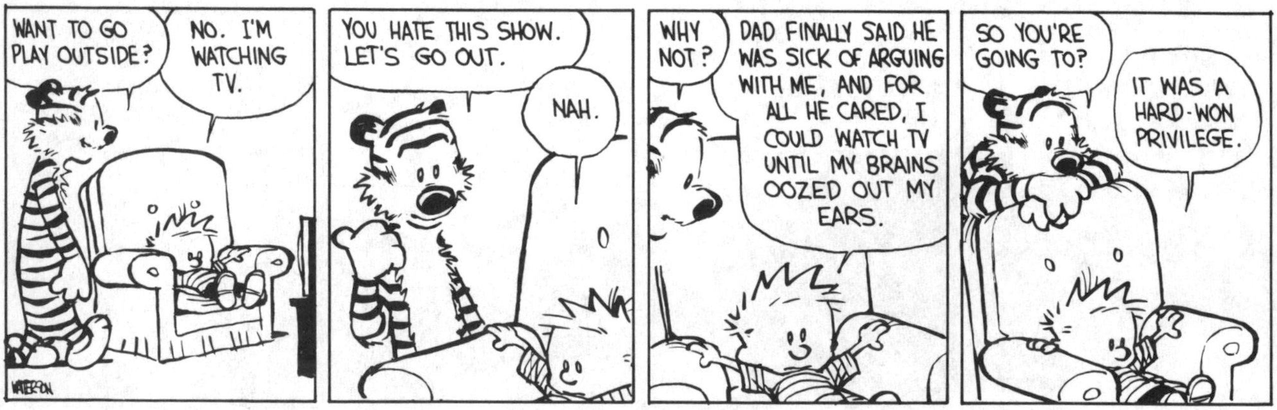
WANT TO GO PLAY OUTSIDE?
NO. I'M WATCHING TV.
WATERSON
YOU HATE THIS SHOW. LET'S GO OUT.
NAH.
WHY NOT?
DAD FINALLY SAID HE WAS SICK OF ARGUING WITH ME, AND FOR ALL HE CARED, I COULD WATCH TV UNTIL MY BRAINS OOZED OUT MY EARS.
SO YOU'RE GOING TO?
IT WAS A HARD-WON PRIVILEGE.

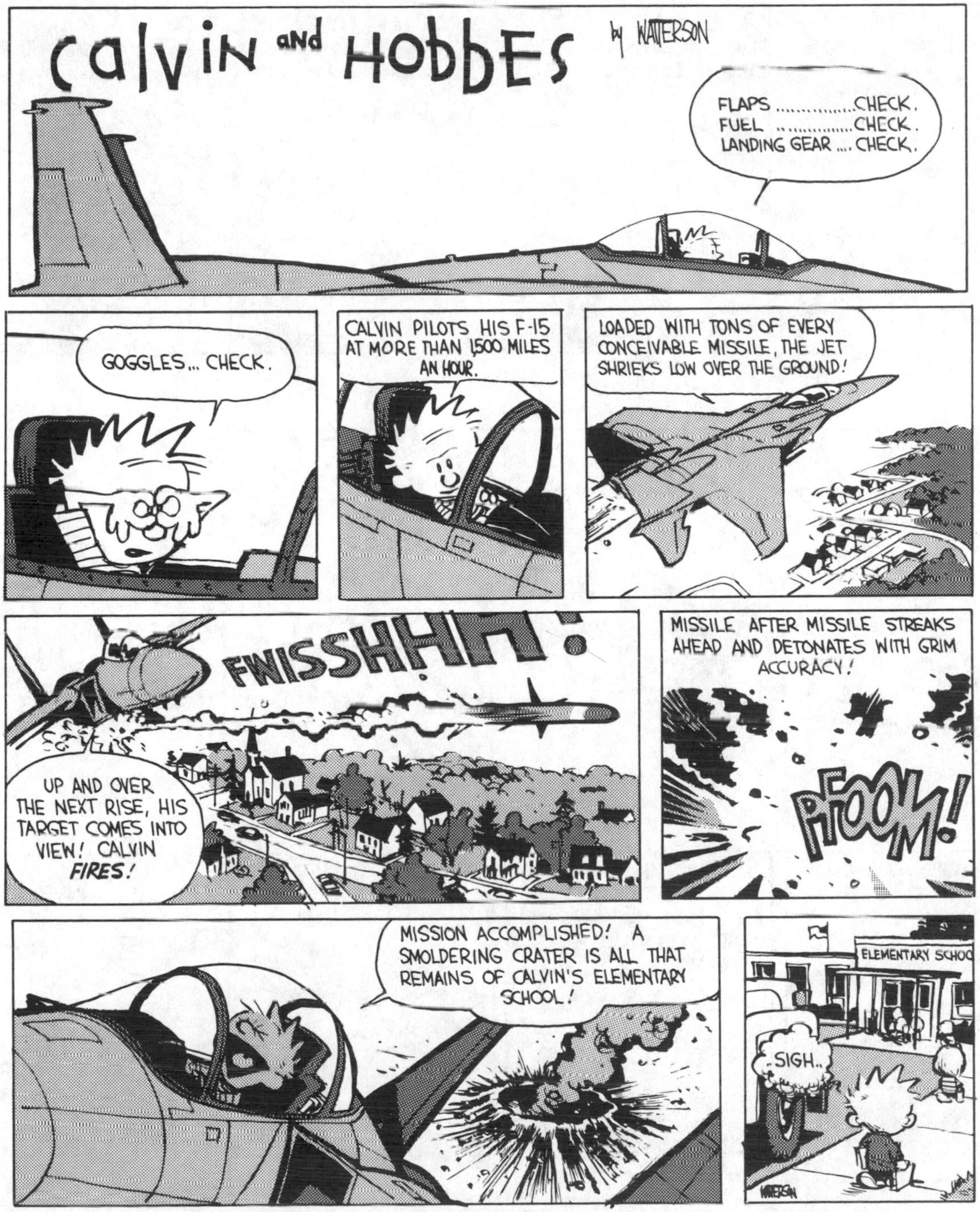
Calvin and HOBBES
by WATTERSON
FLAPS .... CHECK. FUEL .... CHECK. LANDING GEAR .... CHECK.
GOGGLES... CHECK.
CALVIN PILOTS HIS F-15 AT MORE THAN 1,500 MILES AN HOUR.
LOADED WITH TONS OF EVERY CONCEIVABLE MISSILE, THE JET SHRIEKS LOW OVER THE GROUND!
FWISSHHH!
UP AND OVER THE NEXT RISE, HIS TARGET COMES INTO VIEW! CALVIN FIRES!
MISSILE AFTER MISSILE STREAKS AHEAD AND DETONATES WITH GRIM ACCURACY!
PFOOM!
MISSION ACCOMPLISHED! A SMOLDERING CRATER IS ALL THAT REMAINS OF CALVIN'S ELEMENTARY SCHOOL!
ELEMENTARY SCHOO
SIGH..
WATTERSON

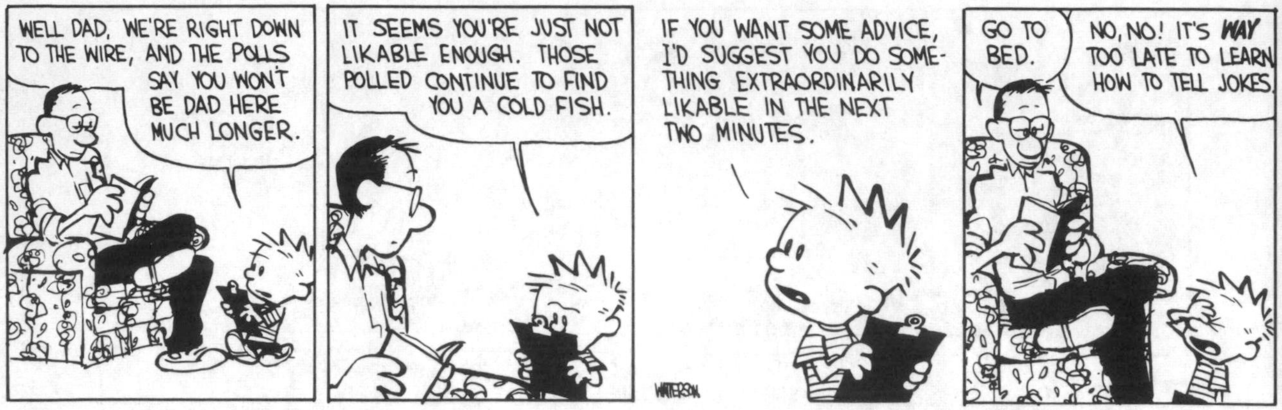
WELL DAD, WE'RE RIGHT DOWN TO THE WIRE, AND THE POLLS SAY YOU WON'T BE DAD HERE MUCH LONGER.
IT SEEMS YOU'RE JUST NOT LIKABLE ENOUGH. THOSE POLLED CONTINUE TO FIND YOU A COLD FISH.
IF YOU WANT SOME ADVICE, I'D SUGGEST YOU DO SOMETHING EXTRAORDINARILY LIKABLE IN THE NEXT TWO MINUTES.
GO TO BED.
NO, NO! IT'S WAY TOO LATE TO LEARN HOW TO TELL JOKES.

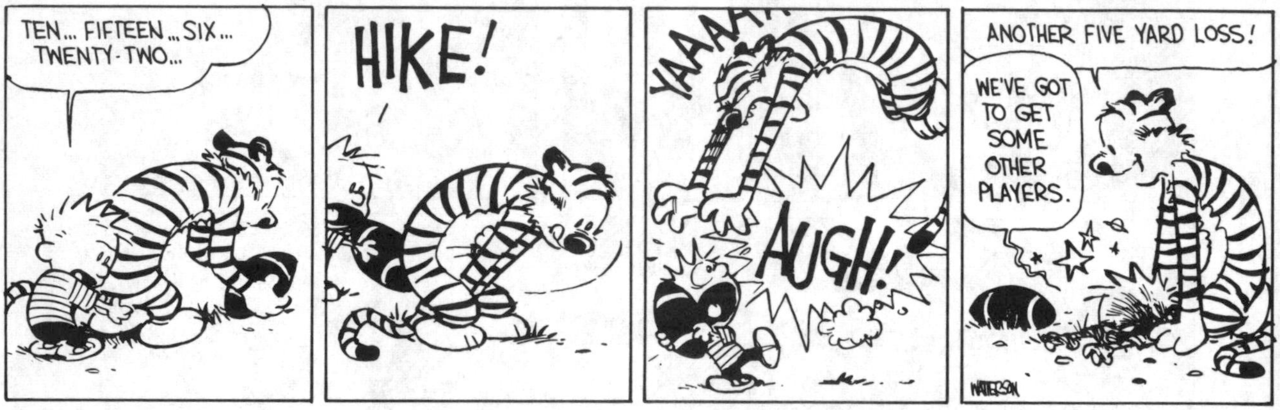
TEN... FIFTEEN... SIX... TWENTY-TWO...
HIKE!
YAAAAA
AUGH!
ANOTHER FIVE YARD LOSS!
WE'VE GOT TO GET SOME OTHER PLAYERS.

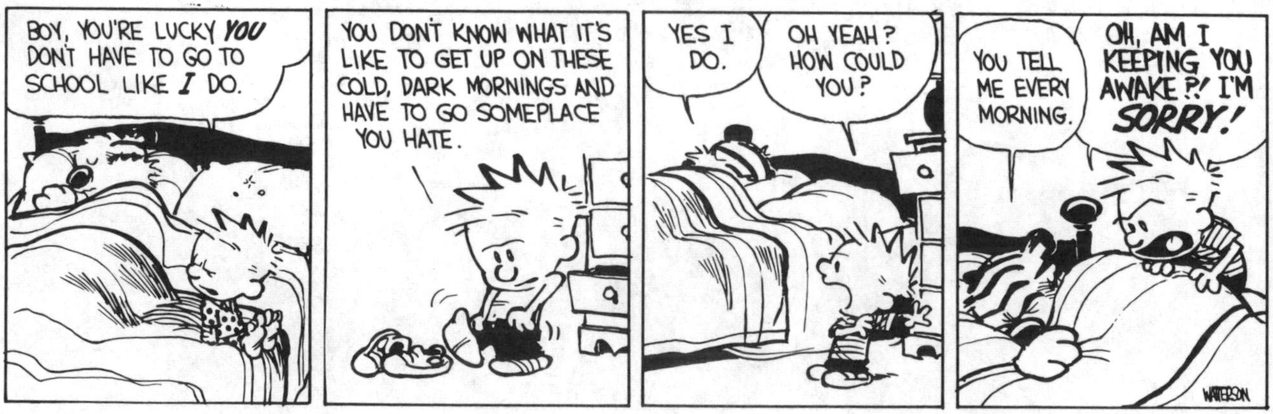
BOY, YOU'RE LUCKY YOU DON'T HAVE TO GO TO SCHOOL LIKE I DO.
YOU DON'T KNOW WHAT IT'S LIKE TO GET UP ON THESE COLD, DARK MORNINGS AND HAVE TO GO SOMEPLACE YOU HATE.
YES I DO.
OH YEAH? HOW COULD YOU?
YOU TELL ME EVERY MORNING.
OH, AM I KEEPING YOU AWAKE?! I'M SORRY!

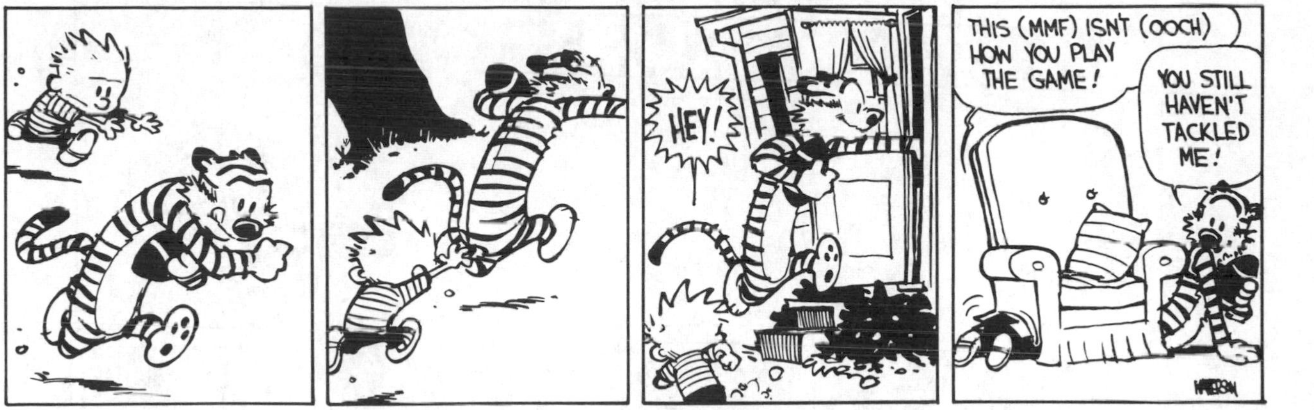
HEY!
THIS (MMF) ISN'T (OOCH) HOW YOU PLAY THE GAME!
YOU STILL HAVEN'T TACKLED ME!

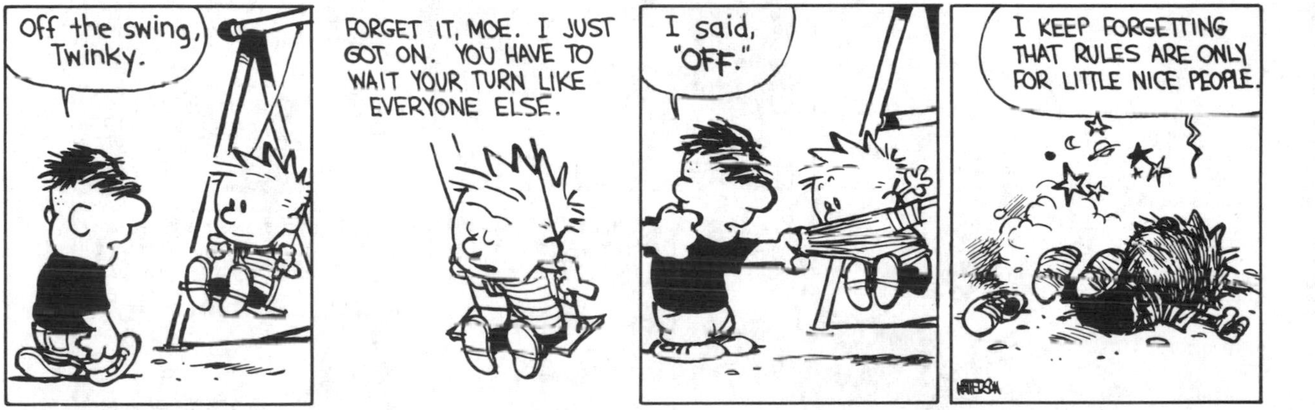
Off the swing, Twinky.
FORGET IT, MOE. I JUST GOT ON. YOU HAVE TO WAIT YOUR TURN LIKE EVERYONE ELSE.
I said, "OFF."
I KEEP FORGETTING THAT RULES ARE ONLY FOR LITTLE NICE PEOPLE.

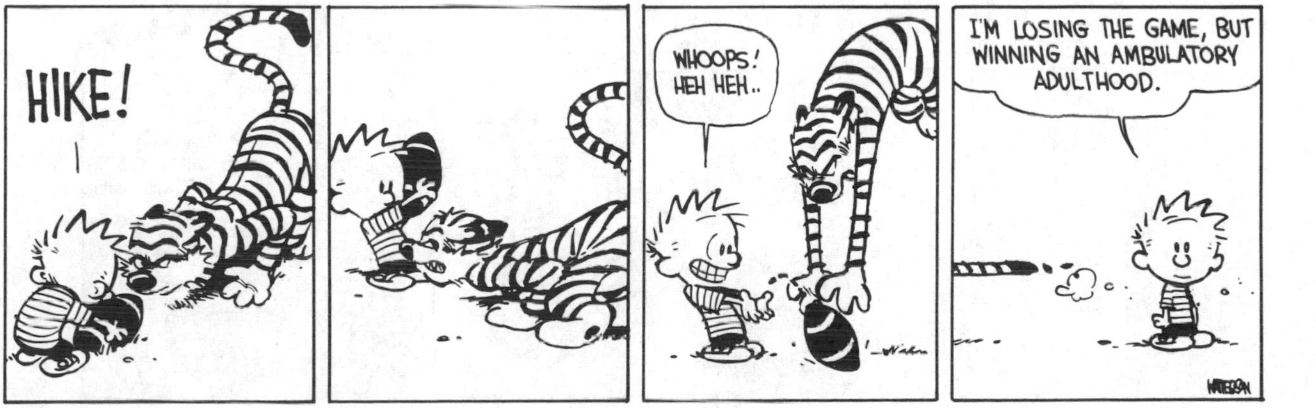
HIKE!
WHOOPS! HEH HEH..
I'M LOSING THE GAME, BUT WINNING AN AMBULATORY ADULTHOOD.

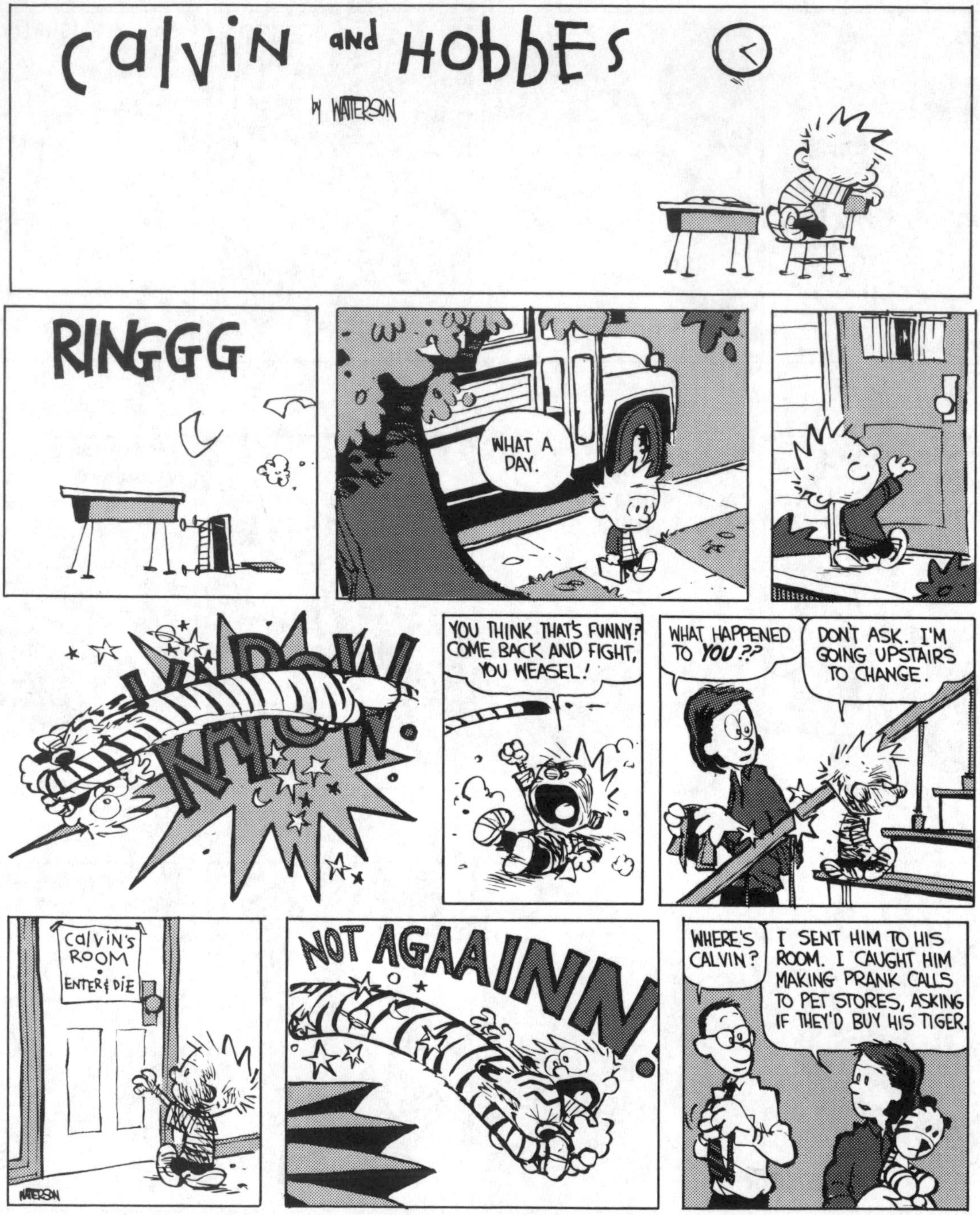
Calvin and HOBBES
by WATTERSON
RINGGG
WHAT A DAY.
KAPOW
YOU THINK THAT'S FUNNY? COME BACK AND FIGHT, YOU WEASEL!
WHAT HAPPENED TO *YOU*??
DON'T ASK. I'M GOING UPSTAIRS TO CHANGE.
Calvin's ROOM • ENTER & DIE
WATTERSON
NOT AGAAINNN!
WHERE'S CALVIN?
I SENT HIM TO HIS ROOM. I CAUGHT HIM MAKING PRANK CALLS TO PET STORES, ASKING IF THEY'D BUY HIS TIGER.

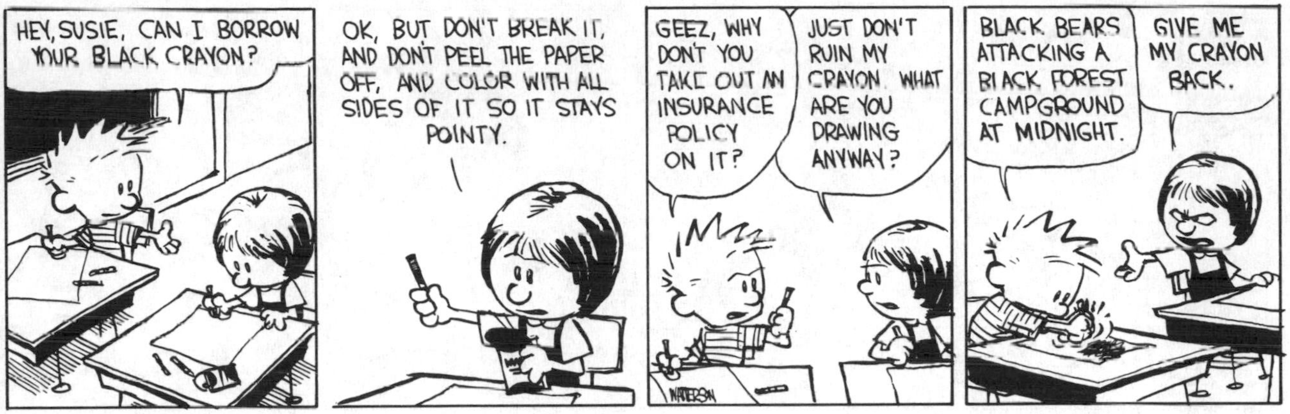
HEY, SUSIE, CAN I BORROW YOUR BLACK CRAYON?
OK, BUT DON'T BREAK IT, AND DON'T PEEL THE PAPER OFF, AND COLOR WITH ALL SIDES OF IT SO IT STAYS POINTY.
GEEZ, WHY DON'T YOU TAKE OUT AN INSURANCE POLICY ON IT?
JUST DON'T RUIN MY CRAYON. WHAT ARE YOU DRAWING ANYWAY?
BLACK BEARS ATTACKING A BLACK FOREST CAMPGROUND AT MIDNIGHT.
GIVE ME MY CRAYON BACK.
WATERSON

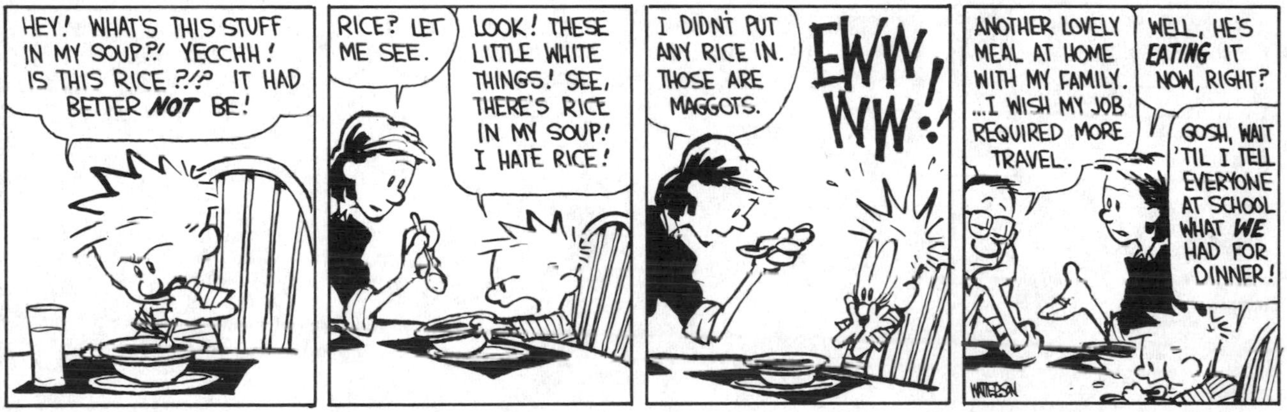
HEY! WHAT'S THIS STUFF IN MY SOUP?! YECCHH! IS THIS RICE ?!? IT HAD BETTER NOT BE!
RICE? LET ME SEE.
LOOK! THESE LITTLE WHITE THINGS! SEE, THERE'S RICE IN MY SOUP! I HATE RICE!
I DIDN'T PUT ANY RICE IN. THOSE ARE MAGGOTS.
EWW, WW!!
ANOTHER LOVELY MEAL AT HOME WITH MY FAMILY. ...I WISH MY JOB REQUIRED MORE TRAVEL.
WELL, HE'S EATING IT NOW, RIGHT?
GOSH, WAIT 'TIL I TELL EVERYONE AT SCHOOL WHAT WE HAD FOR DINNER!
WATERSON

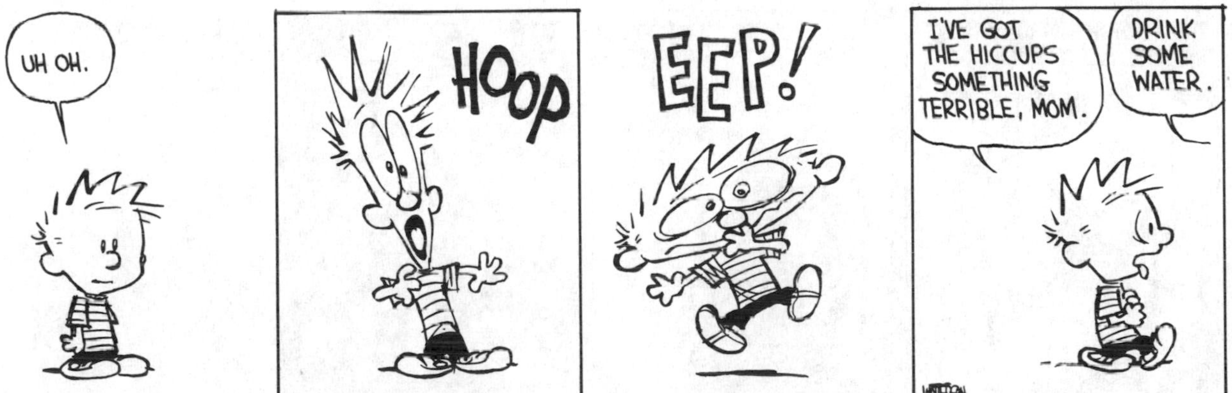
UH OH.
HOOP
EEP!
I'VE GOT THE HICCUPS SOMETHING TERRIBLE, MOM.
DRINK SOME WATER.
WATERSON

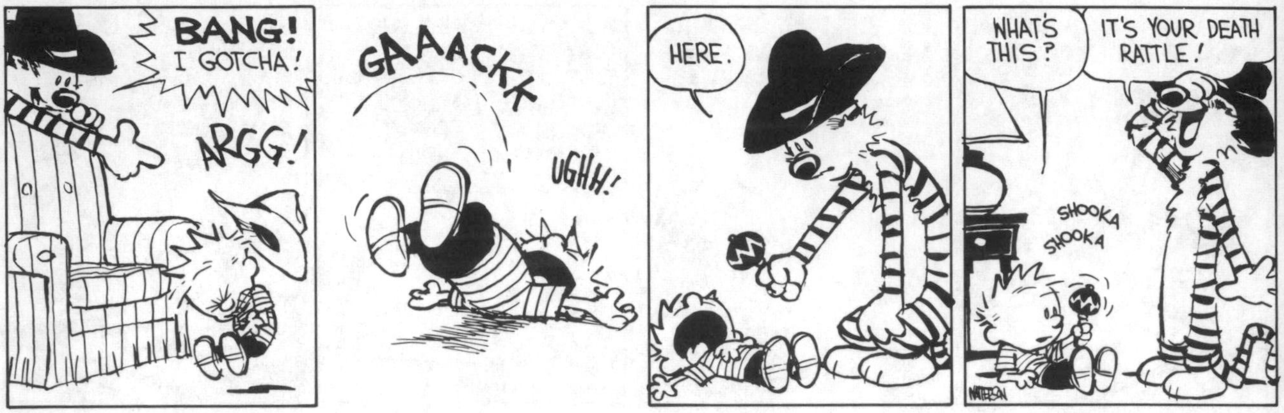
BANG! I GOTCHA!
ARGG!
GAAACKK
UGHH!
HERE.
WHAT'S THIS?
IT'S YOUR DEATH RATTLE!
SHOOKA SHOOKA
WATTERSON

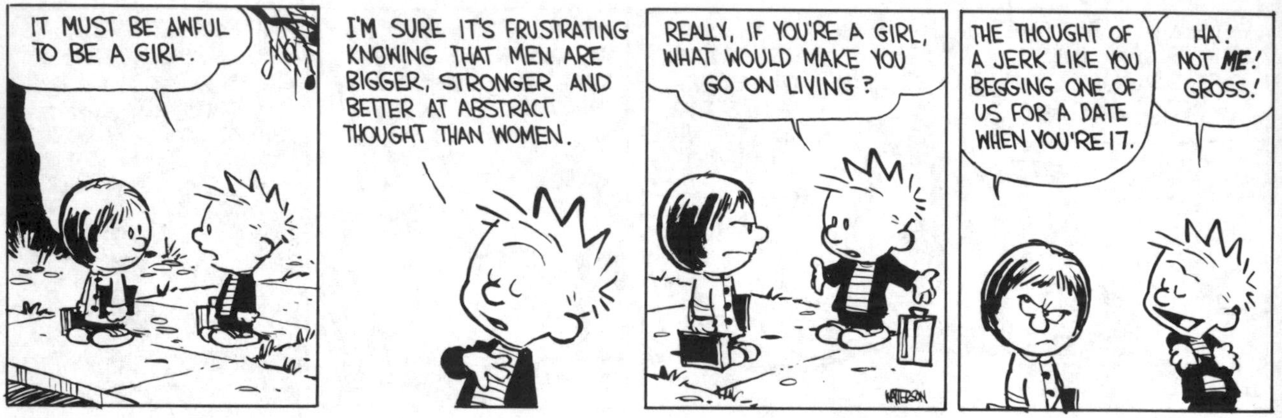
IT MUST BE AWFUL TO BE A GIRL.
I'M SURE IT'S FRUSTRATING KNOWING THAT MEN ARE BIGGER, STRONGER AND BETTER AT ABSTRACT THOUGHT THAN WOMEN.
REALLY, IF YOU'RE A GIRL, WHAT WOULD MAKE YOU GO ON LIVING?
THE THOUGHT OF A JERK LIKE YOU BEGGING ONE OF US FOR A DATE WHEN YOU'RE 17.
HA! NOT ME! GROSS!
WATTERSON

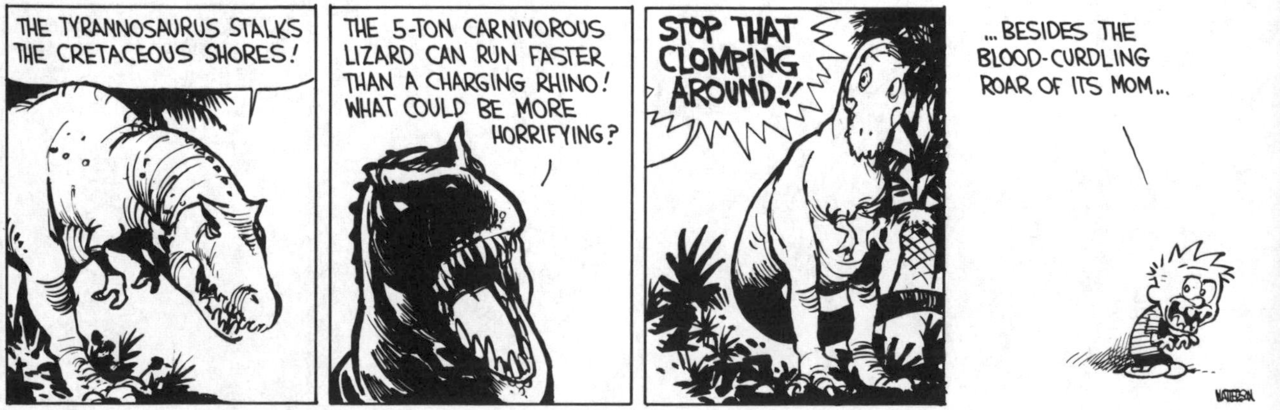
THE TYRANNOSAURUS STALKS THE CRETACEOUS SHORES!
THE 5-TON CARNIVOROUS LIZARD CAN RUN FASTER THAN A CHARGING RHINO! WHAT COULD BE MORE HORRIFYING?
STOP THAT CLOMPING AROUND!!
...BESIDES THE BLOOD-CURDLING ROAR OF ITS MOM...
WATTERSON

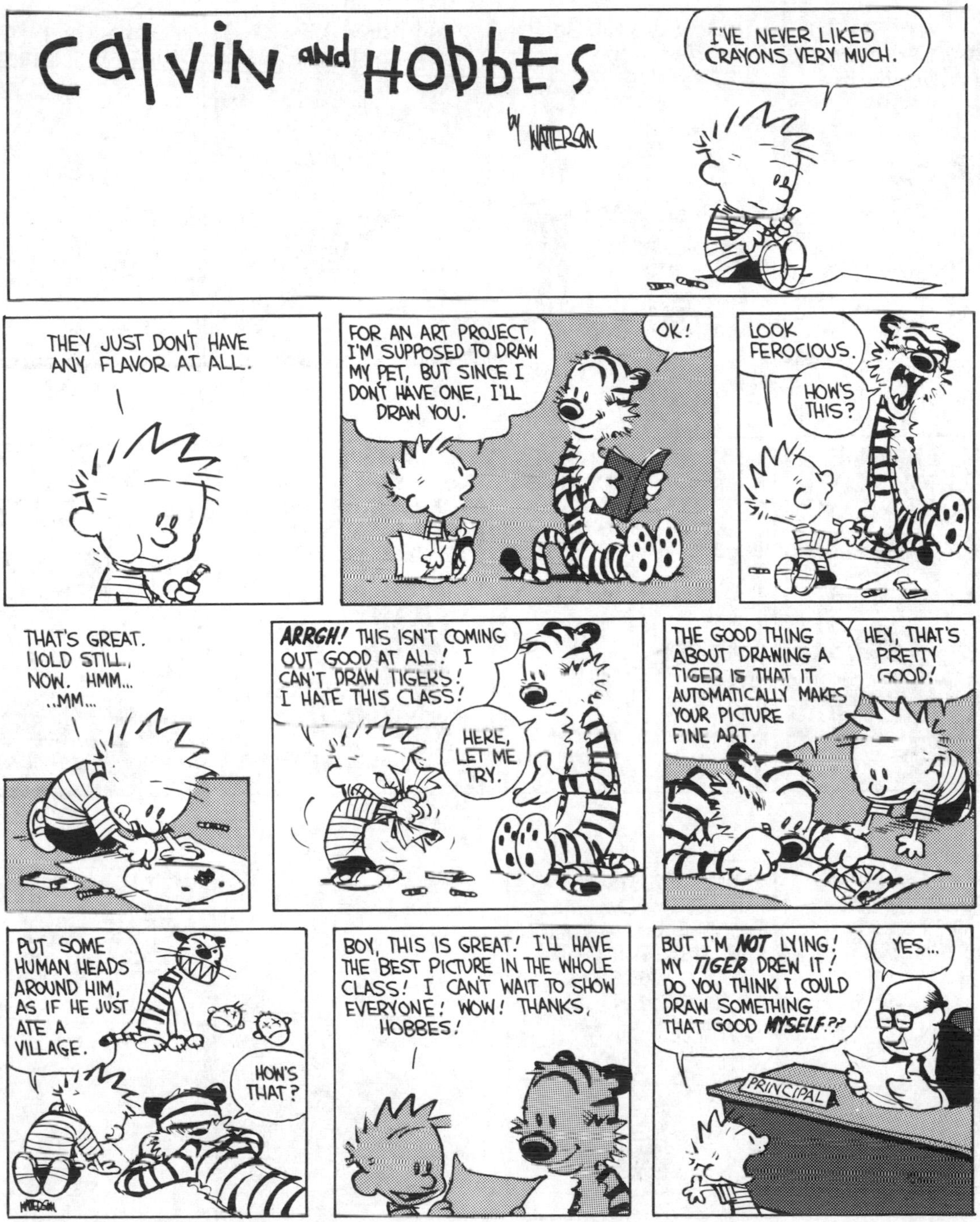
Calvin and HOBBES
by WATTERSON
I'VE NEVER LIKED CRAYONS VERY MUCH.
THEY JUST DON'T HAVE ANY FLAVOR AT ALL.
FOR AN ART PROJECT, I'M SUPPOSED TO DRAW MY PET, BUT SINCE I DON'T HAVE ONE, I'LL DRAW YOU.
OK!
LOOK FEROCIOUS.
HOW'S THIS?
THAT'S GREAT. HOLD STILL, NOW. HMM... ..MM...
ARRGH! THIS ISN'T COMING OUT GOOD AT ALL! I CAN'T DRAW TIGERS! I HATE THIS CLASS!
HERE, LET ME TRY.
THE GOOD THING ABOUT DRAWING A TIGER IS THAT IT AUTOMATICALLY MAKES YOUR PICTURE FINE ART.
HEY, THAT'S PRETTY GOOD!
PUT SOME HUMAN HEADS AROUND HIM, AS IF HE JUST ATE A VILLAGE.
HOW'S THAT?
BOY, THIS IS GREAT! I'LL HAVE THE BEST PICTURE IN THE WHOLE CLASS! I CAN'T WAIT TO SHOW EVERYONE! WOW! THANKS, HOBBES!
BUT I'M NOT LYING! MY TIGER DREW IT! DO YOU THINK I COULD DRAW SOMETHING THAT GOOD MYSELF?!?
YES...
PRINCIPAL

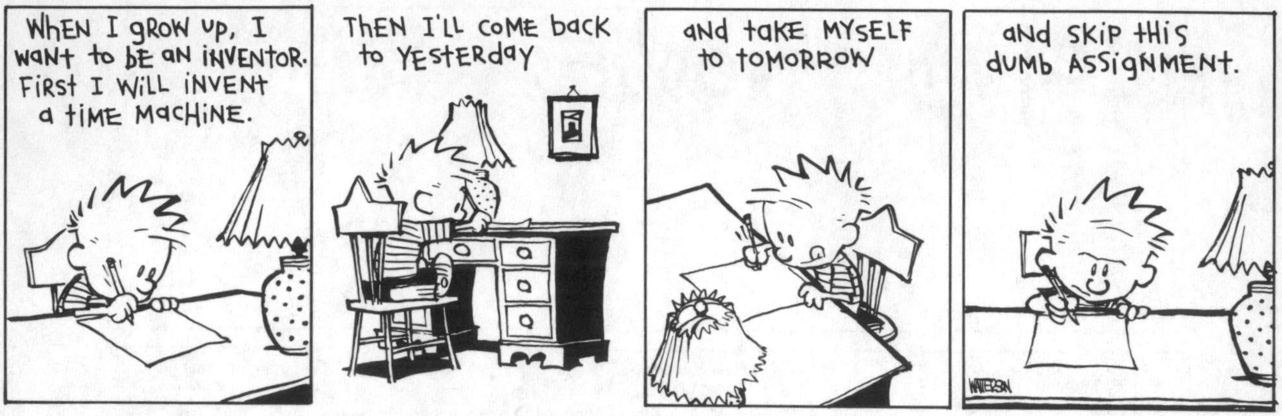
WHEN I GROW UP, I WANT TO BE AN INVENTOR. FIRST I WILL INVENT A TIME MACHINE.
THEN I'LL COME BACK TO YESTERDAY
AND TAKE MYSELF TO TOMORROW
AND SKIP THIS DUMB ASSIGNMENT.

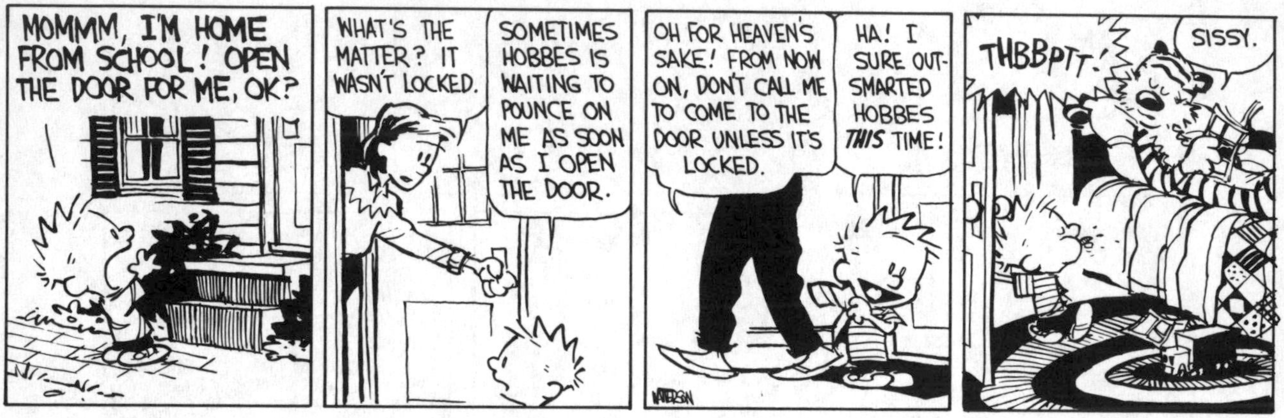
MOMMM, I'M HOME FROM SCHOOL! OPEN THE DOOR FOR ME, OK?
WHAT'S THE MATTER? IT WASN'T LOCKED.
SOMETIMES HOBBES IS WAITING TO POUNCE ON ME AS SOON AS I OPEN THE DOOR.
OH FOR HEAVEN'S SAKE! FROM NOW ON, DON'T CALL ME TO COME TO THE DOOR UNLESS IT'S LOCKED.
HA! I SURE OUT-SMARTED HOBBES THIS TIME!
THBBPTT!
SISSY.

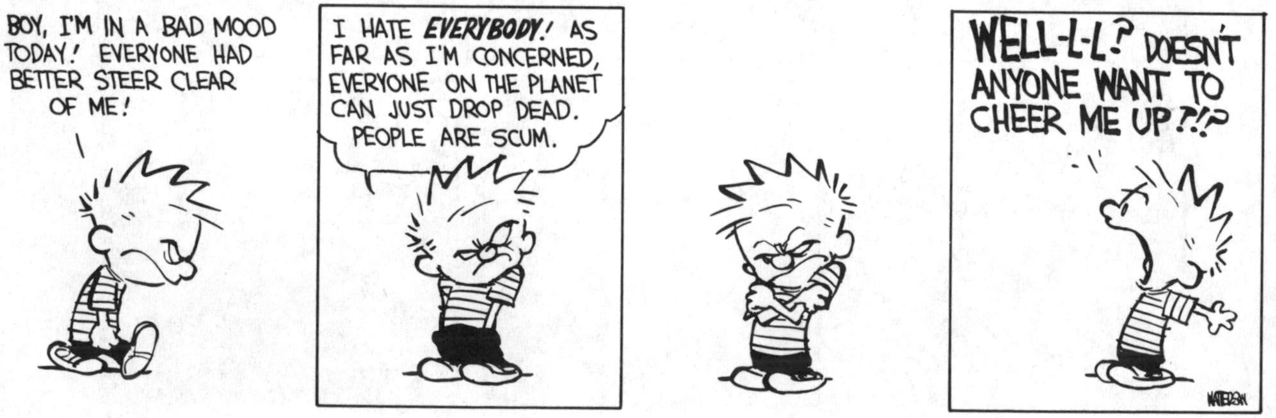
BOY, I'M IN A BAD MOOD TODAY! EVERYONE HAD BETTER STEER CLEAR OF ME!
I HATE EVERYBODY! AS FAR AS I'M CONCERNED, EVERYONE ON THE PLANET CAN JUST DROP DEAD. PEOPLE ARE SCUM.
WELL-L-L? DOESN'T ANYONE WANT TO CHEER ME UP?!?

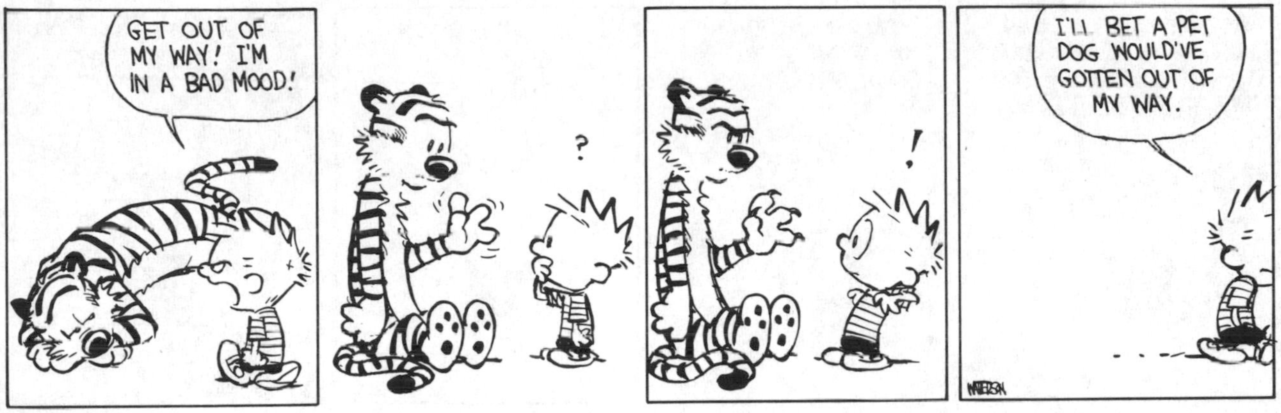
GET OUT OF MY WAY! I'M IN A BAD MOOD!
?
!
I'LL BET A PET DOG WOULD'VE GOTTEN OUT OF MY WAY.

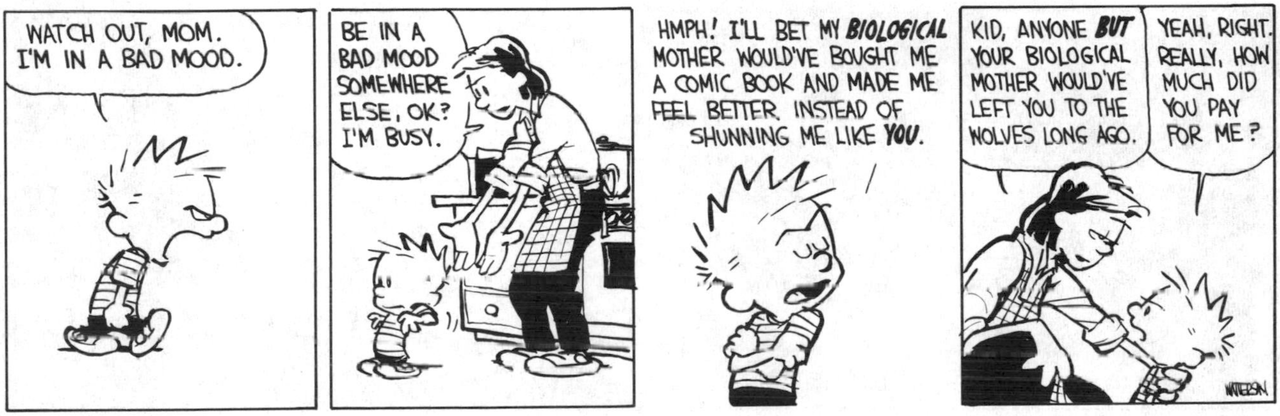
WATCH OUT, MOM. I'M IN A BAD MOOD.
BE IN A BAD MOOD SOMEWHERE ELSE, OK? I'M BUSY.
HMPH! I'LL BET MY BIOLOGICAL MOTHER WOULD'VE BOUGHT ME A COMIC BOOK AND MADE ME FEEL BETTER INSTEAD OF SHUNNING ME LIKE YOU.
KID, ANYONE BUT YOUR BIOLOGICAL MOTHER WOULD'VE LEFT YOU TO THE WOLVES LONG AGO.
YEAH, RIGHT. REALLY, HOW MUCH DID YOU PAY FOR ME?

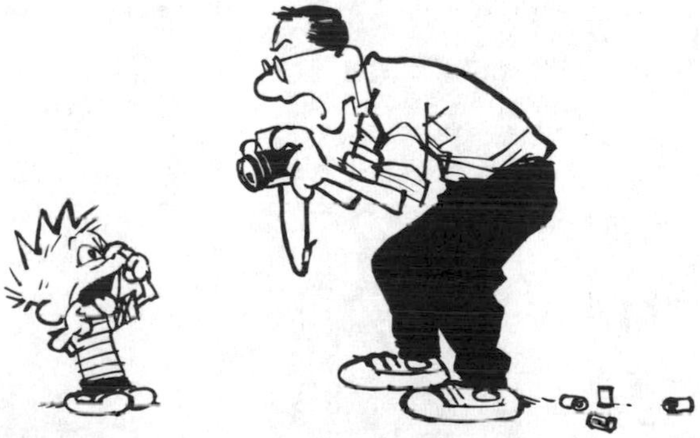

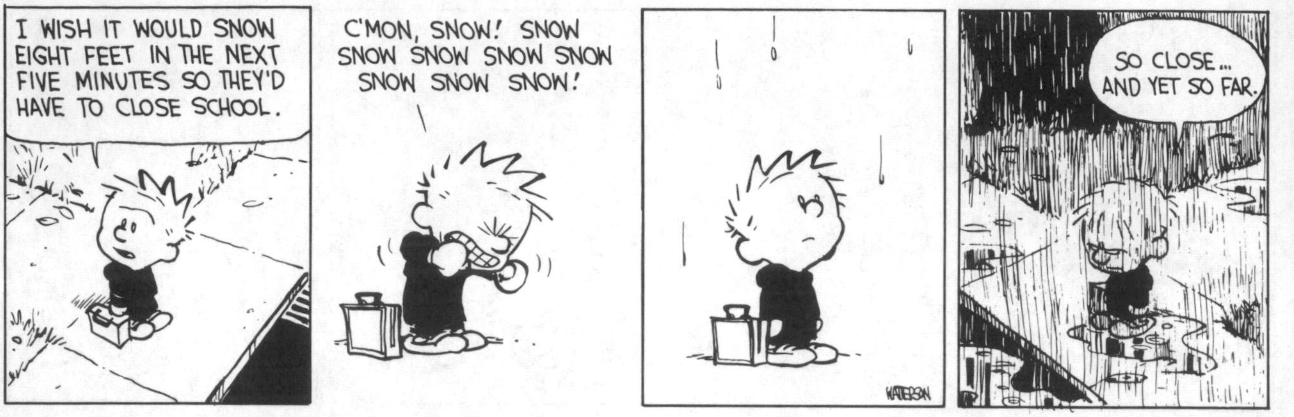
I WISH IT WOULD SNOW EIGHT FEET IN THE NEXT FIVE MINUTES SO THEY'D HAVE TO CLOSE SCHOOL.
C'MON, SNOW! SNOW SNOW SNOW SNOW SNOW SNOW SNOW SNOW!
WATTERSON
SO CLOSE... AND YET SO FAR.

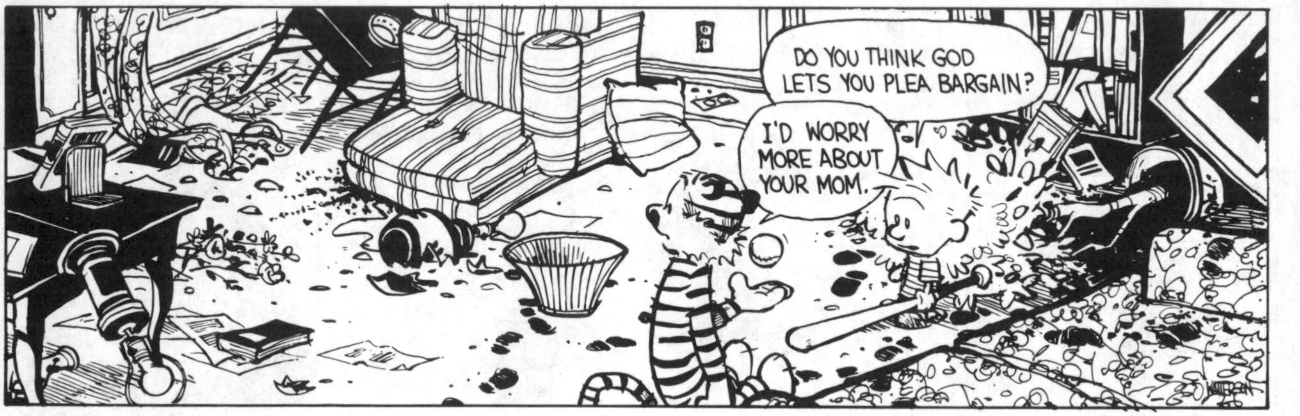
DO YOU THINK GOD LETS YOU PLEA BARGAIN?
I'D WORRY MORE ABOUT YOUR MOM.
WATTERSON

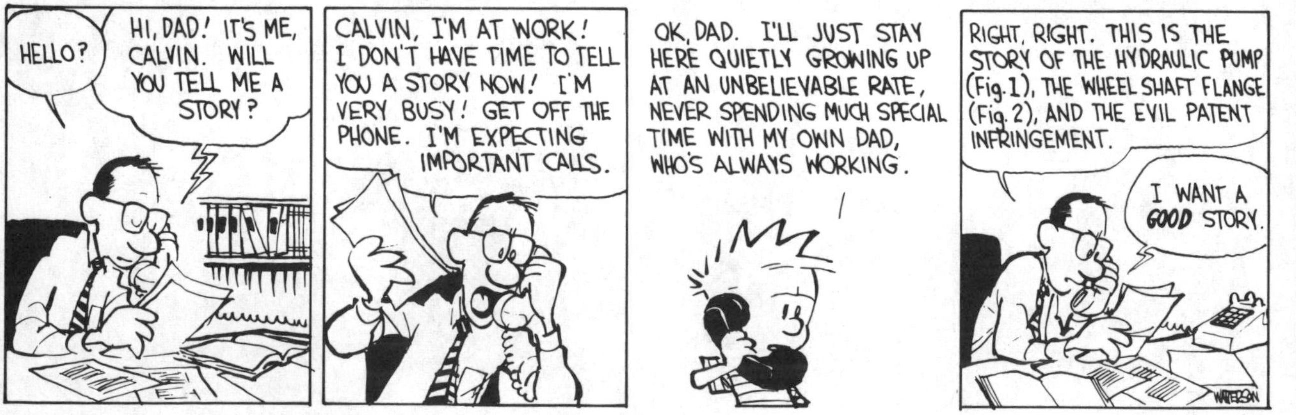
HELLO?
HI, DAD! IT'S ME, CALVIN. WILL YOU TELL ME A STORY?
CALVIN, I'M AT WORK! I DON'T HAVE TIME TO TELL YOU A STORY NOW! I'M VERY BUSY! GET OFF THE PHONE. I'M EXPECTING IMPORTANT CALLS.
OK, DAD. I'LL JUST STAY HERE QUIETLY GROWING UP AT AN UNBELIEVABLE RATE, NEVER SPENDING MUCH SPECIAL TIME WITH MY OWN DAD, WHO'S ALWAYS WORKING.
RIGHT, RIGHT. THIS IS THE STORY OF THE HYDRAULIC PUMP (Fig. 1), THE WHEEL SHAFT FLANGE (Fig. 2), AND THE EVIL PATENT INFRINGEMENT.
I WANT A GOOD STORY.
WATTERSON

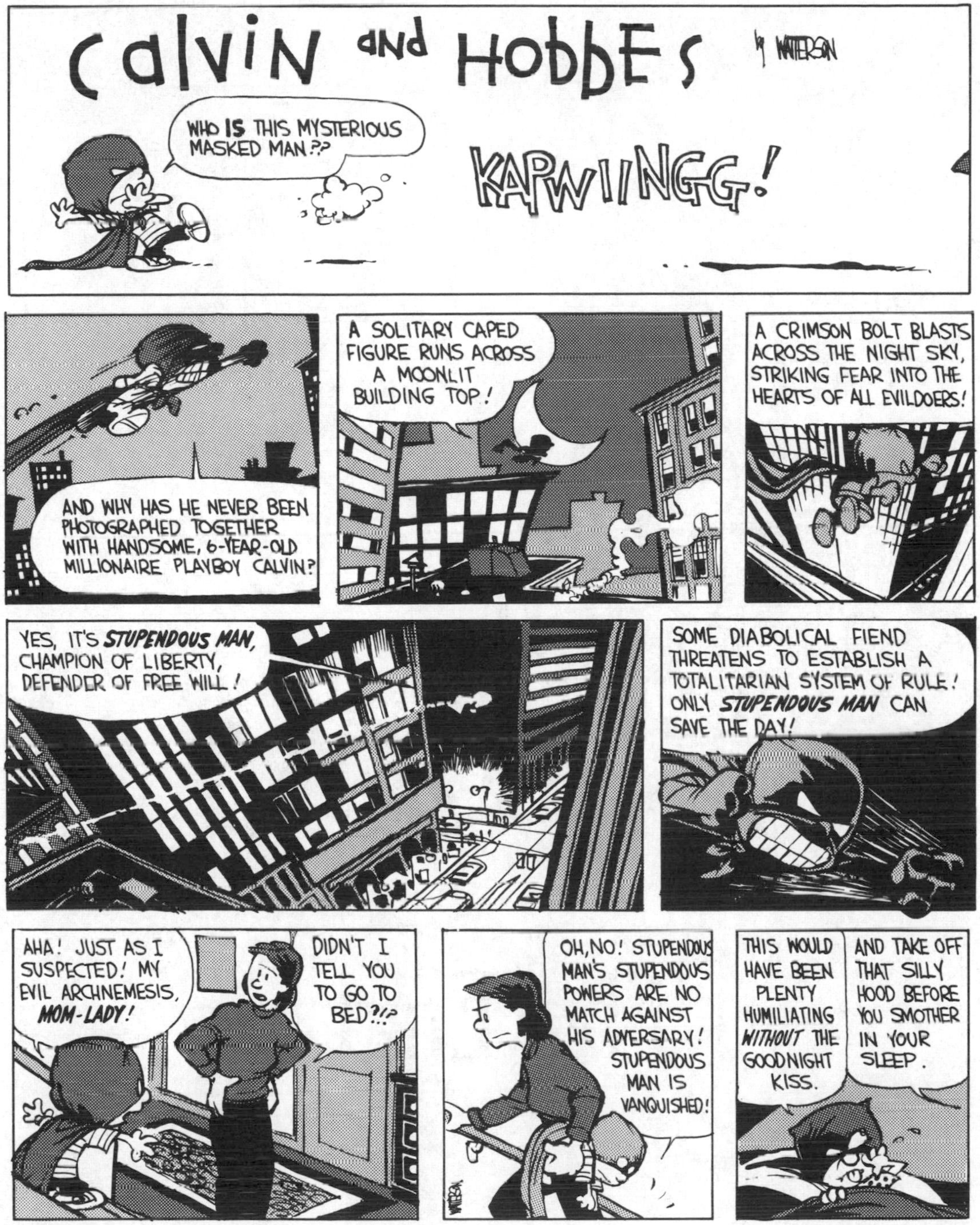
Calvin and HobbEs
by WATTERSON
WHO IS THIS MYSTERIOUS MASKED MAN ?!?
KAPWIINGG!
AND WHY HAS HE NEVER BEEN PHOTOGRAPHED TOGETHER WITH HANDSOME, 6-YEAR-OLD MILLIONAIRE PLAYBOY CALVIN?
A SOLITARY CAPED FIGURE RUNS ACROSS A MOONLIT BUILDING TOP!
A CRIMSON BOLT BLASTS ACROSS THE NIGHT SKY, STRIKING FEAR INTO THE HEARTS OF ALL EVILDOERS!
YES, IT'S STUPENDOUS MAN, CHAMPION OF LIBERTY, DEFENDER OF FREE WILL!
SOME DIABOLICAL FIEND THREATENS TO ESTABLISH A TOTALITARIAN SYSTEM OF RULE! ONLY STUPENDOUS MAN CAN SAVE THE DAY!
AHA! JUST AS I SUSPECTED! MY EVIL ARCHNEMESIS, MOM-LADY!
DIDN'T I TELL YOU TO GO TO BED?!?
OH, NO! STUPENDOUS MAN'S STUPENDOUS POWERS ARE NO MATCH AGAINST HIS ADVERSARY! STUPENDOUS MAN IS VANQUISHED!
THIS WOULD HAVE BEEN PLENTY HUMILIATING WITHOUT THE GOODNIGHT KISS.
AND TAKE OFF THAT SILLY HOOD BEFORE YOU SMOTHER IN YOUR SLEEP.

The End